THE NEW NATION
1865-1917

SIX-VOLUME SET

THE NEW NATION
1865-1917

DUMAS MALONE
COLUMBIA UNIVERSITY
and UNIVERSITY OF VIRGINIA

•

BASIL RAUCH
BARNARD COLLEGE
COLUMBIA UNIVERSITY

APPLETON-CENTURY-CROFTS

DIVISION OF MEREDITH PUBLISHING COMPANY

New York

COVER ILLUSTRATIONS

FRONT: *Top*, Votes for Women
    The Bettman Archive

Right, Theodore Roosevelt
    Brown Brothers

Left, Grover Cleveland
    Brown Brothers

Bottom, Model T Ford
    Ford Motor Co.

BACK: *Top*, Immigrants Arriving from Ellis Island
    Brown Brothers

Right, William McKinley
    Culver Service

Left, Mark Twain
    Culver Service

Bottom, Panama Canal
    Brown Brothers

To

the students we have been privileged to teach —at COLUMBIA, BARNARD, YALE, the UNIVERSITY OF VIRGINIA, the UNITED STATES NAVAL ACADEMY, and elsewhere—*we gratefully dedicate this book.*

PREFACE

THIS IS ONE OF SIX PORTIONS OF OUR WORK OF HISTORY WHICH WAS FIRST published in two volumes under the title, *Empire For Liberty: The Genesis and Growth of the United States of America.* Extended to include the Kennedy-Johnson administration, and also brought up to date in other respects, the work is now presented in six paperbound books for the convenience of students and the public.

Each of these books represents a chronological segment of American history and is a self-contained unit—with bibliography, appendices, and index. To each book we have given a descriptive title because, besides being usable in any combination with the others, it stands alone.

In preparing a new edition we have corrected such errors as were reported to us by those who have used the work and have availed ourselves of various helpful suggestions. The treatment of recent events, of course, is fresh, and minor changes have been made in the text elsewhere as a result of further study. There have been numerous additions to and some omissions from the original bibliographies.

Remaining mindful of the continuity as well as the variety of the American story, we repeat here parts of the original preface in which we tried to sum things up.

We believe that if history is to come alive in the minds of readers it must be presented primarily as a story. Therefore, this work is predominantly narrative in form. Within the inexorable limits of space, we have tried to do justice to all the important aspects of American history—political, economic, constitutional, diplomatic, social, religious, artistic, and intellectual.

In the process of selection, we have laid emphasis on two themes of special interest today. The course of world affairs in our century has magnified the importance of American foreign policy, and in this work we have emphasized international relations. In response to the crucial importance of ideology and movements of thought in our time, we have also given special attention to these. But we do not forget that the American story is one of human beings rather than impersonal forces. We have paid special attention to the people and their leaders in all fields at each stage.

We are wedded to no single thesis, knowing of none by which the whole of our history can be adequately explained. But we do see, as a thread running through the entire fabric, the idea of the free individual. And we repeat, as designating a major historic goal of our growing society, the Jeffersonian quotation from the original titlepage: "Such an Empire for Liberty as She has never surveyed since the Creation." (To Madison, April 27, 1809).

As used here, the word "empire" connotes no exploitation of subject regions on this continent or anywhere else. Its meaning has been newly illustrated by the admission of Alaska and Hawaii as full-bodied members of the Union of self-governing states. The vision of a better life for every human being, with faith that it would result from maximum liberty compatible with public order, inspired all the most fruitful public and private actions of Americans from the beginnings of English settlement. If this vision was temporarily blurred after the Civil War, it has gained renewed life because of events in the twentieth century, especially the rise of totalitarianism in the world.

The threat to the free individual that is implicit in the consolidating tendencies of our generation, both at home and abroad, intensifies the need to grasp the meaning of the American experience. Americans and all others who believe that man fulfills himself in conditions of political, social, economic, and cultural freedom should understand that American history is less important as a success story in material terms than as a struggle to fulfill human potentiality. The authors will be grateful to readers who accept this work as an effort to contribute to such understanding.

In the preface to the first edition, after expressing our gratitude to all those who had helped us through the years to understand our country better, we named a number of individuals who had rendered us special services. The list of helpful friends has now become so long that we must content ourselves with a general expression of thanks, without reference to particular persons. We should be remiss, however, if we did not say that we are more grateful than ever for the good counsel of our publishers.

Since the labor and judgment of both authors have gone into all parts of this history, no precise apportionment of responsibility between them is possible. In the full meaning of the term this is a joint product. In restudying and resurveying the whole of our country's past we have enjoyed a very great experience. We hope that this book will serve as an invitation to others to explore that past and share that experience.

D. M.

B. R.

CONTENTS

Part III: Imperialism and Progressivism, 1896-1917

MAPS and CHARTS

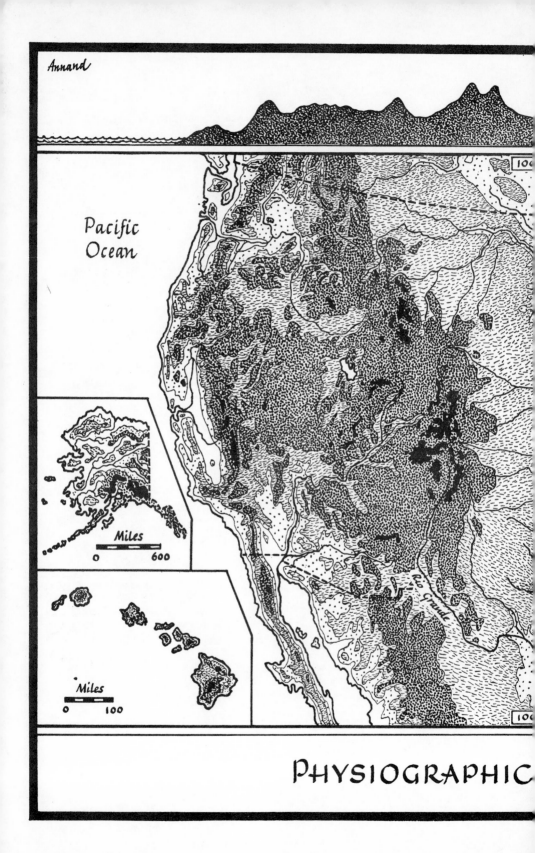

Annand

Pacific
Ocean

Miles

0   600

Miles

0   100

Rio Grande

PHYSIOGRAPHIC

Profile

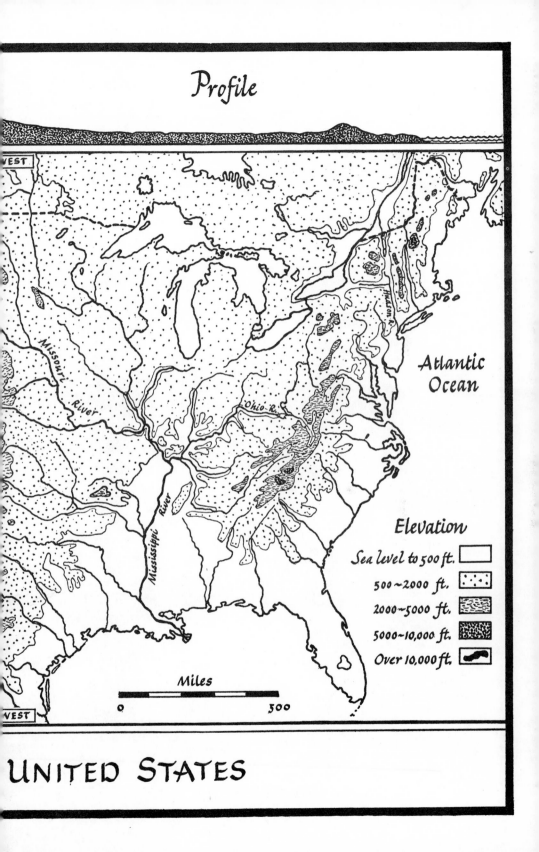

UNITED STATES

Atlantic
Ocean

Missouri River

Mississippi River

Ohio R.

Hudson R.

Elevation

Sea level to 500 ft.

500~2000 ft.

2000~5000 ft.

5000~10,000 ft.

Over 10,000 ft.

Miles

0   500

Part I

THE ERA OF RECONSTRUCTION
1865-1877

CHAPTER 1

Reconstruction of the Union

THE MILITARY CONFLICT CLOSED WITH THE SURRENDER of the Confederate armies in 1865; and the end of the mighty "insurrection" was officially proclaimed on August 20, 1866, when President Andrew Johnson announced that "peace, order, tranquility, and civil authority" now existed throughout the United States. The statement was questionable. Genuine peace between the two sections was not effected until the last federal troops were withdrawn from the South in 1877, ending the era of Reconstruction.

The war had demonstrated that the Union would endure, that the Republic would not be divided in two, that the national government could not be successfully defied by a state or group of states. But the war had not determined the precise relations of the conquered states to the restored Union. It had put an end to slavery but had not determined the status of the freedmen in American society. Over these two unanswered questions the major political battles raged in the turbulent years immediately following the war. Behind them was the even more basic question of the location of political power within the nation and its government. The net results were the consolidation of Northern power over the prostrate South; the dominance, for a time at least, of Congress in the government; the ascendancy of the Republican Party in politics; and the strengthening of the industrial and financial groups which had already been favored by the war. While sectional animosities were kept alive and exploited, the political and economic patterns of a generation were being set and it became clear that the preserved Union was to be a new nation.

NORTH AND SOUTH AFTER APPOMATTOX

The problem of effecting a genuine peace was projected on an economic and social background which varied greatly in the two sections recently

3

at war. In the North the abnormalities of war quickly gave way to a condition of great prosperity, which was soon accompanied by political corruption such as had never before been seen in the Republic. A million troops had to be returned to civil life, normal legal processes had to be restored, taxes had to be adjusted to peacetime conditions, and the currency needed to be stabilized. Meanwhile, the Northern victors were turning with zest and without hindrance to the economic exploitation of the vast physical resources of a peaceful continent. The many problems of the North were complicated and accentuated by the prosperity of the region and the lack of adequate opposition to the dominant political group. The victors suffered from the completeness of their own victory.

The South had not been extensively industrialized, but its capital was now spent and what factories it had were destroyed, along with railroads, houses, barns, and fences. Despite the increased erosion of the lands and the losses in horses, mules, hogs, and cattle, this predominantly agricultural region might have been rather quickly restored had it not been forced to adjust itself to political, economic, and social change for which American experience offered no parallel. Under any circumstances the problems of the postwar South would have been extraordinarily difficult, and the era proved a deeply tragic one when statesmanship showed itself unequal to an unexampled situation.

It is not surprising that the various contemporary commentators on Southern sentiment after Appomattox presented varying judgments. Much of the difficulty of the federal government in attempting to frame policy arose from the conflict of testimony. This was not merely between Northerners and Southerners, but among the Northern journalists, soldiers, and visiting statesmen who viewed the scene. Yet, from the welter of comments and descriptions, which generally reflected the predilections of the observers, certain generalizations emerge. Few historians will question the judgment of General Grant in late 1865 that the mass of Southerners recognized that the questions of secession and slavery had been settled by the tribunal of arms, and that they accepted the decision in good faith. But the former Confederates were not apologetic. In the same year Carl Schurz, whose views were more radical and partisan than Grant's at this stage, had reported to the President and proclaimed to the nation: "Treason does, under existing circumstances, not appear odious in the South. The people are not impressed with any sense of criminality." The ex-Confederates remained loyal to their old leaders —especially their military leaders. The expressions of this loyalty were impolitic at times, but there was little other leadership to turn to, for in most parts of the South the former Unionists were neither numerous nor respected.

Dependent though the Southerners were on federal troops for the maintenance of even a semblance of public order in the months just after the cessation of hostilities, they could hardly be expected to like an army of occupation. They were resentful of the Negro soldiers, who became proportionately more numerous as the white troops were demobilized. They also resented the incoming Northerners—officials, missionaries, and adventurers—whom they came to lump together as "carpetbaggers," while terming their more active Southern collaborators "scalawags." The dominant thought in most Southern minds at first was the need to establish a *modus vivendi;* and, under the realities of the situation, they were convinced that somehow the exhilarated freedmen must be made to work. Nowhere did the former Confederates concede that recognition of their recent slaves as their political equals was a necessary result of the war.

During the summer and fall of 1865, predominant Northern opinion was moderate. Grant and Sherman had set a high standard of magnanimity, and many Union soldiers expressed great respect for their recent foes. The most acute resentment in the North, perhaps, was aroused by tales of horrors in Confederate prisons which haggard survivors brought home. Henry Wirz, the crazed and cruel Swiss-American who was in charge at Andersonville, was hanged in the fall after trial by a military commission, atoning for the unspeakable conditions of that place for which he was partly responsible. No other Confederate officer suffered like punishment. Grant interpreted the terms of surrender as pledging the civil authorities not to prosecute former Confederate soldiers who observed their parole, and actually they were not prosecuted in civil courts.

There was an inevitable revulsion of feeling among Northerners against the South after the assassination of Lincoln. In the presidential proclamation which led to the capture of Jefferson Davis in May, his name was linked with the plot of John Wilkes Booth. President Johnson and his Cabinet soon decided to drop the murder charge, which was wholly without foundation, and to try Davis for treason. This they never did, but by keeping him in prison at Fortress Monroe for two years, before releasing him on bail, they made him a martyr in Southern eyes. Lincoln had hoped that Davis would escape.

In July 1865, nine persons charged with implication in the plot against Lincoln were tried—four being hanged, four imprisoned, and one acquitted. This action, which appears to have been unjust in the case of Mrs. Surratt, was also that of a military commission rather than a regular court. There were no other military executions. The Amnesty Proclamation of May 29, 1865, by President Johnson, offered pardon, with specified exceptions, to participants in the "existing rebellion" who would take an oath of allegiance to the Constitution and promise to support the federal actions against slavery. He excepted more classes than Lincoln had in previous proclamations, but he provided for petitions from individuals falling within them. General Lee, who was in one of the excepted classes, was an early applicant for the "full restoration of all rights and privileges." He was in no real danger of prosecution, as Grant assured him, being covered by his parole. He was never "pardoned" but many others were, and these Executive actions seemed to meet with general approval.

Most people in the North favored a speedy re-establishment of the Southern states and their restoration to the Union—with certain provisos: there must be unquestionable loyalty to the Union, and the freedmen must not be re-enslaved. A radical group went much further, holding that the Southern states had no rights except such as their conquerors chose to grant them, that there must be more signal punishment for rebellion by the complete destruction of the old ruling class, that the Negroes must be given civil and political equality immediately. This was a policy of Reconstruction, not restoration, and it came to be followed because the extreme group gained complete ascendancy in Congress. But Congress was not in session until December 1865 and until then matters were in the hands of the Executive.

PRESIDENTIAL RESTORATION, 1863-1865

The death of Lincoln, at the moment of victory and the height of his prestige, deprived the country of the leader who was best fitted to bring to a close the tragic era of sectional conflict. It was already obvious that the peacetime policies of this wise and compassionate man would be bitterly opposed by extremists, but he spoke the language of humanity and common sense and was in position to command a wide hearing. He wanted to bind up old wounds, not make new ones. The supremely important thing, in his opinion, was not to quibble about theories, but to do what was necessary to *restore* the proper *practical* relations between the defeated states and the Union.

Andrew Johnson inherited Lincoln's policy of restoration, along with the presidency; he agreed with it in all essentials and sought to carry it out with sincerity and devotion. But he lacked Lincoln's political astuteness and had temperamental faults which worked to his disadvantage. The picture of Johnson which persisted in the public mind long after his day was a caricature drawn by his enemies. They described him as illiterate, drunken, vulgar, intolerant, and insolent—as a man without dignity or capacity who disgraced his high office. Now that the clouds of controversy have rolled back, we know that he was a strong, intensely patriotic, excessively industrious, and inflexibly honest man. But he was pugnacious where Lincoln would have been conciliatory; he was stubborn and sounded egotistical; and, while deserving respect, he did not win the hearts of men. His greatest weakness lay in his political isolation. The party which had re-elected Lincoln called itself not the Republican but the Union Party; and the convention put Johnson on the ticket as a

Southern Unionist. Politically, this former Democrat was now a lone wolf. Regarded by the old Confederates as a renegade, he was to the more partisan northern Republicans an unfortunate accident.

Born obscurely in Raleigh, North Carolina, Johnson was in the full sense a self-made man, and he now stands forth in history as the most notable champion of the plain people whom the ante-bellum South produced. Apprenticed to a tailor at the age of fourteen, he made his way at eighteen to Greeneville in East Tennessee. There he soon became moderately prosperous as the proprietor of a small shop. Aided by his wife, he gained the essentials of an education and became an eager reader. Soon getting into local politics, he served as mayor and state legislator, and then spent ten years in Congress. There he introduced a homestead bill in 1846, and he continued to uphold the interests of small farmers; he had antipathy for great planters, of whom there were relatively few in his part of Tennessee. Before the war he accepted slavery, reflecting to some extent the hostility of the poorer whites to Negroes, and he greatly disliked the abolitionists. He defended the constitutionality of slavery, but did not advocate the extension of the system or uphold the institution on abstract grounds. After two very successful terms as Governor of his state, he was elected to the United States Senate, and he became notable by remaining there after the southern states seceded. He performed a thankless but heroic task as war Governor of Tennessee (1862-1865), under appointment from Lincoln. He believed the war had been waged to restore the Union, accepting the emancipation of the slaves as a later purpose, but he was a strict constitutionalist and his conviction that the continuing rights of the states could be safely recognized had been reinforced by his own experience. In Tennessee he had really effected the restoration of civil government, and his own success seemed a justification of Lincoln's policy.

That policy, as described in Lincoln's Amnesty Proclamation of December 8, 1863, offered pardon on generous terms. It permitted the re-establishment of a state government whenever the required oath had been taken by a number of persons equal to 10 per cent of the voters in 1860. It conceded that temporary arrangements might be made for the freedmen as "a laboring, landless, and homeless class." It also recognized that the admission of Representatives was a question which only Congress could settle. But Lincoln stretched Executive powers throughout the war, and the hostility in Congress, as reflected in the Wade-Davis Bill which he checked by a pocket veto, was based in part on the desire of Congress to have a determinative part in the postwar policy. The Radicals insisted on excluding far more Southerners from the privilege of taking the oath, and on raising the percentage of the electorate of 1860 required for the re-establishment of a state government from 10 to 50 per cent. Under the terms of the Wade-Davis Bill, it would have been virtually impossible at

this time to organize a government even in Tennessee, where Union sentiment was much stronger than elsewhere in the South, and the Congress
would have the last word to say in all these matters, including the status
of the freedmen. To the Radicals, Lincoln's policy of leaving so much to
the citizenry of the old slave states seemed far too soft and trusting.

He had gone ahead, nonetheless, and before he died governments had
been set up according to his plan in Tennessee, Arkansas, and Louisiana,
while he had recognized a "reorganized" government in Virginia. A week
after Lincoln's assassination, the new President declared in a public speech
that "treason must be made odious, that traitors must be punished and
impoverished." In his Proclamation of Amnesty (May 29, 1865), he excluded Rebels worth $20,000 or more, thus reflecting his antipathy to large
planters. To the Radicals it appeared that Johnson was going to be a man
more to their liking than his predecessor. But Johnson's early expressions
reflect the severity of war times and the revulsion of feeling that followed
Lincoln's assassination. Shifting his position quickly, he proceeded during
the summer of 1865 to carry out a presidential policy which was practically
indistinguishable from that of Lincoln.

He appointed provisional governors for the remaining southern states,
instructing them to call state conventions. By the time that Congress met
in December, all the states except Texas had taken the steps which the
President deemed essential. The conventions annulled secession, declared
slavery abolished, and nearly all of them repudiated the state debts.
Legislatures were then set up, and in due course these ratified the Thirteenth Amendment, which abolished slavery (proclaimed December 18,
1865). Shortly before Congress met, however, they began to take actions
which aroused forebodings in the North. They began to enact "black
codes" which represented an effort, often crude, to express in law the
transition from slavery to freedom. They actually extended to the freedmen important legal rights, of which the slaves had had none, but by
drawing a distinction in law between blacks and whites and retaining or
imposing special restrictions on the former, they gave occasion for the
charge that the Negroes were being re-enslaved and the fruits of Northern
victory lost. When the Senators and Representatives gathered in Washington in December, newly elected men from nearly all the states of the
former Confederacy appeared with their credentials. The President had
enabled these states to attain the semblance of local government, but
Congress was now to have its inning.

CONGRESS AND PRESIDENT, 1865-1866

The one sure ground of Congressional objection to presidential "restoration" was that Congress had had nothing to do with it. Under the astute
leadership of the implacable Thaddeus Stevens, Representative from

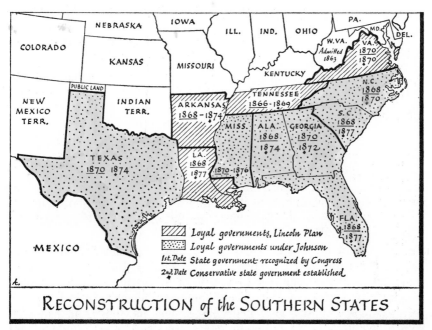

RECONSTRUCTION of the SOUTHERN STATES

Pennsylvania, the Radicals followed a policy of obstruction and delay. Stevens had the clerk of the House, Edward McPherson of Pennsylvania, leave the names of the newly elected Southerners off the roll, pending a determination of their status. Then, immediately after the election of a speaker (December 4), Stevens secured the adoption of a resolution that a joint committee of fifteen, six from the Senate and nine from the House, be appointed to inquire into the condition of the states of the former Confederacy and report whether or not any of them were entitled to be represented. To this the Senate soon agreed (December 12), and the joint resolution required no presidential signature. By this skillful maneuver the Radicals avoided a direct issue with Johnson until the time should be more propitious.

There were enough uncertainties in the situation to make many members of both houses welcome delay. An important unanswered question was what the basis of representation should be in the future. The constitutional provision that representation should be based on free population plus three-fifths of the slaves would not apply after the slaves were freed, and unless something were done the former slave states would be entitled, at the next apportionment, to representation based on their entire population, including the unenfranchised freedmen. That is, as a result of a war which the North had won, the South would actually gain strength in the national government. To many Northerners besides Radicals this was unthinkable. Furthermore, the assumption was that these men would be Democrats, and no partisan Republican could view that prospect with composure.

Most of the members of the Committee of Fifteen were Radicals on the Southern question. Senator William Pitt Fessenden of Maine wanted additional guarantees from the Southern states, but was embarrassed by the presence on the Committee of so many men of extreme opinions. Representative John A. Bingham of Ohio was chiefly concerned to have the federal government assume protection of the civil rights of the people, but was not a vehement partisan. On the other hand, Representative George S. Boutwell of Massachusetts was described by a contemporary, Gideon Welles, as "an extreme radical, destitute of fairness where party is involved." The dominant figure was Stevens, now in his seventy-fourth year and the living embodiment of opposition to the Southern policy of Lincoln and Johnson. He held this Committee and this Congress in the hollow of his hand.

Born in Vermont but now living in Lancaster, Pennsylvania, Stevens had long been a violent antislavery man. He had made a point of befriending hapless Negroes but was no apostle of brotherly love when it came to the white South, which he deeply hated. At all stages he had opposed sectional compromises, and, believing conflict inevitable, he had welcomed its outbreak. He had many times expressed the constitutional and political philosophy of ruthlessness and naked power which he brought to this issue. He summed it up with appalling frankness in a speech soon after Congress assembled (December 18, 1865). "The future condition of the conquered people depends on the will of the conqueror," he said. "They must come in as new states or remain as conquered provinces. Congress . . . is the only power that can act in the matter." Regarding the basis of representation, he held that the Constitution would have to be amended "so as to secure perpetual ascendancy of the party of the Union." This he clearly identified with the Republican Party. "With the basis unchanged the 83 Southern members, with the Democrats that will in the best times be elected from the North, will always give a majority in Congress and in the Electoral college. . . . I need not depict the ruin that would follow." As for the slaves, he said: "If we do not furnish them with homesteads, and hedge them around with protective laws, we had better have left them in bondage." He had previously proposed a plan for the confiscation of the lands of the Southern "arch-traitors" who held more than 200 acres—comprising more than three-fourths of the total acreage. Part of these lands would go to the freedmen, and the rest used to reward the loyal and serve other Northern purposes. These confiscatory policies, which would have carried Reconstruction beyond political to social revolution, were never adopted. Little land was ever given to freedmen, though thousands of them believed they could expect "forty acres and a mule."

A head-on collision between the Radicals and the President occurred in February 1866. Johnson vetoed a bill indefinitely extending the life of the Freedmen's Bureau and enlarging its powers and jurisdiction. This agency of the War Department had been established in March 1865, and its life had been limited to a period of one year after the end of the war. It was directed by General Oliver Otis Howard, often designated as "the Christian Soldier," whom Johnson had appointed commissioner after Secretary Stanton had informed him that Lincoln had intended to do so. The Bureau rendered genuine service in relieving destitution, but most Southern whites regarded it as an "engine of mischief." They viewed it as a species of foreign government, supported by an army of occupation. Northern opinion tended to uphold it, because of the Southern black codes and because of the atrocity stories which were circulating. Johnson was not hostile to the Bureau, but he believed it would encroach on the rights of the Southern states if it were made an authorized guardian of the civil rights of freedmen. He vetoed the bill as unnecessary (since the present Bureau would continue for some months), as unwise, and as unconstitutional. He reasoned that laws so vitally affecting the domestic life of the Southern states should not be passed when they were unrepresented in Congress.

The veto was sustained by a narrow margin, but Johnson had directly challenged the Radicals. He compounded the injury by attacking some of them by name (especially Stevens and Senator Charles Sumner) in a speech on Washington's Birthday. The Senate now joined the House in adopting a resolution that no Senator or Representative should be admitted from any of the Rebel states until Congress had declared that state entitled to representation. Congress passed the Civil Rights Bill in March, and passed it again over Johnson's veto. The Radicals now had a numerical advantage over the President, as the moderates began to abandon him.

The Fourteenth Amendment

The Civil Rights Bill sought to gain for the freedmen, by means of federal law and the operation of federal courts, the same civil status as the whites, regardless of state legislation. Johnson alienated many high-minded Northerners by his veto of it and lent color to the charge that this wartime Unionist was at heart a Southerner. Entirely apart from the merits of the bill, however, the President was on strong ground when he alleged that it was unconstitutional, because the relations of a state with its citizens had hitherto been adjudged to be beyond the authority of the general government. It seemed to many that the constitutional question required an answer, and this was given by the Radicals in the first section of the Fourteenth Amendment. The amendment, which was adopted by Congress and submitted to the states in June 1866, consisted of four parts.

The first part was not the one that Southerners most objected to at the time, but it proved much the most important in the long run. It stated that all persons born or naturalized in the United States are citizens of the United States, and of the states where they reside. That is, it created national citizenship, which had been denied by the Dred Scott decision, and, while affirming state citizenship, made that secondary. This section forbade any state to abridge the privileges or immunities of citizens of the United States; to deprive any person of life, liberty, or property without due process of law; and to deny to anyone in its jurisdiction the equal protection of the laws. The Bill of Rights of the Constitution had been designed to protect individuals against *federal* action, but the federal government was now to become their protector against *state* action. This proposal represented an attempt to uphold individual rights everywhere against potential tyranny.

The second section was an attempt to solve the vexing question of representation. Apportionment was to be based on total population, with a penalty for the denial of the right to vote on any other ground except participation in rebellion or crime. In the case of such denial (denial to freedmen, for example), there should be a proportionate reduction in representation. This ingenious scheme avoided the direct question of Negro suffrage, which actually existed in only six Northern states at the time, and left control of the suffrage with the states.

The third section disqualified for state or federal office any former officeholder, civil or military, who, having taken an oath to support the Constitution, had engaged in rebellion against the United States or given aid or comfort to its enemies. By a two-thirds vote Congress could remove any such disability but otherwise virtually all the Southern leaders of any consequence were ruled out. There was no way to make the third section palatable to Southerners, but the fourth was unobjectionable to them except on the ground that it was now unnecessary. It affirmed the validity of the United States debt, required the repudiation of all Confederate debts, and denied all claims arising from the emancipation of slaves.

Although contending that the Southern states were not now members of the Union, Congress submitted the Fourteenth Amendment to them. In the legislature of Tennessee it gained the necessary majority, though under very questionable circumstances. Following this, Congress admitted the Representatives from Tennessee in July, thus restoring that state to the Union. No guarantee was given, however, that this amendment represented a final settlement of the sectional controversy. Many of the Radicals wanted to go much further. They had drawn a composite document which would serve as a platform in the Congressional elections in the fall. The Report of the Joint Committee (June 20, 1866) was designed to show Southern intransigence and the need for stern federal action.

Radical Victory at the Polls

The moderates, whose number had declined in Congress but who may still have comprised a majority in the North, had nothing to stand on but the policy of Johnson. The political situation of that hapless executive had become increasingly anomalous. Lincoln had shrewdly used the patronage to gain supporters; Johnson did not. The government service was filled with Radicals, and Johnson was not the master of the Cabinet he had inherited from Lincoln. The connivance of Secretary of War Stanton with the Radicals was notorious. The President had no organized party behind him.

In August 1866, a number of moderates of diverse past affiliations met in Philadelphia in what they called a National Union Convention. There was much confusion of terms at this stage, for the Radicals called themselves Unionists whenever they could. A one-time Whig, Congressman Henry J. Raymond of New York, the editor of the *New York Times*, was prominent in the meeting. Senator James R. Doolittle of Wisconsin, a former Democrat who became a devoted follower of Lincoln, was a moving spirit, and among those present was Alexander H. Stephens, former vice-president of the Confederacy. The notorious Copperhead, Clement L. Vallandigham, was finally induced to stay away. As a political rally in support of Johnson this national gathering of moderate men seemed a great success, and one of the incidental results was to bring about the resignation of three unsympathetic members of his Cabinet and their replacement by men willing to be loyal to him. Stanton remained, however, and the effects of the convention were dissipated. No moderate party, deserving to be called a Union Party, was created. The local party machinery remained or passed into the control of Radical Republicans on the one hand and Democrats on the other, with the result that in the Congressional election moderate men had to choose between them.

In the early fall, the President made a trip to Chicago to speak at the unveiling of a statue to Stephen A. Douglas, and extended his tour to several other cities in the Middle West. His extemporaneous utterances, especially when heckled, were in bad taste and an injury to his own cause. Radical campaign orators seized upon these as evidence of his unfitness for his high office. The Radicals also played up race riots which took place in New Orleans and Memphis during the summer, asserting that these proved the necessity for severity in Southern policy.

The Congressional elections did not amount to a referendum on the Fourteenth Amendment as an alternative to Johnson's policy. The issues were not that clear, and the general policy of the Radical campaigners was to evade and obscure them. Their effort was to make the issue seem one between loyalty and disloyalty, between national patriotism and treason. The immediate result was the overwhelming success of the Radicals, who were assured of more than a two-thirds majority against the President. Their success had other unfortunate consequences besides the more radical Reconstruction policy which followed. This campaign, with its excitation of sectional feeling to the ignoring of grave constitutional, economic, and social questions, set the pattern for two decades of election campaigns.

Meanwhile, the Southern legislatures, by overwhelming and often unanimous vote, were rejecting the Fourteenth Amendment—chiefly on the ground that they could indulge in no such repudiation of their own leaders. Furthermore, they argued that there was no real point in helping amend the Constitution of a nation of which they were not recognized as members. Johnson agreed with them in this. He has often been criticized by historians for his attitude, but he had concluded that the Radicals had no intention of stopping with this amendment and believed that the course of events would not be affected by what he and the Southern states now did.

CONGRESSIONAL RECONSTRUCTION, 1867-1868

The refusal of ten Southern states to ratify the Fourteenth Amendment strengthened the determination of the Radicals to employ far sterner measures, while their overwhelming victory at the polls assured them that, throughout the rest of his term, the President would be powerless to prevent them from enacting any laws they liked. In July 1866, by reducing the number of Justices of the Supreme Court from ten to eight, Congress had deprived him of the chance to fill an existing vacancy on the Court and the next one which should occur. The Radicals recognized that the federal judiciary might prove obstructive. The decision in the case *Ex parte* Milligan (December 1866), by a vote of 5 to 4, that military commissions and martial law were unconstitutional when the ordinary courts were open, was described by Thaddeus Stevens as more dangerous than the Dred Scott decision. Some of the Radicals uttered threats against the Court, but their immediate animus was against Andrew Johnson and, after knocking him down, they were doing all they could to gag and bind him.

Two acts of March 2, 1867, are without parallel in American history as legislative attempts to curtail the executive functions of the President and to subordinate him to the legislature. By the Tenure of Office Act, Congress declared that persons holding offices with senatorial confirmation were not removable without the consent of the Senate. By the Command of the Army Act, Congress required that all military orders from the President must go through the General of the Army (Grant), and that this officer must not be removed or assigned elsewhere than Washington without the previous consent of the Senate. The next phase of Congressional policy was to be under military auspices, and Congress wanted to make sure that the President should not control the Army. Behind the scenes Secretary of War Stanton was working to the same purpose.

The Radicals had not regarded the Fourteenth Amendment as a full plan of Reconstruction, but it marked the first and preliminary phase of Congressional policy. The second and much more extreme phase is what is generally meant by the expression, "Radical Reconstruction." As worked out in early 1867 the policy was embodied in two Reconstruction Acts, one passed over a presidential veto on March 2 and the other three weeks later. These acts may be summarized by saying that: (1) the existence of legal governments in ten Southern states was denied; (2) new governments were to be formed on the basis of thoroughgoing disfranchisement of Confederates and full enfranchisement of the freedmen; (3) the process was to be under military control at all stages.

The ten states were divided into five military districts, each to be presided over by an officer of at least the rank of brigadier general. These officers were to oversee the formation of new governments under a prescribed procedure. Voters were to be registered without distinction of race or color, participants in the rebellion being disqualified. Constitutional conventions were to draw up new frames of government embodying Negro suffrage. These constitutions were to be adopted by the new electorates and approved by Congress. Legislatures elected on this basis were to ratify the Fourteenth Amendment and readmission to the Union would follow by congressional action.

In January of this year, Congress had granted the vote to Negroes in the District of Columbia. In Northern state elections in 1867, however, constitutional amendments enfranchising the Negroes in their own states were rejected by the voters of Ohio, Minnesota, and Kansas, as they had been defeated since the war in other states. Thus Congress was imposing on the South, where the Negro population was large, policies which were not imposed on Northern states where the Negroes were relatively few. Undoubtedly the advocacy of universal suffrage by certain Radical leaders, including Stevens and Charles Sumner, was sincere; but a major concern of the omnipotent legislators in Washington was to make the South safe for the Republican Party. One of the maxims of the Radicals was "indemnity for the past and security for the future." The chief indemnity now to be imposed on the South was the enforced acceptance by the white citizens of the political equality of recent slaves. The chief political security of the North was to lie in the votes of the freedmen. With these some vainly hoped that poorer whites, who might expect to gain from social upheaval, would be allied.

President Johnson performed his unwelcome official task by appointing Generals Schofield, Sickles, Pope, Ord, and Sheridan to command the five districts. The existing governments which he had set up were ignored rather than immediately abolished by the two Reconstruction Acts of March 1867, and the laws themselves needed interpretation. The trend of the advice given by the Executive Department through the Attorney General, Henry Stanbery, was to allow the benefit of doubt to the existing civil governments and to limit the military authorities in applying the prescribed oath to prospective voters and in disqualifying participants in the rebellion. But this relatively liberal policy was checked by a supplementary Reconstruction Act of July 19, which subjected state officials to the military commanders in all respects, permitting their removal at will, and declared that the military commanders and officials serving under them were *not* bound by the opinions of civil officers. Final authority was vested in the General of the Army—not the President.

The constitutional theory of Reconstruction to which the Supreme Court afterwards acquiesced in the case of Texas *vs.* White (1869) was that of "suspended rights." According to this view, the power to restore constitutional relations lay with Congress, the earlier acts of the President being regarded as provisional. Congress was undoing Johnson's acts as fast as possible. Except that territorial boundaries were not disturbed, the policy now being followed was virtually in accord with Charles Sumner's "state-suicide" theory, while to Southerners it seemed that their former states were "conquered provinces."

Under military authority the prescribed procedure was followed step by step during the succeeding months. The results of the registration in the summer of 1867 were that Negro voters greatly outnumbered white voters in all the states of the Lower South except Georgia, where there was a small white majority, and Texas, where there was a larger one. The whites were more numerous than the Negroes in Virginia, North Carolina, and Arkansas. In the vote on holding constitutional conventions the whites commonly followed the tactics of abstention, but the conventions were held nevertheless. The tactics of abstention proved more embarrassing to military and Congressional authorities in the matter of ratifying the new constitutions, for the law required a majority of the registered voters. In Alabama this was not attained. Consequently, in March 1868, by a supplementary Reconstruction Act, the requirement was changed to a majority of the persons voting. In three states—Viriginia, Mississippi, and Texas—the prescribed legal processes were not carried out during the year 1868, but by summer Congress recognized seven Southern states besides Tennessee as entitled to representation as members of the Union.

In July of that year, the Fourteenth Amendment was proclaimed, under rather confused circumstances. By that time it had been ratified by 23 "loyal" states, though two of them, New Jersey and Delaware, had rescinded their action after Democratic victories in state elections. Secretary of State Seward, in a proclamation of July 20, stated the facts without committing himself in regard to the validity of the previous resolutions of ratification by these two states. Furthermore, Southern ratifications were necessary to gain the required three-fourths vote of *all* the states, Seward said that the amendment had been ratified in six Southern states by "newly constituted and newly established bodies avowing themselves to be and acting as Legislatures." Congress promptly passed a resolution declaring that the amendment had been ratified, and on July 28, after a seventh Southern state had ratified, Seward categorically proclaimed it a part of the Constitution. Several weeks earlier Congress had come to final grips with the President.

The Impeachment and Trial of Andrew Johnson

From the time that Congress assembled after the elections of 1866, certain Radicals had been seeking grounds for legal action against their enemy the President, but their efforts were vain until Johnson tried to rid himself of Secretary of War Stanton. In discussions in the Cabinet bearing on the administration of the Reconstruction laws, Stanton, who occupied a key position as the civilian head of the Army, was wholly out of sympathy with the President, the Attorney General, and indeed with the Cabinet as a group. Johnson eventually came to the point where he could no longer put up with him, and in August 1867, when Congress was not in session, asked his resignation. When Stanton declined to resign, the President removed him, appointing General Grant Secretary of War *ad interim*. Though Johnson believed that the Tenure of Office Act was unconstitutional, he was in fact keeping within its terms, since it permitted the making of such an *ad interim* appointment with a report to the Senate within twenty days after the opening of the next session. That would be in December.

Some months earlier the Judiciary Committee of the House had been asked to inquire into the desirability of Johnson's impeachment, and in December 1867 this committee finally recommended it by a vote of 5 to 4, submitting more than a thousand pages of testimony. While this testimony heavily underlined the differences in policy between the President and the congressional majority, it offered so little ground for charges of illegal action on his part that the House rejected the recommendation by a vote of nearly 2 to 1 (December 7, 1867). In the following week Johnson's own report of his removal of Stanton was submitted to the Senate.

About a month later (January 13, 1868) the Senate, after a long debate, refused to concur in the President's action, basing its own action on the theory that the Tenure of Office Act was applicable. Grant then withdrew, implying that he agreed with this interpretation. Johnson believed that Grant had let him down. He had hoped that Stanton would have recourse to the courts and that the constitutionality of the Tenure of Office Act would thus be tested. Instead, Stanton resumed office. He held no communication with the President and the latter instructed the General of the Army not to take orders from him. The situation was unendurable. Finally, after about a month, Johnson removed Stanton (February 21, 1868), appointing Adjutant General Lorenzo Thomas Secretary of War *ad interim*. The President's foes retaliated by causing Thomas to be arrested as a violator of the Tenure of Office Act. Released on bail, Thomas again demanded possession of the office and was again refused by Stanton. Under these absurd circumstances an infuriated House of Representatives voted on March 3 by 128 to 47 to impeach the President. Only Democrats supported him.

According to the Constitution, the House of Representatives has the power to impeach—that is, to prefer charges—while the power to try rests with the Senate. The indictment by the House, consisting of eleven articles, dealt chiefly with the removal of Stanton, the appointment of Thomas, and the President's expressions about the Tenure of Office Act. Article X, however, which was included at the insistence of Congressman Benjamin F. Butler of Massachusetts, consisted of quotations from Johnson's speeches, to show a design to set aside the authority of Congress and bring that body into contempt and disrepute. In other words, it was wholly political. Article XI was supposed to be the strongest. Its main idea was that the President had sought to resist the execution of a law, the Tenure of Office Act.

The trial of Andrew Johnson by the Senate, presided over by Chief Justice Salmon P. Chase, began on March 30, 1868. Johnson was ably defended by Henry Stanbery, who resigned as Attorney General for this purpose, by former Justice Benjamin R. Curtis, William M. Evarts, and others. The managers for the House were less able and they were faced with the necessity of proving the President guilty of "Treason, Bribery, or other high Crimes and Misdemeanors," the only grounds provided by the Constitution for the removal of civil officers on impeachment.

The question of Johnson's guilt hinged on the Tenure of Office Act. Even though he regarded this as unconstitutional, did he have any right to resist it? That question remained unanswered because it gave way to another. Did the Tenure of Office Act really apply in this instance? It stated that a Cabinet officer should hold office during the term of the President by whom he was appointed and for one month thereafter. Stanton had been appointed by Lincoln. If Lincoln's term was the one for which he was elected—that is, till March 1869—the law applied to Stanton, but if Lincoln's term ended with his death the law did not apply. This question aroused grave uncertainty in the minds of certain conscientious Senators. Furthermore, the removal of Johnson would have resulted in the accession of Benjamin F. Wade, the President pro tempore of the Senate, to the presidency of the United States, and some of Wade's colleagues did not like the prospect of that.

Since Article XI was believed most likely to carry, it was voted on first (May 16). The result was a vote of 35 to 19 for conviction, which lacked one of reaching the required majority of two-thirds. It seems, however, that others would have voted for acquittal if necessary. Johnson was supported by 12 Democratic Senators and by 7 Republicans who faced ostracism. Senators Fessenden, Fowler, Grimes, Henderson, Ross, Trumbull, and Van Winkle gained honor at the bar of history for their brave action. It now seems surprising, in view of the flimsiness of the evidence, that so many of their fellows voted to convict a President of the United States of high crimes and misdemeanors. After a delay of nearly two weeks and much frantic maneuvering, two other articles were voted on, with the same result. Then the Senate sitting as trial court upon articles of impeachment adjourned *sine die*.

Few episodes in American history reveal more strikingly the extraordinary extremes to which political animosities can go and the depths of unreason to which they can sink. Among other things Senator Charles Sumner said: "Andrew Johnson is the impersonation of the tyrannical slave power. In him it lives again." Historians of our day, while fully aware of Johnson's limitations, cannot recognize him from this description. They can readily perceive, however, the great significance of the outcome as showing that a President could not be removed because of his disagreement with the policies of Congress. Had Johnson been convicted, the historic system of co-ordinate branches would have received a dangerous and perhaps a mortal blow. The presidency, already weakened, would have been wholly subordinated to the will of Congress. In no other case has the framework of the American constitutional system been subjected to so severe a test.

Stanton now withdrew and, on nomination of the President, General John M. Schofield was confirmed by the Senate in his stead. That body declared that Stanton had not been legally removed but had "relinquished" his office. At last Johnson was the head of his own household, though Congress did not admit that he had a right to be. The most offensive clauses of the Tenure of Office Act were removed in 1869, when there was a President more to the liking of Congress, and twenty years later the act was wholly stricken from the laws.

THE ELECTION OF 1868 AND THE FIFTEENTH AMENDMENT

The convention of the National Union Republican Party was held in May 1868. It resulted in the unanimous nomination of General Ulysses S. Grant for the presidency. Schuyler Colfax of Indiana, Speaker of the House, was named as his running mate. The nomination of Grant had been a virtual certainty since his withdrawal from the post of Secretary of War *ad interim*. Earlier, there had been some Republican talk of nominating Chief Justice Salmon P. Chase, whose presidential ambitions were perennial; but this former Democrat had shown slight sympathy with the Radicals in the impeachment trial and really had little in common with them except the advocacy of Negro suffrage. In selecting Grant, a national military hero whose political views were so vague as to be inoffensive, the Republicans were following the tradition of the ante-bellum Whigs.

The Democrats, in their platform, said that Johnson deserved the gratitude of the country. This was very different from the Republican charge that he was a treacherous usurper and the assertion that he was "justly impeached" and "properly pronounced guilty" by the vote of thirty-five Senators. But the Democrats did not adopt the discredited President as their candidate. Meeting in July, they nominated Governor Horatio Seymour of New York for the presidency and General Francis P. Blair, Jr., one of the most outspoken critics of Congressional policy, for the vice-presidency. Seymour accepted the nomination with great reluctance and afterwards regarded this action as his greatest political mistake. He was opposed to the plank in the Democratic platform calling for the payment of government bonds in greenbacks in all cases in which there was not an express statement that they must be paid in coin. This plan was associated with the name of George H. Pendleton, the Democratic leader of Indiana and a major spokesman of Western discontent with the monetary situation. It has been said that in the Democratic convention the West got the platform and the East the candidate.

The greenback question played a part in the campaign, but the Republican position on it was ambiguous, and this was a sectional issue between East and West rather than a political issue between the two parties. It is probable that the tariff was more important in the minds of Republican leaders than they admitted publicly; one reason for wanting to retain political control of the South was to keep the tariff high. But the foremost issue was that of Reconstruction.

In their platform the Republicans congratulated the country on the "assured success" of the Reconstruction policy of Congress, as evinced by the adoption in most of the Southern states of constitutions "securing equal civil and political rights to all." In view, however, of the recent rejection of Negro suffrage in Northern states, it seemed impolitic to press that issue outside the South. The double standard in the two sections was justified as follows:

> The guaranty by Congress of equal suffrage to all the loyal men at the South was demanded by every consideration of public safety, of gratitude, and of justice, and must be maintained; while the question of suffrage in all the loyal states properly belongs to the people of those States.

Though concern for justice to the Southern Negroes was real, Republican leaders counted on the newly constituted electorate in the reconstructed states to cast proper Republican votes in the election. A statement in the platform about the future removal of disqualifications "imposed upon the late rebels" was so hedged about as to be virtually meaningless, but the spirit of magnanimity was properly associated with the name of Grant and he was widely recognized as a man of good intentions. "Let us have peace," he said in his message of acceptance.

The Democrats in their platform arraigned the Radical Party for "its disregard of right, and the unparalleled oppression and tyranny which have marked its career." They favored the restoration of the Southern states, amnesty for past offenses, and the regulation of the suffrage by the states. The vice-presidential candidate said: "The peace to which Grant invites us is the peace of despotism and death." During the next few years many Southern whites were to describe it thus, but in the North the Democrats were still suspect, still identified by many with the Copperheads. Seymour, for all his personal eminence and fine qualities, was open to attack because of the moderation he had displayed at the time of the draft riots in New York at the height of the war. Unjust though the charge of disloyalty was, he was at a great disadvantage when pitted against Grant, the symbol of Union victory.

Under these circumstances the Democratic showing was surprising. The electoral vote was one-sided: 214 for Grant to 80 for Seymour. But Grant's popular majority was only a little more than 300,000. It has been estimated that he got 450,000 Negro votes to Seymour's 50,000. Thus the popular majority was dependent on Negro suffrage. As for the electoral vote, Grant would have had a small margin even if he had lost all the reconstructed states. He carried all of them but Georgia and Louisiana, and in these two states Democratic victory was attributed to the intimidation of Negroes by Southern whites. Out of this political situation emerged the Fifteenth Amendment, which was submitted to the states on February 26, 1869, a week before Grant's inauguration. By means of this the Radicals sought to make Negro suffrage irrevocable. It ushered in the final phase of Congressional Reconstruction.

By this time, in the South, Negro support of the Republicans had been solidified under the leadership of carpetbaggers and scalawags, working through the Union League of America. This order, which began in the North during the war, was extended to the South and opened to the freedmen, who were deeply impressed by its awe-inspiring ritual and proved amenable to its iron discipline. But, by means of the fearsome Ku Klux Klan and various extralegal devices and practices, the Southern whites were deterring the freedmen from voting. There was good reason to believe that they would continue to do so wherever military control was removed or relaxed; and, despite all the safeguards imposed by

Congress, there was no absolute assurance that the provisions for Negro suffrage would be retained in the constitutions of the Southern states after the latter had fully resumed self-government.

The Fifteenth Amendment declared that the right of citizens of the United States to vote should not be denied or abridged by the United States or by *any State* on account of "race, color, or previous condition of servitude." It also declared that Congress should have the power to enforce the article by appropriate legislation. The assumption of this degree of national control over the suffrage in the Northern states was not in accord with the Republican platform of 1868, but it was in harmony with the views of consistent advocates of universal male suffrage like Senator Charles Sumner, and it was justified on political grounds to Republicans as a group. They wanted to assure themselves of votes in the South without maintaining troops there indefinitely. Thus idealism and political expediency joined hands in framing the amendment. As a condition of readmission to the Union, the states which had not completed the procedure already prescribed by Congress were now required to ratify the Fifteenth Amendment. On March 30, 1870, it was proclaimed as part of the Constitution.

By the summer of 1870, when Grant had been more than a year in office, all the states were recognized as entitled to representation in Congress. In framework the Union had been reconstructed. The adoption of the Thirteenth, Fourteenth, and Fifteenth Amendments had weakened the constitutional position of the states, Northern as well as Southern. Congress was dominant, though not supreme, in the federal government; and the anti-Southern party, keenly aware of Northern economic interests, was in the seat of power. The Radicals, capitalizing on sectional animosity, had dictated a peace which was probably more drastic and more partisan than most Northerners realized or had intended. Therefore, when it proved unworkable on the local level, Northern opinion became increasingly acquiescent as Southerners began to break Radical Reconstruction down.

THE SOUTH UNDER CARPETBAG GOVERNMENT

To the great body of Southern whites the most frustrating of the postwar years were those immediately following the recognition by Congress that their states were again members of the Union. Then they had the semblance of home rule without the reality. The state governments were dominated by a few white Radicals (carpetbaggers and scalawags) who were supported by the votes of the newly enfranchised Negroes. The native leaders to whom the Southerners would naturally have turned were still disqualified, and thousands of ex-Confederates were still disfranchised. This situation lasted in a particular state until its Radical government was displaced by a native white government, commonly called Conservative. In the South itself the process went by the name of Redemption and the persons carrying it out were known as Redeemers. During Grant's administration carpetbag government reached its height, and, in most of the states, it fell.[1]

From what were the Conservatives seeking to "redeem" their states? They were trying to rid themselves of rule which they regarded as a travesty on democratic government. Perhaps they detested the scalawags, who were Southerners turned Radical, even more than the carpetbaggers from the North, but they viewed members of both groups, with few exceptions, as unscrupulous adventurers who were exploiting the situation to their personal advantage. The admission of Governor Henry Clay Warmoth of Louisiana that he made $100,000 during the first of his four years as Governor when his salary was $8000, and the estimate of two Congressional investigators in 1872 that he was then worth from $500,000 to $1,000,000, provide a conspicuous illustration. The support of the Radical rulers by the dominant group in the national government was owing in some part to a continuance of the abolitionist psychology— as exemplified by such a man as Charles Sumner—but increasingly to considerations of partisan advantage, as the crusading spirit waned. The Radicals in the South were necessarily identified with the Republican majority in Congress, and the Conservatives with the Democrats.

The Conservatives deplored the deprivation of leading whites of political rights while rights were granted to Negroes just emerging from the bonds of slavery. Some Northern observers of the various constitutional conventions and legislatures agreed with the local judgment. A Liberal Republican, writing in 1871 of the South Carolina legislature, in which the Negroes were in large majority, said: "It is barbarism overwhelming civilization by physical force." Here, he said, "stands the rude form of the most ignorant democracy that mankind ever saw, invested with the functions of government."

In the South as a whole, however, Negro officeholders were far less numerous than their very high proportion of the electorate would have warranted. They served more effectively in many places than might have been expected, in view of their very slight political experience, and the most notorious examples of corruption were provided by white men. In a dozen years 28 Negroes served in Congress as Senators or Representatives, the first being Hiram R. Revels, a Methodist preacher of moderate political views who filled the seat in the Senate previously

[1] For dates, see Map p. 9. Note that Tennessee did not suffer the full rigors of Reconstruction, since its short-lived Radical government was native; and that Virginia, which passed directly from the military phase to Conservative rule, escaped a carpetbag regime. Radical governments were still maintained by federal power in South Carolina, Florida, and Louisiana when Grant left office.

occupied by Jefferson Davis. The mass of Negroes exercised their right to vote with great enthusiasm, but white carpetbaggers and scalawags held the high administrative offices in the states and dictated policy. In effect they constituted an oligarchy. Besides controlling the vote of the freedmen, they could manipulate the returns, by means of electoral returning boards that were set up in many of the new constitutions. They were in the seat of power, passing out the favors, and behind them stood the federal authority.

Judgment on Radical Rule

The interpretation of Radical rule as a complete travesty on government, which became traditional in the South and was generally accepted in the North by the early twentieth century, has been modified in our own time by scholars, including Southern historians. These later interpreters have emphasized the fact that many of the ills of Radical government could be matched in the North at the time, and they have pointed out certain long-range benefits of the era. No one has successfully asserted, however, that this was good government.

Major counts in the indictment of it are financial maladministration and corruption. The extravagance of the Radical regime became a byword. This was manifested in specially ludicrous form in South Carolina, where, along with Louisiana, government was probably at its worst. Not only was there a refreshment room for the state Senators, where gallons of alcoholic liquors were guzzled and innumerable cigars smoked at public expense. Also, virtually anything that a Senator chose to order was included under supplies—wines, armchairs, refrigerators, feather beds, tapestries and linens, gold watches, diamond rings. In Florida in 1869, the cost of printing alone was more than the expenses of the entire state government in 1860. By 1870, in eleven states, taxation had increased to eight times what it was a decade earlier, and in those remaining under Radical rule it grew even heavier. Meanwhile, the debts of states, counties, and cities increased fantastically. The most notorious of all the financial abuses, probably, was the reckless aid given by the Radical governments to railroads. This was done by the purchase of railroad stock, the guaranteeing of bonds, the making of direct grants for miles of line constructed, and other benefits or favors at the expense of the public treasuries.

The actions of Southern states in this regard, however, were similar to those in other parts of the country in this reckless and rambunctious era. Public aid to railroads did not need to be accompanied by so much graft in the South or elsewhere, but speedy construction was contingent upon it. The railroads in the South were backward, and actually there was less construction there than in the Old Northwest and the trans-Mississippi region in this period. In the country as a whole the South did not even hold its own. Furthermore, this was no mere party matter. Many Conservative leaders appreciated the desirability of helping railroads, and these men were involved in the same game as the Radicals, both before and after Redemption. The expenditures of the Radical governments can also be explained in part as the result of contemporary conditions. Taxation had been low in the ante-bellum South, and there was an inevitable increase in public expenses in a period of recovery, inflation, and the extension of public services.

Among the latter none was more important than public education. The clear recognition, in the new constitutions and laws, of the responsibility of the states for public schools has been hailed by many historians as a distinct mark of progress over the ante-bellum regime, and the long-range results were constructive. Unhappily, however, the school systems broke down almost everywhere for lack of funds and popular support. There were many instances of fraud. In one parish in Louisiana, more than half of the money assigned for teachers' salaries and other expenses was embezzled. In education, as in other fields, the practice of the Radical governments fell far below their profession and theory. Northern teachers followed the federal troops and they made real progress in the tremendous task of reducing illiteracy among the Negroes, but the native whites regarded them as foreign political missionaries. Hostility to the education of Negroes was greater at the end of the period than at the beginning —especially among the poorer whites, who had themselves lacked adequate schools. In 1868, General Samuel C. Armstrong, who came of missionary stock, established in Virginia a private institution for the education of Negro youth, the Hampton Normal and Industrial Institute. Booker T. Washington attended Hampton in this period, imbibing there the ideas of industrial education which he afterwards carried into effect at Tuskegee, Alabama, with the support of Northern philanthropists and the sympathy of conservative Southerners.

Among the whites the opinion was practically universal that education suffered a setback during Reconstruction, despite the legal provisions that were made for it. The immediate educational gains of the freedmen, though perceptible, were slight; and their political gains were more apparent than real, since they were so generally under the control of the carpetbaggers and scalawags. Most of the Negroes could have made more effective use of land than they did of votes; but despite the original efforts of the Freedmen's Bureau and the hopes of Thaddeus Stevens, relatively few of them were given land. The breakdown of the plantation system redounded chiefly to the advantage of enterprising white men who had previously been on the outskirts of the planter class. But the forces of economic change enabled a vast body of former slaves to advance at least to the stage of what would be called peasantry in

Europe. White landholders, finding the Negroes reluctant to work as hired laborers, acceded to the establishment of a system of tenancy and share-farming. Since this system bound everybody in an endless cycle of recurring debt it was far from being an ideal solution of the agricultural problem.

In this period, the Negroes gained full control over their own religious affairs through the establishment of separate churches. This was one of many tendencies toward a sharper separation of the races, but the Negroes' churches were an ultimate social and cultural resource which they clung to and developed.

Radical Reconstruction abolished the black codes, but the degree to which it promoted social equality between the races has been exaggerated. In only four states (South Carolina, Florida, Mississippi, and Alabama) were mixed schools legalized, and wherever educational integration was attempted the white children as a group did not attend. Certain politicians played up social equality, but few Negroes sought it and the scalawags had little or no sympathy for it. The "equal rights" issue was more stressed in Washington, where Senator Charles Sumner of Massachusetts was its conspicuous champion. In 1875, Congress passed the Civil Rights Act, providing for equal rights in inns, public conveyances, and places of amusement—not in schools, cemeteries, or churches—and forbidding racial discrimination on juries. A pattern of segregation such as had been impossible under slavery began to emerge in Reconstruction times, and the net effect of the period was to intensify racial antagonism. But the biracial Southern system did not assume rigid form until the last decade of the nineteenth century, when the old-time gentry, traditionally more friendly to Negroes than the poorer whites, suffered a loss of political power.

The Undoing of Radical Reconstruction

The process whereby Radical Reconstruction was undone had both local and national aspects. In the beginning, when federal laws and all political authorities were against them, Southern opponents of the Radical regime resorted to extralegal methods. There was fraud and intimidation on both sides, but the Union League, which regimented the freedmen, was overmatched by the Ku Klux Klan, which terrified them. The latter organization started in 1866 in Pulaski, Tennessee, as a young men's club for social purposes, the name being derived from the Greek word "kuklos," meaning circle. It soon had conspicuous success in playing spooky pranks on the Negroes, and, following the Reconstruction acts of March 1867, it was transformed into a section-wide organization of regulators. General Nathan Bedford Forrest, the noted Confederate cavalry leader, became head of the elaborate organization, with the title "Grand Wizard of the Empire." Its most effective period was 1868-1870, when the hooded "Knights," garbed in white, rode forth at night and counter-acted much of the influence of the Union League.

From the point of view of most white Southerners, its first effects were good, and highly respected men made no bones about joining it. It served to restrain the Radicals and started the whites on the road to political supremacy. Later, lawless elements used this secret organization as a cloak for misdeeds and personal spitefulness, weakening general respect for law and accentuating the disposition to settle affairs extralegally. The lynching habits of later years were a natural outgrowth of Ku Klux prac-tices. Officially, the organization was disbanded in 1869, when states like Tennessee passed laws against it, but it lingered in a number of places for several years. It occasioned the Congressional Ku Klux Klan Report of 1872, after an extensive investigation of Southern affairs. The majority report, by the Republicans, emphasized Southern disorder and abuses, while the minority report, by the Democrats, stressed the ills of Radical government.

Out of these conditions emerged the Enforcement Acts of 1870-1871, one of which was known as the Ku Klux Act. These increased the penal-ties for the denial to any citizen of rights secured by the Fourteenth and Fifteenth Amendments, provided for federal supervision of congressional elections, and authorized the President to suspend the writ of habeas corpus and employ military force in elections and disturbance. Under this authority, in October 1871, nine counties of South Carolina were declared to be in rebellion, the writ of habeas corpus was suspended in them, and many persons were arrested by federal soldiers.

These acts represent the last strenuous attempt by Congress to enforce Reconstruction by federal power. The passage of the Civil Rights Act of 1875—forbidding discrimination in hotels, public conveyances, and places of amusement—was little more than a gesture. The Supreme Court invalidated this measure in 1883, on the ground that the Fourteenth Amendment did not empower Congress to legislate on subjects within the domain of state legislation or to create a code for the regulation of private rights. Earlier in the same year the Court had struck down the Ku Klux Act.

By 1872, there was a definite though not yet decisive reversal in Northern sentiment. This was shown by a notable act of amnesty that year, removing the disabilities of ex-Confederates except in the cases of those who had formerly held high civil or military office under the United States. The Liberal Republicans, who advocated a more generous Southern policy in the election of 1872, were unsuccesssful at the polls, but the Democrats carried the Congressional election two years later, and North-erners were showing unmistakable signs of weariness with the Southern question and the rights of the freedmen. Under these circumstances, the Conservative movement in the South proceeded from victory to victory until, by the election of 1876, only South Carolina, Florida, and Louisiana remained in Radical hands. In those states the federal government had intervened and the Radical regime was maintained by military power. These last troops were not removed until after Grant had been succeeded by Rutherford B. Hayes, but by 1876 the full restoration of home rule to the South was widely recognized as inevitable.

CHAPTER 2

Postwar Economic Expansion

THE ERA FOLLOWING THE CIVIL WAR WAS MARKED BY
economic expansion which exceeded all expectations, despite the severest
depression the Republic had yet suffered. The United States was embark-
ing on a new stage of its growth. Intensive industrial development, for
which the existing territory amply sufficed, superseded extensive
agricultural development as the most dynamic and politically influential
force in American life. The overtaking of the frontiersman by the businessman was apparent in the Plains and Rocky Mountain. There railroad
promoters and mining and cattle corporations did more than small landowners to open up the country.

Businessmen did not need or care for expansionist adventures in foreign relations any more than for Radical reformism in the South or anywhere else. They preferred safe, quiet government which supported confidence in business ventures. The hard-won victory of conservative Republicans in the election of 1876 signified the victory of the businessman's
view. It brought an end not only to the issues which had divided the
nation into two armed hosts, but also temporarily to the broad reformist
tendencies of Jacksonian democracy and the dream of the territorial
expansion of the nation.

COMPLETING THE RAILROAD NETWORK

The most important event in American history from the end of the
Civil War to the end of the century was a great acceleration of the Industrial Revolution. War needs stimulated industrial development along
some lines, while they did not prevent striking advances in others not
directly related to the military effort. The most remarkable example of

this was the starting of the first transcontinental railroad in the midst of war. The completion of the railroad network permitted the nationalization of the market for the products of farms, mines, and factories.

The departure of Southerners from Congress broke the sectional impasse over the location and financing of the transcontinental road. During the Buchanan administration, which catered to the South, federal mail subsidies had supported stagecoach lines such as the Butterfield Overland Express, following the southwestern route to California. Central and northern routes were left to private Northern initiative. The Pony Express which carried mails from Missouri to San Francisco by the South Pass route, the most romantic of these enterprises, lasted only a year and a half, until October 1861. Then the first transcontinental telegraph line, which gained a subsidy from the government, put it out of business.

Prior to secession, Southerners acquiesced in federal land grants to states on the understanding that the lands would be used to subsidize railroads. This policy encouraged railway construction across the tier of states immediately west of the Mississippi River, but, beyond that tier, the Great Plains and Rocky Mountain regions were not yet populated and direct federal subsidy to railroad companies was essential. California was rapidly filling up and its people were eager for improved connection with the East. Its government subsidized the Central Pacific Railroad, and the promoters of this—men like Leland Stanford, Collis P. Huntington, Mark Hopkins, and Charles Crocker—lobbied in Congress to secure federal subsidy for a line to span the Plains and the Rockies and connect with their own road.

The plan seemed likely to increase loyalty to the Union in far-off California. On July 1, 1862, Congress incorporated the Union Pacific Railroad. From Kansas City, Leavenworth, St. Joseph, Sioux City, and Omaha branches were to converge in one line across the mountains. The government gave the road a four-hundred-foot right-of-way, ten alternate sections of land for each mile of track, and a loan of from $16,000 to $48,000 per mile depending on the difficulty of the terrain. Since these handsome terms were not considered sufficient, Congress improved them in 1864. Work proceeded slowly until Chinese coolie labor in the West and Irish immigrants in the East were imported in sufficient numbers. The Central Pacific was authorized to build eastward from California on the same terms of federal subsidy as the Union Pacific, and it actually started first.

After the war the two roads raced to outbuild each other. The nation and the world heard reports of incredible feats of engineering skill and speedy construction. The crews caroused in vice-ridden boom towns as violently as they built the roadbed and strung the rails. The epic contest threatened to end ridiculously as the advance gangs of the two roads

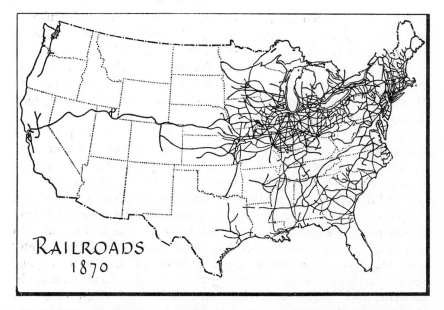

RAILROADS
1870

passed each other without speaking, grading parallel tracks. Ordered by federal authorities, however, they joined at Promontory Point, Utah, in the ceremony of the golden last spike which has passed into folk legend. The whole country celebrated in the spring of 1869 when the telegraph flashed the news. Orators proclaimed that iron ties of Union had replaced the guns of war. Within a generation other transcontinental lines were built with varying amounts of federal aid: in the Southwest the Atchison, Topeka, and Santa Fé and the Southern Pacific; in the northwest the Northern Pacific from Saint Paul, Minnesota, to Portland, Oregon (later to Tacoma, Washington), and the Great Northern, from St. Paul to Seattle. After the sectional controversy ceased to bear on this question the ante-bellum dream of Stephen A. Douglas came true.

At the same time the older regions of the country expanded and consolidated their rail networks at an accelerated pace. The Middle West led all the sections in building new lines. By 1873, Illinois alone contained 5000 miles of track. The South nearly doubled its mileage between 1865 and 1873 while rebuilding the almost totally ruined lines (about 10,000 miles of road) it had possessed before the war. In the nation as a whole the Panics of 1873 and 1893 drastically reduced new construction, but lost time was made up in boom years so that the national mileage which had stood at about 40,000 in 1860 approached 200,000 in 1900. Then the United States had more track than all of Europe.

New methods and inventions brought rail traffic close to modern standards of speed, comfort, and safety in approximately that order of precedence. Wider roadbeds, steel rails and bridges, and more powerful locomotives permitted faster schedules. In 1865, George M. Pullman built the first sleeping car. Its success led the roads to adopt his steadily improved models which by the 1880's were fantasies of baroque decoration. Pullman also developed dining, drawing-room, chair, and observation cars, manufactured them himself and rented them to railroads. The American passenger found that by paying extra charges he could enjoy the luxuries of a palatial hotel.

The railroads resisted measures to increase the safety of their passengers until public clamor against the rising accident rate forced reforms. Observing an accident in 1866, George Westinghouse put his mind to solving the problem of quickly stopping a train. Three years later he patented the compressed air brake. Westinghouse became president of a company to manufacture braking equipment, and the press got behind the campaign. He steadily improved his brake to make it automatic and smooth in operation, and by 1880 half of the rolling stock in the country used his devices. Automatic signal systems and ingenious coupling devices were also developed during these decades. Coal became the preferred fuel, though wood continued to be used wherever it was abundant. By the 1890's, American rail travel had entered a golden age of speed, luxury, and safety.

Subsidies and Abuses

The railroad builders of the post-Civil War decades created a transportation system that was required for the industrialization of the nation's economy and is indispensable to this day. Few would deny that federal, state, and local governmental subsidies were justified as initial spurs to the construction of roads where population was not yet sufficient to assure immediate revenues. State and local cash subsidies amounted to more than a half billion dollars, and federal and state land grants equaled the size of Texas. Federal cash loans were smaller and federal land grants were larger than those of the states. It is estimated that taxpayers bore 40 per cent of the cost of all railroad building prior to 1870.

The unconscionable methods of the promoters quickly turned the public against subsidies. Innumerable devices were invented to loot the companies and cheat the public. A standard technique was disclosed when the Credit Mobilier was investigated in 1872 and 1873. The largest stockholders of the Union Pacific, led by Oakes Ames, Congressman from Massachusetts, had formed the Credit Mobilier as a construction company. As directors of the Union Pacific they awarded a contract to Credit Mobilier that drained the railroad company of both its huge federal subsidy and the funds of private investors; as owners of Credit Mobilier they pocketed enormous profits and disbanded the construction

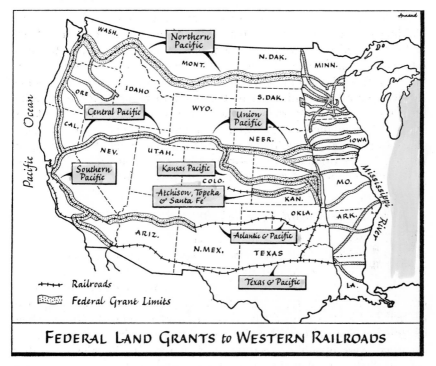

FEDERAL LAND GRANTS to WESTERN RAILROADS

company; as directors of the Union Pacific they ran it into debt and bankruptcy so that the company was burdened with a capitalization which could only be serviced by permanently exorbitant freight and passenger rates. They distributed shares in Credit Mobilier at low prices "where they would do the most good." The recipients included Senators, Representatives, and Vice-President Schuyler Colfax. Perhaps the worst revelation, indicative of the state of public morals, was that many of these "purchasers" of shares refused to admit that they had engaged in anything but a normal business transaction.

Practically all of the railroad companies were looted in one fashion or another by insiders and left to carry the watered debts by charging high rates. Land grants, instead of being used to finance construction, were held until the settlement of contiguous government lands caused a rise in price, and were then unloaded on later settlers for fat profits. Directors of the companies used their power to create artificial rises in the price of their companies' securities by withholding issues from the market and then dumping their personal holdings on small investors. Bankruptcies and receiverships alike were rigged, sometimes by the same group, to profit insiders and exploit the public.

In 1872, the Supreme Court ruled that local governments were liable for debts contracted to subsidize railroads—meaning that the taxpayers

were denied the recourse of default—and this along with the Credit
Mobilier revelations ended the era of governmental subsidies. The Panic
of 1873 pushed many unscrupulous promoters out of business, but they
returned unchastened and fertile with new schemes in the 1880's. By
that time federal and state governments were under pressure from homesteaders, reformers, and users of the roads to regulate the companies;
the directors of these were on the defensive, and corruption of legislators
was chiefly designed to prevent regulation of the companies' financial
and rate policies. The railroads then became the arena of the first great
struggle in the United States between advocates of unlimited free enterprise and proponents of governmental intervention in the public interest.

The Trend toward Consolidation

During both prosperity and depression the steady consolidation of
railroad ownership among fewer and fewer companies went on. Modern
students tend to believe that this process was inevitable because a railroad is a "natural" monopoly, and, granted governmental regulation to
prevent abuse of private power, that monopoly is even desirable. There
seemed to be little chance that a government of limited powers would
be able to control the colossal companies, particularly since "railroad
Senators" were openly or secretly on their payrolls. Popular opposition
was insufficient to stay the monopolistic trend; and, in the eyes of the
railroad men themselves, consolidation was necessary to avoid the
harmful effects of unbridled competition. Uncontrolled building resulted
in unnecessary duplication of carriers between many points. Rate wars
made proper service to the public impossible. The first attempts to end
competition took the forms of "pools," whereby competing roads agreed
to share the traffic, and "gentlemen's agreements," whereby rivals promised not to cut rates. But the only certain means of ending competition
was unified control.

Beginning in 1862, Cornelius Vanderbilt bought up roads between
New York and Chicago along the northernmost routes, creating the New
York Central system. He improved his roads, cut the running time of
passenger trains between the two cities to twenty-four hours, and preferred a sound investment to speculator's profits. The owners of the
Pennsylvania and the Baltimore and Ohio companies kept pace with
Vanderbilt's New York Central in extending their ownership over Middle
Western lines. Competition among the three giants was modified by
occasional agreements, receiverships, and interlocking directorates. This
last became a popular device whereby two companies ostensibly competitors were actually controlled by the same directors who saw to it
that competition did not get out of hand. The fourth largest northeastern
system was the Erie Railroad, the famous victim of Daniel Drew, Jay

Gould, and Jim Fiske, whose rivalry for control of the road included informal civil wars between their employees. In the South, mergers also produced a few great systems, and the operators of the transcontinental lines of the West, giants at birth, fought each other and engaged in deals and mergers with the special gusto of frontiersmen.

The West was the scene of abuses which aroused the deepest hatred of the railroad systems. Farmers who took up homesteads during and after the Civil War quickly shifted from enthusiasm for railroad construction to disillusionment with the results. Not only did the railroads push up the price of land by speculative techniques, they owned grain elevators along their sidings to which the farmer had to sell his wheat at ruinous prices or, if he shipped it by rail to the great city markets, there, too, the railroads owned the elevators. Since Western farmers rarely lived at points served by more lines than one, where rates were reduced by competition, they generally paid higher shipping rates than any other class of users. Farmers of the South suffered from similar disadvantages.

INDUSTRIAL DEVELOPMENTS

It is said that a new industry opening up a new business "frontier" was the secret of every period of American prosperity during the decades of industrial revolution. Steel probably played that role immediately after the Civil War. Formerly steel had been too expensive for anything but fine tools and cutlery. The process of the English inventor, Henry Bessemer, made the product cheap enough to be used for rails and the skeletons of buildings and bridges. The first Bessemer converter in the United States was built in 1864 at Wyandotte, Michigan. For a time Detroit led in steel production, but Pennsylvania coal, needed in enormous quantities for the converters, rather than Minnesota iron ore, determined the location of the industry within a few years. The Cambria Works of Daniel J. Morrell in Johnstown, Pennsylvania, the Bethlehem Works, and, destined to be largest of all, the plants of Andrew Carnegie near Pittsburgh, acquired their own mines, and brought the ore by Great Lakes ship and by rail to the flaming furnaces. Production of steel ingots rose from 2600 tons in 1867 to 929,000 in 1879. By that time the open-hearth process had begun to displace the Bessemer converter.

The meat-packing and flour-milling industries were also spurred by improved processes. They moved west towards the great cattle ranches and bonanza wheat farms of the Plains. Refrigerator railroad cars made possible the sale of fresh meat across the nation from the Union Stockyards of Chicago, where Philip Armour, Nelson Morris, and Gustavus F. Swift developed huge packing plants. The flour-milling industry moved north as well as west when new processes made an improved flour out of the hard spring wheat of Minnesota and the Dakotas. Railroads, water power, and men like Cadwallader C. Washburn and Charles A. Pillsbury made Minneapolis the flour capital.

The oil industry was born during these years. "Coal oil" or kerosene for lamps was at first the most marketable product of petroleum and quickly displaced whale oil and candles in Europe and Asia as well as America. Long regarded as an Indian medicine and mostly ignored, petroleum which oozed out of the ground in western Pennsylvania was first pursued underground by drilling wells in 1860 at Titusville. At the close of the Civil War, proved oil fields and barren regions alike were the objects of feverish speculation. Pithole City grew to 10,000 inhabitants in six weeks in the rush for "black gold." Problems of storage and transportation were solved by building stationary, railway, and water-borne tanks. Refineries clustered at Pittsburgh and Cleveland. By 1870, the latter city, enjoying competition between Lake ships and the New York Central, drew away from Pittsburgh, which was wholly dependent on the Pennsylvania Railroad. But from oil well to oil lamp the young industry was riddled with waste and speculation.

The Emergence of Rockefeller

John D. Rockefeller, a Cleveland merchant, entered the industry in 1865. He saw that refining was the strategic position from which both ends of the industry could be controlled, and that economies could be achieved by large-scale operation. He built and bought refineries, incorporated for a million dollars the Standard Oil Company of Ohio in 1870, and experimented with devices like secret freight rebates from railroads to give him advantage over his competitors. He had a relentless will conditioned by strict Baptist religious faith, an artful brain, and a genius for organization.

Inefficiency, overproduction, and the Panic of 1873 eliminated many small refineries, and Rockefeller was ready with a plan for a partnership with some of his competitors in a pool strong enough to crush all other refiners. He brought O. H. Payne, H. M. Flagler, William Rockefeller, and others into the South Improvement Company, and this combine extorted from the Pennsylvania, New York Central, and Erie railroads secret rebates on payments for its oil shipments. The railroads were further squeezed to pay the combine drawbacks on the freight charges for oil shipments by *other* refiners. This last maneuver enraged the independents so that they formed a counterorganization, gained the support of the Pennsylvania Railroad, and embargoed the Rockefeller combine. The South Improvement Company failed, but Rockefeller used the enormous profits of the Standard Oil Company to buy up competitors and expand his facilities. The Pennsylvania Railroad capitulated; bills in

Congress to regulate interstate commerce and forbid rebates were defeated; and by 1879 Standard controlled more than 90 per cent of the oil refining plants in the nation and practically all the rail and pipeline facilities for the transportation of oil.

Rockefeller's pattern was duplicated in many other industries. The railroads themselves bought up coal mines and established a virtual monopoly over anthracite. A "trust" was more often successful than a pool in efforts to achieve a monopoly position. The trust did not depend on "gentlemen's agreements." The owners of the constituent companies handed over to a committee of trustees control over their voting stock. The trustees could then allocate production, fix prices, and divide markets with assurance that the constituent operating companies would obey their dictates. Trusts generally aimed at "horizontal" monopoly, that is, control over a strategic bottleneck between raw materials and consumers' products. Control over prices at both ends could be achieved only by virtually complete monopoly in the middle, otherwise producers and consumers would hasten to do business with a competitor and quickly by-pass the monopoly. The Standard Oil Company became the greatest of the trusts.

Mechanization itself dictated large-scale enterprise. It transformed old industries and created new ones. Production of ready-made shoes and clothing, cheap watches, sewing-machines, pianos, stoves, and dozens of varieties of small hardware was rapidly mechanized after the Civil War. Monopoly was a minor problem in such industries except as patents conferred legal rights to exclusive use of inventions. Where competition reigned, planning of production to match the market was virtually impossible, and overexpansion by small business was equally responsible with the monopoly practices of big business for the increasing severity of "boom and bust" in the business cycle.

The number of business firms increased from 431,000 in 1870 to nearly 609,000 a year later. The market for their various products could not keep up with such a phenomenal rate of growth. Particularly alarming to observers was the growth of service and middlemen's companies, from railroads and commission and brokerage firms to banking and retailing. They produced no goods but only exchanged them from place to place and from one owner to another, creating a disproportion between the number of people producing new wealth on farms and in factories, forests, mines, and fisheries, and those who exchanged them. During the decade of 1860-1870 the population increased 22 per cent, but the middleman classes increased 40 per cent. Both the productive and the exchange sections of the economy expanded on credit. Banks created credit to help companies and individuals to expand, speculation contributed to the creation of false values, and the structure became dangerously top-heavy.

Panic Follows Boom

The federal government failed to check the inflationary spiral during the boom years. Following a brief period of gradual contraction of the currency, further retirement of the wartime greenbacks was forbidden by the Act of 1868. The value of greenbacks in terms of gold had risen markedly from the wartime low, but the currency was far from stabilized and the uncertainties of the situation encouraged the spirit of speculation. Gold was being drained out of the country to pay interest on public and private debts and to make up the unfavorable balance of trade. In Europe as well as America there was currency inflation and overexpansion of economic activities. Under these circumstances there was danger of an international reaction to a tremor anywhere, and when depression came it was worldwide.

Bankruptcies of American business firms increased drastically in 1872. Early in 1873 the Credit Mobilier revelations and a wave of insurance and banking scandals undermined confidence in government and business. Fear gripped the business community as it was realized that any break in the inflated structure might cause all creditors to demand cash payment at once. Total credit was six times greater than total cash, therefore widespread bankruptcies would inevitably follow.

The break came in September 1873. Jay Cooke's banking firm, grown huge since his marketing of war bonds for the federal Treasury, closed its branches in the leading eastern cities—an admission that it could not obtain cash for its loans and investments, and therefore could not pay back to depositors their savings on demand. The failure of this presumed pillar of the national economy precipitated panic as creditors of every sort demanded payment and debtors unable to pay—individuals, business companies and banks—were ruined. Mob scenes occurred in stock exchanges, where holders of stocks and bonds offered them at descending prices and few had cash to buy at any price. Savings were wiped out as bank after bank barricaded its doors against angry crowds of depositors. The New York Stock Exchange closed them to prevent further hysterical trading from pushing all prices down to nothing. The Panic spread in widening circles from unsound to sound firms, from East to West and South, from bankers and brokers to the ultimate foundations of the economy—farms and factories. Bankers, frantic to realize cash on the paper in their vaults, demanded payment on loans to manufacturers and on mortgages to farmers. Unable to pay, farmers lost their homes and acres, while business men lost factories for which no buyers with cash could be found, and their employees were thrown out of work to join evicted farmers in destitution. Farms and factories that managed to continue operations could obtain only low prices for their products as purchasing power fell, markets were glutted, wages were cut, and hunger beset millions.

Deflation and Recovery

The boom had dazzled Americans into believing they were in a wonderland of eternal prosperity. The frightening collapse caused them to realize that the nationalization of the economy increased the risks as well as the benefits of interdependence among all classes and sections. Moralizers preached that the sins of luxurious living had brought punishment, and they enjoined repentance and frugality on the people. *The Nation* called this a "cheap, sick-bed morality." Far from expecting a rebirth of virtue to result from mass pauperism, secular writers and many clergymen pointed out that the increase in destitution bred a startling increase in crime. Unemployed men and even some women and children took the road as tramps; they organized gangs devoted to thievery, incendiarism, and murder, terrorizing whole districts. Radicalism increased as the practices of Big Business were the most vulnerable target of anger, but it was notable that the majority of the rebellious unemployed turned to the "individualist" way out, that is, to nonpolitical violence rather than anticapitalist revolution.

There was some demand that state and federal governments should assume responsibility for direct relief to the unemployed and provide work on public projects. But it was not until 1933 after two more great depressions that the federal government responded to such demands. Private charity and town and municipal governments, their funds occasionally supplemented by state grants, tried to cope with lengthening breadlines, diseases of malnutrition, and shattered homes. Relief to the unemployed was so inadequate that it could not rebuild the consumers' market for farm and factory products. Another proposal was that the federal government should stem deflation by issuing new quantities of paper currency and coining silver. This was the crucial demand of the Greenback-Labor Party in 1878, and of similar third-party movements in the next depression.

Strict laissez-faire theory required that the federal government should keep hands off the "natural" processes of the business cycle. The depression should be allowed to run its course until all unsound economic activities had been eliminated and a new beginning could be made on a basis of low prices and low wages. Tariffs were a standing violation of this theory because they provided governmental support to protected industries. In its monetary policies the federal government now turned to deflationary measures that favored creditors. This depressed prices and wages still further, and worsened the plight of debtors.

Legislation in 1873 demonetized silver, that is, the federal mints ceased to accept that metal from private owners for coinage into money. Thus the currency could not be swelled by the great new silver mines soon opened in the West. In 1875, the gradual retirement of green- backs began. Though checked a little later, this reduced the quantity of currency. On January 1, 1879, the federal Treasury resumed specie pay- ments. Besides gold, only national bank and federal paper money ex- changeable at par for gold remained in circulation. By 1878, the number of dollars in circulation per capita in 1865 had been cut in half. The drastic reduction in the medium of exchange lowered prices, thereby increasing the purchasing power of the dollar which creditors received. Conversely, it injured debtors, who had to pay back more valuable dollars than they had borrowed.

The painful process of deflation could be read in the failures of 5800 business firms in 1874, 7700 in 1875, 9000 in 1876 and almost equal num- bers during the next two years. In 1878, a new wave of revelations of corrupt practices by bankers increased public anger. The debt-ridden West was the chief scene of outcry against both Wall Street and Wash- ington. In the East, the center of creditor interest, "sound money" policies were defended. Laborers failed to rally to the Greenback-Labor alliance.

By 1880, the tide of depression turned. The downward spiral of wages and prices had caused untold suffering but it also produced an ac- cumulation of savings in the hands of the strongest creditors, and when the purchasing power of money reached a peak, confidence revived and savings were used for increased consumption and investment. Recovery was aided by a series of crop failures in Europe which opened great markets for American wheat, pork, and beef. Between 1875 and 1880, the American farmer who had survived the worst of the Depression was able to make gains against his burden of debt on the strength of bountiful harvests and growing demand for his produce at home and abroad. Granger legislation helped him in some states against the worst abuses of railroads and middlemen. New farm tools—the gang plow, the hay- loader, corn-planter, and steam-powered "combine" which joined harvest- ing and threshing of wheat in one mammoth implement—permitted farmers to reap new rewards for their labor.

In the West recovery came at the expense of the small farmer, who frequently lost his land and turned to tenancy. It benefited the cattle kings and bonanza wheat farmers of the Plains and the owners of smaller but richer plots in the Middle West. In the East recovery was a general upward movement of employment, wages, prices, and production after appalling economic and social costs had been paid by all classes except the most cautious creditors. Everywhere, however, the sunshine of pros- perity after 1880 quickly banished remembrance of disasters and the country moved buoyantly into an era of fabulous expansion which lasted almost without setbacks for twelve years and was hailed as no mere turn of the cycle but as an entrance into eternal economic bliss. False as later events proved this dream to be, the upward turn of recovery carried the national economy during the 1880's far above the levels of production and consumption of the post-Civil War boom. Nor did the downward swing of 1893 wipe out all these gains.

THE WESTWARD MOVEMENT

The victory of the Union in the war etched more deeply than ever the treasured image of America in general and the West in particular as the land of hope and opportunity. Just as the end of the war released businessmen to concentrate on the exploitation of the nation's resources and markets, so it also signaled to thousands at home and abroad to cut old ties and move west for more freedom and more bread.

Federal Legislation and the Last Frontiers

Two federal laws enacted during the Civil War offered specific invitations to Americans and foreigners to populate the West and to swell the labor supply of the East. The Homestead Act of 1862 had little effect during the war. The falling off of European immigration from almost half a million per year during the fifties to 72,000 in 1862 alarmed the federal government and industrialists who feared a labor shortage. Lincoln asked Congress to encourage immigration and the result was the Contract Labor Act of 1864. The operations of the Homestead and Contract Labor Acts meshed by holding out to foreigners who came to America under contract to a private employer the chance to win a farm in the West. Together the two laws formed one grand design providing practical methods to convert the American dream into reality for all comers. The reality was not as rosy as the dream; nevertheless no other government had ever done so much to bestow on any taker opportunity for material competence coupled with political rights.

The Homestead Act provided that any adult citizen or any alien who had filed his first citizenship papers could claim 160 acres of the federal lands upon payment of a $10 registration fee, and obtain final title after living upon or cultivating the farm for five years. Such a law had long been advocated not only by farmers but by Eastern reformers and laborers, and the terms were thought to give genuine effect to the slogan of "land for the landless." Through no fault of the lawmakers, however, it did practically nothing to effectuate the slogan if "landless" meant totally lacking in capital. The majority of the homesteaders were Middle Western farmers who sold their farms and used the money for travel, implements, shelter, seed, and the cost of living during the first years

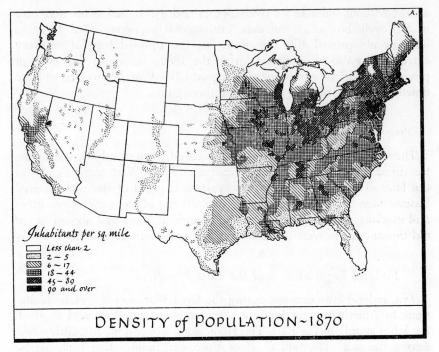

DENSITY of POPULATION~1870

until the new land could be made productive. Eastern laborers whose annual incomes often amounted to less than $300 could not finance the establishment of a farm even on free land. European immigrants who arrived with funds formed a minority of the homesteaders.

Of those who did move into the frontier region of the Great Plains after 1862 more bought their farms from private landowners than took up free homesteads on the federal domain. In violation of the original intention of the Homestead Act, 521 million acres of federal land were given or sold to railroads, states, or large-scale speculative jobbers, while only 80 million acres were obtained by homesteaders, and these tracts were often less desirable. The railroads took possession of choice sections along their rights-of-way and sold them at several dollars an acre to farmers willing to pay for good land close to transportation. By the Morrill Land-Grant Act of 1862 every state government was entitled to 30,000 acres of western land for each of its Senators and Representatives, the proceeds to be used to endow agricultural colleges. Most of the states sold large tracts to speculators who subdivided and sold to settlers at $5 to $10 an acre. The Land Office sold large tracts, usually at $1.25 an acre, and lumber companies, mining companies, and jobbers bought up most of the richest resources of the West before homesteaders could stake out claims. Even Revolutionary land warrants given to veterans and handed down in their families were bought up by jobbers and used to engross vast tracts. As Indian reservations were narrowed down by new agreements with the tribes, their former lands were sold off to speculators.

The Timber Culture Act of 1873 encouraged homesteaders to plant trees on the grassy Plains by giving them an additional 160 acres if they would set out seedlings on 40 acres. The Desert Land Act of 1877, presumably enacted to help the homesteader by giving him a larger farm—640 acres where irrigation was necessary—was actually put through by cattlemen seeking means to take over grazing lands. The Timber and Stone Act of 1878 led to the worst abuses. It permitted the fabulous forests of the Pacific Northwest to be handed out as "unfit for cultivation" and therefore of slight value. The lumber barons of the next decades reaped the harvest.

A host of facts may be adduced to show that the great experiment of the Homestead Act ended in failure and disillusionment. The very region of the Great Plains which was the homesteaders' frontier in the sixties and seventies, became the chief seedbed of the Farmers' Revolt in the eighties and nineties. Nevertheless, land was cheaper in the American West than in Europe even after railroads and speculators reaped their profits. Not all the disappointment of the pioneers was due to failure of the Homestead Act. The Great Plains presented less favorable climate and soils than any earlier belt of settlement and many a settler failed to adopt the necessary dry-farming methods soon enough to avoid defeat. Many districts of the Plains were not capable of supporting the type of diversified family farm that was standard in the Middle West and East. Much of the land could be used effectively only by large-scale cattle ranchers or by small farmers after huge irrigation projects had been built. The Homestead Act did serve to advertise the last American frontiers and to populate them rapidly. Most of the settlers were sturdy enough to survive disillusionment and, with their children, went on to overcome man-made and natural handicaps more severe than any other American frontiersmen had met.

Cattle-grazing, mining, and lumbering became permanent activities of the High Plains and Rocky Mountains because of climate and geography. In the Low Plains (stretching northward from Central Texas) rainfall in good years may reach the twenty inches necessary for crop farming, and there the standard type of family farm with a concomitant growth in industry and urbanism has approximated the pattern of older frontiers. Even so, farming was made hazardous by the frequent years of drought and, once the primordial sod was turned under, by dust storms which often blow away the thin layer of topsoil. The Industrial Revolution hastened settlement of the region by threading it with railroads and providing cheap metal windmills for deep wells, barbed wire to substitute for wooden fences, and heavy machinery to cope with extensive fields. The scarcity of water led to fierce struggles over riparian rights along the inadequate streams. The technique of "dry farming"—deep plowing to encourage capillary movement of moisture upwards, dust mulching by harrowing the surface after rainfall to discourage evaporation—was developed to conserve water, but it required expensive machinery. Added to the costs of windmills and fencing, periodic ravages of hordes of locusts, exorbitant railroad rates, and the exactions of middlemen, this made farming on the Low Plains in the loneliness of empty horizons an enterprise to make any but the stoutest heart quail. All the more remarkable that the belt from western Kansas to the Dakotas was brought under the plow within a few years after the Civil War. Despite periodic contractions of the western limit of cropping after seasons of drought or low prices for wheat and corn, the early sod huts were replaced by frame dwellings, while schools, churches, and trading towns grew up to enrich the farmer's existence.

Indians and Cattlemen

The American Indian staged his last fight against white domination during the dozen years after Appomattox. The tribes of the northern mountains, like those of the Pacific Coast states, were weak and easily subdued by miners backed by the federal government. In the Southwest, federal troops carried on successful forays against the Apache and Navaho tribes during the Civil War. But the tribes of the Plains were stronger and had developed a culture superbly adapted to their environment. The plentiful buffalo provided food, clothing, and shelter. Vast distances could be covered on the captured wild horses which the Plains tribes handled with spectacular skill. Above all, the Sioux, Crow, Blackfeet, Comanche, Cheyenne, and lesser tribes were fighters determined to avoid the fate of their kinsmen and capable of defeating any ordinary efforts by white settlers or soldiers. Even the Colt six-shooter did not completely overcome the skill of an Indian who, while galloping like the wind, could fire from the off side of his pony twenty barbed arrows with enough force to drive them through a buffalo.

Before the Civil War the common conception of the Plains country was signified by its label on the maps of the period as "The Great American Desert." Considering the region useless for white settlement, the federal government in good faith pursued the policy of "One Big Reservation" for the older tribes and for those it pushed westward. The movement of pioneers and forty-niners across the Plains to Oregon and California gradually dispelled the notion that the region was desert; transportation and mining created settlements here and there; and by the fifties the federal government began to demand of the Plains tribes that they accept "Concentration," that is, definite but vast boundaries for each tribe separately. Once more Indian chiefs accepted promises that treaties would be eternal. Surveyors for railroads and prospectors for gold and silver paid little attention to the tribes' titles to their domains, and federal agents constantly demanded of the chiefs acceptance of narrower boundaries.

Following the discovery of gold in Colorado in 1859 and other strikes elsewhere, the Indians perceived that they were caught between miners from California and settlers from the East. They became restless and sullen, and the Civil War encouraged them to resist the distracted federal government. Chiefs who had signed treaties were overthrown by their warriors. Fighting began among the Arapahoe and Cheyennes in Colorado and devastated the settlements there by 1864. Then to an Indian offer of peace, Chief Black Kettle received the answer that the Great Father in Washington would soon win the war against the South and would send his soldiers against the Plains Indians.

This threat was carried out. The Sioux resisted the plan to build the Powder River Road from the east to supply miners at Virginia City, and massacred federal troops. War became general. Criticism of the War Department led to an effort by Congress in 1867 to effect peace by sending a commission to offer the tribes small but permanent reservations where they should give up hunting, turn to agriculture, and be given food and clothing by the federal government while they learned "to walk the white man's road." The Five Civilized Tribes were pushed into eastern Indian Territory (Oklahoma) and the Comanches and other Southwestern tribes were offered the remainder of that area. Apaches and Navahos agreed to settle on small plots in Arizona and New Mexico. Cheyennes and Arapahoes submitted to a treaty giving them inferior land along the Cimarron River. Chief Red Cloud of the Sioux was pacified by a promise that the Powder River Road project would be abandoned and accepted a reservation west of the Missouri River in Dakota Territory.

But many individual warriors refused to turn, at the signing of a paper, from nomadism to wardship under the federal government. In small bands they carried on guerrilla warfare from Canada to Mexico for ten more years. Ready for death rather than submission, they raided settlements and ambushed troops with relentless cunning. Arduous campaigns by equally relentless federal troops commanded by Generals Sheridan and Sherman were necessary to crush them. The Sioux—incited by mistreatment by agents, the violation of their rights by the gold rush into the Black Hills, and the approach of the Northern Pacific Railroad —broke out of their reservation in 1876 under Chief Sitting Bull. On the Little Big Horn River they slaughtered 265 men under Colonel George A. Custer, who had rashly led his men into a trap. He was rewarded with legendary fame as the hero of "Custer's Last Stand." General Terry defeated the main body of Sioux in October 1876, and thereafter no important rebellion occurred. The Nez Percé tribe of Oregon was subdued in 1877 and sent to barren lands in Indian Territory where malaria wiped it out. Small bands of warriors who staged sporadic raids during the following years were hunted down.

In 1890, a strange final incident symbolized the end of Indian strife in America. Sioux warriors invoked the potency of their old gods against the white man in "Ghost Dances" which the Payute Messiah, Wavoka, promised them would make the whites vanish. Army officers tried to stop the fantastic rituals and a few Indians, including Sitting Bull, resisted hopelessly in the face of the new Hotchkiss rapid-fire guns. Their death signified the downfall of their gods.

The destruction of the buffalo by white men as much as military action assured the defeat of the Plains Indians. Where an estimated 13,000,000 of the shaggy beasts had roamed in two great herds, by 1885 zoos had difficulty in finding a few animals for exhibition. Sportsmen had shot thousands, and tanneries financed the slaughter of millions merely for their hides. Once the buffalo was gone, the Indian could not subsist except by agriculture supplemented by federal aid. This aid was usually specified in peace treaties, but in 1871 Congress decreed that no tribe should henceforth be recognized as an independent entity with which the United States might contract a treaty. Thereupon treatment of the Indians depended solely upon Washington and the influences which contending reform groups could bring to bear upon the government in favor of their pet schemes.

No sooner had the back of Indian resistance been broken in 1876 than the Indian became the object of a sentimental cult, typified by Helen Hunt Jackson's *A Century of Dishonor,* which was accurate enough in its details of mistreatment by whites but erroneous in its assumption that the Indian wanted to be converted immediately to the white man's civilization. A leader in the movement, Senator Henry L. Dawes of Massachusetts, put through the Severalty Act in 1887, in effect a homestead law for the Indians. It allocated 160 acres of reservation land to each head of a family and smaller plots to others, held the Indians' farms in trust for their "owners" for twenty-five years, and made each recipient a citizen of the United States, while the state governments were left free to refuse state citizenship. Remaining reservation lands were sold and the proceeds used for education of the Indians. Tribal organization was destroyed as a corollary of conversion to individual homesteading and superposition of federal political jurisdiction. This law was the foundation of federal Indian policy until the growth of anthropological knowledge created respect for the Indians' own culture and was registered in the "New Deal for the Indian" during the Franklin D. Roosevelt administration. Then new federal laws belatedly encouraged revival of tribal ways as an alternative to absorption of individual Indians into white society at large.

The removal of the Indian barrier on the Great Plains was followed by the incursion of cattlemen. The treeless Plains with their rich native grasses were better suited for grazing than anything else. Mexican cowboys and herds in Texas early set the pattern for the steady expansion of the range northward. American cattle were mingled with the ancient Moorish breeds left by the Spanish to produce the famous Texas Longhorn—rangy, half-wild, and able to travel great distances to market without losing meat value. The Civil War blocked markets to the east so that the herds of Longhorns multiplied. With the end of the war fortunes were made by rounding up Texas cattle and herding them north on open range to railheads. The adventurous "Long Drive" of cowboy song and story followed. As settlement and railroads invaded the Plains, the open range available for the Long Drive narrowed westward and southward. The Long Drive similarly retreated along the Sedalia, Chisholm, Western, and Goodnight-Loving Trails successively until mountain forests and deserts, besides the availability of railroads everywhere by 1880, ended the golden age of the cowboy.

While eastern and foreign markets steadily expanded, fatter and more sedentary breeds were developed on vast ranches from Texas to Montana. Often without show of legal right, ranchers appropriated land by the tens of square miles along streams and were upheld in their range and water "rights" by public opinion. Cowboys and ranchers fought off sheep herders whose close-cropping animals made the sod unfit for cattle, rustlers who stole marketable steers, and neighboring ranchers with whose herds their own mingled. The "round-up," an annual branding of calves, replaced the Long Drive as the colorful climax of the cowboy's year.

In the 1880's news and exaggerations of the fortunes made in a few years by ranchers whose capital had been "a steer and a branding iron" created a rush of "tenderfeet" to Wyoming and Montana. This led to the formation of corporations by eastern businessmen to raise cattle, and even caused an influx of British capital whose owners were eager to match the 30 per cent profits of American ranchers. The inevitable result of the boom was a fall in prices resulting from overstocking of the range. Old ranchers formed associations to protect their holdings against newcomers, but the boom ended with a few years of bad weather in the late eighties. Winter blizzards were followed by summer drought, and vast losses of cattle were coupled with low prices. The bankruptcy of most corporations and the ruin of many ranchers, along with incursions of sheep herders and fence-building farmers, closed the open-range period by 1890. In that year, the federal Census declared that the frontier (defined as a North-South belt of land containing fewer than two persons per square mile) was no more. Thereafter the cattleman in less spectacular fashion held his own on smaller ranches. He gave more heed to legality and employed more careful methods, including the provision of feed to supplement the native grass. His work became humdrum, but the cowboy had already made his place in legend.

CHAPTER 3

Foreign Affairs and National Politics

IN THE DOZEN YEARS FOLLOWING THE WAR THE FOREIGN affairs of the United States were conducted with much more gratifying results than the domestic. This was partly because the blighting partisanship and political corruption of the time affected the conduct of diplomacy less than they did the operations of government at home. It was partly owing to the ability of two distinguished Secretaries of State: William H. Seward, whom Johnson inherited from Lincoln, and Hamilton Fish, who was the shining light of the Grant administration. Of the two, Fish was the wiser and more successful. Besides the acquisition of noncontiguous territory which proved more valuable afterwards than was commonly expected at the time, the achievement of American diplomatic statesmanship in the period of Reconstruction was a thoroughly satisfactory settlement of difficulties growing out of the Civil War.

On the home front, the national government floundered in a morass of inefficiency and corruption—as did any number of state and municipal governments throughout the land. The lowest depths were reached during the presidency of a great soldier, sincere patriot, and personally honest man—Ulysses S. Grant. Obviously the nation's hero failed as President to provide the sort of statesmanship that the times required. But this is more than a story of one man's inadequacy. The political ills of the Grant era must be viewed against the background of the existing economic and psychological situation.

In the aftermath of war there had come over the land a spirit of materialism, selfish aggrandizement, and civic corruption for which there is no parallel in American history except perhaps in the 1920's, just after the First World War. Outside of the South, the mood of the country was one of blind complacency and reckless optimism. Still intoxicated with the wine of victory, aggressive men everywhere ruthlessly exploited the opportunities that had come with peace. Not until the depression of 1873 did the sobering process really begin, and not until after that did movements of political protest make much headway. By 1876 a series of public scandals left no doubt that the need for reform of some sort had become imperative.

THE EXPANSIONISM OF WILLIAM H. SEWARD, 1865-1869

Seward continued as Secretary of State throughout President Johnson's term. After the war he decided that a spirited program of expansion would help to reunite the sections and strengthen his own political position against attack by the Radical Republicans. He did not foresee that the absorption of Americans in internal affairs would make them indifferent to external expansion for another generation. His promise in 1867 that, if he were granted thirty more years of life, he would give his countrymen "possession of the American continent and the control of the world" was an empty boast.

Immediately after Napoleon III, in 1867, abandoned Maximilian to his Mexican executioners and removed the French threat against the Monroe Doctrine, Seward visited the Caribbean to study likely locations for naval and coaling stations. In the Dominican Republic he found not only the attractive Bay of Samaná but a hard-pressed government which was willing to sell the harbor and even the whole island. Congress vetoed any such scheme. The attractions of another harbor, St. Thomas in the Danish-owned Virgin Islands, and the willingness of Denmark to sell the whole group led to the amicable negotiation of a treaty, signed in October 1867, to hand over the Islands to the United States for $7.5 million, provided that a plebiscite of the inhabitants was favorable. The Senate ignored the Danish treaty. The net result of Seward's search for islands, besides a great deal of ridicule, was the acquisition of the uninhabited Midway Islands a thousand miles west of Hawaii. Title to them was asserted by an American naval officer. Congress and the public hardly noticed the event. Their strategic value was revealed only in 1942 by the Battle of Midway.

The Purchase of Alaska

The idea of an Alaskan deal originated with Russia. Her despotic government regarded the distant American Republic as no threat to the Czar, but as a counterbalance to the European Powers, chiefly Britain, that Russia feared. Russian officials believed that the territory of Alaska was bound to be taken from their country by the British in case of war, whereas in American hands it would form a flanking position to weaken Canada. The managers of the monopolistic Russian-American

Company who ruled the territory already had information about the gold deposits which were "discovered" in 1897 by the American "sourdoughs." They kept it secret for fear that a premature gold rush from the United States would disrupt Russo-American relations. In this strange real estate transaction the salesmen did not use their best argument.

Seward was nevertheless very eager. In March 1867, after an all-night session with Baron de Stoeckl, the Russian Minister to the United States, he signed a treaty taking title in exchange for $7.2 million. Then the Secretary set about the much more difficult task of convincing Congress that he had done well. News of the treaty was at first greeted by jests against paying so much money for "Seward's Icebox." Gradually opinion changed under a barrage—carefully organized by Seward—of favorable information on the resources of Alaska and eloquent speeches by the influential Senator Charles Sumner and others. The Senate thereupon approved the Alaska Purchase Treaty by a vote of 37 to 2. But the House claimed its right to withhold the necessary appropriation. Opponents of the purchase argued that the United States was too big already and that in time Alaska would fall into the national lap "like ripe fruit" without cost. Supporters revived the Manifest Destiny arguments of the prewar expansionists, and spelled them out in terms of strategic and economic advantages. Perhaps the decisive argument was that to refuse payment under the terms of the treaty would be a serious affront to a government friendly to the United States. The House after more than a year of debate voted to appropriate the purchase price.

This was the first important annexation of noncontiguous territory and many regarded it as a first step in a new journey that would carry the United States flag to the two Poles and the Far East. But special circumstances rather than any inevitable process explain the purchase of Alaska. It was in fact a great bargain. The Gold Rush of 1897 not only uncovered deposits that matched the purchase price many times over but injected new "hard" money into the American economy at a moment of crucial need. The agricultural and commercial potentialities of Alaska made it a frontier beckoning the adventurous, and the huge area with its island appendages skirting northeast Asia amply justified its annexation as a strategic outpost of hemispheric defense.

Anglo-American Difficulties

In the more pressing matter of solving the Anglo-American problems arising from the war, Seward failed. To blame were the inept diplomacy of Reverdy Johnson, the Minister to Great Britain, and intolerable pressure at home for the annexation of Canada as payment for the "indirect" damages to the Union by the Confederate raider *Alabama*.

In 1864, Seward himself had threatened to terminate the Rush-Bagot

Agreement and to fortify the boundary against Canada. In March 1865, he gave the required year's notice to abrogate the Canadian Reciprocity Treaty of 1854. Irish Fenians enthusiastically organized on American soil filibuster expeditions to free Canada as a first step towards the liberation of Ireland. A few hundred Irishmen crossed the Niagara River in the summer of 1866 and were easily scattered by the Canadian authorities, but Fenian "armies" continued to plot raids and occasionally repeated the futile performance. This and American annexationism in general only strengthened the loyalty of Canadians to their mother country, which did its part to cement ties by creating the self-governing Dominion of Canada in 1867. The House of Representatives in 1866 added a threat to that other most accessible British possession, the merchant marine, by unanimously resolving that in future Americans be permitted to sell warships to belligerents. This would release innumerable *Alabamas* against Great Britain the next time she should be at war, and Irishmen saw the resolution as an enormous encouragement to their plans for revolution.

A break in the mounting tension occurred when Earl Russell left office. Charles Francis Adams, the American minister, on retiring after the war had left with Russell a comprehensive statement of the grievances of the United States government. The chief accusation was that the British government had committed a wrong when it failed to strengthen its domestic law in fulfillment of its international obligation to prevent Confederate warships from being built in British territory. Adams declared that Britain should formally admit the wrong and pay for the consequent damages to Union shipping. Earl Russell, who could only defend his own conduct, rejected Adams' argument. But another Foreign Secretary could repudiate Russell's policy. Unfortunately Seward sent an utterly incompetent man to England to negotiate. Reverdy Johnson fawned on the British and signed with Lord Clarendon in 1869 a Convention that said nothing of the wrong committed by Great Britain. It placed the *Alabama* claims on an equal footing with British claims since 1854 against the United States for damages of the ordinary, nonpolitical sort which arise from minor incidents of damage to the properties of foreign subjects in any country.

Only one Senator voted to approve the Johnson-Clarendon Convention. Charles Sumner, in April 1869, made one of the most sensational speeches in the history of the Senate's participation in foreign affairs. He demanded that Britain pay not only for the actual value of the shipping destroyed by the *Alabama* and other British-built raiders, estimated at $15 million, but also for "national losses" of $110 million resulting from increased insurance rates and the flight of shipping to other flags. On top of this Sumner piled an item of $2 billion, representing the total cost of the war during its last two years when, he asserted, the Confederacy would have collapsed but for British moral and material encouragement. Everyone understood that Sumner wanted Canada in lieu of pounds. In this country wild enthusiasm greeted his outburst, while the British met it with offers to fight rather than negotiate. By this time Grant had taken office and he inherited in the foreign field a problem second in difficulty only to Reconstruction.

HAMILTON FISH AND THE RECONSTRUCTION OF FOREIGN RELATIONS

The diplomacy of Hamilton Fish was a bright ray in the murky atmosphere of the Grant administration. A wealthy New Yorker of prominent family, he brought brains, integrity, and superior political and diplomatic skill to a regime otherwise remembered only for inadequacy. He solved the jangling problems of foreign relations left over from the war and from Seward's erratic expansionism with decent regard for the obligations as well as the rights of the United States. He was the chief architect of reconstruction in foreign policy. The statesmanship of Fish did not satisfy the blusterers who stood in the way of a reasonable settlement of the *Alabama* claims, nor was his influence on Grant always a match for that of less worthy advisers. But the bewildered hero of Appomattox came to rely on his Secretary of State as a pillar of good sense and rectitude.

In 1869, they both faced the powerful Senator Sumner, who expected to control foreign policy from his chair at the head of the Senate Committee on Foreign Relations. Sumner's famous speech rejecting the Johnson-Clarendon Convention and in effect demanding Canada as balm for the *Alabama* wounds was his challenge to the new administration. If Sumner had had his way, punishment of Great Britain would have matched the Radical policy of punishing Confederates, and Congress would have dominated the Executive in both the foreign and domestic spheres. He won a preliminary skirmish when Grant agreed to appoint as Minister to Great Britain the distinguished historian John Lothrop Motley, a supporter of Sumner's views.

The new minister inaugurated his mission by violating the orders of the Secretary of State and presenting Sumner's demands to Her Majesty's government. Grant wanted to discharge Motley at once, but Fish talked him into the more diplomatic maneuver of avoiding a premature break with Sumner and transferring negotiations to Washington. Grant, however, favored Sumner's views on indirect damages and was eager to win a few island trophies in the Caribbean. Fish set himself the delicate and formidable tasks of winning Grant away from expansionism as well as from Sumner's indirect damages, of defeating both policies in Congress and establishing his own moderate leadership in foreign relations. He quieted the Anglo-American clamor by postponement, while deeper forces of common interest were operating for a settlement. Sir John Rose, a Canadian financier interested in the stability of the American and Canadian railroad securities sold by his firm to British investors, journeyed as Canadian Minister of Finance from Ottawa to Washington to London and back again in confidential efforts to find a new basis for negotiations of all outstanding Anglo-Canadian-American issues.

Caribbean excitements diverted Grant and created the break between him and Sumner that cleared the way for Fish. Revolution in Cuba, beginning in 1868, opened to Americans the enticing prospect of finally ejecting Spain, freeing the Cuban slaves, and incorporating the island in the family of American republics if not in the United States. Filibuster expeditions repeated on a larger scale episodes of the ante-bellum years, and now Northerners were foremost in sympathy and activities for *Cuba Libre* while Southerners were doubtful that the large Negro population of the island should be liberated either from slavery or from Spain. War with Spain was eagerly demanded by newspapers, mass meetings, and expansionist Congressmen. The latter proposed as a start that the United States recognize the belligerency of the Cuban rebels, and Grant favored the step. Fish tried to distract Grant with the less warlike project of annexing Santo Domingo. He completed with that unhappy republic in 1869 a treaty of annexation that fascinated the President and led him to solicit personally the support of Senator Sumner.

In June 1870, the Cuban and Dominican crises both came to a head in Congress. Grant thought Sumner had promised to support the annexation treaty and was deeply angered when he pronounced against it. Fish at the same time told Grant he would resign if a presidential message to Congress condemning the movement to recognize Cuban belligerency was not sent. Grant, clinging to his Secretary of State, sent the message, and the resolution was narrowly defeated. For good measure, Grant removed Sumner's friend Motley from the London mission and used his influence in Congress to remove Sumner from the chairmanship of the Foreign Relations Committee.

The Treaty of Washington and the Geneva Arbitration

By the time Sir John Rose returned from London with private word for Fish that the British government was ready to make concessions, the Secretary of State was in command of the situation at home. Grant was now willing to abandon the indirect damages claim because it smelled of the hated Sumner. A Joint High Commission of five Americans headed by Secretary Fish, four British representatives and the Prime Minister of Canada, Sir John A. MacDonald, met in Washington during the spring of 1871. Amiable personal relations and mutual concessions resulted in the Treaty of Washington, a document that amounted to a new charter of peace among the three North Atlantic nations. The British agreed to a frank expression of regret for the *Alabama* and to rules of international law which defined the action of the Palmerston ministry as a violation of international obligations. The question of damages was referred for arbitration to a commission of five members appointed by the President of the United States, the Queen of England, and the rulers of Italy, Switzerland, and Brazil. A dispute over ownership of the San Juan Islands between the coast of the state of Washington and Vancouver Island was referred to the Emperor of Germany as arbitrator, who awarded them to the United States.

Two minor matters were also arbitrated. The perennial fisheries problem on the east coast was arranged to give the United States more extensive privileges than ever before and British subjects privileges as far south as Delaware Bay, an exchange to which the Canadians vainly objected as uneven, particularly since the United States refused to relax its tariff barriers and renew the trade reciprocity features of the Treaty of 1854. Other clauses of the new treaty regularized details of relations with Canada in recognition of her new self-governing powers in foreign relations. The only significant concession by the United States was of ambiguous value because it was not pinned down; no mention was made of *Alabama* claims for indirect damages. The British commissioners regarded this as a tacit agreement to ignore such claims, but the Americans wished only to avoid antagonizing die-hards of the Sumner persuasion in the Senate.

The Treaty of Washington was generally welcomed on both sides of the Atlantic, although Canadians feared that their strengthened political position would not prevent Great Britain from sacrificing their interests on the altar of Anglo-American friendship, and American annexationists, of whom Irish Fenians were most vocal, were irritated that Canada had been "awarded" to Britain once more on the same altar. Democratic Senators voted against the treaty, but it was approved by a vote of 50 to 12.

The Tribunal of Arbitration met in Geneva early in 1872 with Charles Francis Adams as the American member. The meeting was the most important in the long series of Anglo-American arbitrations and came closest to disaster. This was because Secretary Fish found it expedient to revive the question of indirect damages in order to get a final settlement of the issue. Entering such a claim seemed to the British monstrous and contrary to the treaty. Amid talk of war, they threatened to leave the Tribunal rather than pay a larger bill than Germany had extorted from recently-conquered France. This threat served to awaken many supporters of Sumner to the practical absurdity and dangers of his claim and they asked for moderation, a policy which Fish was quite ready to adopt. Charles Francis Adams saved the arbitration by agreeing without authority from home that the indirect damages were ruled out. The final verdict was that Britain had failed in her duty to exercise "due diligence" to prevent the escape of the Confederate warships, and $15.5 million damages to American shipping by the *Alabama* and other raiders were awarded to the United States. Sir Alexander Cockburn, the choleric British member of the Tribunal, walked out refusing to sign the award, but the British government and people swallowed the pill with considerable sportsmanship.

In a narrow national sense the Treaty of Washington of 1871 and the Geneva Arbitration were diplomatic triumphs for the United States, satisfying all reasonable grievance by reasonable men arising from British missteps during the Civil War. But their significance far transcended narrow interests. The part of Sir John Rose in the achievement of the settlement is indicative of its meaning. Once more truculent and vindictive spokesmen on both sides who attempted to push their governments into irreconcilable positions had been defeated by those who believed the three countries had far more to gain by peaceful co-operation than by conflict. Anglo-Canadian-American mutuality of economic interest called for an end to disputes over past events for the sake of future opportunities for constructive co-operation.

The Treaty of Washington has been interpreted by the modern historian J. Bartlett Brebner as marking recognition by Great Britain of the emergence of the United States as a great power and recognition by all three nations that the "North Atlantic Triangle" could develop as a free international community. American hatred for Great Britain, and Canadian fear and British contempt of the United States, did not die down for decades after 1871. Still the settlement of the *Alabama* claims was one of the greatest demonstrations in history of arbitration as a technique of settling international quarrels. It gave promise that the nations foremost in the development of free national government would lead also in the development of international institutions for world peace.

Meanwhile, Americans settled down for another generation to their domestic interests and assured themselves that isolation from Europe's troubles was their highest international aim. Excitable naval officers and diplomatic agents occasionally urged that Samoa, Hawaii, and other territories should be picked up by the United States, but both official Washington and the public at large were apathetic. This mood blunted the effect of the last foreign crisis Secretary Fish had to face. In October 1873, a Spanish warship captured the *Virginius*, flying the American flag, and took her to Havana where many of her passengers and crew, including some Americans, were shot as pirates. Americans cried for war and Secretary Fish demanded of the Spanish government an apology and redress within twelve days. Further information, however, revealed that the *Virginius* had been flying the United States flag illegally, that her papers were fraudulent, and that she had been carrying munitions and filibusters from this country to Cuba in violation of American law. Fish toned down his demands and reached an arrangement with the Spanish authorities that brought an indemnity of $80,000 to the families of murdered Americans. Lack of interest in annexing Cuba joined with the moderate diplomacy of the Secretary of State permitted the crisis to be safely weathered. In 1875, Fish proposed that the European Powers mediate between the Cuban rebels and Spain. They refused, but Spain made concessions, including the abolition of slavery in Cuba, which temporarily quieted the rebels.

When Hamilton Fish left office in 1877 he handed on to his successor no foreign problem of importance. In circumstances of the utmost difficulty this great Secretary of State fended off war hawks and expansionists, overcame the extremism of Sumner and the mistakes of Grant, and reconstructed the country's foreign relations so successfully that in following years some Americans advocated dispensing with the diplomatic service altogether.

PRESIDENT GRANT PROVES DISAPPOINTING

Ulysses S. Grant was nearing forty-seven when he was inaugurated as President in 1869. No one had assumed the first office with more general approval since Washington, with whose name his was constantly coupled. The foremost military figure in the Union, he was recognized as the nation's hero by members of both parties. He was viewed with favor by Southerners, who remembered his magnanimity to Lee and his injunction, "Let us have peace." He was virtually free of political commitments. The nomination had come to him unsought, and his personal popularity was probably the decisive factor in the election. Little beholden to anybody, he seemed to be in an ideal position to use his immense personal prestige for great national ends, transcending sectionalism and partisanship, in the tradition of George Washington.

His failure to do so was one of the greatest personal and public tragedies in American history. He had been in office only about a year and a half when a discerning journalist said: "The wreck of General Grant's reputation is a national misfortune." Even at that early date judicious men realized that the great soldier was a misfit in his high office, and time was to show more clearly that he was incapable of grappling successfully with the problems of politics and government.

Actually, the circumstances were unfavorable to the exercise of real leadership by any man as President. Congress had not succeeded in convicting and removing Andrew Johnson, but that body had exploited the reaction against presidential leadership and weakened the presidential office. During the early years of Grant's administration the mood of the country, outside of the South, was one of buoyant optimism. There were many serious problems, even if the Southern problem could have been regarded as settled, but there was no sense of crisis inviting vigorous presidential leadership.

On the pages of history President Grant stands forth as a personally honest man. He did not share in the corruption of his era. But he did not check it; his attitude toward it was essentially negative; he does not seem to have realized that it existed. In a man noted for military deeds and occupying an exalted position, simplicity was an attractive personal quality, but it was a liability among hard-boiled politicians and aggressive men seeking public favors. Only on the fields of war was he a real leader of men and a great commander.

He revealed his naïveté in his ideas about high appointments and in some of the first he made. After his Cabinet got shaken down, however, it contained some strong men. The Secretary of State, Hamilton Fish, was a tower of strength through two terms. George S. Boutwell, an extreme Radical Republican, served as Secretary of the Treasury for one term without distinction but also without serious criticism. The Attorney General, E. Rockwood Hoar, and the Secretary of the Interior, Jacob D. Cox, were outstanding public servants. The former was largely responsible for the excellence of Grant's early judicial appointments, and Cox was notable, in the heyday of the spoils system, for his efforts to attain efficiency in his department and keep politics out of it. Within less than two years, however, both of these admirable officials resigned under political pressure which Grant did not resist. Both had offended Senators whose support the President believed he needed and whose wishes he heeded too often. He was greatly influenced by a senatorial clique including Zachariah Chandler of Michigan, Oliver P. Morton of Indiana, Simon Cameron of Pennsylvania, and Roscoe Conkling of New York —men much more noted as partisans and spoilsmen than as public-spirited statesmen. No member of the House of Representatives had such influence on him as the notorious Benjamin F. Butler of Massachusetts. Grant's judgment of men was poor, and it was charged that he bestowed offices and took them away on mere whims.

It would have been better if he had consulted Hamilton Fish more in matters of official and social propriety. Grant openly accepted gifts, whereas Andrew Johnson had consistently declined them. They were only his due, he thought. It was reliably reported that he knew to the last shilling the sums voted to the Duke of Wellington by a grateful country. Grant, who had been conspicuously unsuccessful in making money, specially admired men who had amassed fortunes, and in this as in so many other matters he was undiscriminating. It was not fitting that the

President of the United States should let himself be flaunted in public as their friend by Jay Gould and Jim Fisk, two of the most notorious manipulators of the time. They were busily engaged in "milking" the Erie Railroad, and during Grant's first year in office sought to corner gold, hoping for the connivance of the United States Treasury. The government, which received gold constantly from import duties, followed a policy of selling it periodically. The precious pair of speculators wanted to keep the Treasury out of the play until they could buy up all the gold offered for sale and artificial shortage should send the price sky-high, and then sell out at a handsome profit.

Grant was the guest of Gould and Fisk on a trip to Boston, and he let himself be taken by the latter to the theater in New York. Besides being an unscrupulous manipulator, Fisk was notorious as a man of pleasure, and it was a shock to sober citizens to learn that the President had been displayed in the box of this gaudy libertine. Along with some minor governmental officials, Grant's brother-in-law was drawn into the unsavory financial operation and through him Gould sought to influence the President. The whole scheme was foiled by the decision of the Treasury to sell gold, but the two stock-gamblers convulsed Wall Street on "Black Friday" (September 24, 1869) and paralyzed legitimate importation business for days. Grant was a party to no plot and he was grieved by the foolish actions of his brother-in-law, but he had given the public a distinct impression of gullibility.

In his first term, which fell in a time of exuberant prosperity, the financial questions of greatest public concern were those of taxation and the currency. By 1870, internal taxes, which had been so heavy and vexatious during the war, were abolished except on liquor, tobacco, and a few other things. The income tax was wholly given up two years later. The high tariff duties of wartime, however, were generally maintained despite the fact that they, as well as the heavy internal taxes, had originally been regarded as temporary. Such reductions as were made were on articles not produced in the country. The removal of the duties on tea and coffee in 1872 clearly marked the trend of policy. This was to get rid of duties designed to produce revenue and to retain those that were protective. Industry had become used to the high protective system and clamored for its maintenance, while the agricultural South was powerless to make effective protest. The most prominent journalistic champion of the system was Horace Greeley, who favored putting a prohibitive duty on everything produced in the United States, so that the people could live wholly within themselves. Perhaps the most conspicuous of extreme protectionalists in Congress was a Representative from Pennsylvania, known as "Pig Iron" Kelly. Far more was said in public about the Reconstruction question, however, than about the tariff. High protection gained victory by default.

The Legal Tender Cases

The currency problem excited more general interest. In Grant's first term it became involved with constitutional questions and the charge that he packed the Supreme Court. The laws passed during the war which authorized the issuance of the greenbacks provided that these should be legal tender for the payment of public and private debts, except for duties on imports and interest on the public debt. But in 1870 the Supreme Court under Chief Justice Chase, by a vote of 4 to 3 (Hepburn *vs.* Griswold), held that all debts contracted before February 25, 1862, must be paid off in coin. The argument was that the Legal Tender Act of that date impaired the obligation of contracts. The decision left doubt whether debts made since then could legally be paid in greenbacks. The practical difficulties resulting from the enforcement of this decision woul·l have been far-reaching, for there were upwards of $350 million in greenbacks in circulation; and the judgment, while agreeable to the creditors affected by it, was highly disagreeable to persons who had contracted debts in good faith and it was embarrassing to the federal government. Grant was no inflationist, but he did not like the decision.

Soon after his inauguration, Congress, which had reduced the Supreme Court in order to prevent his predecessor's making appointments to it, increased it to nine members. There were now two vacancies, and on the very day that Chase announced his decision Grant nominated William Strong of Pennsylvania and Joseph P. Bradley of New Jersey as Justices. With Justice Samuel F. Miller and the two others who had dissented they formed a majority which reversed Chase's decision (January 15, 1872) and ruled the Legal Tender Act constitutional, as a valid exercise of the war power of Congress. The argument was based on broad grounds; as Justice Strong put it, the power to issue bills of credit and make them legal tender is an essential national power. In our own day of controlled currencies, such a declaration does not seem at all surprising, but the circumstances and events served to discredit both the executive and judicial departments. In no strict sense was the Court packed; Grant exacted no promises from his appointees. On the other hand, he probably believed from their past records that they would take the position they did in this particular matter. The episode weakened the prestige of the Court itself, for it took one side, and then hastily took the other. The question of the greenbacks was not disposed of in Grant's first term; it came up again in his second and the problem of providing currency which was both sound and adequate became a major issue in the next quarter century.

No Headway in Civil Service Reform

That Grant should make an important contribution to the solution of financial questions was hardly to be expected, but the former commander of great armies ought to have worked to free the civil administration of his country from political domination and to make the operations of the government more efficient and honest. His relative indifference to this problem was shown by his failure to back his Secretary of the Interior against the senatorial spoilsmen. The resignation of Cox gave impetus to the movement for civil service reform, however, and the Congressional elections of 1870 showed that the American people were becoming less complacent about the state of affairs in Washington. The Democrats gained several seats in the Senate, and the Republicans lost their two-thirds majority in the House.

In his message to Congress soon after the election, Grant urged that measures be taken to elevate and purify the civil service, in order that fit men might be brought into office and kept there. Bills providing for the introduction of competitive examinations, presented in the House by Thomas A. Jenckes of Rhode Island and in the Senate by Carl Schurz of Missouri, failed of passage, but a provision which was incorporated in an appropriations act in March 1871 gave the President a chance to make a start. He was authorized to prescribe rules and regulations for admission into the civil service and to appoint a commission. George William Curtis, noted as the editor of *Harper's Weekly* and a conspicuous advocate of this sort of reform, was appointed chairman. The Commission recommended the establishment of a merit system and formulated rules which Grant said he would put into effect, but Congress neglected to provide the necessary funds. Bowing to the will of the senatorial and Congressional spoilsmen, who had nothing but contempt for the "men milliners," Grant retired from the battle. He accepted the judgment of Roscoe Conkling and Ben Butler in regard to the necessities of politics.

Unfortunately, the crusade for civil service reform lacked popular appeal. The basic reason for bad government in a democratic society was the same in that era as in others—that is, public indifference—and the difficulty of cleaning things up was accentuated by the diversion of attention to issues which, while actually more remote, were more emotional. The most important of all questions, as the dominant politicians kept on saying, was the Southern question; and by the same token virtually anything could be forgiven anyone who was "sound" on that.

Since the Southern issue was employed to obscure all others, Grant could have performed an invaluable service by settling it for once and all. At first it seemed that he was taking the lead. He facilitated the return to the Union of the last three unrecognized states (Virginia,

Mississippi, and Texas). But after that he made no real contribution to the settlement of the continuing sectional controversy. The worst evils of Radical Reconstruction fell within his administration, and he himself was associated in the public mind with the harsh Force Acts and military control of elections.

The Failure of the Liberal Republicans

The inadequacies Grant revealed in his first term as President were not sufficient to prevent his renomination. The party professionals liked him all the better for being manageable, and they believed that his name still carried enough magic to assure his re-election. In his party, however, there were a number of high-minded and intelligent men who were so opposed to what he had come to stand for that they staged a revolt. This is known as the Liberal Republican movement, and it drew to itself men who were against Grant for several reasons. Senator Charles Sumner never joined this group officially, but from the time of the Santo Domingo episode he was bitterly hostile to the President, whom he was now comparing unfavorably to Andrew Johnson. Others opposed him because of their interest in civil service reform or tariff reform. But the most important single issue serving to unify the diverse group was dissatisfaction with the Reconstruction policy. In a real sense, therefore, these Liberals were heirs of the moderates whose voices had been drowned in Andrew Johnson's time.

The Liberal Republicans got their name and had their beginnings as a party in Missouri. Allying themselves with the Democrats, they elected B. Gratz Brown as Governor in 1870 and put an end to the extreme policy of proscribing Confederate sympathizers which had prevailed there. The results were salutary and generally popular. Their best-known leader was the German-American Carl Schurz, whose original views about the Southerners had been considerably less moderate than Grant's. But as a United States Senator Schurz now vigorously opposed the renewed policy of coercion. This group in Missouri, who had attracted wide attention, issued a call in 1872 to a national convention in Cincinnati. They hoped to nominate for President somebody whom the Democrats would be willing to support and who might defeat Grant. The movement gained great momentum in the spring, being strongly supported by some of the best newspapers in the country and many prominent men. It was essentially a movement of leaders, but it inspired large hopes.

The gathering in Cincinnati in April 1872 was more like a mass meeting of citizens than a convention of politicians. Present were an unusual number of intelligent and public-spirited men, along with a sprinkling of disgruntled office-seekers. Its brief platform contained well-phrased resolutions bearing on the Southern question. The Liberal Republicans lived up to their name by calling for the immediate and absolute removal of disabilities imposed on account of the war which had been seven years ended, for a return to self-government in all the states and to peaceful and constitutional practices in the nation. At the same time, they opposed any reopening of the questions settled by the Thirteenth, Fourteenth, and Fifteenth Amendments. In other words, they accepted the principles of Reconstruction as written into the Constitution while believing that the need for external rule and coercive methods was at an end. In an admirable resolution they proclaimed the necessity for reform in the civil service, but on the insistence of Horace Greeley, they took no stand either for or against a protective tariff.

In the opinion of Carl Schurz and many other competent judges, the best nominee would have been Charles Francis Adams, son of John Quincy and grandson of John Adams, who had served the Union so ably in Great Britain during the war. Though he made no effort in his own behalf, he led the field on most of the ballots. Horace Greeley had always been in the running and the nomination went at last to him. He was an earnest advocate of a more liberal Southern policy, and had shown his magnanimity by signing Jefferson Davis's bond when the former Confederate President was released on bail. But Greeley had an equivocal record on civil service reform, he was an extreme protectionist, and he had been castigating Democrats nearly all his life. The brilliant but erratic editor of the *New York Tribune* completely stole the show—to the consternation of Schurz and many others. Governor Gratz Brown, who had favored him, was named for Vice-President.

The Democratic convention, now containing numerous Southerners, swallowed Greeley, who was in so many ways unpalatable, because their main concern was to restore home rule to the southern states. If their acceptance of the Liberal Republican candidate as their own was surprising, their adoption of the platform had more long-range significance, for they put themselves on record as accepting the amendments to the Constitution which they had previously condemned.

The regular Republicans, nominating Grant for a second term as a matter of course, named Henry Wilson of Massachusetts as his running mate instead of Schuyler Colfax. In their platform they conceded the desirability of civil service reform, but they wholly differed from their rivals in their full approval of the Force Acts and they made no bones about their support of protective tariffs.

Greeley, whose many extreme utterances during his long years as an editor had made him highly vulnerable, received heavy blows in the campaign; some of the most damaging were delivered by the cartoonist Thomas Nast, who caricatured him as unmercifully as he did notorious Boss Tweed of New York City. This fantastic candidate never had a chance. Though now somewhat tarnished, Grant was still a popular legend and he seemed safer than his erratic rival; he had a powerful organization behind him; the Southern issue had not lost its potency of appeal in the North as yet, and the carpetbaggers and scalawags were still powerful in the South. The President got 272 electoral votes to Greeley's 66; the latter carried only three border states and three southern states. Grant's popular majority was 750,000, which was considerably larger than it had been four years before. Greeley, who described himself as "the worst beaten man who ever ran for high office," completely broken in body and spirit, died less than a month after his defeat. The regular Republicans regained their two-thirds majority in Congress, and Grant entered upon a second term which was marked by graver scandals than his first.

Public Morals at the Worst

Public immorality may have sunk to no lower depths after Grant's re-election than it had reached already, but it was more strikingly revealed in high federal office. For this reason the years 1872-1876 are often described as the most disgraceful in American national history. But graft and corruption were a characteristic feature of the entire era. Though not universal, they were ubiquitous—infesting the governments of cities and states while pervading the operations of large business enterprises. It is doubtful if the standards of business morality have ever been so low in the United States as they were in this era of defalcations, stock frauds, and downright stealing.

The bulk of the people, while uncommonly confused and restless, were honest and law-abiding, but American society had adjusted neither its laws nor its ethics to the new age of vastly enlarged economic enterprise, and the sense of private and public responsibility had not kept pace with the inordinate increase of the country's scale of operations. Where there are bribe-takers there must be bribe-givers, and political corruption was merely one aspect of a general condition. A major reason for its growth was the huge increase, as compared with ante-bellum days, in the favors, privileges, and money-making opportunities the various governments had to hand out—contracts and franchises, land grants and access to mineral resources, tariff protection and tax relief. This was the time of the "Great Barbecue." Aggressive men sought special favors and negligent or compliant officials granted them—often for a political or monetary price.

The Tweed Ring

The most infamous of all the corrupt city governments of the era was the Tweed Ring in New York. Its overturn came before the election of 1872, though the bloated Boss was not actually convicted until later. There were other infamous city rings, like that in Philadelphia, but the one in the largest city has remained through the years the synonym of civic corruption. Boss Tweed—whose bearded face and projecting stomach became familiar to thousands through the cartoons of Thomas Nast— took care of the poor and sick, befriended immigrants, rigged elections, and ruled the city to his great enrichment and that of his associates. Nominally a Democrat, he had a working agreement with upstate Republican legislators. Not content with that, he had his own man, John T. Hoffman, the Tammany mayor of New York City, elected Governor in 1868. Following this he put through the legislature a bill for a new city charter facilitating his control and his depredations. He admitted that it cost him $600,000.

The Ring was at the height if its power in 1871, the citizenry seeming helpless and the attacks of the *New York Times* and *Harper's Weekly* (with Nast's devastating cartoons) unavailing. In the middle of the year, however, the publication by the *Times* of accounts that unmistakably revealed Tweed's colossal swindling led to the formation of a large citizens' committee and the bringing against him of both a civil suit and criminal action. Outstanding in the successful fight against him was Samuel J. Tilden, who gained thereby national stature as a reformer. Jay Gould provided $1 million for Tweed's bail. The boss had several trials, releases, and escapes but he died in jail in 1878. Estimates of the toll exacted from the city by him and his Ring ran as high as $200 million.

Corruption and the Legislative Branch

Corruption was most shameless in city rings, but there was a great deal of it in state legislatures, especially in connection with grants and aids to railroads. If this was most flagrant in the Radical governments in the reconstructed South, conditions were comparable wherever there was much land to be granted or many miles of track to be built. From the point of view of the federal government, the most notorious railroad scandal was the affair of the Credit Mobilier. Stories about the distribution of stock of this construction company of the Union Pacific among influential public men were circulated during the campaign of 1872 but too late to affect the result. When Congress assembled in December after the election, an investigating committee, headed by Luke P. Poland, was appointed in the House of Representatives. In late February 1873, it recommended the expulsion of Representatives Oakes Ames of Massachusetts and James Brooks of New York. The deaths of these two men, both of which occurred before summer, were probably hastened by their disgrace. A Senate committee about the same time recommended the expulsion of John W. Patterson of New Hampshire, but this was deemed unnecessary since his term expired in March. Vice-President Colfax, who had been Speaker of the House when these unsavory events occurred, gave the impression of untruthfulness when questioned by the Poland Committee, and the reputations of other prominent public men were smirched. Some of them frankly admitted taking stock at a low price. They helped create a general impression that public ethics and propriety had sunk to a dangerously low point.

The disfavor in which Congress was held at this juncture was increased by the Salary Grab Act in March 1873. By this the salaries of high federal officials were increased, the salaries of members of Congress being advanced 50 per cent and made retroactive. The Constitution provides that no Senator or Representative shall be appointed to any *civil* office which is created or the emoluments whereof are increased during his legislative term. If the Salary Grab Act was not in direct conflict with this provision, it was certainly contrary to its spirit. The salaries of public officials needed raising, and fortunately the increases stuck in the cases of the President and the members of the Supreme Court, but the next Congress reversed the action about its own members and thus reduced the public clamor.

The President himself showed no conception of the need to purify the government. Early in Grant's second term, George William Curtis, the deeply discouraged chairman of the Civil Service Commission, resigned from that body. Grant appointed a good man in his place, but Congress failed to take positive action in support of the Commission's activities, and by the end of 1874 Grant said in so many words that efforts to reform the civil service must be abandoned.

Scandal Invades the Executive Branch

The Secretary of the Treasury, William A. Richardson, who succeeded Boutwell, ran into great trouble in the matter of contracts whereby John D. Sanborn of Massachusetts, a friend and supporter of Benjamin F. Butler, was empowered to collect delinquent taxes at a fee of 50 per cent. A Congressional committee recommended the abandonment of this sort of practice and the "severe condemnation" of Richardson. He escaped impeachment by resigning. Grant appointed him to the Court of Claims.

His successor, Benjamin H. Bristow, did much to clean up and reorganize the Treasury Department. He broke up the Whiskey Ring in St. Louis, a combination of officials and distillers to avoid payment of internal revenue taxes. In his innocence and blindness, Grant let himself get involved by accepting hospitality and rich presents from the supervisor of internal revenue in St. Louis, whose federal salary was only $3000 a year. The President's private secretary, Orville E. Babcock, was indicted by a grand jury for alleged connection with the Ring, but Grant made a strong deposition in his favor and he was acquitted. Babcock finally resigned in 1876, but so did Bristow since the President failed to support this energetic and courageous public servant.

In March 1876, a Congressional committee recommended the impeachment of the Secretary of War, William W. Belknap, and he escaped this only by hasty resignation. His difficulty arose from the acceptance of a bribe in connection with the post leadership at Fort Sill, Indian Territory.

In 1876, also, the Mulligan Letters, involving James G. Blaine in a dubious railroad deal, received dramatic attention in Congress. We shall recur to this famous episode in the account of the election of that year. One reason for the rash of exposures toward the end of Grant's second term was that in the Congressional elections of 1874 the Democrats gained control of the House of Representatives. The political upset was definitely connected with the Panic of 1873, and it was accompanied by a growing clamor for expansion of the currency. In 1874, the President vetoed a bill which would have increased the volume of greenbacks; and in 1875, under the leadership of Senator John Sherman of Ohio, an act was passed providing for their gradual reduction and the resumption of specie payments on January 1, 1879. Grant took a stand against inflation and for "sound money," but he left the currency question unsettled, as he did the Reconstruction question, and through the years his passive administration has continued to be best remembered for its scandals.

It was while these were at their height that the centennial of American Independence was celebrated by a great exposition in Philadelphia, to which exhibits were sent by the nations of the world. The Declaration of 1776 was read there by a descendant of a famous Signer. But many sincere patriots whose eyes were open to the evils of their day confessed with shame that the most conspicuous current product of American freedom was corruption. James Russell Lowell, writing in 1875, gave examples and could have given more a few months later.

> Show 'em your Civil Service, and explain
> How all men's loss is everybody's gain, . . .
> Show your State Legislatures; show your Rings;
> And challenge Europe to produce such things
> As high officials sitting half in sight
> To share the plunder and to fix things right;
> If that don't fetch her, why you only need
> To show your latest style in martyrs—Tweed:
> She'll find it hard to hide her spiteful tears
> At such advance in one poor hundred years.

Grant's tragedy arose from the fact that he was confronted with evils he did not know how to combat—that he did not even recognize. No single man was responsible for the forces of evil which were rampant in the country in this dark period, but the dominant political leaders in Congress had served to perpetuate and increase many of the ills of the time. They ignored or obscured questions bearing on the integrity of the national government itself while keeping the sectional controversy in the forefront of public consciousness. By continuing to concentrate attention on the issue of Reconstruction in the South they diverted attention from national questions which were now more vital. They did more than punish the South; they left the whole country open to the ravages of spoilsmen and freebooters. But the public scandals provided an inescapable danger signal, while the exposures themselves showed that the political climate was changing and the national conscience awakening.

CHAPTER 4

The End of an Era

THE SECTIONAL SETTLEMENT OF 1877 MARKED THE END
of the long period of strife between North and South. In effect the North
let the problem of race relations go by default, yielding it to the Southern
states themselves. The question of the position of Negroes in American
society became national and international a half century later, but in
the meantime the sectional truce was generally observed. The particular
circumstances of the disputed presidential election of 1876, and the
crisis created by it, were much more favorable to the reaching of an
agreement than they seemed on the surface. That Rutherford B. Hayes
fairly won the presidency over Samuel J. Tilden is still doubtful, but
unquestionably it was better that the final peace settlement should be
made by a Republican than a Democratic President. As the titular head
of the party which was so closely identified with the war and the cause
of the Union, he could not be charged with lack of national patriotism as
readily as Tilden and there was less likelihood that his work would be
undone.

The circumstances also turned out to be favorable to the perpetuation
of Republican rule, despite all the scandals which had accompanied it;
and that party generally dominated national politics for another generation. The Republicans did not cease to exploit the sectional issue. This
continued to yield political dividends until it was crowded off the market
by the financial issues of the 1890's. Its appeal in the North grew weaker
as the bonds of spiritual unity with the South were progressively restored.

A basic reason why a sectional truce was acceptable in the North was
that it really involved the recognition by the South that the Northern
economic system had triumphed. Many of the Southern leaders were
attune to the spirit of the new business age, and most Southern whites
were chiefly concerned to regain local control of local affairs. The events
of 1876-1877 marked another and important milestone in the development
of a society and a government in which business assumed the central

place. Afterwards, many farmers in the South and West were convinced that the country was under the rule of Eastern industry and finance and made vigorous protests, but this was not because they were against business; it was because they were seeking for themselves a fuller share of the benefits of a business civilization. At the moment Eastern industrialists and financiers were strongest. They enjoyed the support of Eastern Republicans, and, in matters vital to them, they were rarely opposed by Eastern Democrats or Southern Redeemers.

Except in the matter of political morality there was little literary protest against the dominant politico-economic group during the era of Reconstruction, and the prevailing literary tone was one of gentility. This was not a time when American civilization was realistically appraised by American writers; and critical scholarship, which was eventually to lead to less partisan historical works and more searching social analysis, was only in its beginnings.

THE DISPUTED ELECTION OF 1876

The depressed economy of the country and the scandals in the federal government, which the Democratic majority in the House of Representatives had done so much to expose, put the Republicans at a disadvantage in 1876. The Congressional leaders of the party squelched the talk of a third term for Grant, realizing that they could not successfully campaign on the record of his administration. Using an old but effective device, they tried to change the subject—that is, to revive the Southern question. James G. Blaine, whose political brilliance and personal popularity made him the leading candidate for the Republican presidential nomination, sounded the keynote in the House of Representatives early in 1876, when he proposed an amendment to a general amnesty bill which had been expected to have easy passage. He proposed to except Jefferson Davis, specifically because of the horrors of the Andersonville prison. Blaine expatiated on these, while pointing out that there were more than sixty ex-Confederate soldiers now in the House. His effort to bait the Southerners and distract attention from public corruption worked to his personal disadvantage, however, for in the spring the Democratic majority scrutinized his own public conduct.

Blaine had previously defended himself against charges of receiving favors from railroads after he had made a ruling (as Speaker of the House in 1869) which was not improper in itself but which saved a federal land grant to the Little Rock and Fort Smith Railroad. Blaine sold bonds for this company to friends, under terms very favorable to himself, and when the securities turned out badly he redeemed them— apparently with the aid of other railroads, including the Union Pacific. To his admirers it seemed that he had cleared himself, but in 1876 the investigating committee learned that one James Mulligan had certain letters of Blaine's relating to the Little Rock and Fort Smith. Blaine visited Mulligan, got possession of the letters, and refused to deliver them to the committee. Instead, in a dramatic scene, he read them in part to his colleagues in the House, while claiming that the attack on him was owing to the hostility of Southerners and charging that the chairman of the investigating committee was withholding testimony favorable to him. He achieved a histrionic triumph, but the parts of the letters he had read aloud actually showed that his conduct had been of very dubious propriety.

Presenting Blaine's name at the national convention in one of the most famous of nominating speeches, Robert G. Ingersoll described him as the man who had "torn from the throat of treason the tongue of slander," who had "snatched the mask of Democracy from the hideous face of the rebellion," who, as a "plumed knight," had thrown his bright lance "against the brazen forehead of every traitor to his country." Since they wanted to keep talk of public scandal out of the campaign, the Republicans were wise in not nominating Blaine. They might have named the former Secretary of the Treasury, Benjamin H. Bristow, who had done so much to expose corruption, and he was favored by many in the reform group. But he was weak among the regular politicians and the choice finally fell on Rutherford B. Hayes. He had served two terms as Governor of Ohio and then, after two years' retirement, was again elected in 1875. In his latest gubernatorial campaign, financial questions were central. Hayes strongly supported the Resumption Act of 1875, calling for the return to specie payments in 1879, and was regarded in the East as an advocate of "sound money." His excellent record as an administrator and his strong support of civil service reform commended him to the Liberal Republicans, and this brevet major general of volunteers had done long and honorable if not conspicuous military service.

The Democratic nominee, Governor Samuel J. Tilden of New York, who had gained renown as a civic reformer after attaining wealth as a corporation lawyer, was as conservative as Hayes on the monetary question, though his running-mate, Thomas A. Hendricks of Indiana, was regarded as a "soft-money" man. The currency issue was not pressed in the campaign, except by the Greenback Party. It put a presidential ticket in the field, headed by Peter Cooper of New York City. He got fewer than 100,000 votes. To advocates of clean and effective government there seemed little choice between the major contenders. Both of them were inactive in the public campaign. Tilden, who was sixty-two and in frail health, was regarded by his partisans as indifferent. The campaign was unusually bitter, nonetheless. The Republicans made all they could of the Southern issue, and the expression "waving the bloody shirt" came into use about this time.

Tilden or Hayes?

By the morning after the election Tilden was sure of 184 electoral votes, needing only one more for victory. At no time thereafter was there any doubt that he had a popular majority; in the final count this was about 250,000. Besides his own state of New York, he carried Connecticut, New Jersey, and Indiana along with all the states of the former Confederacy in which the Radical regimes had been overthrown. But there were three southern states where Radical governments were still in existence, supported by federal troops—South Carolina, Florida, and Louisiana—and returns from these were delayed. If Hayes carried all of them he would have an electoral vote of 185 and a majority of one. Soon the Democrats discovered a technical irregularity in Oregon, which Hayes unquestionably had won; one of his electors was found to be ineligible as a federal officeholder. Never since the adoption of the Twelfth Amendment has a presidential election been so close. It was nearly three months before the American people knew who the next President would be.

It soon appeared that Hayes had a small majority in South Carolina, although a Conservative was elected governor. Supported by federal troops, the Radicals refused to yield the office, with the result that there were rival state governments, both claiming to be legal. Upon the face of the returns, Tilden carried Florida and Louisiana, but the returning boards threw out enough votes to give a majority in both states to Hayes. They sought to justify this action on the ground that there had been widespread intimidation of Negroes in the election, while white Conservatives maintained that this had been matched by wholesale registration frauds by the Radicals. The Louisiana board carried on its important deliberations in the presence of visiting statesmen from the North who had the net effect of emboldening it to disregard fierce local criticism. The Radicals could not prevent the setting up of a rival Conservative state government in Louisiana, however, and the Conservatives took over the governorship in Florida. As a result of these confusing developments two sets of election returns went to Washington from each of these three states.

Congress met in December under conditions of great excitement. Throughout the country the Democrats asserted that they had won the election and the Republicans were trying to steal it. In the *Louisville Courier-Journal*, Henry Watterson soon said that 100,000 citizens would march on Washington to make sure that Tilden would be inaugurated. These were to be unarmed, but some historians believe that more people expected bloodshed in 1876-1877 than had expected it in 1860-1861. If there had been a rebellion, Tilden would not have led it; he seemed befogged and contributed nothing to the solution of this problem. Some of his ill-advised supporters, without his knowledge, confused the situation further by negotiating with members of the returning boards. How

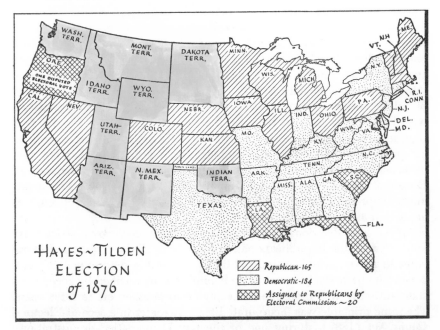

HAYES~TILDEN
ELECTION
of 1876

Republican-165
Democratic-184
Assigned to Republicans by
Electoral Commission ~20

close they came to a corrupt transaction is difficult to say but they put ammunition into the hands of their political enemies. Hayes, the major beneficiary of the actions of the returning boards, repudiated none of them, arguing that he would unquestionably have carried the disputed southern states in a fair election. It does not seem likely that he would have carried all of them.

Counting the Electoral Votes

In this unexampled situation the constitutional provisions were inadequate. The Constitution requires that the electoral returns of the various states, properly certified, shall be transmitted to the seat of the federal government, addressed to the President of the Senate, that they are to be opened by him, and that they are to be counted at a joint session. But who should do the counting—that is, who should decide between the disputed returns? His fellow Republicans claimed that the President of the Senate should count them. The Democrats, with a majority in the House, claimed that joint action of the House and Senate was necessary, or reference to the Representatives. State-rights arguments changed sides, the Republicans arguing that there should be no going behind the actions of legally-constituted state returning boards, while the Democrats took the opposite position.

Out of this confusion emerged, late in January 1877, a statesmanlike measure, the Electoral Count Act. This set up an electoral commission of fifteen—five members from each branch of Congress and five from the Supreme Court. To this body the rival returns were to be presented, and its decisions could be rejected only by the concurrent action of both houses. The general reason for the adoption of this procedure was to avoid civil war and anarchy. But at the outset the Democrats were rather more pleased with it than the Republicans because of the merit of Tilden's case. It was assumed that the members of the commission would be evenly divided between the two parties, except for the final representative of the Supreme Court, Justice David Davis, supposedly an independent with Democratic leanings. Davis got off of that hot spot by accepting election to the United States Senate by a combination of Democrats and Independents in Illinois. There were no more Democrats on the Supreme Court, and Justice Joseph P. Bradley, a Republican, was appointed as the fifteenth man.

All the vital decisions of the commission were made by a strict party vote of 8 to 7, the Republican majority assigning all the disputed electoral votes to Hayes. Accident and political partisanship determined the outcome. The basic decision not to go behind returns certified by recognized state authority was thoroughly acceptable to Southerners in later years. The same principle was incorporated ten years later in a second Electoral Count Act (1887), during one of the few Democratic administrations. According to this act the determination of electors by state authority, under laws passed before the election, is conclusive. Congress may act only in the case of a conflict of state tribunals, and concurrent action of both houses is then required. In the case of disagreement between the two houses, the returns certified by the governor of a state must be accepted.

By the time the decision for Hayes and against Tilden was finally made, it was less objectionable to Southern than to Northern Democrats. This was partly because they, in particular, were opposed to renewal of strife from which they had already suffered so greatly, and partly because of certain negotiations with Hayes of which we shall speak hereafter. The only hope of blocking the work of the commission was to resort to filibustering, and this the Southerners declined to do. Accordingly, on March 2, 1877, the count was finally completed in Congress, and Hayes was declared elected by a majority of one. His legal title was clear and he probably made a better President than Tilden would have, but the cry of fraud was often raised against him in the next four years.

THE SETTLEMENT OF 1877: THE REDEEMERS AND SOUTHERN HOME RULE

Before the election of Hayes was assured, many Southern political leaders had become confident that it would be followed by the withdrawal of federal military support from the remaining Radical governments. With the abandonment of the policy of coercion, home rule would be fully re-established. The conduct of the Southern Representatives during the bitter struggle in Congress attracted much favorable comment in Republican circles in the North, being described as brave and noble in newspapers hitherto noted for their anti-Southernism, and it had an appreciable effect on Northern opinion. In his last week in office President Grant stated that the country was opposed to the continued use of force in support of state governments. During the four months between the casting of the vote in November and the end of the electoral count in March, public sentiment had so crystallized in support of a change in policy that perhaps one might have been expected in any case. Furthermore, the Democratic majority in the House had deliberately weakened the hands of the future Commander-in-Chief by failing to pass an army appropriations bill. President Hayes afterward said that he had no army with which to support the Radical governments. That was not literally true, but until Congress assembled in the fall the one he had was unpaid and discontented.

In late February 1877, a confidential conference was held in Washington between friends of Hayes and Southern representatives—the so-called "Wormley Conference." At that time the Southerners were told that federal support of the Radical governments would be withdrawn by Hayes if not by Grant, and in turn they said that they would not filibuster against the electoral count or seek to prevent the inauguration of Hayes. A trade whereby they conceded the presidency to the Republicans for four more years in return for noninterference with their own state affairs was one which most white Southerners would have been glad to make. It seemed more important to them to gain and maintain home rule than to have a Northern Democrat in the White House, and for this reason they generally approved of the Settlement of 1877 when it was effected. For their part, Northerners welcomed a return to the historic American policy of political compromise after years of strife had demonstrated the costliness of coercion.

For weeks certain Democratic leaders had been negotiating, not merely for home rule, but also for future aid to Southern economic projects such as had been given to so many in the North and West. These included not only levees on the Mississippi River to control floods, but also railroad projects, especially the Texas and Pacific Railroad. President Thomas A. Scott of the Pennsylvania was also president of this road, and this powerful financier was anxious to resume construction, which had suspended because of the Depression of 1873. His ambitious plans called for a line across Texas to the Pacific with eastern termini at New Orleans, Vicksburg, Memphis, and St. Louis. The association of leading Southerners with this huge promotion scheme is shown by the actions of L. Q. C.

Lamar of Mississippi, who had played a conspicuous part in the Redemption of that state from carpetbag rule. He had attracted national attention in 1874 after the death of Charles Sumner, when he delivered a magnanimous eulogy of that statesman in Congress. In January 1877, the distinguished Mississippian presented to the House of Representatives a Texas and Pacific bill calling for federal aid of such scope that it suggested the Union Pacific, and for just that reason it was objected to by reformers and discreet politicians who remembered the Credit Mobilier.

Lamar was typical of the first leaders of the New South—generally known as the Redeemers and sometimes designated as Bourbons. They were not all alike, except in their Confederate background, but to a notable degree they were seeking to adjust themselves to the new economic order in the nation; and, apart from racial questions, they had much in common with Eastern Republicans. This was especially true of the old Wigs, and it was with them chiefly that the friends of Hayes dickered. Through them he hoped to build up support for his administration in the South which would prove more durable than that offered by carpetbaggers and scalawags. To this end he agreed to appoint a Southerner to his Cabinet, and he was given ground for hope that, when Congress assembled in the fall, enough Southern votes would be available to overcome the small Democratic majority in the House and enable the Republicans to organize that body.

In the various southern states during Reconstruction men of divergent political views allied themselves against external rule, just as they did against the Republicans as a sectional party in the years immediately preceding the war. This was an uneasy alliance, however, and only on the issues of home rule and the status of the freedmen did the events of Reconstruction create a "Solid South." The name Republican became even more unpopular than it was already, but the old Whigs, who were in the tradition of Henry Clay's American System and had been relatively Unionist in sentiment, were less anti-Republican than the old Democrats. In the course of Redemption a disproportionate number of former Whigs came into political prominence; many of them were now in Congress and they had not failed to observe that the Republicans were more favorable than the Northern Democrats to federal aid for Southern internal improvements. Regardless of party labels, the Redeemers—that is, the leaders—almost everywhere were more sympathetic with the ideas of the new age of business than with agrarian ideals.

The Conservative governments established in the South in the 1870's were much more reputable and generally less wasteful than the Radical governments they succeeded, but as a rule they were more sensitive to the desires of corporations and the claims of creditors than to the needs of the plain people. Thus the "New Order" in the South was compatible with

Eastern Republicanism, from which concern for the freed Negroes was rapidly disappearing. Only on the Southern question had the Radical Republicans been really radical, and as applied to economic matters the term was a misnomer. By enacting high tariffs during the war and maintaining them afterwards the Republicans became the party of industry; through land grants and other favors they became associated with railroads; and whenever they followed a deflationary policy they were working in the interest of creditors. Important features of prevailing policy, such as currency deflation, were strongly opposed within the party, but its history in the next generation was to mark it as the bulwark of the new economic order. There was far less danger that the Southern Conservatives would upset this than that the urban masses of the North and the depressed farmers of the West would. Good reason existed for supporters of "sound money" and untrammeled business enterprise to welcome the full attainment of home rule in the South.

Within the two months following his inauguration President Hayes withdrew the troops from South Carolina and Louisiana, as he had agreed to do and as public sentiment now permitted. He was also withdrawing federal support from the freedman, an action deplored by William Lloyd Garrison and other old abolitionists, but he was relying on the promises Southern leaders had made to respect the rights of the Negroes. These were respected more in the next decade or two than afterward; the Redeemers engaged in no wholesale disfranchisement of Negroes but tried to organize their votes, and they were not responsible for the "Jim Crow" laws which were enacted later.

In his inaugural address Hayes suggested that the national government should consider the economic needs of the South, hinting at federal aid, but he shied away from the Texas and Pacific scheme. When Congress assembled the Southerners found that the Great Barbecue was over. If Hayes did not keep his full bargain with respect to internal improvements it was because of the temper of the times, and also because the plan to gain political support in the South went awry. He appointed Senator David M. Key of Tennessee as Postmaster General, as he had promised, and that official distributed much patronage to hungry Southerners. But the Northern politicians did not approve of such generosity, and the old Southern Whigs were unable to deliver the necessary votes to permit the Republicans to organize the House of Representatives and elect James A. Garfield speaker. The hope of winning over white Southerners to the Republican Party by a policy of conciliation proved empty, and virtually all the Conservatives became nominal Democrats in national affairs. When this trend became unmistakable, the Republicans again waved the bloody shirt before the voters.

But the issue of loyalty had lost its vitality, and unquestionably the restored Union was here to stay. The real issues of the time were economic and they cut across party lines. The role of the South in connection with them was to be essentially negative. As has been well said, the road to reunion that the defeated section took had two forks, one leading eastward and the other westward. At times the Southerners ventured down the fork to the West, where there were so many discontented farmers, but generally, until the days of the Populists, most of the leaders looked to the East, where the financial and industrial interests centered. The New South proved to be a bulwark of the new economic order. It is not surprising that, in the next decade after Reconstruction, when Southern writers like Thomas Nelson Page and Joel Chandler Harris recreated the romantic tradition of the Old South, Northerners were eager to accept it. Generous impulses could be given free play now that fear was gone. The planter class which that tradition glorified had become only a memory, and the New South offered little menace as it slowly emerged from its poverty. In the new nation it was to remain for half a century a subordinate part of the nationalized economy.

CULTURE IN THE GILDED AGE

The Civil War strengthened the national consciousness of the American people while chastening the facile prewar optimism that the American story would be exempt from tragedy. Too many men had been killed, too many veterans were maimed for the people to forget that the idealism of the previous generation had not prevented death and destruction. Spiritual energies were exhausted if not discredited. Cynicism and crass materialism won unforeseen victories after Appomattox and the defeat of Lincoln's plan of Reconstruction. By 1876, the costs of Union victory included not only those of the war itself, terrible as they were, but also the delivery of the nation into the hands of Northern businessmen and Southern Redeemers in an alliance that tolerated when it did not foster corruption of governments, exploitation of men and resources, and cultural stagnation.

Still the idea and forms of democracy, however abused, were preserved for future generations, and not every one forgot that democracy was the chief justification of that ideal of American nationalism whose triumph was one unqualified result of the Civil War. Francis Lieber, German-born professor of political science at Columbia University and one-time professor in South Carolina College, formulated a new concept of American nationalism. Rejecting the view, which had been based on eighteenth-century philosophy and invoked by the Confederacy, that the Union was a compact among states, he asserted that its essential reality was organic, growing out of geographic, human, and institutional relations by a process of gradual evolution. The acceptance of this view by Southerners as well as Northerners, and by the Supreme Court itself (Texas vs. White, 1869), signified the supersedure of Webster's as well as Calhoun's legalistic conception of the Union. Lieber's philosophy corresponded by analogy with the Darwinian doctrine of biological evolution, whose influence on the thinking of the country during the next generations consolidated the hold of the organic-evolutionary concept of the American nation. The disruption of such a nation has become a thought impossible for any American to entertain.

Voices of Disillusionment

Lieber answered the question of the purpose of the nation by proclaiming its world mission to solve for humanity the ancient conflicts between national sovereignty on the one hand, and individual liberty, local government, and international order on the other. Obviously the postwar decades grossly caricatured this mission. The very fervor of faith in the historic mission, so nobly proclaimed by Lincoln, produced bitter disillusionment in the minds of the most sensitive observers of the actual postwar scene. Mark Twain gave the period a fitting name in the title of his novel, *The Gilded Age* (1873), but he himself was so entranced by the dream of fortune that his satire of Colonel Sellers (who decided that bribery was only "a harsh term" for a necessary means to success) was blunted by affection. Like most Americans of the time, Twain forgave businessmen who corrupted officials and reserved his contempt for politicians who co-operated with them.

Henry Adams in his anonymous novel, *Democracy* (1880), more consistently pilloried the whole complex of interests that degraded democracy during the Grant administration. He hopelessly concluded that the historical energies which had created the American Republic must be running down, exhausted according to inexorable physical law. Walt Whitman in his prose study, *Democratic Vistas* (1871), recognized that democracy had not yet justified itself:

> I say that our New World Democracy, however great a success in uplifting the masses out of their sloughs, in materialistic development, products, and a certain highly-deceptive superficial popular intellectuality, is, so far, an almost complete failure in its social aspects, and in really grand religious, moral, literary, and esthetic results. . . .
>
> Did you, too, O friend, suppose democracy was only for elections, for politics, and for a party name?

All three of these men knew wherof they spoke from personal experience in Washington. Mark Twain had given up in disgust his post as secretary to a United States Senator; Adams found that the corruptionists of the Republican Party were debarring him from the political career for which he longed and had been trained by family tradition;

Whitman was deprived of his clerkship in the Interior Department because of the frankness of his poems.

These writers carried into the cold climate of the new age the warm idealism of the prewar Republic and were distinguished by their refusal to ignore unpleasant facts. Mark Twain extracted most of the pain from them by representing them as farce; Adams turned to irony and history; Whitman virtually stopped writing. But the writers whose work—in their own opinion and that of the public—comprised the main stream of the official tradition in American letters deliberately turned away from the realities of the postwar scene. The Transcendentalism of Emerson and Thoreau had been impregnated with perceptions of the actual world. Now with Thoreau dead and the aged Emerson a mere shadow of his old self, all grittiness was strained out of their idealism by their followers, leaving a thin ideality. The romances of Hawthorne had been allegories of very grim experience—human, moral and passionate. Now romance was purged by his followers in favor of gentility.

The Escape into Gentility

The masters of genteel ideality moved the official headquarters of American literature from Boston to New York. Richard Henry Stoddard, Bayard Taylor, Thomas Bailey Aldrich, and Edmund Clarence Stedman formed there a tight oligarchy controlling the most elevated literary markets of the period. They were horrified by the vulgarity of the "champagne aristocracy," and thought to combat materialism in society by suppressing realism in literature. To both they opposed an *Ideal Poetry* in which only the refined was true and only dreams were beautiful. Rough-hewn creators of industrial fortunes gladly accepted this poetry as an ornament for the delectation of their wives. Through succeeding decades the makers of the Genteel Tradition fought hard and with much success against the rediscovery of realism, which one of them called "a miasmatic breath blown from the slums." Stedman was the most competent critic in the group and made his standards prevail, particularly in the academic world, by means of studies and anthologies of English and American poetry.

In architecture, too, these "Brown Decades" reached a dead center of confusion between gentility and art. The centuries were ransacked to find forms which appeared cultured in proportion to expensiveness and uselessness, and these were imposed on buildings to hide actual function. Most popular were French Renaissance forms with their thick crusts of pillars, pilasters, mansards, cornices, and ledges. The federal government sanctioned this style in the State, War, and Navy building in Washington. The Equitable Life Assurance Society building in New York, towering 130 feet, was a forerunner of the skyscraper; it contained elevators and used structural steel to carry the weight which otherwise would have required stone walls of impossible thickness. But the metal skeleton was nevertheless clothed with French Renaissance stone ornament of colossal size. Richard Morris Hunt refined this style to create châteaux for millionaires.

The influence of John Ruskin in popularizing authentic imitations of Gothic was seen in the 1870's in the Boston Museum of Fine Arts building, Memorial Hall at Harvard and generally in churches, collegiate structures, breweries, and steam plants. The greatest engineering triumph of the period, the Brooklyn Bridge, designed in 1869 by the naturalized German, John A. Roebling, used steel wire cable to span the longest distance yet bridged between piers. The taste of the times required that the noble piers from which the lacy cables and arc of roadway were suspended be ornamented with Gothic arches and buttresses. Homebuilders who could not afford stone ornaments employed carpenters to turn out wooden fancywork of any or no historic style. This was the age of the "brownstone front" for city dwellings. Interior walls, windows, and furniture were covered with thick layers of textiles, tables and "what-nots" with heterogeneous objects. Late in the century the threat of suffocation enforced a revolution in taste.

Sentimental allegories were considered the perfection of art. The emotions of the Civil War received inadequate expression in the pictorial arts, with the exception of Francis Bicknell Carpenter's portraits of Lincoln. Sculptures to commemorate the dead were duplicated in hundreds by factories, and virtually identical monuments to the soldiers of the sixties sprang up everywhere. The state of national taste was summed up in Henry James's story of an American whose first purchase of a painting was a copy of Murillo's *Madonna* which he liked better than the original.

The most influential person in the theatrical world was Dion Boucicault, an Irish playwright, manager, and actor who performed a service in organizing the "road show" to carry drama into every corner of the country. He prepared the version of *Rip Van Winkle* which Joseph Jefferson acted until after the turn of the century, while his own melodramas, which were travesties on classical tragedy, and his Irish comedy dramas were popular until the mid-seventies. The apotheosis of Victorian romanticism in music arrived with the first American performances of Richard Wagner in New York during the sixties. The Civil War gave rise to admirable popular music, most notably the "Battle Hymn of the Republic," but the United States as yet had produced no composer of importance in more complex forms.

The Growth of Higher Learning

In public elementary and secondary education the decades just after the Civil War saw little progress except in the South. In higher education, however, there were notable developments. The university assumed its modern form and functions. Agricultural and engineering schools founded in the Middle West and Far West with the aid of federal land grants under the Morrill Act of 1862 were the nuclei of higher education in those sections. The older state and private universities increased their attention to science. Most significant was the development of professional graduate study in the arts and sciences. Yale University awarded the first American degree of doctor of philosophy in 1861. The Johns Hopkins University opened in 1876 under Daniel Coit Gilman as an institution devoted solely to graduate study. Besides these two, Harvard, Columbia, and Michigan Universities were the chief early training grounds of professional scholars and scientists. They developed extensive laboratory facilities for the sciences and the first seminars for the training of scholars in literature, languages, and history. Germany was the source of much of the new enthusiasm for objective research in all fields.

What happened to historical writing was typical. Henry Adams organized the first graduate seminar in history at Harvard in the early seventies and the system was rapidly installed elsewhere. Adams himself produced historical works combining artistry comparable to that of a Francis Parkman with Germanic devotion to objective research. The hundreds of doctors of philosophy in history who were turned out by the new graduate seminars by the end of the century added enormously to the scope and soundness of historical knowledge, and they taught expanding numbers of undergraduates. But history virtually gave up claim to inspiration by Clio. Interest in the leading individuals who made history gave way to study of impersonal forces which were thought to explain individual careers if not to determine them. Historians themselves ceased to be public figures. They organized themselves into a professional society, the American Historical Association (1883), and history as a specialized field of knowledge gained ground. But the general public ceased to read works of history and took to historical novels instead. So also literature, philosophy, and the other disciplines were removed from the public as they were taken into the graduate schools.

The prestige of science and growth of specialization had something to do with the revolution in undergraduate education which President Charles W. Eliot of Harvard initiated when he introduced the "free elective" system. This allowed undergraduates almost unrestricted choice of courses. The system was "scientific" in that it rejected value judgments and "democratic" in that it substituted the teacher's ability to convince his students for his disciplinary authority; but it also fragmentized the cultural inheritance. Students drifted towards entertaining teachers and "practical" subjects. While the graduate colleges began to turn out learned specialists, the undergraduate colleges almost all

adopted the free elective system and increasingly turned out businessmen. Women's colleges grew in number and in enrollment, but in cur-
ricula they followed the lead of the men's colleges.

Science and Theology

The social sciences acquired some prestige as their methods were
refined and their conclusions harmonized with the status quo. The "pure"
sciences were enthroned in the public mind as well as in halls of learning. This was the broadest meaning of the chief intellectual battle of
the period, that between the queen of the old learning—theology—
and the most vigorous new science—biology. The idea of the evolution
of the earth and all life on it during eons of time was not new in 1859
when the great Englishman, Charles Darwin, published *The Origin of
Species*, but his formulations opened the final attack on literal interpretation of the Biblical story of creation. Darwin's evidence suggested that no
absolute superiority of man over animals exists, and this seemed to
conventional minds a blow to humanity's status and morale. Enthusiasts
pointed out that, on the contrary, Darwinism encouraged man to believe
that his history was not a decline from innocence in paradise to sinfulness, but progress by his own efforts from less to more complex
forms, functions, and achievements.

The first response of religious leaders in America was a challenge
to all-out battle between theology and science. They declared that if
organic evolution was true, the Bible and faith in the existence of God
and immortality must be untrue. Essentially this was a challenge to
scientific method, because Darwin appealed not to faith but to facts,
and it might have ended in total defeat of theology, had not scientists
themselves offered a compromise. Asa Gray of Harvard, the leading
American botanist and a friend of Darwin, championed the latter's work
while asserting that nothing prevented a Darwinist from believing that
God instituted evolution as His plan. Other scientists elaborated this
view. In 1885, Henry Ward Beecher published *Evolution and Religion,*
reconciling the two, and his immense influence turned the tide for
"liberal" clergymen and laymen. But the evangelical sects were relatively
unaware of this treaty of peace between science and religion, and
many believed that atheists and traitors to religion were teaching that
"man is descended from the monkeys."

The idea of evolution opened new vistas in the natural sciences.
Astronomers patiently collected observations which gained significance
from the hypothesis of the evolution of the universe. Henry Draper in
1872 made the first successful photograph of the spectrum of a star.
Sensational finds of the bones of prehistoric animals had occurred earlier
in this country, but Darwinism suggested to Othniel Charles Marsh,

the renowned Yale paleontologist, that collections of such remains be arranged in series to illustrate the evolutionary process. Eloquent exhibits of this sort became standard in museums of natural history. One of the most eminent American scientists of all time, Josiah Willard Gibbs of Yale, did his most important work in the 1870's and 1880's. Living obscurely in New Haven, he wrote for a tiny audience papers on chemistry and mathematics which laid foundations for modern physics.

In the train of New England Transcendentalism, the idealist philosophic systems of Kant and Hegel dominated American philosophy and reigned throughout the remainder of the century, particularly in the universities. But, as we shall see in a later chapter, Americans were developing a new system of thought, pragmatism, which carried into philosophy the experimental methods and spirit of the scientist. The pragmatists applied to ideas the tests of action and experience, and found "truth" in ideas that "worked." It has been said that Americans were pragmatists without knowing it.

A remarkable new development in religion, Christian Science, may be regarded as evidence of this. Its founder, Mary Baker Eddy, offered as proof of the truth of her doctrines the curing of physical disease. This won the approval of William James as an example of the pragmatic truth that ideas are true if they "work" for those who believe them. There is no doubt that Mrs. Eddy's assertion of the absolute power of mind over matter "worked" to the satisfaction of many followers. Born in New Hampshire in 1821, she became familiar in early life with various Transcendentalist ideas and faith-healing practices. Making a remarkable recovery from an injury through "divine revelation, reason and demonstration," she practiced faith-healing on others and in 1875 published *Science and Health*. With her great personal power and organizational talent, she soon gained a large following, chiefly drawn from the urban middle classes. The Church of Christ, Scientist, was organized in numerous branches of the Boston Mother Church. Christian Science made converts abroad as well as at home. Its stress on science was a portent and a tribute as well as a claim. Observers who could not believe that Christian Science readers made cures ultimately learned caution from the successes of modern depth psychology.

In varying degree the churches submitted their claims to scientific tests in the movement called the Higher Criticism. Originally in Europe but presently in the United States, numerous scholars subjected the historicity of the Bible to objective study. It was not difficult to demonstrate that the Bible contained factual errors, but this had little more permanent impact than had the earlier attacks of Deists. Religionists quarreled for a time over the findings of the Higher Critics, but the outcome was no more decisive than that of the battle between Darwinists and theologians. Belief in the literal infallibility of the Bible was abandoned by many, while its truth as a moral masterpiece was preserved. Fundamentalists simply rejected the Higher Criticism as they did evolution.

In 1875, Madame Helena P. Blavatsky, a Russian noblewoman who had sojourned in India, founded the Theosophy Society in New York. This cult joined spiritualist practices and doctrines, which had been familiar in the United States for a generation, with mystical doctrines drawn from the masterpieces of Hindu religion. A small but persistent group of devotees, chiefly middle-aged and well-to-do women, were attracted by the exotic and esoteric teachings of Theosophy and more or less imitated the way of life of Hindu initiates.

For the great majority of people, either the traditional rituals of Catholicism or the evangelistic revivals of the Protestants satisfied religious needs. The agnostic Robert G. Ingersoll tried to win the masses away from religion, and crowds were titillated by his challenges to God to strike him dead, but larger and more sincere crowds listened to Dwight L. Moody, the latest in the long succession of American revivalist preachers, and to many lesser exhorters.

Not only did evangelicalism manifest vitality in its traditional revivals; it inspired a great new effort in popular general education—the Chautauqua movement. This began as a brief summer assembly of Sunday School teachers on Lake Chautauqua, New York. It was instituted in 1874 by a Methodist minister, John H. Vincent (afterwards Bishop), who was a leader in the Sunday School movement, and an Ohio manufacturer, Lewis Miller, a Sunday School superintendent and enthusiastic promoter of religious education. The session of two weeks was lengthened to two months, lecturers on a great variety of subjects were brought in, and the camp-meeting ground developed into a noted resort for study. Regular courses were drawn up, correspondence courses were instituted, and the movement became nationwide as local Chautauquas developed elsewhere and study circles spread. The movement commanded the services of scholars like William Rainey Harper, later president of the University of Chicago, and attracted noted speakers—including, in the course of time, six Presidents of the United States and William Jennings Bryan.

The institution was chartered by New York State in 1893 to grant degrees, but its chief academic significance lay in the stimulus it gave to the establishment of summer schools and extension courses in universities. The Chautauqua movement was a notable response to the widespread thirst for knowledge at a time when academic opportunities were restricted. It was also a sign that the American democratic faith was still very much alive, despite all the economic, social, and political discouragements of the Gilded Age.

Part II

THE TRIUMPH OF BUSINESS
1877-1900

CHAPTER 5

The Leadership of Industry

IN THE LAST QUARTER OF THE NINETEENTH CENTURY industrialism provided the dominant economic pattern of American life. Then it could not be doubted that business was more important than agriculture in shaping the destinies of the American people and nation. This victory was apparent in the statistics of production, in the shift of population to cities, in the prestige and power of businessmen, and in the preoccupation of thinkers with the question of the values and the dangers of industrialism. Henceforth the central question was not whether industrialism would rule, but how it should rule.

During these first years of industrial maturity politics did not offer an edifying spectacle: the corruption of local, state, and federal officials by legitimate and illegitimate business interests seemed to prove the thesis of Jefferson that business and public virtue are incompatible. The condition of labor suggested the frightening possibility that a host of Americans would be turned into proletarians. The condition of the farmer suggested that the machinery which industrialism offered him would make him a victim of his very productivity. The new moguls of industry undermined the positions of former aristocracies in the South and New England and offered in their stead only their own appalling manifestations of the principle that money is culture.

An observer of the American scene like Henry Adams could be pardoned for concluding that the dream of the Fathers was played out, that plutocracy in society, corruption in politics, and mass brutalization were all that could be expected in the future. But from our present perspective we know that the dream of the Fathers was not dead, that plutocracy would be checked and business would acquire a more civilized character, that the farmer would recover and the laborer acquire status in society, and that proletarian radicalism would be defeated in the United States

by the people themselves. Therefore the years from the end of Reconstruction to the end of the century must be searched for more than
Henry Adams saw. They must be searched for the signs that industrialism
would not defeat liberty in America.

Trusts: Oil and Steel

The recovery of industry in the later seventies from the Panic and
Depression of 1873 was followed by a boom in the eighties which carried
the American economy far above the levels of production and consumption of the post-Civil War boom. Although the disparity in wealth between North and South, which had become more pronounced during
the era of Reconstruction, was little altered, and the states of the former
Confederacy remained predominantly rural and agricultural, the most
notable economic developments in them were in the field of industry.
A downward swing in 1893 did not wipe out all these national gains.
Each new period of prosperity more than made up for losses during the
preceding period of depression. It is also notable that the prosperity of
the late nineteenth century was not related to war needs at home or
abroad. For these reasons the central American faith in progress survived
depressions despite their increasing severity.

The world watched in wonder the piling up of evidence that the
American experiment was at least in material terms a prodigious success,
giving promise that the United States would emerge as the most powerful
of all modern nations. In the country itself a golden glow of self-confi-
dence and hope set in with the last quarter of the century. Union, industrialism, the rule of the people—these were keys that Americans
expected to unlock infinite possibilities of civilization and glory. Union
was in truth unbreakable now. The rule of the people was, however,
thrown into doubt by the very triumph of industry. This was because
this great era of industrial expansion was also the era in which giant
monopolies took form.

By 1880, the Standard Oil Company demonstrated the efficacy of
the trust form of monopoly, and during the next two decades most of
the main branches of American industry were consolidated under trust
control. The essential cause of this development was the productivity
of industry. Manufacturers learned how to increase their output while
reducing their costs, and these individual triumphs of business ability
added up to possible disaster for business as a whole because output
increased without sufficient increase in consumption to absorb it. Producers of the time saw this problem as one of overproduction, but
modern students tend to describe it as one of underconsumption. The
problem was intensified during the years of returning prosperity after

the Depression of 1873. Capital accumulation was so rapid that investors eagerly bought stocks without much regard for soundness. As a consequence, industrial plants and equipment were enormously expanded. Leading manufacturers and financial promoters believed the risks of price collapses and bankruptcies resulting from the operation of free competition to be intolerable. No businessman of importance as yet ventured to act on the principle that free competition resulting in low prices to consumers, coupled with high wages to labor, would create an expansion in the market to match the expansion of productivity. Instead they turned to the easier program of making profits secure by restricting production, and maintaining artificially high prices and low wages.

The most useful tendency of the monopoly-builders was to effect savings in costs by means of efficiency and then pass on a fraction of these savings to consumers in the form of moderate prices. Such a policy, pursued with such genius for organization as was displayed by a Rockefeller, partially justified the trust movement by giving the nation a marvelous industrial plant along with a moderately expanding market and rising level of consumption. But for every Rockefeller there appeared at least one sheer pirate of the Jim Fisk type who exploited investors, employees, and the consuming public with the utmost impartiality, adding nothing useful to the permanent structure of industry, and often leaving looted companies in a state of bankruptcy.

Rockefeller himself and seven of his associates were indicted in 1879 by the state of Pennsylvania, on the complaint of the Petroleum Producers' Union. They were charged with conspiracy to achieve a monopoly through domination of pipeline facilities, extortion of rebates from railroads, and other devices. In the next year, however, the Producers, recognizing their inability to cope with Standard Oil, made a settlement out of court. This resulted in some reform in the practices of Standard's pipelines, but did not appreciably affect the discrimination in railroad rates in favor of the trust. These Producers in Pennsylvania continued to assert that it was the duty of the government to protect the people against the dangerous power of monopolies. But the lesson was clear: the state governments were too weak to control the new combinations of economic power. Meanwhile, the federal government was in the hands of believers in laissez faire—that is, of men opposed to any unfriendly action towards big business, though quite willing to grant special favors to "infant industries" in subsidies and tariff protection.

Rockefeller and His Ways

Rockefeller and his associates now refined more than 90 per cent of the nation's oil. He would have worn out his energies over trifling matters if he had been a lesser man, but Rockefeller also had vitality and imagination to spare for the largest projects. What he really sought, as other great men have sought God or political power, was economy resulting from improvements in operations. He fought free competition because it meant uncertainty and waste. Only if a single plan were imposed upon the entire industry could production be brought into efficient relation to consumption, duplication of effort and costs be avoided, inferior products be banished from the market, and rational procedures resulting in sure profits, which in turn guaranteed availability of necessary capital, be established in the industry.

He cared nothing for money as such, but lived in a kind of puritanic splendor that was suited to his great wealth though quite free of ordinary indulgence in luxury. His children he brought up on principles of a new Spartanism combining plain Baptist morality and sound business habits. He neither gave nor accepted the lavish entertainments in which the ordinary Society of the wealthy exulted. A round of golf with the ball presented as a souvenir to his partner afterwards; consultation with his architects for the improvement of one of his homes; dinner with his family; evening prayer with all the servants in attendance: such was a day of relaxation. Many of his associates regarded him as inhumanly cold, and the public came to think of him as a species of fiend, but he was rather ordinary in everything except his business life. In this he showed great and growing talents. The profits of his enterprise were almost all poured back into it. Rockefeller was the archetype of the new American monopolist who used his power to expand production. The major effort of his rivals to compete against Rockefeller began in 1879, when oil-well owners combined in the Tidewater Pipe Company to build a pipeline over the Allegheny Mountains from the oil fields to the seacoast. This would by-pass Rockefeller's network of subservient railroads and pipelines. In the east they could sell their crude oil to refiners not in the Rockefeller group and obtain a better price. The Standard companies campaigned against this heroic plan to pump oil over mountains, fought Tidewater's titles along the right-of-way, and tried to prevent sales to rival refineries. This convinced the Tidewater group in 1883 that they should accept an offer from Standard of a "gentlemen's agreement" to abandon competition. Still a few producers of crude oil held out against the giant. They combined in a Protective Association in 1887, began to build their own pipeline and storage facilities, and compelled an important change in Rockefeller's policy. He began to buy oil wells for the first time and thus to convert his system from a horizontal to a vertical combination, that is, integration under single control of all stages of the industry from the well to the ultimate consumer. In 1891, the few remaining rivals of Standard organized the Producers' Oil Company and in turn struggled for transportation, refining, and distribution facilities. They were countered by harsh tactics, including violence, but emerged as the Pure Oil Company, which was small but genuinely independent.

Standard developed its marketing organization both as a means of destroying competition and expanding consumption. A network of agents not only sold Standard products but provided information about rivals' sales which was used to put them out of business. The most common method was a price war strictly confined to a local area where Standard would sell products at a loss until the rival was forced to give up, whereupon Standard's price returned to its highly profitable normal level. At the same time Standard offered a line of illuminating and lubricating oils so well designed that it encouraged a general expansion of the market. In places where the kerosene lamp was unknown—in this country, in Latin America, and later in Asia—salesmen would present a householder with a lamp filled and lighted. Very few could resist purchasing oil to keep it burning. Then, as gas and electric illumination began to displace oil, the development of the automobile in the last decade of the century opened greater markets than ever for petroleum products. Standard's technology was pre-eminent chiefly because Rockefeller was determined to manufacture a product for every possible use, and to find a use for every by-product of crude oil. The displacement of beeswax by paraffin in candles and sealing compounds was a typical exploit.

The expansion of the size and number and the increasing diversity of the companies comprising the Standard group posed a problem of control for Rockefeller and his associates. Their lawyers by 1882 had solved it. The owners of stock in the 77 constituent companies turned over their certificates, including their voting rights which constituted actual power over the companies, to nine trustees—Rockefeller and eight partners—in return for trust certificates entitling the stockholders to dividends but nothing else. The profits of the 77 companies were pooled and paid out equally to all stockholders, virtually guaranteeing high dividends because the mammoth system as a whole could hardly fail to succeed even though one part of it might operate at a loss. This is the only form of monopoly properly called a trust, but the apparition of Standard Oil in this guise so shocked Americans that "trust" became their term for every form of monopoly.

Actually the era of the trusts, narrowly defined, was short-lived. During the eighties a few more industries imitated the Standard Oil trust, notably whiskey distilling, sugar refining, cottonseed oil, linseed oil, and lead. But the trust was vulnerable to state legal action because its organization and obviously monopolistic purpose were matters of written record. The Supreme Court of Ohio in 1892 ordered the Standard Oil Trust to dissolve. Rockefeller and his partners employed evasive tactics until 1899 when they found the laws of New Jersey ("the mother of trusts") favorable to reorganization of their system as a holding company. A single corporation, the Standard Oil Company of New Jersey, bought the stock of the other companies in the combine in sufficient quantity to obtain voting control over them. In practice the same men, led by Rockefeller, retained the same powers over the whole Standard system. With New Jersey amenable, only the federal government could move against the giant, and this it did not do until after the turn of the century.

The holding company form was used to consolidate a number of industries, and the merger was employed in other cases. The latter was the simplest device of all, namely, the purchase and extinction of one company by another. This could lead to monopoly if virtually all competing companies were merged into one. A notorious campaign to achieve this end was waged by the National Cordage Company, which was a merger of the "big four" in the rope industry. A large competitor, Plymouth Cordage Company, refused to sell to National, therefore the latter used its control over the world's supply of manila hemp to face Plymouth with an ultimatum: either sell out or pay exorbitant prices for hemp. But Plymouth defended itself militantly and maintained its independence. Nevertheless it took full advantage of the high prices for manufactured rope which National imposed on the market, and consumers learned from this and other instances that consolidation need not be complete for the benefits of competition to disappear.

Carnegie and Steel

The greatest of all mergers occurred in the iron and steel industry. Andrew Carnegie came out of the Depression of the seventies as the leading organizer of the industry. He displaced the old ironmasters by manipulating financial control of his mills. He had a sensitive feeling for public opinion and a genuine warmth towards humankind. But he allied himself with associates who were less sensitive, notably Henry C. Frick, who achieved marvels of production by using cheap imported labor, working his men twelve hours a day seven days a week, fighting trade unionism to a standstill, and making Pittsburgh and lesser steel towns models of industrial efficiency as well as nightmares of soot and slums. Almost a thousand competing companies were absorbed by a few corporations, of which the Carnegie Steel Company was the largest.

Like Standard Oil, Carnegie Steel was a vertical combination owning its own raw materials, transportation facilities, mills, fabrication plants, and distribution agencies. The assembling and integration of this system made Carnegie the peer of Rockefeller as a genius of modern industrialism. In 1900, his companies paid profits of $40 million, of which $35 million went to Carnegie personally, free of any corporate or personal, federal or state income taxes. The percentage of profit on invested capital paid by these companies was exorbitant by modern standards, but it did not preclude prices for finished goods low enough to insure enormous expansion of the market. Superior efficiency of production, along with severe exploitation of labor, accounted for Carnegie's success. Structural steel became universal for larger buildings and for bridges; barbed wire displaced wooden fences; wire nails displaced cut and forged nails; steel coaches displaced wooden ones on the railroads; and the United States Navy in 1887 began to use steel armor plate. These successes occurred because the steel product was cheaper than the old one, or better, or

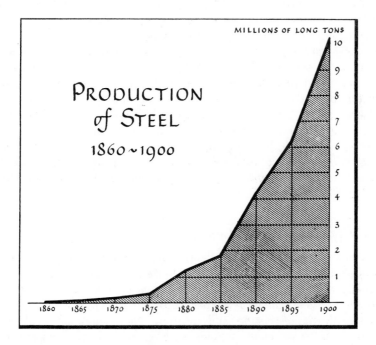

both. Metallurgical scientists steadily improved qualities of metal and devised new alloys for specialized uses. The availability of very hard and heat-resistant steel was basic to the development of electric motors and dynamos, gasoline engines, and the machine-tool industry that made possible mass production of many consumers' articles.

Carnegie relied on competitive ability to maintain his position in the industry. He did not attempt to combine with such important rivals as the Tennessee Coal and Iron Company which had its headquarters in the Birmingham district, the Colorado Fuel and Iron Company in the Rocky Mountains, or the Illinois Steel Company in the Middle West. These and other companies vied to achieve vertical independence, all the way from coal and iron mines to distribution agencies, and to outpace the great Scottish steelmaster. But the horizons of Carnegie's ambition lay beyond the "game" of production which satisfied most businessmen. He was the first of the American industrial titans to view productivity and wealth as means to social goals. Nor did he attribute his business success entirely to his own competitive superiority. In 1886, he published *Triumphant Democracy,* in which he attributed the supremacy of American industry to the superiority of democracy over monarchy and described the growth of education, churches, and libraries as the best fruit of American economic progress. He experimented with methods of improving the lot of labor, on one occasion helping his employees establish a co-operative store. He condemned stock-jobbers and promoters—notably when they organized inefficient and speculative tin-plate mills to exploit the protection given by the McKinley Tariff of 1890.

In 1892, Carnegie retired from active management of his company, leaving that to the tough-minded Henry C. Frick, and from Skibo Castle in Scotland he deplored the Homestead Massacre, writing to William E. Gladstone that "the Works are not worth one drop of human blood." He did not doubt that a law of nature gave him the right to his enormous fortune, arguing in *The Gospel of Wealth* (1900) that, once a man had accumulated wealth, his duty was to use it to benefit humanity, for to die rich was a disgrace. In this mood he was open to an offer when J. P. Morgan set out to organize the first billion-dollar company, the United States Steel Corporation.

Morgan and Finance Capital

This gigantic merger marked the triumph of the finance capitalist over the industrialist as the dominant figure in the American economy. Morgan with his partners, organized as a private bank in New York City, was the leading investment banker in the nation. By a system of interlocking directorates in the largest banks and insurance companies, he was able to determine the investment policies of a great network of institutions. Business companies needing capital could obtain it if Morgan and his associates decided that the banks and insurance companies controlled by them would buy the stock and bond issues. The profit of the Morgan interests came from resale at a higher price than they paid. Their concern was to preserve their reputation for marketing only the safest investments. Therefore the House of Morgan, along with lesser investment bankers, opposed the piracy, speculation, and gutting of business companies' values by insiders which had marked the growth of industrialism.

Morgan represented probity and power in a new combination. His dealings were never shady, but the power of his bank resembled that of an economic government of the nation. The son of an international banker, he was well educated, had thought of becoming a mathematician, and maintained the position of a highly respectable member of St. George's

Episcopal parish in New York City. He was self-conscious about his ugly nose, bulbous and red; he avoided publicity, and seemed to the public mysterious and remote. Next door to his house on Manhattan he built an exquisite Renaissance palace to contain the literary and art treasures for which his agents combed the world. His steam yacht he named the *Corsair,* and in it he traveled as a dignified potentate. In his manners he was a gentleman on the English model, but there was nothing gentle about his way of doing business, or collecting art, or bestowing his limited philanthropic gifts; it was only the logic of power and money honestly but bluntly applied.

United States Steel

By the nineties, J. Pierpont Morgan had developed his power over the nation's money markets to such a level that he was initiating new combinations instead of waiting for industrialists to come to him. The steel industry offered the most tempting field. The United States was now overtaking Great Britain in the size and efficiency of its ferrous metal industry. Judge Elbert H. Gary, counsel of the Illinois Steel Company, advised its directors that it should gain ownership of iron and coal resources and transportation facilities so as to become strong enough to defeat Carnegie in foreign markets. Morgan decided to support this program, and a series of mergers in 1898 resulted in the Federal Steel Company, a vertical combination capitalized at $100 million. But the Carnegie Company could produce more and better steel and sell it cheaper than any other in the world, and Morgan did not like his companies to engage in price-cutting competition even when they might win. He assembled representatives of ten other great steel companies and finally approached the laird of Skibo Castle. The negotiation was epical, the outcome awesome. Carnegie sold out, and began to dispose of his hundreds of millions of dollars by philanthropy, while Morgan in 1901 organized the United States Steel Corporation, a "combination of combinations," as a holding company under the laws of New Jersey. Rockefeller properties were soon brought into the amalgamation by the purchase from the Oil King of rich Mesabi orefields in the Lake Superior district; for these $80 million was paid in stock.

The securities issued for the new colossus amounted to $1.4 billion, which was twice as much as the actual value of the properties. The syndicate organized by Morgan to underwrite these securities took $62 million clear profit for its trouble. The overcapitalization was said to be justified because the new company was bound to be fabulously profitable, and so it was. Although a number of steel companies sufficient to account for almost half of the total national production remained legally independent, their resources of iron ore were too small to permit them to challenge the giant. Judge Gary, chairman of the board of the new corporation, made sure of working agreements by arranging "Gary dinners" of the leaders of all steel companies. In 1911, he sought understandings with the leading steel producers of all other nations besides.

Gary stated that "moral principles" are the basis of all business success, and that the purpose of his understandings with American and foreign competitors was to make sure that all obeyed the "Golden Rule." Because of its command of ore supplies and its high efficiency the United States Steel Corporation earned steady profits of 12 per cent from the beginning, and enough of this was plowed back into the company to absorb much of the original water in the securities. Exploitation of labor in the steel mills remained as severe as ever. Immigrants from Central Europe were used for the roughest work, and unions were ruthlessly suppressed. The twelve-hour day and the seven-day week were standard in the mills.

During the next decade the percentage of steel produced by independent companies actually increased, and this seemed to confound those who accused the great company of monopoly. Modern economists have coined the phrase "price leadership" for the crucial policy of the United States Steel Corporation. An example of its technique in handling details was the very high rate charged for carrying ore by the only two railroads operating from the Mesabi Range to Lake Superior. The Corporation owned these railroads, independent steel companies had to use them, and the more they used them the more the United States Steel Corporation profited. An example of the interrelations among Morgan interests was the payment by the Steel Corporation of high rentals on iron ore lands owned by the Great Northern Railroad, whose builder, James J. Hill, depended on the Morgan Bank for financing. In the new era the financiers wielded the dominant power.

John D. Rockefeller and his partners in the oil industry also became influential in investment banking towards the end of the century because their huge profits outran the capacity of the oil industry to absorb them, even at its great rate of expansion. Certain leading banks and insurance companies consequently came under the influence of this "surplus" oil money, and it was a question whether the masters of oil and the titans of steel would fight or combine. Either alternative was breath-taking. The new century witnessed some skirmishes between Rockefeller and the Morgan interests, and also a good deal of co-operation. The most decisive struggle, which occasioned the federal government to assert the supremacy of public interest, was waged on the old battlefield of the railroads.

THE RAILROADS AND THEIR MASTERS

During this period the railroads, too, came under the control of investment bankers. Because of the special opportunities for chicanery opened by governmental subsidies to railroads, a particularly crude type of potentate had appeared in this branch of industry; and because railroads by their nature tended to be monopolies, they posed a more immediate question of public interest than manufacturing industries. The period opened with campaigns by regional railroad leaders to achieve national control. Most of these men were predatory, a few were constructive in their policies, but none wielded financial power sufficient to integrate the vast congeries of the country's roads. Hence they yielded increasingly to the masters of capital.

From Freebooting to National Consolidation

After nearly ruining the Erie, Jay Gould invaded the West, bought up small roads, threatened to unite and extend them to compete with the Union Pacific, and thereby forced the big company to buy his roads on his own exorbitant terms. This made competition a form of blackmail. Gould's extortions helped drive the Union Pacific into bankruptcy in the nineties. The technique was used by many other freebooters, notably the builders of the "Nickel Plate," or New York, Chicago and Saint Louis Railroad, who had no purpose other than that of selling it to the New York Central—at a price so high that Cornelius Vanderbilt grumbled that the rails must be made of nickel plate.

Exceptional in his methods was James J. Hill, who created the Great Northern during the eighties. This road eventually extended from Saint Paul to Seattle and paralleled the Northern Pacific. Hill worked without government subsidy, followed sound financial practices, and served rather than exploited the public. He realized that the welfare of the settlers along his railroad would determine its prosperity, and he helped them build schools, improve their farms, and obtain loans at low rates. Hill was an "empire-builder" in the best sense. Not far behind him in vision and probity was Henry Villard, who was president of the Northern Pacific (1881-1884) at the height of his career. He brought tens of thousands of European immigrants into the Pacific Northwest. Hill relied on Morgan for financing, and Villard went begging for capital.

Morgan also gained dominant influence in the railroads of the South. Consolidation there proceeded to a climax after the Depression of 1893, when he created the Southern Railway out of more than a score of companies and united lines covering the region from Washington to New Orleans. East of this system was the Atlantic Coast Line, itself the product of the consolidation of more than a hundred roads from Virginia to Florida and equally controlled by the House of Morgan. In the East, Morgan was most influential in the New York Central after Cornelius Vanderbilt's son William had inherited control. Its main line from New York to Chicago was extended by branches reaching Boston and Saint

Louis. The Pennsylvania, which was well managed by J. Edgar Thompson, built a tunnel under the Hudson River to gain access to New York City at the turn of the century. Then it bought the Long Island Railroad, connected its lines with the New Haven road to reach New England, and celebrated its invasion of the Metropolitan district by building a great terminal in New York modeled on the Baths of Caracalla. The Pennsylvania's prosperity centered on its monopoly of traffic—including oil, coal, iron and steel—between Philadelphia and Pittsburgh, and this tempted various others, notably George F. Baer and his Reading Railroad, which was backed by coal interests, to enter that rich territory. The Baltimore and Ohio was unable to gain entrance into New York City and lost position to the Pennsylvania. The Erie after its fourth bankruptcy came under Morgan control and was used chiefly to carry coal.

By the late nineties, Morgan emerged as the greatest influence in the American transportation system. He used his influence to end competition and to secure orderly management and stable revenues for the sake of converting into a source of safe investments the railroads which so often came bankrupt into his hands. His reorganizations all followed the pattern of requiring that he or his associates be placed on boards of directors. The generation of builders and freebooters accepted his medicine, both because he commanded access to the money markets and because he did not insist on squeezing the water out of existing securities. Rather, he guided the policies of the companies he reorganized so as to make efficiency and monopoly pay dividends on all the wastage of the disorderly years.

Morgan's remaining rival for national influence over the railroads was Edward H. Harriman. Beginning as a broker in Wall Street, Harriman learned how to get control of a bankrupt line, reorganize it, obtain new capital, improve its equipment and services, and make it return profits. He was particularly adept in establishing "community of interests" among erstwhile competitors. His operations were backed by Rockefeller money. After gaining control of the Illinois Central he moved into the West. Favored by the Depression of 1893, which could not be weathered by the Western buccaneers, he made himself the master of two great continental roads—the Union Pacific-Central Pacific, and the Southern Pacific. To these he joined coastal railroads from Portland, Oregon, to southern California, and steamship lines from New Orleans to the West Coast. At the same time Morgan backed Hill and the Great Northern in gaining control over Villard's Northern Pacific. Then the Morgan-Hill interests strove for control of the Chicago, Burlington, and Quincy, which tied Chicago to all the central and northern transcontinental roads. The contest that followed was the final competitive struggle between two consolidated systems for unified control of the nation's railroads.

Harriman asked for a share in the C B & Q for fear that he would be shut out of Chicago, but he was turned down. He then tried to wrest the Northern Pacific from the Morgan-Hill group. Generally it was not necessary to own a majority of the voting stock of one of these corporations in order to control it. Ownership was so scattered that holdings of 40 or 30 per cent or less sufficed to decide its policies. But this left open the possibility that a determined rival could buy majority control by assembling small blocks of stock. Such was Harriman's method. There followed a fantastic episode as the Morgan-Hill group became alarmed and the competition of these masters of money forced up the price of Northern Pacific stock in one hour on May 9, 1901, from $350 to $1000. Brokers had "sold short" and no more stock was to be had. Ruin for many firms threatened. None of the principals believed in competition anyway, so they arranged a superconsolidation as a treaty of peace.

The Rockefeller-Harriman and the Morgan-Hill groups organized a new holding company, the Northern Securities Corporation, under the friendly laws of New Jersey, to own controlling interests in the Northern Pacific and the Great Northern, which in turn controlled the C B & Q. Harriman and two of his fellow executives of the Union Pacific became directors of the holding company. Its purpose was frankly admitted to be the "establishment of permanent harmony" among the major railroads from Chicago and the Mississippi Valley to the Pacific Coast. Harriman subsequently tried to win for his western roads connections on the Atlantic through the Baltimore and Ohio. In conjunction with the Morgan interests in the eastern roads, this meant that the railroads of the entire nation were coming under a community of interests managed by a handful of financiers. But the Northern Securities Corporation was so bald an example of monopoly that President Theodore Roosevelt and the Supreme Court acted against it in the new century.

The Golden Age of Railroad Transportation

A significant policy of the financial magnates was to destroy the competition which waterways offered railroads. Speed sufficed to give the latter the cream of passenger traffic and also the small-bulk freight of high value. But for many bulky commodities of low value, such as grain, the slowness of water traffic was more than compensated by cheapness. To deny even these cargoes to shipping, the railroads, once their control was sufficiently unified to pursue consistent policies, added to their advantage of speed ruinous methods of competition. During the summer, when the Erie Canal operated, railroad freight rates were lowered; during the winter, when ice stopped traffic on the old canal, the railroads raised their rates. Railroad rates from ports on rivers, especially the Mississippi, where steamboats were available, were lowered, and compensated for by high rates from inland points without regard for mileages.

In this way, during the last quarter of the nineteenth century, the death blow was delivered to almost all internal water transportation except that of the Great Lakes. There the steel companies, ultimately the United States Steel Corporation which was itself controlled by Morgan, found it convenient to carry the iron ore of the Mesabi Range to the mills at the southern ends of Lakes Michigan and Erie by ships, and these were permitted to carry coal on their return voyages. Some grain from Minnesota and the Dakotas also moved east by Lake ship. But the Pittsburgh Steamship Company, a subsidiary of the United States Steel Corporation, dominated the traffic on the Lakes and prevented any competition from smaller shipowners. The steamships on the Lakes amounted to one-third of the nation's merchant marine because the coastal trade, too, was reduced by railroad competition, and American-owned oceanic shipping did not recover from the setback of the Civil War.

The last decade of the nineteenth century which witnessed the victory of the railroad system over the waterways, also saw the obscure beginnings of the gasoline-powered automobile and truck which would give the railroads their severest competition in the new century. For a few years, however, the railroads enjoyed a golden era of profits under the control of financiers, and the public enjoyed greatly improved passenger and freight accommodations. Trains became splendid affairs in the grandiose decorative style of the period, replete with gilt and plush. Even freight cars were improved by increased use of steel, and new types such as gondolas, and livestock and refrigerated cars were built. Roadbeds were improved, and locomotives became more powerful. The trains ran on time, they became fairly safe, they provided heat, light, sleeping, dining, and lounging accommodations, and the great transcontinental lines invited enjoyment of the scenic wonders of their terrain in "observation cars." The great financiers rode about in private cars of regal luxury. Under their conservative control, the railroads successfully performed the every-growing tasks of transportation in the United States. It remained questionable whether "Wall Street" charged too high a price for its admittedly valuable service in putting an end to the era of the "robber barons"; whether financiers had not taken into their hands power over the nation's economy too vast to be safely confided to any private group; whether they had not superseded government itself in effective power.

The Uses of Electricity

The achievements of Big Business enthralled Americans as much as the specter of monopoly frightened them. While freebooters and financiers outdid their European counterparts in dazzling maneuvers, American manufacturers continued to outpace the rest of the world in the provision of convenient devices for consumers. The first great examples of this, the sewing machine and the reaper, depended on nothing more wonderful than foot and horse power. During the last quarter of the nineteenth century two marvelous new kinds of power, electricity and gasoline, were first applied to the tasks of the home and the farm as well as to transportation and manufacture. For a time it seemed that electricity would reign without a rival; then the internal combustion engine won importance and finally the use of both kinds of power was expanded, each according to its applicability.

The oldest use of electricity was the telegraph. Dozens of local companies and several competitors for national position were taken over by the Western Union Company. Under the presidency of Norvin Green, Western Union doubled its wire mileage between 1878 and 1883, reaching 400,000 miles. Profits doubled to more than $7 million during the same brief period, but charges were reduced by only an ironic seven-tenths of a cent per message. Railroads, newspapers, and businessmen were the chief users of the telegraph. A great strike against Western Union by operators from New York to New Orleans and Omaha won public sympathy for the strikers against the unscrupulous policies of the company, but nevertheless failed. The Postal Telegraph Company and the Commercial Cable Company held out with difficulty against Western Union, and in 1887 the former accepted a truce offer under which rate competition ceased. The possibility of governmental regulation was fended off chiefly by means of petty bribes to legislators, mayors, aldermen, and judges in the form of franking privileges—the same weapon as the railroads' free passes. Postmaster General John Wanamaker in 1892 argued for government ownership of the telegraph system on the ground that the companies were serving only one-sixtieth of the people, as contrasted with the virtually universal postal service. But this proposal pointed towards socialism and was ignored.

Western Union fought against the coming of the telephone, which was destined actually to serve the people as effectively as the post office. Its inventor was Alexander Graham Bell, a Scot who came to America in 1870 at the age of twenty-three and devoted himself for some years in New England to teaching the deaf to talk by means of a system of "visible speech" which his father had developed in London. Study of acoustics and experiments in telegraphy led Bell to perceive the possibility of the electrical transmission of speech; and in 1876 in Boston he gave the first successful demonstration of the magneto-electric telephone. His first telephone patent was issued that year. Bell offered to sell his rights in the invention to Western Union, but that company declined.

The early organization of the telephone business was largely the work of Gardiner G. Hubbard, who soon drew Theodore N. Vail into it. Hub-

bard had been attracted to Bell because of interest in the education of
the deaf which was occasioned by his daughter's total loss of hearing
from scarlet fever. The inventor married that daughter about the time
the Bell Telephone Company was formed in 1877. Western Union set up
the American Speaking Telephone Company to exploit the claims of a
rival inventor and prevent the outmoding of the telegraph. The Bell
Company met this and all other competition by successfully defending
the validity of its patents in the courts and by pursuing an energetic
policy of service to the public under the general managership of Vail.
When copper wire was developed, conversations between cities became
practicable.

After 1888, the Bell Company paid dividends of over 15 per cent.
Its service was not cheap but it was popular. Telephones became a
commonplace in the United States, alone among the nations. By 1900,
nearly a million and a half of them were in use in the country. The Bell
Company established one of the first industrial research laboratories, and
the improvements and inventions it turned out enabled the company
to maintain its ascendancy even after the original patents expired in
the 1890's. Many local companies sprang up, however, and this competitive situation led to the creation in 1900 of the American Telephone and
Telegraph Company, a holding company in which the Bell Company
and lesser systems were consolidated. In this field service could be most
effective under a monopoly, but the new Company, capitalized at a
quarter of a billion dollars, was still free of any regulation by government.

The telephone brought the age of electricity into the average American
home. It was followed by the incandescent electric lamp and eventually
by small electric motors attached to tools for the performance of almost
every chore in barn and household. Thomas Alva Edison was the hero
of this revolution. He was the last great example of the earlier kind of
inventor who had not so much scientific knowledge as talent for tinkering;
they made hunches based on other men's scientific discoveries come true.
He was a failure at school in West Orange, New Jersey, and received his
education at home and by selling newspapers and candy on trains. He
worked for Western Union and soon invented an electric vote recorder. In
1876, he built his famous laboratory at Menlo Park, New Jersey, where the
next year he produced the phonograph, and in 1879 improvements that
made possible the manufacture of incandescent lamps. He foreshadowed
the co-operative era of invention by surrounding himself with collaborators. His various devices were manufactured by the Edison General
Electric Company which became the nucleus of the giant corporation,
General Electric of Schenectady, New York. Living on into the fourth
decade of the twentieth century, Edison was partly or wholly responsible
for the storage battery, dictaphone, Sprague motor, electric dynamo,

moving pictures, electric locomotive, and other applications of the marvelous new power. His career was one of the most admirable of all examples of the American success story. His accomplishments were measurable not only in money for himself and for investors but in terms of service to humanity.

The electric motor rounded out the series of American applications of the new power source. Its principle had been discovered by Joseph Henry and Michael Faraday. In 1835, Thomas Davenport invented the first workable motor. But its use depended upon the generation of electricity by the converse principle of the electric dynamo, and this was first developed for outdoor lighting at Cornell University in 1875. Great expansion followed the introduction of the steam turbine to turn the dynamo in 1890. Hydroelectric power was first obtained from the Falls of Niagara in 1894. In the meantime Nikola Tesla produced the inventions which made the electric motor practicable. A Hungarian immigrant, he was highly educated in European science before he went to work in the United States in 1884 to put theory into practice. He discovered the principle of the rotary magnetic field, applied it to the induction motor, and made possible the transmission and use in the motor of alternating current, which was economical and feasible for long lines.

The electric street car was invented by Stephen Dudley Field and used in New York City in 1874. William Morrison designed in 1891 a private vehicle powered by batteries. Factories were slow to turn from steam to electric power to run their machines, the new source accounting for less than 2 per cent of total factory horsepower in 1900. But a wave of electric-trolley building gave the citizens of every city cheap urban transportation by that time—and a new problem of political corruption in the handing out of traction franchises. It remained for innumerable minor inventions and the development of mass production of electric motors and tools to decentralize power consumption into the factory, farm, and home. Then the concomitant centralization of power production, whether by steam- or water-driven dynamos, with all the economic power of a natural monopoly, gave the twentieth century one of its crucial problems of public policy.

Personal Transportation

Decentralization of modern means of transportation began during this era. Steamboats, railroads, and trolley cars left people dependent upon the routes and schedules that the companies believed suited to maximum traffic. The horseless carriage, driven by electric motor, was the first successful application of modern methods to individualized transportation. To keep horses in the cities was very expensive; the new "electric" consumed nothing except when actually operated. It was designed as a carriage completely banded by glass, and its interior appointments often included such elegant touches as silver vases for flowers. Women especially loved the new vehicles because they were safe, simple to operate, and handsome. They were restricted by battery capacity to trips no longer than a round of urban shopping and social calls. In 1900, electrics accounted for almost half of automobile production.

Vigorous young women as well as men who could afford neither horse nor automobile expanded the market for bicycles when the coaster gear and safety brake made them trustworthy. The bicycle became a fad in the nineties with significant meanings. The liberation of young people from home and parents was one thing; the insistence of young women that they had a right to wear "daring" costumes and to ride freely with casual companions of both sexes was another. The swooning Victorian girl, pale and sheltered, gave way to the healthy and gay pioneers of a new era. An important consequence of the bicycle craze was that it established an industry and developed mechanical skills which were quickly applied to the gasoline-driven automobile.

Several Europeans had built vehicles powered by engines in which an electric spark exploded gasoline mixed with air, when a bicycle designer, Charles Duryea, with his brother Frank built in 1892 the first one in the United States. Others, including Elwood Haynes and the Apperson brothers, one of whom was a bicycle repair man, built home-made "gas buggies." The greatest of these tinker-builders was Henry Ford. In 1892-1893 at Detroit, he made a motor with a gas pipe for cylinder, mounted it on bicycle wheels, and made it run. He allied himself to a firm that built automobiles to order like hand-tailored clothes, but soon put his restless mind to work on the task of mechanizing the production of the new machines. In him the new century found the genius who more than any other one man solved the problem to which all the greatest American industrialists had dedicated themselves: to make a machine everyone could use at a price everyone could pay.

THE FREEDOM OF ENTERPRISE

Virtually all American business enterprise came under the influence if not the control of investment bankers by the end of the nineteenth century, which thus serves as a general boundary between the eras of industrial capitalism and finance capitalism. Even in the twentieth century Henry Ford clung to the conviction that an enterprise was not free if it depended on bankers' control of investments, but among the great industrialists he was a solitary figure. Most businessmen, merchants, transportation magnates, and manufacturers were reconciled to the decisive voice of bankers in their affairs. In this they differed from farmers, who relied on mortgage loans to finance their enterprises but periodically lashed out against those who lent them their capital. Small businessmen constituted a rather inarticulate group who were often exploited by bankers as severely as farmers were, but whose pride of status seldom permitted them to identify themselves with antibusiness groups or ideas.

Until the last decades of the century the attitude of most Americans towards businessmen most of the time was one of admiration verging on worship. No one begrudged inventors the rewards they garnered; in fact, few of them gained much profit. Next to them in public favor were the in-dustrialists who personally organized production and were identified with superior products. Stern traditions of personal integrity, practical intelli-gence, managerial skill, and honest workmanship were embodied in the products of business families, who, like the Lawrences and Lowells of earlier New England, emerged at the top of the social structure in cities across the nation. Though sometimes envied, they were too closely identi-fied with the excellence of their product to be hated.

So long as American enterprise was dominated by merchants and manu-facturers, antibusiness opinion remained relatively unimportant. Since the days of Jefferson and Jackson, not businessmen as such but bankers and stock manipulators had been the targets of political attack. Hatred of the parasite who took for himself the rewards of others' work was the essential reason for the antibusiness movements that got underway during the last years of the nineteenth century. The "Robber Barons" and "Trust Kings" seemed to make no genuine contributions to the na-tion's productivity. Modern historians and economists view the integration of vast industrial and financial operations as useful. But at the time the abuses of the process were more apparent than the long-range benefits, and the reaction against the leaders was essentially Jeffersonian. It pic-tured the makers of combinations as mere manipulators who were re-warded for their cunning with wealth and power out of all proportion to their labor.

The facts on which opposition fed were essentially the same as those which led Andrew Jackson to declare war on Nicholas Biddle and the Bank of the United States: the money-power of a few was growing stronger than the political power of the many. City and state organizations of both political parties were known to be more amenable to manipulation by businessmen seeking special favors than to the desires of the mass of voters. The growth of business monopoly and its merger with finance capitalism occurred with bewildering speed. But a J. P. Morgan worked quite differently from a Nicholas Biddle, and this fact generally escaped the early opponents of Big Business.

It was unnecessary for the finance capitalists to corrupt government. Their power over the nation's money supply superseded that of the federal government itself, and in fact made it necessary in emergencies for government to "bribe" the bankers. The most remarkable demonstration of this new relationship occurred when the Treasury's gold reserve declined dangerously in 1894, and individuals drained the Treasury by presenting government paper to it for redemption. The Cleveland administration appealed to the ultimate American master of gold, J. P. Morgan, to rescue it. Morgan agreed, for a generous profit, to buy an issue of bonds with gold which would not be drawn from the Treasury. He kept his part of the bargain, and the government was enabled to rebuild its gold reserve as prosperity returned. But in this episode Morgan dealt with the federal government as one sovereign might deal with another that was weaker. Corruption of government, bad as it was, had been surpassed by something worse: weakness in the face of financial power so great that corruption was unnecessary. This defined the climax of the freedom of enterprise in the history of the United States.

Government had failed to develop its powers in proportion to the growth of private industrial and financial power. The state governments and the Congress did something in response to popular unrest, but every effort to assert new modes of governmental authority over business enterprise and growing private wealth was defeated, first by the inadequacy of the legislation itself, second by the disinterest of the executive branch in enforcement, and conclusively by the decisions of the federal judiciary.

The Supreme Court and Business Enterprise

Before the Civil War, the Supreme Court under Marshall's leadership had used the contract clause of the Constitution to protect business enterprise from governmental action. But the state governments learned to be forehanded. In their constitutions and statutes they specifically reserved authority to alter or amend charters and franchises so that state regulatory measures might not be called violations of contract. The contract clause therefore declined in usefulness as a protection of business from state regulations.

The due process clause of the Fourteenth Amendment was used by the courts to take its place. This is one of the most profound ironies of American history, because that Amendment was intended to protect not businessmen but the newly-freed Negroes. In 1882, Roscoe Conkling, who as Senator from New York had helped frame the Amendment, argued as attorney for a railroad before the Supreme Court that the word "persons" had been used in the Amendment in order to extend the protection of due process to corporations as legal persons. No evidence to support his argument has been found, but the Court began to develop new doctrines which interposed judicial authority between business corporations and all governmental efforts to restrain them.

In the Slaughterhouse Cases (1873) the Court had adhered to the traditional Anglo-American doctrine that due process was limited in application to procedural matters. That is, the requirement that no state shall "deprive any person of life, liberty, or property, without due process of law," did not mean that the substantive regulatory powers of the states were restricted, but only that the process of enacting and enforcing laws must be fair. In the same decision, Justice Miller for the majority declared that the Fourteenth Amendment protects only those rights which derive from national as opposed to state citizenship. He declared civil rights to be under the protection of the state governments. The immediate matter at issue, a grant of monopoly privilege by the legislature of Louisiana to a slaughterhouse company, was decided in favor of the grant as a purely state matter.

In Munn vs. Illinois, the leading Granger case (1877), Chief Justice Waite denied that a state law fixing maximum rates for grain storage was a violation of due process, but now the decision assumed that due process involved not merely procedure but also the substance or regulatory purpose of the law. Business affected with "a public interest," he declared, was subject to state regulation, and appeal from this regulation was not to the courts but to the polls. The ruling opened the door to future invalidation of state regulations of business enterprise which the Court might regard as unfair either in procedure or in substance. It marked a momentous break with traditional understanding of the meaning of due process.

In the Civil Rights Cases (1883) the Court denied that the Fourteenth Amendment empowered the Congress to legislate affirmatively or directly to secure equality of rights for Negroes. Late in the century, in Plessy vs. Ferguson (1896), it denied that segregation constituted inequality and upheld a Louisiana law requiring "separate but equal" railroad accommodations for whites and Negroes. The majority opinion referred to segregation in public schools as an accepted practice the constitutionality of which was unquestioned.

While the Supreme Court set these limits to federal authority over the states in the area of race relations, it steadily narrowed the authority of states in dealing with business enterprise. The decision in Munn vs. Illinois favorable to state regulatory authority was virtually reversed in Wabash, St. Louis and Pacific Railroad Company vs. Illinois (1886). This case involved a state law designed to prevent the long-and-short-haul abuse by railroads. The Court ignored its earlier emphasis on state power to regulate any business affected with a public interest, and used federal authority over interstate commerce to invalidate the state law. In the Minnesota Commission Case (1890), the Court reversed itself on the question of jurisdiction over the reasonableness of railroad rates fixed by a state commission, declaring that not the polls but the courts should be made available to railroad companies complaining of unreasonable rates, otherwise the companies would be denied substantive due process of law. This interpretation was steadily developed towards its climactic statement in Smyth *vs.* Ames (1898). The Court invalidated a Nebraska law fixing railroad rates, calling it a violation of substantive due process, and took the occasion to lay down the rules of economics which a legislature must follow in determining rates. These rules seemed to support railroad owners in their contention that the presence of "water" in a company's securities should be ignored when deciding what constituted a fair return on investment. The decision not only enlarged the due process clause as a substantive protection but made it into a grant of legislative and executive authority to the courts.

Federal legislation unfavorable to business or wealth was not immune from a judicial veto. The Interstate Commerce Commission, established under the Act of 1887 presumably to implement federal authority over interstate commerce in the form of railroads, was shorn of its authority by decisions of the Supreme Court during the nineties which left the Commission no power beyond the collection of statistics. The Sherman Antitrust Act of 1890 was declared by Chief Justice Fuller in United States *vs.* E. C. Knight Company (1895) to be inapplicable to manufacturing monopolies which carried on their business inside state boundaries. Commerce, he wrote, follows manufacture but is not a part of it. The case involved the acquisition by the American Sugar Refining Company of refineries which gave it virtually total control over the industry, with operations extending into many states. The Court's decision amounted to a charter of liberty to the organizers of manufacturing trusts.

In Pollock *vs.* Farmers' Loan and Trust Company (1895), the Court declared unconstitutional a federal income tax law of 1894. The Constitution forbids a direct tax unless it is apportioned among the states according to population. The phrase "direct tax" had been understood by the framers of the Constitution and thenceforward to mean a tax on land or on persons. Taxes on property, such as the early one on carriages which the Court found valid in 1796 (Hylton *vs.* United States), and the Civil War income tax which the Supreme Court found valid in 1881 (Springer *vs.* United States), were understood to be indirect. To apportion an income tax among the states according to population would defeat its purpose. This was to obtain revenue from those most able to pay, who were concentrated in the northeastern states. A future Chief Justice, Charles Evans Hughes, called the Pollock decision a "self-inflicted wound" upon the Court.

The prevailing theory was that constitutional law is a system of absolute truths dependent not upon time or place, interests, or changing needs or circumstances, but upon abstract operations in logic. The duty of the Supreme Court justices was simply to place challenged statutes alongside pertinent clauses of the Constitution and by comparing them find whether the fundamental law was violated. But in fact the Supreme Court during this period, as before and since, expressed the political philosophies of the justices. They had been appointed mostly by conservative Republican Presidents; they had almost all matured as attorneys for businessmen; and they modified and reversed former decisions of the Court and developed new interpretations of the Constitution in harmony with the interests of Big Business. On this level there was no question of corruption. The justices believed they were serving the best interests of the nation. They believed they were defending freedom of enterprise from violations of individual and property rights guaranteed in the Constitution. But their decisions were so consistently favorable to the new forces of wealth and monopoly, and so consistently unfavorable to all other groups and to legislation designed to redress the balance among groups, that public faith in the Court's impartiality began to be undermined.

The development of a favorable system of constitutional law, which reached its climax during the last few years of the nineteenth century, may be regarded as the culminating triumph of Big Business. The personnel of the other branches of government might change rapidly, but the tenure of the justices ensured a long life for the new system of constitutional interpretation. A generation was to pass before the Supreme Court went to work methodically to dismantle this. That body became a chief target of reformers as a citadel of privilege, but it is a remarkable evidence of the enduring American faith in constitutional processes that the Supreme Court *as an institution* emerged unscathed. It suffered no lasting injury from its "self-inflicted wounds."

Much the same thing can be said of American capitalism. Despite all the abuses accompanying the concentration of wealth and power, and despite the glaring contradiction between monopoly and the doctrine of freedom of enterprise, the vast majority of Americans retained their belief that private property in the means of production is a sound institution. Class differences did not precipitate "two nations," as they did in many countries of the Old World. The United States moved much faster and farther than any other country in the creation of a business civilization. This pace imposed severe strains upon institutions originally designed for an agrarian society, and these developments endangered the individual liberty for which all other American institutions existed. But the new business civilization had scarcely taken form before many Americans went to work to safeguard their ancient ideal.

CHAPTER 6

Labor and Immigration

A GRAVE DANGER ACCOMPANYING THE GROWTH OF business monopoly was the possibility that laborers would lose faith in American freedom because of their own exploitation. If such exploitation could not be checked by traditional institutions, laborers might turn to new weapons. The trade union was by this time sufficiently naturalized in the United States to provide the normal alternative when the results of individual bargaining with an employer failed to satisfy an employee. The main questions to which events of this period gave initial answers were two: To what extent would unionism spread among American workers? Would their unions support traditional American institutions or turn against them in favor of different forms of economic and political institutions?

The period is called in labor history "The Great Upheaval." It was a time of unprecedented violence in labor relations and of crucial experiments in organization and doctrine. One effort was to establish national unity among labor organizations. After failures by the National Labor Union (1866-1872), and the Knights of Labor (1878-1893), the American Federation of Labor (founded in 1886) was successful. Partly because of the continuing influx of immigrants, however, most of the workingmen, particularly the unskilled, remained unorganized.

DEPRESSION AND VIOLENCE, 1873-1877

Prior to the Depression of 1873 there were from twenty-five to thirty national trade unions in the country. The most influential of these just after the war was the Iron Molders' International Union. Its head, William H. Sylvis, was the outstanding American labor leader until his death in 1869. The National Labor Union was organized in 1866 and Sylvis served briefly as its president in 1868-1869. His policies and those of the other leaders were changeable, but the trend was distinctly toward political action and reform. The National Labor Union supported the movement for an eight-hour day and in 1872 it sought to transform itself into a party, advocating currency reform. That year the party nominated Judge David Davis of Illinois for President, but he suddenly withdrew, disrupting the organization.

The Depression of 1873 destroyed what slight bargaining power the unions had enjoyed and their membership dropped from perhaps 300,000

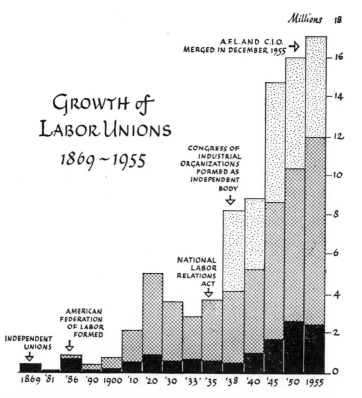

GROWTH of
LABOR UNIONS
1869 ~ 1955

SOURCE: Department of Labor

to about 50,000. Unemployment and the sufferings of hungry and homeless men and their families led to violence and opened the door to radicalism. A few Irish miners in Pennsylvania turned against the mine owners the weapon of assassination they had used against English landlords in their native land. Their secret organization, the "Molly Maguires," was penetrated in the middle of the decade by Pinkerton detectives hired by mine owners, and broken by the conviction of twenty-four Mollies and the hanging of ten. A few Socialist followers of Karl Marx and Ferdinand Lassalle, meeting with anarchist followers of Mikhail Bakunin in New

York and other immigrant centers, set afoot plans to organize laborers for class struggle and revolution. Headquarters of the Marxian First International moved to New York in 1872, when it was moribund. Frederich A. Sorge, a collaborator of Karl Marx, organized the Socialist-Labor Party in 1876. This organization still exists as a cadre of would-be leaders of the American working class. Under the fiery guidance of Daniel DeLeon it formulated a policy that afterwards won the praise of Lenin, the leader of the Soviet Revolution. Johann Most, a German immigrant, called for immediate violence and revolution according to the anarchist prescription of attaining socialism by destroying all government whatever. His supporters founded the Black International in the eighties and gained some support among immigrant workers in Chicago.

The great body of Americans were slow to realize that self-appointed radical leaders would be helpless unless exploitation and suffering drove workingmen into their arms. In 1874, a meeting of unemployed in Tompkins Square, New York, was broken up by charges of mounted police because the city authorities had heard that members of Karl Marx's International Workingmen's Association were going to speak. The *New York Times* reported that the scrambles of the mob before the police were "not unamusing," and put the blame on foreigners. In 1875, the "long strike" of anthracite coal miners in eastern Pennsylvania was accompanied by violence which was to a considerable extent instigated by mine owners in order to discredit unions. They succeeded in breaking the strike.

Before the Depression of the seventies ended it produced the most severe strike in American history. Railroad workers had formed Brotherhoods of Engineers (1863), Conductors (1868), and Firemen (1873). The companies cut wages but continued to pay high dividends on watered stock. The public sympathized with the workers when spontaneous strikes broke out in the summer of 1877 on the Baltimore and Ohio, and spread quickly to the Pennsylvania, the New York Central, the Erie, and finally to the great western lines. The country faced the possibility of a general strike. Rioting occurred in many cities. Federal troops restored order at Martinsburg, West Virginia, but in Baltimore strikers attacked the state militia and set fire to the railway station to which the troops retreated. Federal soldiers were used again to put the strikers down.

Pittsburgh was the scene of events which the press compared to those of the Paris Commune of 1870. The Pennsylvania Railroad was generally disliked because of its policies towards passengers and shippers as well as workers. When the state militia was called out to put down strikers who had stopped trains and seized railway property, the troops would not obey orders but joined the strikers. Militiamen from Philadelphia were therefore sent to Pittsburgh, and a pitched battle with strikers followed, the soldiers killing twenty-five persons. Miners and factory workers then joined the railroad workers, armed themselves by breaking into gun shops, and besieged the troops in the roundhouse. They rolled blazing freight cars into the building and forced the soldiers to retreat. Tramps and criminals now joined the strikers and for several days mobs controlled Pittsburgh, looting and burning property at will. President Hayes had to order all available federal troops to the city before order could be restored. Lesser outbreaks in other cities were also dealt with by federal forces. Sympathy for the strikers gave way to public fear and anger. Communists were said to be the instigators of the trouble, and the genuine grievances of the workers were forgotten. They went back to work on the companies' terms.

The degeneration of union activity into mob violence was actually a result of weak rather than strong organization, but it set back the labor movement by alienating the public. State legislatures revived old laws banning unions and strikes as conspiracies. Employers organized blacklist machinery and required employees to sign the "iron-clad oath" against union activity. The federal government could not well do other than impose order against mobs, but by restricting for another generation its participation in labor disputes to this function, it seemed to side against employees. One workingman, the cigarmaker Samuel Gompers, observing the Tompkins Square Riot, drew the conclusion that organized labor could succeed only by avoiding all connection with radicals and violence. But such a far-sighted policy required education and discipline on the part of union members as well as a new kind of leader.

Labor Begins to Organize, 1878-1896

The Knights of Labor

A different response to the defeat of the railroad strike gave sudden prominence in 1878 to an organization called the Noble and Holy Order of the Knights of Labor. Its secrecy was designed to meet the antiunion policies of employers and governments, and its principle of industrial unionism was designed to unite the growing number of unskilled workers with the skilled and with farmers to overcome the weaknesses of separate craft unions. Terence V. Powderly, who had been elected mayor of Scranton, Pennsylvania, on a labor ticket in 1878, became head of the Knights in 1879. A general assembly governed the national body. Local assemblies emulated the rituals of social secret societies with ceremonies to dignify the meaning and position of labor while strengthening brotherhood without regard to skills, sex, race, or creed. For a time, secrecy and idealism enabled the Knights to gain wide membership. By 1886, nearly 6000 local assemblies had a total membership of more than 700,000. The organization supported the eight-hour day, preferred boycotts and arbitration to strikes, advocated a national income tax, and organized producers' and consumers' co-operatives, extending to the ownership of coal mines.

The minor Depression of 1884-1885 led local groups of Knights to

engage in strikes and boycotts, with some success. They forced the buc-
caneer Jay Gould to negotiate with them and to end discriminations
against union labor on his Wabash Railroad. But this only led Gould to
organize a counterattack that resulted in defeats for the Knights at
the hands of frightened employers.

In 1886, the Haymarket Riot in Chicago turned the tide against the
Knights. The secrecy of the order now worked against it. Ironically,
Powderly had tried to end strikes by the Knights in Chicago. But strikes
at the stockyards and at the McCormick Reaper works had been shorten-
ing tempers. A national movement was under way for general strikes in
favor of the eight-hour day, and when May 1, 1886 (the original May
Day as a radical labor holiday) was set for such a strike in Chicago,
anarchists led by Johann Most exploited the situation to make propaganda in favor of revolutionary violence. This permitted newspapers and
employers to condemn all organized labor as leagued with anarchism.
Two days after the strike for an eight-hour day began, violence occurred
between strikers and strike-breakers at the McCormick plant. The Black
International members, actually speaking for only a tiny group, made
the most of it. They tried to stir up counteraction against the police,
spread incendiary leaflets, and called a protest meeting for the evening
of May 4 in Haymarket Square. The meeting proceeded peacefully
enough, and had begun to break up in the rain, when a detachment of
police suddenly appeared and ordered the remnant to disperse. A bomb
burst in the ranks of the policemen, killing one and injuring others. They
opened fire on the workers and a number were killed on both sides.

To this day it is uncertain whether one of the anarchists threw the
bomb or whether a *provocateur* in a nearby alley was guilty. But precise
consideration of evidence was impossible during the trials of anarchists
which followed, because a storm of anger broke out against all radical
agitators. Eight anarchist leaders were charged with murder. No evidence
connecting them directly with the bombing could be produced, but they
were shown to have advocated violence, and this was enough for the
jury as it was for many citizens. The state's attorney demanded that the
jury find them guilty as examples to "save our institutions," ignoring the
truth that the rules of evidence were important among those institutions.
Seven were sentenced to death and one to life imprisonment. Four of the
seven were executed. In the opinion of William Dean Howells and Henry
Demarest Lloyd, who obtained wide support for petitions, and many
other eminent persons, this was a miscarriage of justice. Finally, in 1893,
Governor John Peter Altgeld freed the remaining prisoners on the ground
that the trial had been unfair.

The leaders of the Knights of Labor struggled hard to dissociate themselves from the odium that attached to the Haymarket anarchists, going
so far as to call for their conviction, but they failed. It was easy to lump

the secret order with the revolutionary anarchists, and in the public mind the distinction between them was insignificant. The Knights of Labor never recovered from the effects of the Haymarket Riot. In 1893, Powderly turned over the small remainder of his organization to an Iowan under whom it lingered on as an unimportant organization, chiefly of farmers. Although the discrediting of the Knights of Labor for the Haymarket Riot was unjust, nevertheless the public was warranted in objecting to a secret organization. Furthermore, American industry had not advanced far enough in mass production to form a body of unskilled labor ready for industrial unionism.

The American Federation of Labor

Most craftsmen did not want to ally their economic fate with that of the unskilled. This was one reason for the success of the American Federation of Labor, the first permanent national American union organization. Crafts unions had tried to unite in a national organization several times before, and the chief reason they succeeded this time was because they found leaders who refused to dissipate the strength of the movement or alienate the public by advocating any utopian, radical, doctrinaire, or political program whatsoever. Instead they formulated a policy of "business unionism." This was unique in the world history of the labor movement and correctly geared to the realities of the American scene. The new organization was founded in 1886, when the disaster of the Knights of Labor, added to all the earlier failures of the labor movement, made clear the necessity for new methods. In December, delegates of twenty-five unions with about 150,000 members met in Cleveland, organized the American Federation of Labor on the principle of the autonomy of each trade, and elected as first president Samuel Gompers, the head of the Cigar Makers Union. Except for the year 1895 he held the office until his death in 1924, and his career is perhaps the most significant in American labor history.

A Jewish immigrant from England, Gompers learned as a worker, and as a leader he applied in his own craft, the lessons that turned out to be essential for the success of organized labor in the United States. These were that American laborers were not and could not be made class-conscious in the Marxian sense. Rather they were "job-conscious," wishing to improve their wages, hours, and conditions of work. They were not antagonistic to capitalism as such but only desirous of making capitalism serve their interests as well as those of capitalists. Most important, they considered themselves to be Americans first and laborers second, and they wished to make good their claim to equal standing with members of other classes. Gompers and Adolph Strasser built up the International Cigar Makers Union from near-collapse in the Depression of the seventies to great strength. Their policy called for high dues, financial probity, aid by strong locals to weakers ones, and the avoidance of strikes except as a last resort when there was reasonable chance of success. They worked for uniform regulations throughout the industry, the use of the union label, better wages, and a short workday. They offered to employers responsible co-operation in carrying out sound labor practices.

Cigar makers were particularly well-educated, perhaps as a result of their tradition that one worker in each shop read aloud while the others worked. But Gompers faced a long struggle to extend "pure-and-simple" trade unionism to the entire labor movement. Communists, anarchists, advocates of co-operatives to displace capitalism, and other doctrinaires often gained leadership in particular unions. Employers, especially those who financed the National Association of Manufacturers (founded in 1895) and other antiunion groups, often regarded the American Federation of Labor as a threat to their position and fought the new conservative trade unionism as bitterly as any other variety. But the stubborn and tireless Gompers steadily made headway against opponents on both sides. He came to be recognized as a valuable national spokesman for labor as a whole, and with him organized labor came of age as an accepted American institution.

The first success of Gompers and the new organization was in displacing the Knights of Labor and rescuing a number of unions from its failure. The second success was in weathering the major Depression of 1893-1896. The American Federation of Labor was the first national labor organization to prove strong enough to survive the losses of membership and of bargaining power which mark such a period. Thereafter it rapidly acquired members, reaching two million by 1910 and gaining strength particularly in the coal, railroad, and building industries. By that time the conservatism of the leadership led to somewhat supine collaboration with employers and continuing refusal to organize semiskilled and unskilled workers. The doctrine of "business unionism" came to include "job ownership," which often meant unwillingness to permit apprentices or any outsiders to enter a trade and the refusal to allow technological progress to make particular jobs obsolete. Thus some policies of the AFL turned out to be a drag on the progress of the labor movement.

THE TURMOIL OF THE NINETIES

The Homestead Strike

In the meantime, the principle of industrial unionism never completely lost support. The conservative tactics of the national AFL leaders often seemed futile to local leaders. The narrow limits within which the AFL could succeed when faced by some employers were sensationally demonstrated at Homestead, Pennsylvania, a company town of the Carnegie Steel Company, in 1892. The skilled workers of the Homestead plant were organized in the Amalgamated Association of Iron, Steel, and Tin Workers. Supported by the unskilled ranks, the union refused to accept wage cuts. Henry Clay Frick, general manager of the Carnegie Company, who strongly opposed unionism as an infringement of his authority, refused further negotiations, shut down the plant, and had deputy sheriffs posted around a barbed-wire fence to protect company property. The workers knew he was getting ready to reopen the plant with strikebreakers, and they ran the deputies out of town. Frick then employed three hundred Pinkerton detectives with rifles as a private army to protect the plant. When the Pinkertons tried to take possession, barricaded workers engaged them in battle in which seven men were killed, defeated them, sent them back to Pittsburgh, and maintained their strike lines for six days. But Frick induced the Governor of Pennsylvania to send 8000 militiamen into Homestead to reopen the plant and protect strikebreakers. With this support he won a struggle which warned Americans that class warfare might be in store for them. Carnegie himself professed much sympathy for unionism as part of his "gospel of wealth" that great financial power imposed social responsibility on capitalists. He had signed a contract with the Amalgamated, but had left for Scotland before its expiration and had given authority to Frick, whose attitude toward unions he knew quite well. Long after 1901, when Carnegie sold out to J. P. Morgan's United States Steel Corporation, labor conditions in the steel industry were unmitigated by either benevolence or unionism.

The aftermath of the Homestead massacre destroyed much of the remaining public sympathy for the workers. Two anarchists who had no connection with the strike, the union, or the strikers, Alexander Berkman and Emma Goldman, decided that Frick should be punished to make "propaganda by deed" against tyranny, just as during these years anarchists assassinated various European rulers and early in the next century a President of the United States. Berkman forced his way into Frick's Pittsburgh office and shot and stabbed him. Frick recovered and Berkman was sentenced to twenty-one years in prison. Later he and Emma Goldman, Russian citizens, were deported. The anarchist attack on Frick convinced many Americans that unions and strikes were inseparable from violence and anarchism, and therefore had no place in American life. The conservative policies of Gompers, who had supported the Amalgamated, could not easily obtain a fair hearing.

The Pullman Strike

Wage cuts were generally the first resort of employers to meet the beginning of general economic depression in 1893. Strikes broke out across the country, and militia forces were used to break a strike of railroad workers in Buffalo, New York, and one of coal miners in Tennessee, while federal troops were used against miners at Coeur d'Alene, Idaho. In 1894, the Pullman Strike, climaxing this era of labor disputes, opened the widest issues of the relation of government to labor problems. It also shattered illusions regarding paternalistic labor policies on the part of employers. Company towns were coming to be ominous symbols of the triumph of industry. Homes, streets, schools, churches, stores, and even the police forces in unchartered company towns were totally owned by the corporation and manned by its employees, so that the workers inhabited a new kind of feudal domain. Most towns of the sort offered no pretense that the company was interested in anything but profits. It was convenient for a company to be able to expel recalcitrant workers, union members, or strikers, from their homes and the town itself as trespassers on private property.

George M. Pullman in 1880 founded a widely admired company town a short distance south of Chicago. Good houses, pleasant parks, excellent services, and cultural amenities such as rental libraries and theaters made it possible to publicize Pullman, Illinois, as a model town. Few observers objected to the complete absence of self-government. The company policy of charging workers very high rates for rents and services made the blunt Mark Hanna advise admirers of Pullman to go and live in it and find out the profits it paid to the owners. But until 1894 the town regularly entertained commissioners of labor from other states who went home to plead with their employers to emulate Mr. Pullman. That year the Pullman Palace Car Company tried to overcome the Depression by taking orders at a loss and restoring some laid-off employees. It did not restore a 25 per cent wage cut, although the rents it charged had not been reduced and shareholders received dividends. A few of the workers joined the American Railway Union, which was attempting to organize an industrial union to include all categories of white railroad workers. Its leader was Eugene V. Debs, a former locomotive fireman with long experience in the railroad craft brotherhoods, who was a man of great eloquence and strong convictions. The union men asked the company to restore the wage cut. Officials refused, while admitting that the arguments they used to justify the wage cut would not be considered in relation to rentals on company houses. The next day three of the union leaders were discharged from their jobs. The union local called a strike and the company immediately closed down the shops. Pullman himself expressed gratitude that he was no longer responsible for the daily bread of 4000 employees and their families.

A convention of the national union proposed arbitration of the Pullman dispute, but the company refused to receive any communication from it. The convention then decided that no member of the American

Railway Union should handle any of the company's cars, which were operated by the railroads under license from the Pullman Company, until it consented to arbitration. The membership of the union was confined to employees of railroads running into Chicago. These railroad companies were united in the General Managers' Association. It, too, refused to negotiate with the union. Switchmen throughout the region between the Ohio River and the Great Lakes then refused to attach Pullman cars to trains. They were discharged. Train crews thereupon joined the strike and the transportation of the Middle West was at a standstill.

Railroad owners demanded that the state and federal governments protect them in their right to operate trains. Governor Altgeld of Illinois refused either to call out the state militia or to appeal for federal aid, saying that no violence was occurring. In this situation the federal government could act only on the constitutional grounds of interference with its own functions or with interstate commerce. A great majority of the country's newspapers sided with the railroad managers. They pointed fearfully to the great strength of Debs' union, whose membership was greater than that of all the railroad craft brotherhoods. Even the AFL unions sided against the rival ARU. Debs himself was vilified although later opinion is agreed that he was a sincere and selfless leader. In this power struggle between the united railroad managers and the united workers, victory was at the disposal of the federal government.

The federal government possessed no means of intervention except force. The managers invited federal intervention by importing strike-breakers from Canada and secretly instructing them to connect United States mail cars to Pullman cars so that when strikers cut out the latter they could be accused of interfering with the United States mails. The Managers' Association induced United States Attorney General Richard Olney to authorize the swearing in of 3600 special federal deputy marshals to maintain order. These men were in many cases criminals and thugs. They were recruited by the companies, paid by the companies, and under the authority of the company officials. After they entered the scene, violence occurred and some railroad property was destroyed. The Managers' Association then appealed to President Cleveland to send federal troops to restore order and to protect the mails and interstate commerce.

The President had formerly advocated arbitration of labor disputes, but his policy now was confined to quelling disorder without regard for its causes. He was reported to say that if it took every federal dollar and every federal soldier to deliver one postcard in Chicago, that postcard would be delivered. Over the protest of Governor Altgeld, he ordered federal troops to Chicago. Disorder increased as the strikers held firm and won new adherents in the East and Far West. They tried to prevent the movement of trains guarded by deputies or troops. Hoodlums took advantage of the situation to loot and burn railroad property. The press identified the strike with anarchism and revolution and demanded that it be suppressed. Attorney General Olney appointed a railroad lawyer as special United States counsel in Chicago, and he obtained from the federal district court an injunction forbidding Debs, the other leaders, and all other persons to interfere with the mails or any other interstate commerce.

Debs turned for support to the American Federation of Labor, but Gompers refused it and advised any of the AFL members who were on strike to give up. Debs then offered to call off the strike if the companies would promise not to punish strikers, but they refused to grant any "recognition of anarchism." A jury called by the federal district judge indicted Debs and three other union leaders and, when they did not call off the strike, they and two hundred others were jailed for contempt of court in disobeying the injunction. Deprived of leadership, the strikers gave up. Thus the federal government seemed in practice to support capital against labor. The public approved at the moment, but a revulsion of opinion eventually required the federal government to devise other means than force to settle labor disputes.

The federal circuit court to which the case of Debs was appealed held that the strike was a conspiracy in restraint of trade within the meaning of the Sherman Anti-Trust Act of 1890. In 1895, the Supreme Court (*In re* Debs), denying the petition of Debs for a writ of habeas corpus, preferred to base its decision on the broader ground that the federal government possesses inherent power to protect the mails and interstate commerce. But it did not dissent from the earlier conclusion that a law, designed to abolish businessmen's monopolies, which the courts had found largely unavailing to achieve that object, was applicable to labor unions.

After six months in jail Debs emerged a martyr and was welcomed by a mass meeting of over 100,000 admirers. He dedicated his life thenceforth to labor unionism and to socialism, becoming the most effective leader the latter cause has ever found in the United States. Even the AFL leadership saw that "government by injunction" could be used by employers to break any strike and make all union organizations futile. Gompers and his followers entered the battle against the use of injunctions in labor disputes and it became an issue in the election of 1896 and thereafter until the Norris-LaGuardia Anti-Injunction Act passed in 1932. Another unforeseen result of the companies' victory was the collapse of the public's hope that a model company town like that of Pullman, Illinois, might help solve the problems of labor relations.

Coxey's Army

While the Pullman Strike represented the climactic defeat of organized labor, the same years of depression produced a parallel demonstration of the plight of unorganized labor under the new industrial order. At least three million laborers were unemployed in 1894. The great majority of them were unaccustomed to union organization and knew only that the businessmen who had been so highly praised for the industrial expansion of the eighties had failed in leadership. While those with a bent for theory tried to analyze the causes of depression and formulate cures, the mass of the unemployed simply wanted jobs. When businessmen failed to provide these, the unemployed turned to the government to do something. Common despair led men to band together in spontaneous organizations to present their case. To them the emergency was equal to that of a war, and the militia tradition and memories of the citizen armies of the Civil War, in which many of these men had fought, suggested that an "army" was the proper form of organization and a "march on Washington" the best strategy. In another country, this sort of action might have meant the outbreak of revolution, but to the American unemployed it was merely a way of exercising their right to be heard by the government and to influence its policy.

Such armies sprang up in many districts. Leaders emerged with equal spontaneity, and among them Jacob S. Coxey of Massillon, Ohio, came closest to achieving general recognition. He was a quiet man who had worked in steel mills but followed the rags-to-riches path and did not personally suffer from the Depression. It was all the more impressive that he sympathized with the unemployed and advocated federal public works to relieve them. He was a Populist and his scheme was marred by the standard panacea of inflation of the currency: he wanted the government to pay for public works with paper money which would not be redeemable. Such schemes turned out to be most popular among mortgage-ridden farmers. When Congress paid no attention to his plan, he called upon the unemployed to form a "petition in boots." The excitement his army caused as it marched from Ohio to Washington was out of proportion to its size. Only four hundred men reached the capital in April 1894. The police allowed them to parade, and then arrested Coxey when he tried to make a speech on the capitol steps. "Kelly's Army," which set out from California, was larger than Coxey's, and other groups straggled into Washington, but these demonstrations were without immediate effect. They were important because they aroused considerable sympathy and convinced many thoughtful people that industrialism was creating human problems at least as fast as it was solving mechanical ones. People also saw that the government was less responsive to demands for reforms than in former periods and more influenced by conservatism and wealth.

Native Forms of Radicalism

In this era reformers turned to more extreme doctrines than had ever gained a hearing in the United States. Only a few advocated anarchism, but Marxian socialism won strength and, with the emergence of the Debs generation, it freed itself of earlier immigrant leadership. Most important was the emergence of several native-American varieties of radicalism. Of these, Populism was chiefly identified with the farmers, while the "Single Tax" of Henry George was the most popular program among urban radicals. Socialism seemed for a moment to find an American accent in Edward Bellamy's *Looking Backward,* which became a best seller following its publication in 1888. The book pictured current America as a land of capitalist absurdity from the vantage-point of the reasonable socialist society of the future. Significantly, the book never used the words socialism or communism, and the methods of transition from capitalism to socialism were slurred over as casually as the problem of control in the integrated utopia, all on the assumption that reason would create agreement and end conflict. "Nationalist Clubs," manned chiefly by well-meaning middle-class people, sprang up everywhere to further public admiration of Bellamy's vision. But within a few years the movement collapsed for lack of a concrete program and concrete accomplishment.

The economics of Henry George and his program were not so shallow and the movement he founded was not so ephemeral. Born in Philadelphia, he gained wide experience as a merchant sailor, printer, gold miner, and newspaper editor. After seeing wild speculation in land values in both California and New York City, he formulated an economic theory that wealth is nothing more than the product of labor applied to land and its fruits. In 1879, he published *Progress and Poverty: An Inquiry into the Cause of Industrial Depressions and of Increase of Want with Increase of Wealth.* In this he sought to explain how capitalists became wealthy by appropriating the most valuable lands and reaping unearned increment from them. He proposed to correct all the evils of the economic system by imposing a single tax on land. While his indictment of capitalism was severe, George taught that its virtues could be rescued and its evils eliminated by the Single Tax. The book deeply impressed many Europeans as well as American laborers and labor leaders. In 1886, George and his followers in the United Labor Party staged an exciting campaign for mayor of New York. He ran ahead of Theodore Roosevelt, but was defeated by Abram S. Hewitt on the Democratic ticket. He continued to agitate tirelessly, gained his widest influence during the Depression of the nineties, and died in the middle of a second campaign for mayor in 1897. The Single-Tax advocates remain to this day an organized group, but George's chief influence was in formulating criticisms of the American industrial system as the destroyer of humane economic relations. Many successful reformers of later years traced their education to Henry George, even though they rejected the Single Tax as a panacea of limited value or positive danger.

Strikes, demonstrations of the unemployed, and radical movements were symptomatic of the growing pains of American industrialism. These phenomena convinced some observers that American labor history would duplicate that of European countries and culminate in rejection by the industrial working class of existing institutions as indelibly tainted with exploitative capitalism. In this they were proved to be wrong. The vast majority of American laborers remained loyal to American institutions and at most asked that these be used to meet the new problems industrialism had projected into society. After four years of depression, it turned out that farmers were more impatient in their demands than laborers. Rather than join the farmers, and far from supporting still more radical solutions of their own, in the election of 1896 most American laborers voted for the candidate of the businessmen, the Republican William McKinley.

THE NEW IMMIGRANTS

An influx of immigrants facilitated the triumph of industry. In depression years the numbers fell, but in the boom year 1882 almost 800,000 came in, a record which was not surpassed until 1905. The advance of mechanization in industry increased the proportion of unskilled laborers needed, and most of the newcomers were prepared to do only the roughest and simplest work. Prosperity in northwestern Europe and the achievement of democratic rights in most of its countries reduced immigration from that region. During the eighties, the countries of southern and eastern Europe became the chief source of immigration. In 1850, the center of emigration to America had been the British Isles; in 1870, it was the eastern shore of the North Sea; in 1890, it was the border of Austria, and it continued to shift in the southeasterly direction until the quota system of recent decades, besides reducing the total numbers, sought to restore northwestern Europe as the chief source.

The problems created by the "old immigration" of Irish, Germans, and Scandinavians seemed mild to Americans who witnessed the coming of the Italians, Hungarians, Slavs, and Jews. Managers of industry wanted a steady supply of cheap and docile labor. The device of placing immigrants under contract to particular employers before they left Europe had been permitted under the Contract Labor Act, passed during the shortage of labor in the Civil War. In 1885, the law was replaced by a strict prohibition of the entrance into the country of laborers under contract, and even of those with an informal promise of a job. In 1882, the increasing numbers of undesirable persons entering the United States led to a federal immigration act which excluded criminals, paupers, and the insane. Those with contagious diseases were excluded in 1891.

In 1882, the government also undertook the first discrimination against

a racial group—the Chinese. Railroad builders used Chinese laborers
and these settled in groups in some cities, especially San Francisco and
New York. Their presence was resented, as their strange appearance and
customs and low standard of living made them easy targets of prejudice.
Riots in San Francisco in 1877 were the background of an exclusion bill
which President Hayes vetoed because it violated the terms of the Bur-
lingame Treaty of 1868 between the United States and China. A new
treaty in 1880 paved the way for the Chinese Exclusion Act of 1882.

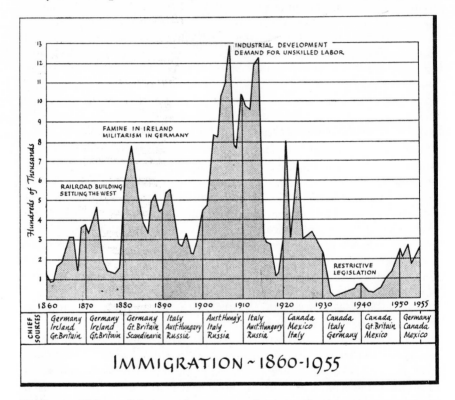

IMMIGRATION ~ 1860-1955

Under it Chinese laborers, but not students or businessmen, were excluded. It was a first indication that Americans, after the failure of Radical
Reconstruction in the South, increasingly identified their institutions with
the presumed characteristics of the white race. During the next years
historians and social scientists as well as journalists went farther and
elaborated the theory of "Teutonic" superiority to account for the current
triumphs of the German, British, and American nations, as compared with
the "decadent" white nations of southern Europe.

This theory did not discourage businessmen from welcoming "non-
Teutonic" immigrants, any more than federal regulations or the end of
the contract system discouraged them from coming. On their part economic improvement was the chief incentive. The wages of the lowest paid

groups in the United States seemed utopian to people who knew the pangs of continual hunger. But many who belonged to the oppressed nationalities came to America for political and religious liberty as well as for bread; from the Austro-Hungarian Empire, particularly Czechs and Slovaks; from the Russian Empire, particularly Poles and Ukrainians; and Balkan nationalities of the Ottoman Empire, along with Jews from all these areas but chiefly from Russia. When the repeal of the Contract Labor Act prevented American employers from conducting advertising campaigns for immigrants, the letters sent home by firstcomers turned out to be equally or more effective. One such letter, addressed to a brother, read: "Michael, this is a glorious country; you have liberty to do as you will. You can read what you wish, and write what you like, and talk as you have a mind to, and no one arrests you." Sometimes a community in Europe would be virtually depopulated by the letters of a single pioneer. The pioneers furthermore sent home money to enable relatives to come. Out of the total population of 76 million of the United States in 1900, more than 10 million were foreign-born.

Like most earlier groups, the new immigrants in great majority had agricultural backgrounds, but a smaller percentage than ever took up farming in America. The vast majority settled in the cities and industrial and mining centers of the North and West. There they took the least desirable jobs. Italians gravitated towards pick-and-shovel work, often under Irish-American foremen whose fathers had wielded the same tools. Jews became numerous in retail trade and in clothing factories. Hungarians and Slavs of many varieties filled the unksilled categories in steel mills and mines. In many industries the hardest and lowest-paid types of work were called "foreign jobs."

The difficulties of the new immigrants were greater than those of earlier groups, but they received no more sympathetic understanding even from the children of Irish and German immigrants than the parents of the latter had received from descendants of old stock. The new immigrants were divided from each other as well as from the older inhabitants by their numerous languages, and one-third of them were illiterate even in their own language. Some employers, in order to prevent unity in their labor forces, deliberately selected nationalities which brought to this country not only the language divisions but the intense hatreds of the Old World. Among the new groups there were almost no Protestants to form a religious tie with the majority of Americans. Most of them were Roman Catholics, a few belonged to unfamiliar varieties of Eastern Orthodox Christianity, and Judaism now for the first time acquired significant numerical representation in America. The new immigrants had practically no experience of liberty or self-government in the religious or civil spheres, with the exception of Jews who had long conducted their internal affairs in the Old World as a separate community. It required a generation before the new immigrants could acquire American-trained religious, intellectual, and political leaders. The Marxists and anarchists among them were not typical immigrants. Predominantly they accepted the American economic system and hoped to share the opportunities of free enterprise. At heart they were capitalists, even while living in slums. Some were inspired by the desire to save money and go back to their old homes with enough of it to become landowners or businessmen. The new immigration produced the first important reverse flow, particularly to Italy.

Family units were less common than in earlier groups. Boarding houses for men became a standard feature of dismal company towns and slum districts of the cities. The various nationalities clung together tightly and the processes of assimilation correspondingly slowed down. A native American walking through the new and bewildering language and nationality districts could wonder whether he had strayed entirely outside his own country. Employers with consciences dulled by contempt for foreigners could exploit such laborers. Skilled workers of older stock could support the conservative unionism of the American Federation of Labor because it was easy to hold the unskilled immigrant in disrepute. Racism could become a stronger ingredient of American nationalism in the presence of candidates for citizenship who seemed so deficient in proper qualifications. Many doubted that the melting pot could dissolve such large masses of foreign material. Perhaps the most poignant aspect of the problem appeared when the individual immigrant was eager to Americanize himself but found that exploitation and isolation left him with no real opportunity to participate in American life after he had eagerly shorn himself of the Old World culture he had brought with him. An Italian gave up the language of Dante but acquired only a gross caricature of Shakespeare's and Lincoln's tongue. A Pole lost his intimacy with his parish and its priest in Poland but felt little attachment to the priest of Irish or German descent in America, while the Protestant churches disdained him in favor of missionary work in Asia. A Russian Jew gave up the customs of his fathers without gaining acceptance as an American. Bitter conflict became the rule between immigrant parents, who clung desperately to their own language groups, and the first American-born generation which worked harder to achieve Americanization and was aided by the greatest agency of assimilation, the public school.

"Mick" and "Dutchman" had been fairly good-natured names for Irish and German immigrants, but the slang names for new immigrants were epithets and these were spread by newspapers and other media without restraint. Nevertheless it is notable that antipathy towards these newcomers did not lead to the organization of a native-American political party, as it did before the Civil War. On the other side it is equally notable that no discouragement slowed down the arrival of further millions or reduced the yearning to become Americans on the part of those who stayed.

CHAPTER 7

The Politics of Business
1877-1890

THE POLITICAL HISTORY OF THE DOZEN YEARS
following the inauguration of President Rutherford B. Hayes was relieved
by no inspiring national policy. To give business what it wanted and
distribute government jobs with an eye to the cementing of party machines
was the whole wisdom of most politicians, and the few who wanted to
reform the civil service or the tariff bored most voters. Business was the
chief interest of the most ambitious men, and voters as well as politicians
believed in the rightness of business rule. The South now seemed to fall
into line with the national ideal. Some old-fashioned Southerners warned
their people against the temptation to imitate their conquerors by adopting
industries and banks as gods; but spokesmen of the "New South"—of
whom Henry W. Grady, editor of the *Atlanta Constitution,* was the most
eloquent and appealing—commanded a wider hearing. They were seeking
to adjust the ways and mind of the region to what Edwin L. Godkin called
"the industrial stage in social progress."

The result of these circumstances was that the Democratic Party offered
no serious opposition to the rule of Big Business until, late in the century,
it was swept by forces of agrarian discontent. Another reason why it
offered no real alternative during these years was the corruption of the
local party organizations in the cities, of which Tammany in New York
was the prime example. Local Democratic machine politicians co-operated
with local business interests large and small, legitimate and illegitimate,
from railroads to corner grocers, from great factories to saloons.

The policies of Democrats and Republicans offered little choice to the
voter. Thus the game of politics revolved around personalities more than
platforms. But real distinctions existed within each of the major parties.
Reformers whose heroes were Jefferson and Jackson in the one case and

Lincoln in the other struggled to reduce the control of business over government and to recall their parties and their country to moral idealism. The bosses despised all reformers as "men milliners." The Republican left wing were eventually called "Mugwumps," and the center "Half Breeds," while the dominant group arrogated to themselves the virtues of "Stalwarts," which meant that they always remained loyal to the nominees and office-holders of the party, and to the alliance of business and government.

THE HAYES ADMINISTRATION, 1877-1881

When President Hayes, soon after his inauguration, removed the Federal troops from South Carolina and Louisiana, he enabled the Redeemers to complete the establishment of Southern home rule. He appointed a former Confederate colonel, David M. Key of Tennessee, to the office of Postmaster General, which controlled the largest amount of federal patronage. This did not result in building up fresh Republican strength in the South, as he and his friend Representative James A. Garfield had hoped, nor did it commend him to the extreme Republican partisans in the North. Hayes was notably independent of the extremists in his own party. If the Democrats repeated the cry of fraud in connection with his election, they could point to no scandal in the conduct of the government by him or those close to him. This conscientious man was the first president after the war to make a serious effort to purify the civil service and weaken the grip of politicians on it.

The President Challenges the Spoilsmen

Hayes believed that the establishment of home rule in the South would lead to better government there, and he wished to match this by ridding the federal administration of the abuses which had infested it while public attention focused on the problems of Reconstruction. He appointed four Liberal Republicans to his Cabinet, headed by Carl Schurz as Secretary of the Interior. On the issue of civil service reform Senator Roscoe Conkling, head of the Republican machine in New York, was the chief antagonist of Hayes. The President announced his belief that party bosses should have no more influence in appointments than other "equally respectable citizens," and that standard techniques of assessing office-holders for contributions to party treasuries, padding federal agencies with job-holders who had no real duties, and putting office-holders in charge of party activities should all be stopped. On June 22, 1877, an Executive Order required obedience to these idealistic rules. In Conkling's view this was the gush of ladies' magazines.

The worst corruption was found in the New York Customs Office, where the Republican machine gained profits from importers by a system of bribery to violate the tariff laws. Secretary of the Treasury John Sherman (brother of the General) ordered the collector of the port, Chester A. Arthur, and the naval officer, Alonzo B. Cornell, to clean up these notorious conditions. Taking courage from their master, Senator Conkling who publicly defied the administration, they refused to obey orders. When the President demanded their resignations, the Tenure of Office Act permitted them to refuse. In the summer of 1878, after Congress had adjourned, Hayes suspended them and installed his own appointees. In the fall, with Democratic help, he secured their confirmation. Hayes had won a point and had done something to restore Executive authority, which had been so much weakened since the war, but his party remained divided and the Stalwarts thirsted for revenge.

The Currency Issue

During the first half of the Hayes administration, when the country had not yet recovered from the Depression that started in 1873, the monetary issue was pressed by debtor groups favoring currency inflation and by silver-mining interests. Westerners and Southerners in Congress combined to pass the Bland-Allison Act over a presidential veto in 1878. At a time when the price of silver was falling, this called for the purchase of silver bullion to the value of at least $2 million a month, and the coinage of it into dollars. The action was mildly inflationary. Determined to stabilize the currency, the administration itself followed a deflationary policy. According to the Act of 1875, specie payments were to be resumed on January 1, 1879. In the Congressional elections of 1878 the Greenback-Labor Party, which had won less than 1 per cent of the total vote in 1876, staged a vigorous campaign, predicting that disaster would follow resumption. It polled over a million votes in 1878, electing more than a dozen members of the House of Representatives. At the same time the Democrats gained control of both branches of the next Congress.

Nevertheless, specie payments were resumed on schedule. Secretary of the Treasury Sherman brought this about by building up the gold reserve—a process which was facilitated by a turn in the tide of foreign trade. As exports began to exceed imports, gold was drawn back into the country instead of being drained abroad. By the resumption date the greenbacks stood at par with gold, and nobody was in a hurry to present them for redemption. The Secretary of the Treasury made conservative use of his authority under the Bland-Allison Act, and the inflationary effects of this proved slight. Administration policy was much more favorable to creditor groups (chiefly banking) than to debtor groups (chiefly farming), and Hayes showed little understanding of the difficulties of the latter. But the greenback question was settled and returning prosperity reduced the pressure of agrarian demands.

The Election of 1880

The announcement of Hayes that he would not run for a second term reduced his influence among party leaders. Late in his term the Democrats, now in control of both Houses, tried to take advantage of Republican disunity and presidential weakness by attaching riders to Army appropriation bills which nullified the laws of 1865 and 1874 authorizing the President to use federal troops in Congressional elections. Hayes, resenting this improper way of bringing Congressional pressure on the Executive, vetoed them all, and his vetoes were sustained. But neither Hayes nor any future President actually used the Army to protect voters in the South or anywhere else. Henceforth the issues of the Civil War were revived chiefly at election time to distract voters from current issues which divided the Republican Party and to create unity by the demagogic technique of "waving the bloody shirt."

The Republican National Convention of 1880 witnessed an open fight between Stalwarts and Half Breeds. The party platform advocated civil service reform, the protective tariff, aid to veterans, and restriction of Chinese immigration. Conkling and the Stalwarts were unable to win a majority of votes for a third term for ex-President Grant even though he led for thirty ballots. James G. Blaine and John Sherman, the leaders of the Half Breeds, who had both been contenders for the nomination, finally secured a majority for the "dark horse" Half Breed, James A. Garfield of Ohio, minority leader in the House of Representatives, by turning over the vice-presidential nomination to the Stalwart, Chester A. Arthur. The Democratic Party was unable to present any opposition on principle to the Republicans except a tepid statement in favor of tariffs for revenue only. Winfield Scott Hancock of Pennsylvania, one of the outstanding Union commanders at Gettysburg, was nominated for President and William H. English for Vice-President. Neither one had shown any particular ability in statecraft. The Greenback Labor Party drafted a program that went beyond the inflation demand and attempted to appeal to discontented and reformist elements by favoring woman suffrage, federal regulation of interstate commerce, and a federal income tax. This party nominated James B. Weaver of Iowa for President and B. J. Chambers of Texas for Vice-President.

Returning prosperity allayed discontent. The Greenback-Labor candidates received less than a third of a million votes and presently that party ceased to matter. The Democrats came within 7000 votes of a popular majority out of a total vote of 9 million, showing how evenly divided the electorate was. Garfield won 214 votes in the electoral college to Hancock's 155. Still the campaign had brought forward nothing more important than the desire of each party to win power and control over patronage.

National political life had reached a nadir. Its condition was dramatized by a political crime that had no motive except hunger for spoils of office.

THE GARFIELD AND ARTHUR ADMINISTRATIONS, 1881-1885

President Garfield refused to make peace with the Stalwarts. He appointed James G. Blaine as Secretary of State and other Half Breeds to all the offices at his disposal, including the collectorship of the port of New York. Senator Thomas Platt of New York, who helped run the Republican machine from the barroom of the Fifth Avenue Hotel (called the "Amen Corner") joined Senator Conkling in a maneuver. They resigned from the United States Senate and applied to the New York State legislature for re-election as a mandate against the President. But the legislature refused to dance to their tune and Conkling gave up politics. At this point, on July 2, 1881, President Garfield was shot at a Washington railroad station by Charles J. Guiteau, a Stalwart who had failed to gain a minor office he wanted. Standing over the wounded President, he said: "I am a Stalwart and Arthur is President now."

Civil Service Legislation

This degradation of the Republic caused a revulsion of opinion during the long weeks while the President struggled vainly for life. He died on September 19. The murderer was tried, convicted, and executed. President Arthur himself was chastened. Although the Half Breeds of the Cabinet resigned when he took office, he showed considerable independence of the Stalwarts in his appointments and policies. The most important consequence of the assassination was the passage in 1883 of the first civil service reform legislation. The law was drawn by a Democrat, Senator George H. Pendleton of Ohio, and the Democrats had won the elections of 1882 before the outgoing Republican Congress passed the law, but President Arthur advocated its principle of appointments based on "ascertained fitness." Public opinion had been further exacerbated by revelations of the "star route" frauds in which Stephen W. Dorsey, the secretary of the Republican National Committee, was shown to have profited from mail contracts in collusion with Assistant Postmaster General Thomas J. Brady.

The Pendleton Act provided for an independent and bipartisan Civil Service Commission of three men to conduct competitive examinations to determine fitness for office. Only about one-tenth of the total number of federal offices were placed under the civil service, and the rules governed future appointments only, but the President was empowered to extend the list. Once a civil service appointment was made, the employee could not be dismissed for political reasons, and the levying of contributions to political parties was forbidden. No one advocated the application of civil service rules to the highest levels of office, which are concerned with policy making. Opinions differ as to where the line between policy-making offices and the others actually lies, but even today the civil service list does not cover all the offices which everyone agrees lie below the line. The grip of the spoils system on American government is relentless even now, and for many years after the Pendleton Act little more was accomplished than the laying down of a principle and a foundation.

The hope of achieving bipartisanship in another agitated area of public policy led Arthur to recommend the establishment of a tariff commission. Congress approved but secured the appointment of protectionists as the first commissioners. After hearings and studies they nevertheless recommended reduction of the rates. Congress was not enthusiastic. The Tariff Act of 1883 changed the rates of 1875 very little and increased some of them.

Foreign Affairs

While contented isolationism was the rule in foreign policy, the Samoan Treaty of 1878, by which the island chieftains granted the United States rights to a naval station at Pago Pago, was a small and almost unnoticed step towards a strong naval policy. The Treaty of 1880 with China permitting the United States to suspend immigration of Chinese laborers showed that internal preoccupations governed the Far Eastern policy of the United States. Blaine, though his term was brief, was the only Secretary of State between Hamilton Fish and Richard Olney (1895-1897) who can be said to have had a positive program. He believed that in Latin America the United States should assume the role of leadership. But Blaine's attempts to arbitrate the War of the Pacific between Bolivia and Peru and disputes between Costa Rica and Colombia, and Mexico and Guatemala, were all failures. He tried to reduce British influence in Latin America, chiefly in relation to the Isthmus of Panama. Despite the equal rights of Britain in a canal, secured in the Clayton-Bulwer Treaty of 1850, Blaine announced in June 1881 that the Monroe Doctrine gave the United States a "paramount interest." Earl Granville, the British Foreign Secretary, answered that Her Majesty's Government stood on its Clayton-Bulwer Treaty rights.

Blaine's largest scheme was to organize all the American republics for commercial and cultural co-operation under the leadership of the United States. He invited the Latin-American governments to a conference for these purposes, and nine of them had accepted when he gave President Arthur his resignation in December 1881. His successor, Frederick T. Frelinghuysen, withdrew the invitations. But Blaine had the satisfaction of presiding over the first Inter-American Conference when he was again Secretary of State in 1890

The Election of 1884

On his third try, in 1884, Blaine gained the Republican nomination for the presidency. The unquestioned leader of the Half Breeds, he was the most conspicuous man in the party, and his friends hoped that the charges against him of receiving favors from railroads had by this time grown dim. The charges had been dramatically aired in the episode of the Mulligan Letters in 1876, when Blaine himself read into the record evidence which served considerably to substantiate them. The Stalwarts were lukewarm in support of him for other reasons, while the reform element among the Republicans, led by Carl Schurz, Charles Francis Adams, Jr., and E. L. Godkin, could not stomach his record. They bolted to the Democratic candidate, Grover Cleveland of New York, and became known as "Mugwumps." The nomination of Cleveland was made in expectation of their support.

The reputation of Cleveland at the time is suggested by the best-remembered comment on him, made in a seconding speech at the Democratic National Convention: "We love him most for the enemies he has made." As sheriff of Erie County he was relentless in pursuit of evildoers, as mayor of Buffalo he was known as the "veto mayor," and as governor of New York he added the name of John Kelly, leader of Tammany Hall, to the list of his enemies. He did not glitter like Blaine nor attract the personal loyalty of other men, but Cleveland, now in his later forties and weighing some 250 pounds, was a man of character.

The campaign of 1884 still stands out as one of the dirtiest in American history. It was not fought on issues, for there was little to choose between the public professions of the rivals. Cleveland had no war record, and he was caricatured as a Southern sympathizer with Jefferson Davis and the Confederacy behind him. In cartoons Thomas Nast showed Blaine with plumes emerging from his top hat and quotations from the Mulligan Letters. To counter the devastating Democratic attacks, the Republicans dug up an episode from Cleveland's personal life as a young man and aired charges that this bachelor was the father of an illegitimate son. These he did not deny, but one Mugwump said: "We should elect Mr. Cleveland to the public office he is so admirably qualified to fill and remand Mr. Blaine to the private life which he is so eminently fitted to adorn."

An episode in this campaign may possibly have lost the election for Blaine. He had gained popularity among the Irish by his supposedly anti-British sentiments and had a sister who was a Catholic nun. Nevertheless, he listened without comment in New York when a Protestant clergyman characterized the Democrats as the party of "Rum, Romanism, and Rebellion." These words, constituting an open affront to the Irish and other Catholics, made the headlines in the metropolitan press on the eve of the election. Cleveland could not have won without the vote of New York, which he carried by a very small margin. He had a popular majority of only 60,000 in the entire country, and an electoral majority of only 37.

The Democratic victory, slight as it was, scotched the notion of Republican politicians that the record of their party in the Civil War entitled it to permanent possession of the White House. With all his honesty and courage Cleveland was too conservative to effect any fundamental reform. The change he represented was therefore not drastic, but it was wholesome.

Democratic Interlude: Grover Cleveland, 1885-1889

The first Democratic President after the Civil War was one of the most independent men ever to hold that high office. Grover Cleveland was ponderous in language as well as person. Few gems adorned his polysyllabic speech, but out of his campaign utterances emerged an epigram which has been associated with him ever since: "Public office is a public trust." He administered his office under the conviction that it belongs to the public rather than to any party, but he lacked the arts of showmanship which were afterwards employed by both of the Roosevelts to popularize their leadership. He did not think that his private affairs should concern the public, specially resenting the attention these received at the hands of prying reporters on the occasion of his marriage in 1886 to Frances Folsom, who brought fresh beauty and grace to the White House. He increased the prestige of the presidential office. It is significant that the Tenure of Office Act, by means of which Congress had shackled and humbled Andrew Johnson, was finally removed from the statute books in this administration.

In the matter of appointments, Cleveland did not truckle to partisan spoilsmen. But the hunger of the Democrats for office had been whetted by their long absence from power, and he yielded to political pressure more than the civil service reformers liked, while failing to satisfy his own party. He lacked Lincoln's skill in the use of patronage to strengthen his position, and one of the penalties of his independence of spirit was a considerable degree of political isolation. During the years of Republican dominance the Democrats had produced a meager crop of leaders, and, partly for this reason, his major appointments were relatively undistinguished. But they were respectable, and his administration was unmarred by scandal in high places. The Cabinet appointments which aroused greatest protest were those of two Southerners, L. Q. C. Lamar of Mississippi as Secretary of the Interior, and Augustus H. Garland of Arkansas as Attorney General.

The partisan charge that, as a Democrat without a war record, the President was pro-Southern and unpatriotic was intensified by the stand he took with respect to Civil War pensions. These had become unconscionable, but few politicians dared say a word against them. Private pension bills were often trumped up by unscrupulous lawyers; some of them were filed in behalf of actual deserters. The conscientious President set himself the task of reading these bills and he vetoed a great many of them. In 1887, he vetoed a general pension bill which he believed to be unsound in principle. He compounded his offense by issuing in that same year the Rebel Flag Order, calling for the return to Confederate regiments of their battleflags still in the possession of the War Department. This order, which he regarded as routine and a mere matter of common sense, aroused a storm of indignation in the huge and powerful veterans' organization, the Grand Army of the Republic, and was seized upon by patriotic orators. It had to be rescinded. The war had been over for more than twenty years, but nearly that many more were to pass before a Republican President, Theodore Roosevelt, accomplished without protest what the first Democratic President after the war should never have attempted.

Cleveland courageously vetoed "pork-barrel" bills for rivers and harbors. He ejected ranchers, lumber barons, and railroad companies from almost a hundred million acres of public lands which they had occupied fraudulently. He achieved considerable success in his effort to administer his public trust in the public interest, but his chief fight, for the reduction of the tariff, was a failure, while the most important legislative achievement of his term, the Interstate Commerce Act, owed nothing to his initiative.

Raising the Tariff Issue

The tariff had not been open to serious question since the Republicans took over the government in 1861 and its traditional Southern critics had been silenced during war and Reconstruction. The immediate occasion for making an issue of it now was the surplus in the Treasury, which had been growing since the resumption of specie payments and the return of prosperity. The situation created a temptation to indulge in governmental extravagance, as the pension legislation showed, and pointed to the desirability of reducing taxes. The heaviest taxes, though concealed, were the customs duties, and these were the largest source of federal income. Cleveland seized upon this fact to add a forceful practical argument to the historic antiprotectionist principle of his party, from which many Democrats had departed.

High tariffs had been adopted by the administration during the abnormalities of wartime, partly to balance heavy war taxes on industry which were afterwards removed. During the political excitement

of Reconstruction the tariff largely escaped public notice, though
the maintenance of high rates was an important underlying reason for
the Radical Republican policy of excluding Southerners from national
affairs until continued Republican dominance was assured. The net result
was that, despite occasional legislative actions and proposals, the tariff
remained at its wartime level and came to be largely taken for granted.
Meanwhile, leading protected industries in the country, notably iron and
steel, had matured well beyond the "infant" stage which had originally

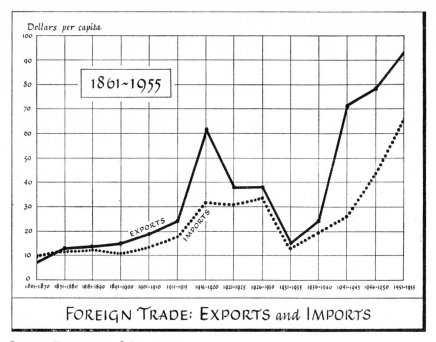

FOREIGN TRADE: EXPORTS and IMPORTS

SOURCE: Department of Commerce

justified protection against foreign competition. It could be argued
that certain protective rates now served only to make it easier for trusts
to charge high prices and reap extra profits, which they did not use to
increase the wages of labor. Furthermore, even if the philosophy of protection was accepted, there were many inconsistencies such as duties on
raw materials. "It is a condition which confronts us—not a theory," said
Cleveland. Determined to put the facts before Congress and the country,
he devoted his entire State of the Union Message in 1887 to the subject.
This was an unprecedented effort to influence legislation and he made it
at a time when his party controlled only the lower house of Congress.

The result was that the Democrats in the House of Representatives
passed the Mills Bill, which the Republicans all opposed, while the

Senate Republicans, under the leadership of Nelson W. Aldrich of Rhode Island, proposed even higher duties. No final legislation resulted and enthusiasm for tariff reform was not conspicuous at the Democratic National Convention of 1888. The difficulty lay deeper than any facts or arguments. Most Republican politicians and many Northern Democrats were protectionists, not on principle, but as a matter of collusion with some of the numerous protected interests. Cleveland sought to advance the general interest, as he saw it, but the result of his dramatic gesture was just the opposite of what he intended. The Republicans seized upon the issue, and when they returned to power they raised the rates, inaugurating an era of even higher protection.

The Interstate Commerce Commission

The Interstate Commerce Act of 1887 came out of the recommendations of a special Senate Committee on railroads of which Shelby M. Cullom of Illinois was chairman. It was made politically expedient by public demand for federal action when the Supreme Court in the Wabash Case (1886) virtually denied the states any authority to regulate railroads. It set up the Interstate Commerce Commission as a permanent and independent federal administrative board, the first American agency to attempt national regulation of business enterprise. The law provided that railroad rates should be reasonable and required the publication of rate schedules. It did not authorize the Commission to fix rates, though it empowered that body to issue "cease-and-desist" orders against carriers violating the law. Such railroad abuses as pooling, drawbacks, rebates, and higher charges for short than long hauls were specifically forbidden. But the railroads were able to evade the Act by exploiting the weaknesses of its terms, and by 1898 the conservative Supreme Court reduced the Commission to the function of collecting statistics.

Cleveland's position on the question of railroad regulation was essentially negative. In truth he was a consistent believer in mid-nineteenth century liberalism, whose credo of low tariffs and noninterference with private business was inadequate to the emergent era of those unforeseen products of free competition—trusts and monopolistic railroads.

The Navy and Foreign Affairs

In foreign relations his policy did not differ essentially from that of the Republicans. His Secretary of the Navy, William C. Whitney, took steps to reorganize his department and modernize the fleet. A rapid building program began to equip the Navy with the latest guns and steel-armored vessels. Close co-operation with the American steel industry ended the Navy's dependence on European makers of armor plate and big guns.

In 1880, the United States Navy had been weaker than that of Turkey, standing twelfth in the world; by 1900 it was third, ranking after Great Britain and Germany. The decisive steps were taken during Cleveland's first term, although most "big Navy" advocates were Republicans.

Pago Pago in Samoa and Pearl Harbor in Hawaii were the best sites for naval bases in the entire Pacific Ocean. Their value both for the defense of the United States and for extending United States influence into the Orient was perceived by navalists, notably Captain Alfred Thayer Mahan and the young Theodore Roosevelt, and by businessmen who believed the United States should not fall behind in the race of the industrial nations for Far Eastern markets. In 1887, the Senate approved a treaty with the Kingdom of Hawaii that provided for trade reciprocity and gave the United States naval rights at Pearl Harbor. Agents of Germany, Great Britain, and the United States were all active in Samoa. When Germany turned to armed intervention and Britain acquiesced, President Cleveland advised Congress that the interest of the United States was threatened. Subsequently the United States took part in the Berlin Conference of 1889 and agreed to a condominium by the three powers over the islands. This held the issue in suspension for another ten years.

Another policy chiefly identified with Republican leaders was advanced in 1888 when Secretary of State Thomas F. Bayard, on instructions from Congress, revived Blaine's plan for an Inter-American Conference and issued invitations which led to the first such meeting in 1890.

Election of 1888

Only on the tariff did Cleveland's policy differ greatly from that of Republican Presidents, and the tariff became the chief issue in the election of 1888. The President was renominated, and the Republican Convention named Benjamin Harrison of Indiana, who had emerged from the war as a brevet brigadier general and had recently served a term in the United States Senate. He was the grandson of William Henry Harrison, who had held the presidential office for one month. His chief contribution to the campaign consisted of a series of "front-porch" speeches to visiting delegations. He was a rather colorless candidate. The dominant factor in the campaign was Senator Matthew S. Quay of Pennsylvania, chairman of the Republican National Committee. An astute and cynical politician, he never had any doubt that he made Harrison President. Besides promising new high levels of tariff protection to businessmen and farmers, the Republicans vowed to renew the policy of generous pensions which Cleveland had tried to confine to cases of merit. They raised the unheard-of amount of $4 million for campaign purposes, and used most of it to buy votes.

A Republican posing as a naturalized Englishman elicited from the incautious British Minister to the United States, Sackville-West, a letter containing advice that by voting for the low-tariff candidate he would best serve the interests of Britain's free-trade policy. The Republicans gleefully spread this letter across the country. The administration handed Sackville-West his passports, but harm had been done Cleveland's cause among Irish voters. He received almost 100,000 more popular votes than his opponent, but the Republican operators had concentrated their efforts better. Harrison carried New York and other key states by small margins, gaining 233 electoral votes to 168 for Cleveland.

THE ASCENDANCY OF REGULAR REPUBLICANISM: HARRISON AND THE LEGISLATION OF 1890

The Harrison administration, during the brief but significant period of two years when the Republicans controlled both houses of Congress, seemed bent on substantiating the accusations of reformers and radicals that the rule of Big Business meant the perversion of government. The President exercised little leadership, allowing the party bosses to go their own way. Only Secretary of State Blaine stood out among the nondescript holders of high office in the executive department. The appointment as Postmaster General of John Wanamaker, a wealthy Philadelphia merchant who had contributed heavily to the campaign funds, was sharply criticized by reform elements. He was a better administrator than most, but spoilsmen feasted on the patronage of his department. Harrison appointed Theodore Roosevelt as Civil Service Commissioner, but that energetic and colorful young official could make little headway in his efforts to further the merit system.

Probably the most notorious of Harrison's appointments was that of James Tanner as Commissioner of Pensions. "Corporal" Tanner, who had been active in the Grand Army of the Republic, was determined to raise all pensions, saying that his critics might pray, "God save the surplus!" His service was brief and Harrison afterwards regretted his appointment, but the President signed a dependent pension bill which Cleveland had vetoed. This measure encouraged a boom in marriages of young ladies to elderly veterans and saddled the federal government with payments running well beyond the lifespan of the Union soldiers. During his four years in office, expenditures for pensions increased more than 50 per cent. Because of its hostility to reform, the dominant Republicanism of these years is commonly called conservative, but it showed little desire to conserve the financial resources of the government.

The most influential leaders were in Congress—notably Speaker Thomas B. Reed of Maine and Senator Nelson W. Aldrich. Under the powerful and often arbitrary leadership of "Czar" Reed, the House of Representatives adopted rules which did much to expedite legislative procedure and permit the carrying out of the will of the Congressional majority—with the inevitable result that the power of the Democratic minority was curtailed. Aldrich moved more quietly in the Senate, but he and a little group of elder statesmen, including the resourceful Quay, controlled the deliberations of that body to an extent which has rarely been equalled. These men formed the nucleus of what came to be called the "Old Guard" or the "Stand-patters." As a result of their efforts the first Congress of the Harrison administration enacted an unusual amount of important legislation. The three major enactments, all in the year 1890, were the McKinley Tariff, the Silver Purchase Act, and the Sherman Anti-Trust Act. The two first conferred favors on special-interest groups, while the last law was a nominal concession to the reform spirit and was destined to be ineffective.

By raising duties to a new level, sometimes prohibitory, and by extending protection to products not previously encouraged, the McKinley Tariff introduced a new phase of protective policy. At the same time, by reducing rates on certain articles which were relatively little produced in the country but which had previously brought in large revenues, and by raising other duties so high as to cut down imports, it resulted in a very considerable decrease in the income of the government.

Rates on some agricultural products such as wheat were meaningless gestures because the American farmer produced export surpluses of these. The case of sugar was different since only a small part of this was produced in America. The desire of the Havemeyer Sugar Refining Trust for the free importation of raw sugar was met, American growers being quieted by a bounty of two cents a pound, while refined sugar was protected by the high tariff rate of one-half cent per pound. In this way the grower of cane or sugar beets was subsidized by the taxpayer to provide the Trust with raw materials at low cost, and the taxpayer as a consumer paid an additional tribute to the Trust in the form of a high price for refined sugar.

The law provided for a coercive type of reciprocity with Latin America. It placed certain products imported from that area, which did not compete with American products, on the free list and stipulated that the President could place duties on them if the countries did not reduce their rates on American exports, while it maintained the rates against the same goods coming from third countries. Latin Americans concluded that this was actually a policy of economic imperialism.

The Sherman Silver Purchase Act of 1890 was linked to the McKinley Tariff Act in a deal whereby some Congressmen from farm states abandoned their resistance to the tariff in return for Eastern votes in favor of silver. The silver-mining interests amounted to a special-interest group which the Republican leadership was willing to favor like any other, but the fears of Eastern creditors were aroused by the demands of farmers that the government use silver to inflate the currency. The new law was a concession that pleased the mining interests without satisfying the inflationists. It required the Treasury to buy 4.5 million ounces of silver per month and to pay for them with paper money which the Secretary of the Treasury could redeem in silver or gold at his discretion.

The combined effects of the administration's pension policy, the McKinley Tariff, and the Silver Purchase Act were unfortunate for both the government's financial stability and the Republican Party. Pensions reduced the Treasury surplus while the tariff resulted in a net decline in the revenues from customs duties. Depletion of the Treasury in the face of the new silver policy created fear in the minds of holders of paper money that the Treasury might be unable to redeem it in gold. They steadily increased pressure on the Treasury's gold supply during the next several years by presenting paper for redemption, and in 1892 the situation was worsened by the flow of gold to Europe to pay unfavorable trade balances resulting from the decline of United States exports. This spiral helped to bring on an economic cyclone in 1893.

The third major enactment of the Harrison administration was the Sherman Anti-Trust Act. Its passage signified not so much effective opposition to the monopolization of industry as a token to the small businessman and farmer. It put the Republican Party on record as theoretically favorable to competition. Government prohibition of business monopoly as a conspiracy in restraint of trade was as old as the English common law and had been inherited by the state governments in this country. But the nationalization of industry had now made effective state action against great interstate corporations out of the question, particularly since some states made a special effort to invite such corporations to make their legal "residence" inside their boundaries. The monopolistic movement was accelerating in 1890. The Sherman Act did nothing to slow this. Congressmen who voted for it understood that it would not be effective.

The key sentence of the law read: "Every contract, combination in the form of trust or otherwise, or conspiracy, in restraint of trade or commerce among the several States, or with foreign nations, is hereby declared to be illegal." No definition of the terms was provided, only the Attorney General could initiate a suit againt a monopoly, and it was left to the courts to determine what the law meant. During the eleven years before Theodore Roosevelt became President, only eighteen antitrust suits were brought before the courts and four of these suits were against labor unions. In 1895, the Supreme Court decision in the case of the United States vs. E. C. Knight Company denied that the Sugar Trust restrained trade even though it controlled upwards of 90 per cent of the sugar refined and sold in the United States. This amounted to a warning that suits against trusts were useless so long as businessmen observed a few legal rituals. Nevertheless the existence of the law with its assertion of principle opened a door for future action.

In the Congressional election of 1890 the voters repudiated the Republican Party more thoroughly than they ever had before, giving the Democrats a large majority in the House of Representatives. The ostensible reason for the Republican debacle was the adverse reaction of the public to the McKinley Tariff. But the political unrest of the late eighties and early nineties had other causes and other expressions. In the West and South debt-ridden farmers had long been discontented with the economic system which had been consolidated since the war, and they were rebelling in a variety of ways against a political order which they believed to be betraying their interests.

CHAPTER 8

The Rebellious Farmers 1873-1892

UNLIKE LABORERS, WHO WERE SO OFTEN RECENT immigrants, American farmers were highly experienced in self-organization and politics. Furthermore, they were deeply conscious of a tradition to which almost everybody paid lip-service in public—that the husbandman is nature's nobleman and society's benefactor. They were convinced that the American farmer, especially the small farmer, had always been and always should be recognized as the most important citizen of the Republic. Farmers felt that the triumphant surge of industry had reduced them all to the position of second-class citizens. They believed that the American Republic which had been dedicated by their fathers to liberty and virtue was being prostituted to the service of wealth and corruption. Despite some efforts to associate industrial workers with their programs, they developed very little sympathy for labor. Rather, they held to Jefferson's belief that "city mobs" were untrustworthy material for citizenship in a free republic; and labor disputes, spreading slums, and the swelling ranks of immigrants from southeastern Europe did not quiet their fears.

The "revolt of the farmers," which built up in the seventies and eighties and reached a great climax in the nineties, was a rebellion against the power of Big Business and in favor of the restoration of the farmers to their ancient position as the most influential class of Americans. They were fervent supporters of capitalism and wanted simply to insure that small property-owners, especially agriculturists, were not crushed by huge corporations. To gain such security, they did not hesitate to turn to government with demands for new types of intervention in the economic system, and the formulation of such programs turned out to be their most permanent political contribution. The acutely dissatisfied farmers, castigated as rebels at the time, turned out to be the pioneers of the characteristic new policies of American government in the twentieth century.

145

Emotionally, the recovery of status was probably the most powerful motive of the farmer-rebels. This can be seen in the fervor with which the Grangers carried out rituals symbolic of the spiritual glory of the farmer, in the farmers' anger at the arrogance of many of the new masters of industrial wealth, and in the passion with which they followed leaders who preached to the nation on the theme of the farmer's moral worth. Emotional factors, however, were inseparable from economic conditions, and these varied with localities and products. The plight of farmers was worst in the staple-producing districts of the South and West—especially those given over to the chief export crops, cotton and wheat—and among those most burdened with debt because of overextension or an inescapable credit system. It was least in the Northeast, where markets were predominantly domestic and there were the fewest transportation problems. As time went on, conditions became more favorable in those portions of the Middle West which turned to dairying or corn-hog farming. The farmers were predominantly of the older ethnic groups and, more than any other major economic group, they tended to look backward. But discontent about status declined whenever a farmer gained a place in the new economic order as a successful businessman. That proved to be much easier in the twentieth century than in the generation following the Civil War.

GRIEVANCES OF THE FARMERS

The economic and political grievances of farmers accumulated in proportion to the rise of industry. Their prosperity declined in proportion as they invested in improved machinery, which they did particularly in the West, and produced more food and fiber. This paradox frustrated individual effort. In the last three decades of the century, while farmers were expanding the acres under cultivation from about 500 million to almost 850 million, they increased their investment in implements and machinery by almost three times, from $271 million to $750 million. To earlier inventions were added such new ones as the twine-binder, disc-harrow, corn-binder, cotton-planter, gang-plow, and centrifugal cream-separator. The use of commercial fertilizer was multiplied more than eight times, from 321,000 to 2,730,000 tons. The farmer eagerly adopted the businessman's gospel of efficiency and turned his vocation into a business. The accentuated trend from self-sufficient farming to commercial agriculture resulted in increased emphasis on marketable crops and products: oats, corn, hogs and wheat in the Middle West, wool in the Mountain states, cotton and tobacco in the South. Rice culture moved to Louisiana, and dairy production spread to Wisconsin and beyond.

American farmers, as a group, could not be accused of lacking energy or failing to apply progressive methods. But all their great accomplish-

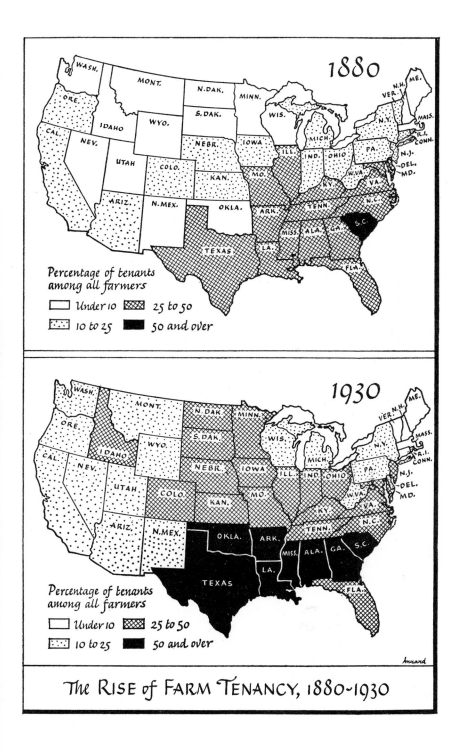

1880

Percentage of tenants
among all farmers

☐ Under 10   ▨ 25 to 50
⬚ 10 to 25   ■ 50 and over

1930

Percentage of tenants
among all farmers

☐ Under 10   ▨ 25 to 50
⬚ 10 to 25   ■ 50 and over

Annand

The RISE of FARM TENANCY, 1880~1930

ments resulted in a fall in the prices they received for their crops. The index (1910-14 as 100) of wholesale prices of farm products dropped not only from the high of 140 at the end of the Civil War to 89 in 1876. During the following years of industrial prosperity, farm prices continued to fall, to 71 in 1890, and still farther during the depression of the nineties, to 56 in 1896. During these same years when the Homestead Act was intended to strengthen the family farm in the United States, farmers steadily increased the mortgage debt on their property and tenants displaced owners. The mortgage and tenant problems were most pronounced in the Plains states which had been settled under the Act. In Kansas alone, 11,000 farms were lost by mortgage foreclosure during the "prosperity" years from 1889 to 1893.

Problems of the Commercial Farmers

Specialization in cash crops and dependence on bank credit combined to make the Western farmer a businessman. For his old independence founded on diversified-subsistence land use, he now exchanged the chance to get rich and the risk of failure. Some of the new commercial farmers did get rich, but most of them found that besides the ordinary commercial problems of buying and selling wisely which all businessmen must meet, they faced risks peculiar to their calling. The vagaries of climate introduced an unpredictable factor which made it impossible for them to plan their production. To this was added the inability of any particular producer to know what quantities would be thrown onto the market in a given year by others. There were far too many farmers and they were far too individualistic to permit co-operative regulation of production or other measures of price control such as industrialists were successfully developing for themselves. The farmer simply followed his instinct to raise as much as possible. When he was most successful in raising a good crop, the price was most likely to fall, because other farmers with equally good crops oversupplied the market. When he failed to raise a good crop, the price with the same perversity went up and he had little to sell.

These hazards were those attending a thoroughly competitive economic process, and they were "natural" in the classical economists' sense which most Americans supported at least theoretically. But the farmer became angry when he saw that he was being isolated as the only important producer in America who actually lived up to the theory of the natural law of competition. The railroads which had been subsidized to help him were coming under the control of exploitative monopolists. Their managers not only favored great industrialists with rebates and drawbacks but charged more for short hauls from a rural point to a market city than for longer hauls between two cities. Middlemen, grain-elevator owners, commission merchants, various wholesalers and jobbers, and traders in "futures" increasingly intervened between the producer and the consumer, buying cheap from the former and selling dear to the latter, taking the cream of the profits of a crop for themselves and using speculative methods to exaggerate the movement of prices.

Most protective tariff rates on agricultural products did the farmer no good, because he did not restrict his production to the quantity which could be absorbed by the American market. Most years in nearly all the chief cash crops, but especially in wheat and cotton, the farmers poured into the market more than Americans could consume, whereupon some of the crop had to be sold abroad in competition with the producers in other countries, and the low prices of the world market determined the prices at which the entire American crop was sold. Industrialists, who were organized in fewer units and increasingly coming under centralized control, were better able to restrict their production to the amount the market would absorb without ruining prices, therefore they could gain full advantage from tariff protection. The countryman complained bitterly that he sold his crops for low prices in a free world market but was forced to buy manufactured goods at high prices in a protected American market. Sons of the American farmers who had been won over to the principle of protection in the time of Henry Clay turned against the principle.

The farmer saw that it was not merely tariff protection that raised the prices he had to pay for tools and clothes, but also the monopolistic methods of the masters of the mines and factories. To the railroads he added the trusts as his enemies. The greatest of the trusts was that of the masters of capital, the bankers and financiers whose control of credit gave them an octopus-grip on the entire economy. The farmer found himself at a severe disadvantage in the money market. Faced with no other way of getting land or of holding on to it after a crop or price failure, the Western farmer mortgaged his property in return for a loan. The terms of this were fixed by the banker, running from 8 per cent to an exorbitant 25 per cent and occasionally to 40 per cent, and failure to repay on time was dealt with ruthlessly. "Wall Street" as the center of the financial system became the best-hated symbol in the farmer's litany of grievances. To his strictly economic reasons for hatred was added moral loathing as he learned how the new generation of millionaires flaunted their wealth arrogantly and—what was most objectionable to the old-fashioned Protestants of the farms—in sinful ways.

Special Difficulties of the Cotton Farmers

More even than the producers of wheat and corn, the cotton growers suffered from low prices, and their difficulties were accentuated by distinctive local conditions which lasted long after the period of Reconstruction. To the external view it appeared that one of the results of the war was the breakup of the old plantation system to the advantage of the small holder. In the two decades, 1860-1880, the number of farms in the cotton-producing states doubled, while the average size of these was cut in half. But there was also a great increase in tenancy and, more characteristically, share-cropping. It is less accurate to say that the plantation system was destroyed than to say that it lost its "system"—that is, the close supervision of labor which had marked it wherever it was most efficient. Also, it tended to pass from the hands of the old planters to a new group. Under the share system, which was preferred by the freedmen to either wage labor or straight tenancy, the owner's proportion was generally half the crop if he provided tools, mules, and seed; it was less if he merely provided the land. The share-cropper had gained freedom from supervision but he was still bound to the soil.

Parallel with the share-cropping system, which affected Negroes more than whites, the crop-lien system, which affected all classes, arose out of the need of farmers for supplies before the marketing of the crop. Either merchants or owners provided these, taking a lien or chattel mortgage on the future crop as security. The two groups tended to coalesce, since merchants acquired land and large owners were likely to move to town and become merchants. The net result of the crop-lien system, in an era of falling agricultural prices, was to plunge the debtors into perpetual economic bondage. Supplies were provided at high prices with heavy interest charges, but the merchants ran great risks and themselves paid high interest. The tendency of the system was to perpetuate the specialization in cotton culture, regardless of the state of the market, and its paralyzing effects on southern agriculture were comparable to those of slavery.

As a permanent debtor class the great body of cotton farmers advocated currency inflation. The decline in the price of their staple in the twenty years following the accession of Hayes in 1877 was greater than that of corn and wheat. Cotton fell as low as 5.8 cents per pound. A price of at least 8 cents was necessary for a profit and when it fell below 7 cents a loss was sustained. Cotton culture was actually conducted at a loss in the 1890's. More consistently than the Westerners, the Southern farmers opposed a high protective tariff. Also, under the rule of the Redeemers, they lacked state governments sensitive to their special needs. Their eroded lands were fertile in discontent in this era of regnant industrialism in the nation. In certain respects the Southern agrarians were more radical than the Western. Because of the degree of their poverty, however, many of these tillers of the soil were apathetic until aroused by violent voices.

THE FARMERS ORGANIZE: FROM THE GRANGE TO THE FARMERS' ALLIANCES

The Grange and the Granger Laws

In an age of industrial consolidation and growing urbanism, the farmers were at a disadvantage since their physical isolation restricted their personal opportunities and made co-operation among them difficult. To better their condition and make their influence felt in public matters they needed organization. The first nation-wide agency for the advancement of the interests of farmers was The Patrons of Husbandry, popularly called the Grange, a secret fraternal order of men and women with an elaborate ritual. This was conceived and originally organized by Oliver H. Kelley, a former clerk in the Bureau of Agriculture in Washington. During the years 1867-1874, the order grew rapidly throughout the country, especially in the Middle West and the cotton South, but it declined rapidly thereafter. At the peak there were more than 21,000 granges and nearly a million members. Not the least of the services of the organization was its provision of social intercourse for isolated farmers and their families, and it still survives as a fraternal order.

The Grangers created numerous co-operative enterprises—buying and selling agencies, co-operative stores, factories of agricultural implements, even banking and insurance establishments. For a time these resulted in considerable saving to members, but they were too hastily set up and proved to be beyond the power of their debt-ridden sponsors to maintain. Their failure was one of the reasons for the decline of the Grange.

The Grangers opposed middlemen and monopolists, while advocating agricultural education, cheap textbooks, and railroad regulation. Their political influence was greatest in the Middle West, where their most eloquent voice was that of Ignatius Donnelly of Minnesota, afterwards one of the noted orators of Populism. Many Grangers were sympathetic with national third-party movements, such as the Greenback movement, but they operated on the state level and left their chief mark on political history by influencing state legislation. In the Granger Laws the first important legislative steps were taken toward railroad regulation.

In Illinois, Wisconsin, Iowa, Minnesota, and other agricultural states of the Middle West, laws were passed in the early 1870's fixing maximum freight and passenger rates for railroads. While the farmers regarded the attitude of the monopolistic railroads as high-handed and intolerable, the railroad corporations viewed the Granger movement as an attack on private property. One able legal writer soberly declared it to be "sheer communism." Nonetheless, these laws, along with an Illinois law fixing rates for grain elevators in Chicago, were upheld by the United States

Supreme Court in 1877. In the best known of the cases, Munn *vs*. Illinois, the elevator case, Chief Justice Waite declared that the grain-storage business in Chicago, a virtual monopoly bearing on the commerce in grain in seven or eight states, was "affected with a public interest" and therefore subject to public regulation. The Chief Justice applied the same principle to a number of railroad cases on the same occasion, denying that the fixing of maximum rates by state legislation infringed on the right of the warehouse and railroad owners to due process of law. This view was challenged by Justice Field in a dissenting opinion, which pointed the way to later judicial interpretation.

The attack on state regulation of railroads was pushed aggressively in the courts thereafter, but the failure of the Granger laws can be attributed more immediately to practical conditions. The railroads could be limited in rates but they could not be compelled to render sufficient service. Toward the end of the decade, therefore, these laws were repealed; and they were followed by laws creating state railroad commissions. This legislation represented a more intelligent approach to the problem of regulation, but the farmers ran into other difficulties arising from the fact that the railroad business was interstate in character. In 1886, in the case of Wabash, St. Louis, and Pacific Railroad Company *vs*. Illinois, the Supreme Court held that a state law prohibiting greater charges for short hauls than long violated federal authority over interstate commerce, even when the regulation applied only to the part of the commerce within the state. This decision played a direct part in the passage of the Interstate Commerce Act of 1887, but, as we have seen, the Commission established under that law had little power and was presently shorn of that by the federal courts. By that time farmers saw that only federal regulation could be effective, and their demand for it became vociferous. By that time, also, the Grange had ceased to be a political force.

The Farmers' Alliances

With the decline of the Grange, a new crop of farmers' organizations sprang up in the West and South, many of them short-lived. The two most important ones are generally designated as the Northern and Southern Farmers' Alliance, though each of them had the word "National" in its official name. Both of them were started in the late 1870's and they had enormous growth in the late eighties. The former had greatest strength in the Middle West beyond the Mississippi, the first state alliance being in Nebraska. In 1887, when seven states were represented in a national convention, a national constitution was drawn up. Growth thereafter was rapid, so that by 1890 there were ten fully organized state alliances, with others in process, and hundreds of locals. The largest membership was in Kansas.

The Southern Alliance originated in Texas, where it was incorporated in 1880 as a "secret and benevolent association," and had its greatest growth after 1887, when it received a national charter in the District of Columbia. Under the leadership of a remarkable man, Dr. C. W. Macune, it was spread with evangelical fervor throughout the South, especially in the cotton-growing districts. Within a couple of years it was consolidated with another organization known as The Agricultural Wheel, and by 1890 it was said to comprise about half the agricultural population of the South. In size it exceeded the Northern Alliance two or three to one. Closely associated with it was the Colored Alliance, organized by a white man. This consisted of a dozen state organizations and more than a million members by the early nineties.

These large agricultural organizations constituted the farmers' response to the consolidation of industry and transportation. An unsuccessful effort to merge them into a single group was made in December 1889, when the two major organizations held their national conventions in St. Louis. One difficulty was that the Southerners insisted on maintaining the practice of secrecy, which had enabled their leaders to act with speed and effectiveness. Furthermore, there were real differences in sectional problems. The Southern Alliance expected to continue to draw the color line in the South. It agreed to leave that question to state decision and to permit Negro membership in the Supreme Council, but Northern suspicions had not disappeared. The Northern Alliance, furthermore, did not like the idea of being absorbed in the larger Southern body. Kansas and the Dakotas, where agrarian distress was most like that in the South, did join the Southern Alliance, and the Knights of Labor approved its program.

Like the Grange, the Alliances admitted women as well as men and offered much-needed social opportunities to isolated people. In the South, especially, membership was limited to "dirt farmers" and their friends. Lawyers, merchants, and bankers were rigidly excluded and every effort was made to maintain this as a country order. In that sense it promoted class-consciousness. Both in the North and South the Alliances sought to perform an educational function. By lectures, by the circulation of books and papers, and by other means they spread knowledge of improved agricultural methods and provoked discussion of political and economic questions. Among the hundreds of agricultural periodicals, many of them ephemeral, the most influential was the *National Economist*, official organ of the Southern Alliance, edited by Macune. By means of these educational activities thousands of farmers were made more conscious of their needs and interests.

The Alliances were much less successful in the attainment of the business purposes which they emphasized as their main ones at the outset. They engaged in a great variety of co-operative projects—stores, grain elevators, cotton gins, insurance schemes, and others, most of them abortive. The most elaborate of these "business agencies" was the Texas Exchange, established in 1887 by Dr. Macune and housed in a huge four-story building in Dallas. Farm products were sold through this and farm supplies bought. It ran into difficulties because of the farmers' shortage of cash and lasted less than two years. The banks did not regard the joint-notes of Alliance members as sound security, and quite obviously this grandiose scheme had insufficient capital to meet the farmers' credit needs. Other exchanges, operating chiefly on a cash basis, were more successful and lasted longer, saving a good deal to individuals, but for the solution of this problem public aid was required which that generation was unwilling to provide.

The most constructive proposal involving direct federal action was the "subtreasury plan," which Macune fathered. This called for the setting up of government warehouses and subtreasury offices in agricultural counties. Under it, farmers might withhold their crops from a glutted market, store them in the warehouses, and secure short-term government loans on them in legal-tender paper up to 80 per cent of their value, paying a low rate of interest. This bold plan directly attacked the existing banking and monetary system. Numerous bills to carry it into effect were introduced in Congress, but nothing came of them. It was greeted in Eastern financial circles as the fantastic proposal of "hayseed Socialists," but in important features it resembles measures enacted in the twentieth century.

THE FARMERS IN POLITICS: THE BEGINNINGS OF POPULISM

Since many agricultural organizations in the past had been wrecked by political dissension, the leaders of the Alliances tried to keep them non-partisan and to emphasize their business aspects. But as time went on it became increasingly clear that their objectives could not be attained without political action. When the farmer turned to his state and federal governments for redress of grievances, his anger mounted because he found that both federal and state legislatures were indifferent to his needs if not actually allied with interests which he regarded as inimical to him. His anger was the greater because he thought of himself as belonging to the American majority. Historically, the farmers had always been that and they were now sufficiently awakened to be aware of their power at the polls. The question confronting their leaders in the late eighties and early nineties was how best to employ their political strength.

The rebellious farmers had two fundamental convictions: the capitalists —trusts, railroads, banks, loan sharks, merchants—were bleeding them; and the currency of the country was insufficient. By 1889, when the two great Alliances met in St. Louis, these groups had gone beyond the point of seeking merely to restore competition or regulate corporations. Among their demands were public ownership and operation of railroads. As inflationists the farmers probably preferred paper money. Both Alliances put at or near the top of their demands the abolition of national banks and the substitution of treasury notes for national bank notes of legal-tender, issued in sufficient quantity to meet the growing needs of the country. They saw no reason to base the currency on gold, and the more radical Southern Alliance was already demanding the free and unlimited coinage of silver. These members of a debtor class wanted more money in circulation, any way they could get it, and they were drawn into the silver movement by a working alliance with Western mining interests which were not at all agrarian in spirit. In the end the farmers were engulfed by the silver movement. It bulked very large in their minds by 1890, but they were then concerned with many other things, including political procedure. Should they or should they not form a new and independent party in their localities? The immediate answer to the question was negative in the South and affirmative in the most distressed portions of the trans-Mississippi West.

The leaders of the Southern Alliance believed that with the farmers' votes they could gain control of the Democratic Party, and they seemed to realize their hopes richly in the elections of 1890. In five states governors backed by the Alliance were chosen, including two conspicuous popular leaders with whom it joined forces, Benjamin R. Tillman of South Carolina and James S. Hogg of Texas. It gained control of eight legislatures and elected nearly fifty sympathetic men to Congress, including Thomas E. Watson of Georgia. In regional history these developments are significant as marking the beginning of the end of the Redeemers, and the appearance of a new group of Southern political leaders more aware of the needs of farmers. But the Alliance had not sufficiently calculated the possibility that instead of its annexing the Democratic Party, the party might annex it, weakening if not destroying it in the process. These governors and legislatures proved unwilling to go as fast or as far as the Alliance demanded, and from the point of view of the latter the immediate results of the changes in state governments were distinctly disappointing. In 1891, the South Carolina Alliance went so far as to take formal action repudiating Tillman.

Meanwhile, certain developments in Congress played into the hands of Democratic Party leaders in the South and helped solidify the region. In June 1890, Senator Henry Cabot Lodge of Massachusetts introduced the Force Bill, threatening to invoke the Fourteenth Amendment and calling for even greater federal control of elections than under Reconstruction. The bill was defeated early in 1891, but it created more alarm in the white South than anything that had happened in Washington since Hayes withdrew the troops, and it greatly lessened the prospects of creating a new party in the cotton country. The bill served the political purpose of making co-operation more difficult between radical agrarians of the South and West. Also, it tended to weaken the ties between the white and colored Alliances within the South, and played into the hands of Tillman and others who exploited the race question for political advantage. It helped create the psychological situation which permitted, in the next two decades, the disfranchisement of Negroes by ingenious state laws and the enactment of "Jim Crow" legislation.

It was in the wheat-producing West that the distressed farmers set up independent state tickets and started the People's Party on the local level. This was in the summer of 1890, when prices of grain were abysmally low and the Middle Border was parched from drought. The initial step was taken at Topeka, Kansas, at a convention in which Alliance members predominated but which Knights of Labor and Patrons of Husbandry attended. This called for a new organization based on the principles proclaimed at the meetings of the Alliance in St. Louis the year before, and it named this the People's Party. In Kansas, Nebraska, the Dakotas, and contiguous states third-party tickets were entered, and the political campaign was waged in the spirit of a religious revival. The uprising in Kansas has become a part of American folklore. The most spectacular of the agrarian haranguers, Mrs. Mary Elizabeth Lease, urged the farmers "to raise less corn and more Hell!" The immediate local successes of the hastily organized and highly emotional new party were gratifying to its supporters and disturbing to the regular parties. But, as in the South, the results in state legislation were slight; and it seemed to many in the trans-Mississippi wheat country that the People's Party, in order to compete with the Republicans and Democrats, must become a national organization.

Forming a National Party

The Southern Alliance, which the state Alliances of Kansas and the Dakotas had joined, held a convention at Ocala, Florida, in December 1890. The Western representatives were favorable to the formation of a national party, but it did not yet seem feasible to the Southerners, who feared the Force Bill and still hoped to bend to their will the Democratic Party in the South. By way of compromise it was agreed to defer decision on the crucial question of a national party until early in the presidential election year (February 1892), when a convention composed of delegates from "all organizations of producers" should be held. Also, the convention drew up a fresh set of "Demands," known as the "Ocala Platform." This included the subtreasury scheme, free silver, and other radical proposals of the Southern Alliancemen.

The Northern Alliance, which met soon thereafter, also favored delay until February 1892, but many Westerners were impatient. Some of them

brought about a convention in Cincinnati in May 1891 which announced
the formation of a national People's Party and appointed a national committee. This was a decisive step, but the support of the great farmers'
organizations, the Southern Alliance being the largest, was of such importance that further important action was delayed until the meeting in
February 1892.

Meanwhile, agitation in the Western farm states again reached fever
pitch. Farmers neglected their fields to gather at crossroads and listen to
orators blast Wall Street, the gold standard, the railroads, the trusts, and
stand-pat politicians of both old parties. The movement was likened to
a prairie fire, and to staid Easterners the farmers of the newer West
seemed to be running wild, while sober economists blanched at the
"crackpot" economic theories and reckless measures the homespun leaders
advocated. The Westerners precipitated the national third-party movement and forced the hand of the Southern agrarians. The leaders of the
Southern Alliance, disillusioned by their failure to attain their ends
through the Democrats, fell in with the Western groups though uncertain about the attitude of their own following.

Southerners predominated at the meeting in St. Louis in February 1892,
and the Colored Alliance was strongly represented, as were the Knights
of Labor. This convention described itself as "the first great labor conference in the United States," and it adopted an impressive platform.
Candidates were nominated at a gathering in Omaha in July, which was
described as the first national convention of the People's Party of America,
and adopted still another platform. But for his death, Leonidas L. Polk,
of North Carolina, president of the Southern Alliance, might have been
nominated for president, for this unusually able man was much talked
about. The choice fell on General James B. Weaver of Iowa, who had run
for the presidency as a Greenbacker. The second place went to General
James G. Field of Virginia, who had lost a leg in the service of the
Confederacy.

The candidates were relatively moderate, but the oratory at these
meetings was hot. Among the firebrands were Ignatius Donnelly of
Minnesota, "Sockless Jerry" Simpson of Kansas, and the redoubtable Tom
Watson of Georgia. In tone and emotion their oratory was a transmutation
of evangelical Protestantism and self-righteousness against the materialism
and sinfulness of the mighty and the rich. Such an appeal was very
potent among plain people in rural districts, but they enjoyed it more
than they respected it, and it exposed their cause to the derision of other
groups.

The final platform of the People's (or Populist) Party included oft-
repeated demands in extreme form. It advocated inflation of the currency
to a minimum of $50 per capita, by means of free silver and paper money
issued by the federal Treasury; and it called for the abolition of the right

of national banks to issue paper money. Government ownership of all transportation and communication facilities was demanded. More prophetic of later developments were demands for a graduated income tax to force the rich to contribute a larger share to the cost of government, a postal-savings system to relieve citizens from dependence on privately-owned banks, direct election of United States Senators, a secret ballot to free voters from intimidation, and the initiative and referendum to give voters more direct control over legislation. The demand that the ownership of land by aliens be forbidden reflected the nativistic spirit of the farmers, as did their proposal that immigration be restricted. They expected the latter to appeal to organized labor, and they coupled with it demands for a short working day and the abolition of strikebreaking agencies.

Apart from the planks bearing on the currency and banks and the ownership of railroads the platform would not startle most Americans today, but it was radical in the conditions of 1892. A statement in the preamble had a specially ominous sound in conservative ears: "Wealth belongs to him who creates it, and every dollar taken from industry without equivalent is robbery." By "industry" the Populists meant not factories but all varieties of working people, and they thought their crusade one to restore rights, not to destroy property. They looked chiefly to the American past for their social ideals, but they were significantly forward-looking in challenging the prevailing political doctrine of laissez faire. "We believe," they said, "that the powers of government—in other words, of the people —should be expanded . . . as rapidly and as far as the good sense of an intelligent people and the teachings of experience shall justify, to the end that oppression, injustice, and poverty shall eventually cease in the land."

The abiding significance of the farmers' crusade lies in such sentiments as these, rather than in the specific proposals they made or the oratorical excesses which accompanied them. But the immediate question was how they would fare in the national political arena which they had now boldly entered.

CHAPTER 9

From Populism to High Republicanism

In the last decade of the nineteenth century, national political battles were waged with much greater intensity than in the 1880's, and they were of far greater concern to the electorate. Politics ceased to be a game in which the stakes were little more than the spoils of office.

When the showdown came in the tariff fight, Cleveland found that Eastern Democrats were very much like Harrison Republicans; and in 1896, when the money question was the main one, many of them had more in common with McKinley Republicans than with Bryan Democrats from the West and South. In this period political sentiment tended to follow class and sectional lines. The Populists, who directly challenged the regulars in both camps, constituted an agrarian party that vainly sought to identify industrial labor with its cause but was drawn into alliance with western silver-mining interests. Then it fused with the Democrats under Bryan and lost its national identity. In the great battle of 1896 the alignment was predominantly sectional.

The silver question obscured the issue between "producers" and Big Business, but never since the Civil War had the ruling economic group been defied so openly by so many people. Discontent increased during an economic depression such as the country was not to know again until the 1930's, and this found political expression in the most important reform movement since the war. That it failed is the most significant political fact of the decade. The movement associated itself with what most Americans regarded as financial heresy. The preservation of "sound money" was a major result of the victory of William McKinley over William Jennings Bryan, and for this the next American generation was grateful. But the triumph of the Republicans in 1896 permitted a consolidation of the posi-

159

tion of the economic groups whose power had been growing for a generation. Big Business reached its political zenith in the administration of
McKinley.

THE ELECTION OF 1892 AND THE POPULISTS

The defeat of the Republicans in the Congressional elections of 1890
was the most decisive the party had suffered since the war; and the
Harrison administration, during its last two years, failed to regain the
confidence of the public. The net effect of the financial measures of
the government was the virtual annihilation of the Treasury surplus. This
occasioned concern in conservative financial circles where Republicanism
was normally so strong. Besides the rising tide of agrarian discontent
there was a wave of strikes in 1892. The best-known, the Homestead
Strike in Pennsylvania, was put down by state troops, but federal troops
were used on several occasions and the administration was commonly
regarded as unfriendly to labor. Bosses like Matthew S. Quay of Pennsylvania, Tom Platt of New York, and "Czar" Reed in Congress had turned
against the President by the middle of his term, while the public found
him cold and unappealing. His party could not deny him renomination in
1892, however. They completed the ticket by naming Whitelaw Reid,
editor of the *New York Tribune,* for the vice-presidency. Reid was a man
of personal distinction, but was disliked by Boss Platt and had gained
enmity of labor groups by his longstanding opposition to attempts to
unionize the *Tribune.*

Since the Congressional victories of the Democrats in 1890 were attributed to public reaction against the high McKinley Tariff of 1890,
minds naturally turned to Grover Cleveland who had made the tariff a
major issue. It was, indeed, the only issue which sharply differentiated
the two major parties in 1892. The Democrats in their platform denied
the constitutional authority of the government to impose duties for any
purpose except revenue, while the Republicans frankly espoused the
protective principle. This commended them to industrialists, but in many
respects Cleveland was more acceptable to financial groups than Harrison, who had distributed pensions so lavishly and signed the Silver Purchase Act.

During his four years of political retirement, Cleveland had practiced
law in New York, serving great corporations and making friends in high
financial circles. He remained a living symbol of honesty and courage,
but he had become more conservative with age and personal prosperity.
He seemed less a man of the people, less a champion of civic reform,
than he had previously. Ben Tillman undoubtedly voiced the sentiments
of many when he described Cleveland's nomination as a surrender of
popular rights to the "financial kings." The portly former President was

not one to surrender to anybody, but he was more unyielding on the currency question than Harrison and he had shown no special concern over the difficulties of farmers. For the vice-presidency the Democrats nominated Adlai E. Stevenson of Illinois, who, besides being a man of personal charm and conciliatory spirit, was more sympathetic with the agrarians than the urban-minded Cleveland. But the party platform yielded nothing to the demands of Western and Southern farmers, and the net effect of the actions of the Democratic National Convention was to stimulate rather than retard the movement for a third national party. Adherents of the People's Party, which nominated Generals James B. Weaver and James G. Field, were now commonly referred to as "Populists," sometimes as "Populites" or "Pops."

Victory at the polls went to Cleveland, who received 277 electoral votes to Harrison's 145, with a popular plurality of about 360,000 out of a total of some 10 million. Weaver got 22 electoral and more than a million popular votes. For a third party in a country wedded to the two-party system the Populists made an impressive showing, despite their sad lack of campaign funds, and they held the balance of power in a number of states. In the West and South many successful candidates for state office or for Congress accepted their program, as a whole or in large part, while running as Republicans or Democrats. But the Populist leaders ran into great difficulties in their effort to create an effective national party dedicated to the interests of the lower-income groups.

The election showed unmistakably that the appeal of Populism was regional, not national, and that it did not extend to the labor group. In the northern states east of the Mississippi, where most of the industry of the country was concentrated, the party did not get 5 per cent of the popular vote in a single state. The *spirit* of Populism was very strong in the cotton-producing districts of the South, especially among the poorer farmers. The Democrats incorporated many of the Populist demands in their state platforms, even though these were ignored in the national platform, thus making it difficult to wean voters from their customary allegiance. Nevertheless, the Populists set up tickets of their own in state after state, and it has been estimated that perhaps half of the members of the Southern Farmers' Alliance went along with the new party.

They encountered terrific opposition from the existing Democratic organizations, even when these were in the hands of men relatively sympathetic with the Populist program. In South Carolina, for example, Ben Tillman prevented them from making any headway, and despite his denunciation of Cleveland he supported that candidate in 1892. In its nonpartisan days the Southern Alliance had co-operated with the Colored Alliance, even though the poorer white farmers were particularly antagonistic to Negroes. Populist leaders now appealed to small farmers of both races as members of the same economic class. They desperately sought Negro votes and were drawn into co-operation with Republicans. The regulars outmatched them, however, in the old game of intimidation and ballot-stuffing. As a rule the Democrats collected more Negro ballots than the Populists, and the extent of fraud is suggested by the fact that in the Congressional election in which Tom Watson was defeated in Georgia, the total vote was twice that of the legal voters. Democratic leaders admitted that in many places they "counted out" the Populists. The attempts of the latter to fuse with the Republicans afterwards brought local success in certain localities, notably in North Carolina, but in the end they proved the undoing of the new party in the South. In 1892, Weaver carried no southern state, though he got more than a third of the popular vote in Alabama.

In the agricultural states west of the Mississippi, the Populists as a party were strongest in Kansas, Nebraska, Minnesota, and the Dakotas. They did best in the wheat belt and did not fare well in Weaver's own Iowa, where the emphasis was on corn-hog farming. In several states, notably in Kansas, they gained success by fusing—not with the Republicans as in the South, but with the Democrats. They elected several governors, but not even in Kansas did they gain control of the entire state government.

Though the Populists were identified in most minds with the interests of farmers, in 1892 their party got its largest percentage of the popular vote in the mountain states—especially Colorado, Idaho, and Nevada, all of which Weaver carried. These were mining states, relatively uninterested in the People's program except as it pertained to silver. As a prospective national party, therefore, the Populists had to face the facts that they had virtually no following in the East or in the ranks of labor, that they had not dented the Solid South, and that their national ticket had fared best in the silver country. Even in the wheat belt the parts of their platform which proved most appealing were the proposals regarding the currency. These experiences had fateful consequences, for henceforth they minimized the other features of their program of reform and concentrated on the money question.

THE SILVER ISSUE, 1873-1892

Following the election of 1892 the monetary issue resolved itself into the silver question, and this overshadowed the national political scene until the "battle of the standards" was fought to a national decision in 1896. To champions of gold, the theoretical issue was between sound and unsound money, while to those espousing the cause of silver it was between an adequate and an inadequate supply of money. We can understand the terms and slogans better if we review briefly the monetary history of the two decades before Grover Cleveland was inaugurated as President for the second time. The silver orators generally went back at least as far as the demonetization of silver, which they called the "Crime of '73."

Throughout American history there had been advocates of paper money backed merely by the credit of the government, and that was what the true Populists really wanted. The famous greenbacks were money of this sort until 1879, when the Treasury assumed responsibility for redeeming them in coin upon request. Then, literally, they became as good as gold. Many inflationists saw no necessity for this action, but in the orthodox fiscal thinking of the time true money was hard money. This had intrinsic value which paper money lacked and it was acceptable in world trade. The soundness of paper money depended, therefore, on its convertibility into a precious metal.

Until 1873, the government recognized both gold and silver as standard. Its mints would coin either of them into dollars when bullion was presented, and before the Civil War the ratio between them was established by law as 16 to 1. That is, sixteen ounces of silver were recognized as equal in value to one ounce of gold, and the weight of a dollar in either metal was fixed accordingly. Silver was somewhat undervalued at 16 to 1. Being worth more as bullion than as coin, it was not brought for mintage. Therefore, in a routine law in 1873, the silver dollar was dropped from the list of coins. Though this action was afterwards excoriated as the "Crime of '73", no evidence has been found that a creditors' conspiracy against silver existed.

The situation soon changed with respect to silver. Rich new mines in this country and limitations on the coinage of silver elsewhere caused the price of this metal to fall. American producers of it would have profited if the "free and unlimited" coinage of silver at the ratio of 16 to 1 had been restored, while debt-ridden farmers in the West and South saw advantage to themselves in the increase in the amount of money in circulation. Under the Bland-Allison Act in 1878, coinage of silver dollars was resumed, but it was limited. Producers sold to the government at the current price, which in 1878 was not a sixteenth of that of gold but approximately an eighteenth. In the next year, 1879, when the resumption of specie payments went into effect, the country really went on the gold standard.

By 1890, the value of silver had declined further. The Silver Purchase Act of that year required the purchase of 4.5 million ounces of this metal per month, approximately the entire output of American silver mines. This was a substantial sop to the producers, but they were to be paid not at a ratio of 16 to 1 but at the low current price in a falling market. Payment was to be made in legal-tender notes, redeemable in coin— either gold or silver. The policy of the Treasury actually was to redeem them in gold, that is, to support the gold standard, whereas both the silver producers and the agrarian inflationists were clamoring for bimetalism. The Treasury policy required the maintenance of a sufficient gold reserve and this was assumed to be at least $100 million.

Many of the arguments of the silverites in the course of their crusade were absurd. Two metals are better than one, they said, just as two eyes are for a man, two wings for a bird, and two wheels for a bicycle. They were correct in their basic contention that an increase in the money supply was necessary to carry on the business of a rapidly expanding economy. The world production of gold, on which the money system rested, had fallen far behind the increase in marketable goods produced by American farms and factories. Indeed, in a period of twenty-five years, annual gold production actually decreased; in 1866, it was about $130 million, and in 1890 about $119 million. The country's monetary system was not flexible enough, and in the long view this was not even good for creditors. But the proposed remedy amounted to uncontrollable inflation.

By 1896, the price of silver on the market had sunk to about 32 to 1. If the government now offered to accept all of it at 16 to 1, the price would be so wondrously attractive that mining operations would be expanded to the limit and all the silver of the world would be presented to the United States Treasury in return for gold. An indefinite inflation of the currency would result. Prices of other commodities would rise and debtors would pay off their obligations with corresponding ease. It was precisely to pay off mortgages with cheap money that American farmers supported "free and unlimited coinage of silver at 16 to 1;" and the prospect frightened creditors and many others who were concerned to maintain the stability of the financial system.

Cleveland Bucks the Storm, 1893-1896

Grover Cleveland's troubles began immediately after he returned to the White House and did not end until he left it—discredited but undismayed. He did not understand all the forces that beat upon him, but he steered a fixed course with inflexible determination, and he brought safely to port the part of the ship's cargo that seemed to him most indispensable. He saved the country its precious but dwindling store of gold until this could be replenished.

Depression and the Currency Question

He inherited a desperate fiscal problem from the Harrison administration, whose spending policies had depleted the Treasury while the redemption of the legal-tender notes authorized by the Silver Purchase Act dangerously reduced the gold reserve. This fell below the level of $100 million in April 1893. Since the law stipulated redemption in coin without expressly requiring gold, many bankers and importers feared that the government might have recourse to silver, under pressure of necessity. Then, according to Gresham's famous law, bad money would drive out good, and gold would vanish altogether. Cleveland gave assurances to the contrary, but these uncertainties, which were accentuated by others arising from the international financial situation, brought on a panic. In May and June prices on the New York Stock Exchange suddenly plummeted as investors lost confidence and stampeded to sell their holdings at any price. Meanwhile, throughout the country, frightened depositors were taking their money out of banks.

From the time of the so-called "Baring Panic" in England in 1890, international trade and finance had been in a troubled state; and in June 1893 the British closed the mints of India to the free coinage of silver, with the result that the price of that controversial metal fell rapidly. Americans tended to interpret the economic difficulties of the time in terms of the money question, and advocates of silver often asserted that it was the victim of an international plot. They overlooked other important factors—such as the collapse of the bubble of European overseas investment, which had been dangerously extended. In the United States, depression followed panic as the holders of money refused to take risks, credit shrank, businesses went bankrupt, prices fell, markets dried up, and employees were thrown out of work.

Cleveland tried to halt the downward spiral by correcting one cause of the trouble which was of immediate concern to him as the guardian of the national Treasury—the drain on the gold reserve resulting from the Silver Purchase Act. He called Congress, which was controlled in both branches by the Democrats, into special session in August and asked it to repeal that law. The House of Representatives acceded promptly and the Senate agreed at the end of October. Strong opposition was offered, however, by Western and Southern Democrats, among whom a young congressman from Nebraska, William Jennings Bryan, was conspicuous in debate. So far as the Treasury was concerned, the damage was already done and beginning in 1894 there was a deficit; repeal merely prevented further drains on the shrunken gold reserve. The action had no immediate effect on general financial conditions, hence the silver people could say that it was unnecessary and undesirable.

Cleveland followed the traditional policy of dealing with a depression by shoring up creditor interests and allowing deflation to run its course. This policy required that the government do nothing to halt bankruptcies, or to stop the decline of prices, wages, and employment. The President sent troops to Chicago to break the Pullman Strike in 1894, and Coxey's Army of unemployed dissolved that year when the police arrested its leader in Washington. Private charity was left to deal with the hungry and homeless at a time when some 3 million laboring men were out of work. Cleveland acted only to maintain public order and save the country's gold reserve.

Bond Sales and the Silver Crusade

In 1894, two bond issues were sold for gold to syndicates of bankers, but since the subscribers obtained the gold by presenting paper money to the Treasury for redemption, the maneuver only cost the government money without strengthening the gold reserve. After the second issue enforced the lesson, the Treasury in early 1895 made an agreement with J. Pierpont Morgan to sell him a bond issue for gold, on the understanding that he would get half of this from Europe and would draw none of it from the Treasury. Morgan made a handsome profit on the transaction by reselling the bonds to investors at an advance, but the fiscal crisis was surmounted. In 1896, the Treasury by-passed the bankers entirely by selling a fourth bond issue in small denominations directly to investors. By then the new lode-mines of South Africa were beginning to relieve the world shortage of gold, and new discoveries in Alaska soon served a like purpose.

The administration of Cleveland saved the gold standard in the United States. In the course of time his countrymen gave him full honor for the disinterested patriotism and the stubborn persistence he displayed under extraordinarily difficult circumstances, but during his presidency his services were not appreciated by impoverished farmers in the Western wheat belt and the Southern cotton country. Among them his operations, which were climaxed by the deal with Morgan, strengthened the conviction that he had permitted the "money power" to victimize the government.

In the minds of many unhappy men and women gold was now personified as the tool of predatory interests and the enemy of the people, while silver was the people's friend. The most popular presentation of the cause of the friendly metal was *Coin's Financial School* (1894), a paper-covered and crudely illustrated little book which had thousands of avid readers. The author, William H. Harvey, claimed that he had set up a school in Chicago, to which bankers and business leaders came only to be confounded by this engaging young man who presented the theory of money in elementary terms. Readers of the dialogues from which Coin always emerged triumphant rarely realized that his school was wholly imaginary and they accepted his fallacious logic as unanswerable. The enormous influence of this work was attested by William Jennings Bryan; it became a catechism of "Free Silver." Numerous imitations of it followed, the most notable being *The American People's Money* (1895) by Ignatius Donnelly.

Complicated economic issues were thus simplified into moral terms, and the abstruse monetary question was taken up in the spirit of a crusade. The debtor farmers and the coinage of the people were arrayed in battle against predatory bankers and investors whose evil instrument was gold. Despite widespread unemployment, the issue had little appeal to labor but it cut across party lines, tending to tie Westerners and Southerners together against the East.

The Failure of Tariff Reform

The Depression and the currency question overshadowed all other issues, including the tariff. Yet, if the Democrats had a mandate from the electorate on any question it was on that, and Cleveland wanted to make tariff reform the outstanding accomplishment of his second administration. But he believed it necessary to meet the currency crisis first, and the repeal of the Silver Purchase Act weakened his influence in the party. Furthermore, the Democratic margin in the Senate was slight. The tariff bill that passed the House of Representatives under the sponsorship of William L. Wilson of West Virginia, constituted a modest move in the direction of freer trade, but Eastern Democrats in the Senate, led by Arthur P. Gorman of Maryland, joined the Republicans to make many increases in the proposed rates which the House accepted. The resulting bill was so unsatisfactory to Cleveland that he failed to return it within the specified ten days, letting it become law without his signature.

The Wilson-Gorman Tariff of 1894 accomplished little one way or the other. The most important departures from earlier policy were the placing of raw wool on the free list and the restoration of a duty on raw sugar. The sugar duty was designed to increase revenue, and it aroused popular objection because it fell on a necessity of the poor. It was offset by the imposition of a tax of 2 per cent on incomes above $4000, which meant in that day a tax on the well-to-do. Popular opposition to the tariff was chiefly grounded on the belief that it favored trusts. But the Populists were strongly advocating an income tax, and many champions of the people saw in this provision some justification for the measure as a whole.

In the case of Pollock *vs.* Farmers' Loan and Trust Company (1895), the Supreme Court declared the income tax unconstitutional on the ground that it was a direct tax in the meaning of the Constitution, and could only be levied when apportioned according to population. This was a reversal of earlier judicial acceptance of the income tax of the Civil War period, and it was one of many indications of the economic conservatism of the highest court. The legal difficulty was not overcome until the adoption of the Sixteenth Amendment in 1913.

The Political Isolation of Cleveland

Nothing that the President did in the domestic sphere contributed to his political strength and public popularity. The Democrats suffered overwhelming defeat in the congressional elections of 1894, and by 1896 he had become virtually a man without a party. He denied patronage to Congressmen and Senators who opposed his monetary policies, and his stubborn independence of spirit led him to alienate men who agreed with him. Party bosses in the East had long disliked him and he became notoriously unpopular in the Democratic South. Not only did Ben Tillman call him an "old bag of beef" and promise to stick a pitchfork in his fat ribs, but a relative conservative like Senator John T. Morgan of Alabama was driven to say: "I hate the very ground that man walks on." His name was hissed at state party conventions in 1896.

For all his honesty and courage, Cleveland failed in political leadership in his second opportunity. He was most unfortunate in the times during which he served, but this strong and resolute man was himself out of date. His negative, old-fashioned liberalism was incapable of contending with the problems of private industrial and financial power or of meeting the real needs of human beings. He failed to effect the only reform he really championed, but a low tariff was no sufficient solution of the ills of the time anyway. He saved the gold standard, but his unwillingness to promise anybody anything, while magnificent, was certainly not good politics, and at last the unbending President stood alone.

FAILURE OF A CRUSADE, 1896

The Republicans: Hanna and McKinley

Both of the major parties contained members infected with the silver virus, but the Republicans were more strongly anchored in financial conservatism. In the Congressional elections of 1894 they had been the chief political beneficiaries of the dissatisfaction with the administration, and their course in 1896 was plotted by the astute Marcus A. Hanna of Cleveland. Now in his late fifties, Hanna held no public office but he had long been a power in Republican circles and he personified the alliance between business and politics. He rose to wealth in the coal and iron, banking, and street-railway businesses; and, clearly perceiving the interrelations between government and business, he turned to politics, for which he had extraordinary talent. He believed that all other groups in the nation would prosper if business did, and he regarded protective tariffs and a stable monetary system based on gold as essential. He was more farsighted than many industrial leaders of his day in his attitude toward labor, condemning employers who would not meet employees half way in negotiation and regarding reasonable treatment as the best security for industrial peace. Not the least of his services to his party was the reconciling of labor groups to it, by convincing them that their well-being was contingent on the prosperity of business, and by associating the "full dinner pail" with high protective tariffs. This is one explanation of the resistance of labor to the blandishments of the agrarian inflationists.

Hanna's chosen instrument was William McKinley, who, in his opinion, best exemplified the virtues of sound Republicanism and to whom he was personally devoted. McKinley, who emerged from the war as a major, had a business background, but early in his career as a lawyer he attracted attention by defending and gaining the acquittal of strikers who had been jailed in Canton, Ohio, where he lived. On this occasion he opposed Hanna's own firm, and neither Hanna nor labor ever forgot the episode. Elected to Congress thereafter, McKinley made a special study of the tariff and as chairman of the Ways and Means Committee was the person most responsible for the Tariff of 1890. As a protectionist, he was notably consistent and thoroughgoing. He spread the mantle of protection over the widest possible area, trying to give something to everybody, and he impressed his contemporaries as being not only amiable but fair-minded. Following the reaction against the tariff that bore McKinley's name, Hanna guided his successful candidacy for the governorship of Ohio and afterwards rescued him from personal disaster when he fell into financial difficulties. Hanna organized McKinley's candidacy for the Republican presidential nomination so skillfully that he got it on the first ballot. The vice-presidential nomination went to Garret A. Hobart of New Jersey, a businessman who had become a power in local politics and was an unwavering supporter of the gold standard.

McKinley himself had voted for both the Bland-Allison Act and the Silver Purchase Act and was regarded as a bimetalist. He did not expect the currency issue to dominate the campaign and preferred to emphasize the tariff. The party declaration of allegiance to the policy of protection as "the bulwark of American industrial independence and the foundation of American development and prosperity" fully accorded with his convictions. He believed, as the platform stated, that this policy put the burden of revenue on foreign goods, while securing the domestic market for the American producer and upholding the American standard of wages. On the currency question the Republicans, who met in advance of the Democrats, went on record as unreservedly supporting "sound money" and unalterably opposing any debasement of the currency. The platform said: "We are therefore opposed to the free coinage of silver, except by international agreement with the leading commercial nations of the earth, which agreement we pledge ourselves to promote, and until such agreement can be obtained the existing gold standard must be maintained." The bimetalist gesture enabled McKinley to save face and it was designed to reduce the loss of Western votes.

There was no doubt that the campaign would be well managed on the Republican side, for Mark Hanna stepped into the chairmanship of the National Committee. He proceeded to raise an unprecedented campaign fund of $3.5 million by a process that he called "frying the fat out of the rich," and he illustrated the virtues of gold by distributing it lavishly. The representations of Hanna by hostile cartoonists from this time onward as a bloated plutocrat made him a symbol of all that sensitive citizens feared and hated in the rule of Big Business.

Bryan and the Democrats

The Republican monetary plank lost the party a group of Western Silver Republicans, led by Senator Henry M. Teller of Colorado. The Democratic National Convention in Chicago in July offered a startling contrast to the adroitly managed Republican assembly. It was one of the most dramatic national conventions in American history. Rebels against Cleveland were in control and the administration was completely repudiated in the platform. This condemned the bond issues and the "trafficking with banking syndicates" to their enormous profit, and it objected to "government by injunction." It condemned trusts and pools and called for effective regulation of railroads. It denounced the Republican policy of protection and approved a tariff for revenue, while disapproving the action of the Supreme Court in invalidating the income tax. But the Democrats minimized the tariff issue and placed first emphasis on the money question. They denounced "gold monometalism" as a British policy, not only un-American but anti-American. The convention demanded the free and unlimited coinage of both silver and gold at the ratio of 16 to 1 "without waiting for the aid or consent of any other nation." This plank was adopted after the delegates had been excited almost to hysteria by the oratory of William Jennings Bryan, whom they promptly nominated for the presidency.

Bryan, who was thus catapulted to fame at the age of thirty-six, was a native of Illinois now living in Lincoln, Nebraska. His national public service had been limited to two terms as a Representative in Congress and he had failed of election to the Senate in 1894. What prominence he gained in Washington was owing to his advocacy of silver. On March 5, 1895, immediately after the expiration of his Congressional term, he and Richard P. Bland of Missouri drew up "An Appeal to the Silver Democrats" which was signed by a considerable number of Representatives. Some of the phrases of this document reappeared in the platform of 1896. Meanwhile, he gained wide renown as an orator on the Chautauqua circuit. His appeal was to the ear and heart, not to the mind; his own intellectual limitations are suggested by the enthusiastic approval he gave to the fallacious logic of *Coin's Financial School*. A devout man, he translated the currency question into purely moral terms and set these forth in the spirit and manner of a religious revivalist. The people listened gladly to his rich, strong voice and warmed to his humanity.

Bryan had little interest in the tariff and was not disposed to engage in what he regarded as a minor conflict on McKinley's chosen ground. He challenged the Republicans to a battle between gold and silver. In the familiar peroration of his speech at the convention he said: "You shall not press down upon the brow of labor this crown of thorns, you shall not crucify mankind upon a cross of gold." In the manner of the Populists he defined labor as all the "producing masses," but his heart was with the sons of the soil rather than with factory workers. Indeed, his speech contained the concept of agrarian primacy that was as old as Jefferson: "Burn down your cities and leave our farms, and your cities will spring up again as if by magic; but destroy our farms and the grass will grow in the streets of every city in the country." To him the chief enemies were the "idle hoarders of idle capital," and quite obviously he spoke for country against city. He detested Big Business, but used the American idiom, not foreign terms, speaking for a people who hungered for a better share in the opportunities and fruits of a business civilization.

Eastern Democrats who were conservative on the currency question were swept aside by these powerful currents of emotion. A group of "Gold Democrats" in a later convention nominated John M. Palmer of Illinois for President and Simon B. Buckner of Kentucky for Vice-President, but this ticket received only a small vote. Offsetting this defection was the endorsement of the regular Democratic candidates by a convention of Silver Republicans, and the nomination of Bryan by the Populist convention at St. Louis.

While the Populists had not succeeded in electing many of their candidates in the Congressional elections of 1894, the total vote cast for them was 1,500,000 and the party was far from impotent. Western Populists, who had grown accustomed to fusion with Democrats, were strongly for accepting Bryan, but Southern Populists, who had been fusing with Republicans and had suffered injuries at the hands of local Democratic organizations, were much more reluctant.

The Democratic platform included a number of characteristic Populist demands, but many feared that the Democrats would swallow up their party. A more immediate difficulty was raised by the presence on the ticket with Bryan of Arthur Sewall of Maine, who had been put there to balance it. He was favorable to free silver but as a banker and railroad director he was an offense to dyed-in-the-wool Populists. What finally happened was that the convention at St. Louis, after adopting a platform

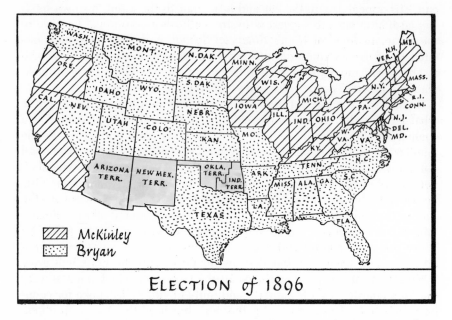

ELECTION of 1896

of its own, nominated Thomas E. Watson of Georgia for Vice-President
and then nominated Bryan for President. The situation was odd and
confusing, but the net result was that Bryan had all the Populists behind
him even if his running mate did not.

The Election

The presidential campaign abounded in contrasts and became one of
the most exciting on record. McKinley staged a front-porch campaign,
presenting an image of homely dignity as he received visitors, and wisely
refrained from competition with the oratory of Bryan. Mark Hanna was
more mobile and organized a vigorous counterattack. In this, the "Boy
Orator of the Platte," whom admirers called the "Great Commoner," was
designated by Republican campaigners as an anarchist and a revolution-
ist. Bryan traveled 18,000 miles in an unprecedented effort to carry his
gospel to every voter in the land. No other American voice had ever been
heard by so many people. His campaign elicited a great outpouring of
the traditional evangelical fervor of the countryside, and towards the end
of the campaign many Eastern businessmen became panicky. McKinley
reduced the abstruse economic doctrines of the gold standard to the
simple formula that it and Republican rule meant economic prosperity.
Businessmen enforced this by inserting in contracts clauses to annul them
in case of Bryan's election, and in workers' pay envelopes they enclosed
notice of dismissal in the same contingency.

The struggle for the labor vote was crucial. In 1896, labor was disposed to believe that tariff protection and the gold standard were conducive to general prosperity. The Depression had occurred after the Democrats had won the last election, and prosperity was at length beginning to return— seemingly as a result of the conservative policies of Cleveland whom the Democrats had repudiated in favor of wild experiments. Besides, the prestige of businessmen had not been sullied by publicity of abuses that later turned opinion strongly against them.

The outcome of the election was that McKinley got 271 electoral votes to Bryan's 176, the plurality of the former in the popular vote being about 570,000. The Republicans carried all the states north of the former Confederacy and east of the Mississippi. They also won Iowa, Minnesota, and North Dakota beyond that river and Oregon and California on the Pacific Coast. Bryan carried all the rest of the farming and mining states in the West and South in a solid block—from Virginia and down the coast, westward to the Plains and northward through the mountains to Puget Sound. He failed to win the electoral vote of a single state in which the industrial working class was important. Such a political alignment of sections according to agrarian-industrial antagonisms had never before and has never since been seen. The defeat of Bryan gave resounding proof that industrialism was in truth triumphant.

McKinley and the High Republicans, 1897-1900

Before President William McKinley reached the mid-point in the term to which he was elected in 1896, he was drawn into unexpected war with Spain, and this led to imperialistic ventures overseas such as that conservative gentleman had not dreamed of. His administration marked the beginning of a new era in the international affairs of the United States. In the domestic field, however, it represented the culmination of trends which had been pronounced for a generation. It marked the heyday of business government and may be termed the era of High Republicanism.

Mark Hanna, the engineer of the victory over the farmers and silverites who had challenged the supremacy of industry and finance, continued to symbolize the alliance between government and Big Business as he stood in 1897 at the peak of his career. He was offered the office of Postmaster General in the new Cabinet, from which he could have dispensed abundant political patronage, but this highly successful man of affairs preferred to go to the Senate. He was appointed to the seat vacated by John Sherman when that aged statesman accepted the Secretaryship of State, and soon he was regularly elected by the Ohio legislature. He was still the President's most intimate adviser, and in domestic matters he was recognized as the chief power behind the throne.

McKinley, who was fifty-four when inaugurated, looked like Napoleon, but in other respects this devout and kindly man did not at all resemble the imperious conqueror. Essentially he was a defender of the new industrial order. He was chiefly concerned to consolidate its position and that of the Republican Party. Unlike Cleveland, he was conciliatory in manner and recognized the exigencies of politics. Being thoroughly aware of the ways of Congress, he got on well with that body, which his party controlled comfortably in the House and less comfortably in the Senate—owing to the presence there of a number of "wild men" from the Western farming and silver states. He came into office at a propitious time, for the Depression had been weathered during the last year of Cleveland's presidency and times were getting better. He inherited a Treasury deficit, however, and he promptly called Congress into special session to consider the problem of revenue. The result was the Dingley Tariff, the purposes of which were to increase both protection and revenue. It was more successful in attaining the former than the latter, and the net result was a higher level of rates than in any previous measure.

Raising the Tariff

In domestic legislation the chief fruits of the Republican victory were the Dingley Tariff Act of 1897 and the Gold Standard Act of 1900. That these measures were adopted in that order, and that long apart, seems surprising, since the election had been fought on the currency question and the electorate had expressed itself unmistakably. The tariff issue had been overshadowed and the administration had no mandate from the people on it. But it came first in the mind of McKinley and he took it up at the first possible opportunity.

Flushed with their victory at the polls, the Republicans had no hesitancy in blaming the Depression on the policies of Cleveland, though it would have been fairer to charge it against the policies of the Harrison administration. To blame hard times on the Wilson-Gorman Tariff was absurd, since that was enacted after the Panic, and the economy had not yet had time to adjust itself to the minor changes in the protective system which this measure wrought. Modern students believe that the influence of the tariff on the economic cycle was much exaggerated by the politicians of this time. As things turned out, the Dingley Tariff was followed by a period of more general prosperity than Americans had enjoyed since the Civil War. It gained greater credit than it deserved and lasted longer than any of its predecessors.

It may be doubted if any considerable revision of the tariff was desirable in 1897 if one considers the interests of consumers and of the economy as a whole. Heightening the level and broadening the scope of protection, while increasing revenue, involved conflicts and contradictions. Rates can be so high that importation is discouraged and revenue from customs decreased, while favors granted one group of interests can neutralize these bestowed upon another.

These difficulties are well illustrated by the cases of wool and woolens. The Wilson-Gorman Tariff had put raw wool on the free list, but the Dingley Tariff reimposed duties on it. The action in 1897 was taken in the interest of wool-growers and was a political gesture to agricultural districts by a party which had been charged with being primarily concerned with industry. But free wool was to the advantage of manufacturers of woolens, who had to import much of their raw material. They successfully clamored for compensating increases in duties on woolens, so the prices consumers had to pay for cloth and clothing were pyramided. Similarly the duty on raw sugar was raised, chiefly for purposes of revenue, and the duties on refined sugar were advanced accordingly. No notable change was made in the existing duties on iron and steel. In this branch of industry American producers were fully capable of meeting foreign competition at home and even abroad.

American industry as a whole had now reached such a point of development that a general increase in protection was hard to justify on rational grounds, but among industrialists as a group there was a common desire to get the maximum of protection. The Republican Party of McKinley retained their support by trying to gratify as many of them as possible. The new rates, along with the flow of new gold into the currency and a new wave of industrial consolidations resulted in a rise in the prices of protected articles which fell at last on the consumers. Wages also rose, but not so fast. The protective system which the High Republicans were now extending offered no tangible benefits to the agricultural groups which had suffered most from the Depression—the wheat and cotton farmers who produced so largely for the foreign market. Their situation improved markedly in the next few years chiefly because of changes in the world situation.

In this phase, Republican protectionism was insular and directed to the domestic market, with relative indifference to world trade. It made, however, one gesture to the future. In the Dingley Act the reciprocity features of the McKinley Tariff Act of 1890 were renewed, with a view to the development of trade with Latin America.

Settling the Money Question

McKinley believed the money question required cautious handling in view of the passions which had been generated by Bryan's campaign and the inflationist tendencies which persisted among Western Republicans. Availing himself of the platform promise to promote international agreement on the free coinage of silver, the President sent a commission to Great Britain to investigate the possibilities. This action dramatized what everyone knew: that the leading powers had no interest in a silver or a bimetallic standard, and that silver was supported only by such producing countries as Mexico and China, which had even less influence on world policy than the bloc of Congressmen from silver-mining states had within the United States. The truth was that in the emergent era of finance capitalism, when bankers were displacing industrialists as the most influential group in every industrialized nation, the creditors' interest in "dear" money, whose purchasing power would be proof against inflationary floods of silver, was bound to prevail. At the same time it happened that new gold from Alaska and South Africa relieved the currency shortage enough to moderate the passions of the farmer-inflationists.

When these factors had all matured, the Gold Standard Act was passed in 1900. It resolved the questions of the status of silver, the ratio between it and gold, and the redeemability of paper money and bonds by declaring that gold and gold alone was the standard of value for all currency. Its value was defined simply in terms of quantity: a dollar, the law determined, was 25.8 grains of gold of a purity nine-tenths fine, and this unit was the standard controlling all other monetary units. To assure the redemption of national paper money in this medium, a special fund of $150 million in gold was set aside in the vaults of the Treasury. Knowledge of its existence reassured the public and made calls on it insignificant.

The law made a gesture to agrarians who were crying for more currency: it authorized the chartering, in towns with fewer than 3000 people, of national banks with smaller capital than was ordinarily required. Since national banks were entitled to issue paper money to an amount exceeding their capital, the law permitted a token quantity of inflation in the farm districts. Silver interests were similarly granted a token by the mint's coinage of some of the metal into impressive dollars as well as lesser coins. The "cartwheels" circulated in the West where they pleased local fancy, as they do to this day.

No real inflation was permitted. The new gold supplies only partially closed the gap between increasing production and the currency supply. But the farmers' share in the general rise in prosperity was sufficient to make the extreme inflationary program of 1896 moribund as a political issue.

The Gold Standard Act of 1900 symbolized the end of the Populist Revolt. But other items of the Populist program showed a remarkable vitality. The McKinley administration pushed them aside, but after the dawn of the new century progressive men revived demands which the Populists had made and which the silver issue had overshadowed—for railroad regulation, the direct election of United States Senators, a federal income tax, and other reforms which are now so old that we take them for granted. The "wild men" of the Western plains and Southern farms left a rich heritage to the nation.

CHAPTER 10

The Beginnings of
Critical Realism

IN THE LAST QUARTER OF THE NINETEENTH CENTURY
a new ferment began to work in most areas of American intellectual and
artistic life. The term "critical realism" is a convenient designation of this
new movement. It was critical inasmuch as it subjected existing beliefs,
forms, and methods to searching analysis. It was realistic because it
denied all tests of truth except those based on objective facts, and all
tests of value except those bearing on the purposes of human beings.

For a few years historians, economists, philosophers, novelists, and
artists assured the country and the world that facts proved the American
millionaire to be the best type of human being, and the system which enabled him to make his millions to be the best type of social, economic,
and political organization. Almost immediately this conclusion was attacked by critics who asserted that the facts proved no such thing; rather
they proved that other goals than money-making and other values than
money expressed the true nature and destiny of man. Since both groups
appealed to verifiable facts, rather than to inherited dogmas or subjective
ideals, this struggle for men's minds was the first completely "modern"
episode in American cultural history. In this sense the beginnings of critical realism may be regarded as the beginning of our own time.

THOUGHT: FROM SOCIAL DARWINISM TO PRAGMATISM

The evolutionary hypothesis was so attractive that thinkers extended
it beyond the field of biological organism. They used it to explain the history of human society, though nothing in the original Darwinist conception justified any identity between organic evolution and social history.
In Social Darwinism the theory of evolution was popularized and dis-
torted.

Social Darwinism

Darwin himself had been influenced by current economic and political doctrines of free competition and laissez faire. Later biologists pointed out that co-operation among members of particular animal species is fully as important as competition, which prevails chiefly between different species. But in the meantime social philosophers, economists, and political scientists greeted with fervent admiration Darwin's emphasis on competition among animals as the way of progress and appropriated it as a scientific sanction of business competition and the noninterference of government in the economic system. The Englishman Herbert Spencer was the greatest of the Social Darwinists. Beginning in 1864, he set forth his "synthetic philosophy" in many volumes. His books had large sales in the United States. In 1882 he enjoyed a tremendous personal success in a tour of the country. It was climaxed by a banquet in his honor at Delmonico's in New York which a remarkable group of outstanding Americans attended. At this banquet Spencer was called the greatest thinker of all time, and Henry Ward Beecher said that he expected to meet him again in heaven as the final proof of the survival of the fittest.

Spencer's synthesis embraced man's past, present, and future history. He asserted that this history illustrated evolutionary progress towards perfection, but that this progress took place only when "fit" men were left utterly free to overcome the "unfit." The accumulation of wealth or attainment of power and success proved "fitness," while disease, poverty, and failure to gain improved status in society were evidence of "unfitness." It followed that governmental measures to protect the weak against the strong, the poor against the rich, the defeated against the successful were violations of "scientific law" and impediments to progress. Men were born unequal, and any attempt to equalize them by means of "artificial" man-made legislation was contrary to the laws of nature. Spencer's logic carried him even to the point of opposing such governmental interference with the processes of natural selection as free public schools and measures against the spread of contagious disease.

American industrialists, led by Andrew Carnegie, hailed this doctrine as ultimate truth. They supported the untrammeled right of the strong to dominate the weak even to the point of justifying industrial monopolists who *eliminated* competition. Yet they were not opposed to governmental interference in the economic system that favored themselves. Examples of this were protective tariffs and laws of inheritance which guarded the descendants of millionaires against the test of their capacity to survive in a genuinely competitive system.

More consistent was the American academic disciple of Spencer, William Graham Sumner of Yale University. He lectured and wrote against tariff protectionists as well as against humanitarian reformers. He championed, not the poorest classes, who were unfit, nor even the wealthiest classes, who used government to protect themselves against genuine individualism and competition, but rather the "forgotten man" of the middle class who relied on his own ability and hard work without governmental help of any kind. Sumner's greatest contribution was his sociological study of "folkways," demonstrating that human values and institutions are relative to time and place. He argued that the mores of a people are subject to slow evolutionary change but beyond the reach of legislative reform.

John Fiske popularized Social Darwinism in numerous historical works, essays, and lectures. Before George Bancroft had finished his *History of the United States* in 1876, proving that Divine Providence had sponsored the American nation, Fiske had begun to publish studies of early American history, seeking to prove that the nation was a natural result of the operation of Darwinian laws. The "fittest" nations survived the international struggle just as the "fittest" individuals survived the struggle within a nation. This doctrine gave new prestige to racism. Along with Fiske in developing the racial interpretation of American history were the Reverend Josiah Strong, the historian Herbert Baxter Adams of the Johns Hopkins University, and John W. Burgess, founder of the graduate Faculty of Political Science at Columbia University. With like-minded scholars in England and Germany, they taught that the "Teutonic" race was superior to all others. This superior stock carried its institutions from the forests of Germany successively to Great Britain, to the English colonies, and to the American West. These men decried as softness, which was likely to cause degeneration of the race, any humanitarian scruples with respect to weaker races. Social Darwinism provided a supposedly scientific sanction for American as well as for British and German imperialism during the last years of the century.

A generation of historians and publicists fixed these ideas as accepted truth for most Americans, though there was no genuinely scientific basis for them. By arguing that might made right, the conservatives and imperialists opened the door to the possibility that their opponents would prove themselves right by becoming more powerful. Lester F. Ward laid the intellectual groundwork for the overthrow of Spencer, Sumner, and their school in his book, *Dynamic Sociology* (1882). Ward was self-educated and not impressed by academic prestige. He worked for many years as a government official and was not averse to governmental regulation of economic affairs. His central idea was that human intelligence, human will, and human ideals are themselves facts of history capable of influencing social evolution to whatever extent men determine to use them. He declared that the fallacy of the Spencers and the Sumners lay in restricting evolutionary influence to genetic phenomena which lie outside human purpose. He asserted the importance of telic phenomena which are controlled by human purpose. If the competitive and laissez-faire economic systems frustrated human progress, as Ward believed they did, they were themselves products of human will and planning and could be modified by human will and planning through the agency of government. Ward's ideas made headway slowly, but in 1906 he was elected the first president of the American Sociological Society and appointed professor at Brown University. The next generation of sociologists worked in the light of Ward's restoration of man as the measure of all things.

New theories in economics which destroyed the hold of classical economic theory by overthrowing its Darwinian rationalization also got under way, but they lacked a leader of Ward's caliber until the twentieth century. Meanwhile, leading exponents of laissez-faire theory pointed out that free competition was actually being destroyed by the monopolists who were loudest in condemning any government intervention harmful to themselves. John Bates Clark of Columbia University, although a classicist in economics, taught that genuine competition could be restored only by government intervention against monopolies. At the same time the foundation of classical economic theory, which Adam Smith had asserted to be natural law and valid for all societies and all times, was undermined by the evolutionary concept that different times and different societies have different needs. This way of thinking led to the view that economic "law" is relative and subject to human will and purpose.

It became important in America with the return of a number of young economists who had studied in German universities and adopted the historical approach. Outstanding among them were Richard T. Ely of the Johns Hopkins University and the University of Wisconsin, who taught that Christian ethics should influence economic activity, and Simon Nelson Patten of the University of Pennsylvania, who held that laissez-faire principles had been suitable to the era of economic scarcity but were not appropriate to the age of abundance which the revolution in production now brought into sight. These and other evolutionary economists founded the American Economic Association in 1885. They formulated principles which condemned laissez faire as "unsafe in politics and unsound in morals," and approved positive action by government as an indispensable condition of progress. By the end of the century an original American school of economics had emerged with Thorstein Veblen as its leader, research into the facts of economic behavior as its chief activity, and reformist legislation designed to humanize the economy as its aim.

Outside academic halls the radical doctrines of Edward Bellamy and Henry George also claimed to find their sanction in scientific evolution. But the influence of *Looking Backward* and *Progress and Poverty* was not so important in making their respective utopias attractive to Americans as in making the current practices of capitalists unpopular. In their scathing criticisms of the unregulated capitalist system they appealed to moral values rather than economic theory, and on this level Bellamy and George were very influential. They supplemented the work of the academic economists in creating a new public opinion ready for governmental regulation of the economic system. Orthodox Marxist economic theory, on the other hand, had practically no influence in the United States, alone among the industrial nations of the world.

William James and Pragmatism

In the allied areas of psychology and philosophy there appeared one of the most brilliant thinkers America has produced, William James, brother of the distinguished novelist Henry James. Their father, Henry James, Senior, had lived an experimental life on the income of a family fortune gained in the region of Albany, New York. He had extraordinary religious experiences, adopted unorthodox—chiefly Swedenborgian— ideas, wrote voluminously, associated with the Transcendentalists, and created a family atmosphere of daring intellectuality that more than compensated for the irregular schooling his children received in Europe and this country. William overcame early nervous ailments, tried painting but gave it up in favor of medicine, taught physiology at Harvard and in 1880 transferred to its Department of Philosophy. Taking the Darwinian idea that mind is an instrument of survival, he explored its consequences in some of the first laboratory experiments in psychology.

These experiments did not lead James to a reductionist or behaviorist view of man as nothing but the most complicated of the animals. In his great *Principles of Psychology* (1890) he showed that man's mind is not only an instrument enabling him to adjust to his environment, as in the case of the other animals, but also an instrument capable of transforming his environment. Therefore man was far more than a bundle of mechanical reflexes. James emphasized the capacity of man to exercise free initiative and spontaneously to introduce novelty into the evolutionary process. He rejected the materialism of Social Darwinism, and even the traditional rationalism of British philosophy which left too little room for free will, emotion, and ethical idealism. On the other hand, he rejected the metaphysical idealism of German philosophy. Ideas are true, according to James, only as they are proved to work when carried into practice. In a series of very readable essays and books he built the system of pragmatism on suggestions first advanced by his Harvard colleague, Charles Sanders Peirce.

In lectures and papers, Peirce explored the implications of the experimental method of science for the traditional concepts of philosophy. Though much influenced by Darwinism, he rejected mechanistic notions and asserted the creative roles of chance and of human emotions and thoughts in evolution. Truth he saw not as eternal but as itself a product of evolutionary development. Ideas should be judged "true" accordingly as they stand the test of action, and rejected for better ones as experience dictates. In just this way the scientist submits his hypotheses to experimental test. Pragmatism, as Peirce called his philosophy, virtually eliminated metaphysics and substituted scientific methodology. His disciple, William James developed the new philosophy and made it popular during the next generation.

Critics declared that pragmatism was not a philosophy but a way of doing without one, and that the equating of truth with workability reflected the American temper of excessive practicality. But James by no means ruled out spiritual values. He advocated faith so strongly that he was accused of arguing that any belief that makes a person feel happy is thereby proved to be sound.

His grace of style and personality helped to make him more influential than any American thinker except Emerson. Like Emerson he gave new scope and validity to man's most generous and creative impulses, while substituting the modern objective experimental method of science for Emerson's romantic and subjective intuition. Pragmatism was an original American contribution to philosophy, and its marriage of ethical idealism to utilitarianism and science was a significant reflection of American experience. In the early decades of the twentieth century it was less important as an influence on philosophers than on leaders of thought in "practical" fields such as law and economics. It released them from the necessity to conform to absolutist systems and encouraged them to become creative relativists. James had not identified himself with reformers, but in the hands of his greatest successor, John Dewey, pragmatism became a doctrine of reform in many fields and completely destroyed the intellectual standing of conservative Social Darwinism.

Interpretations of American History

While William James was doing this work in philosophy, Frederick Jackson Turner made a notable contribution to the interpretation of American history. He opposed a western environmentalism to the prevailing idea that American institutions were derived from Europe by racial heredity. Himself a son of the frontier who grew up in a Wisconsin fur-trading town, he had observed the evolution of society from near-barbarism to civilization. He reacted against the Teutonic-heredity theory of American history which Herbert Baxter Adams taught him at the Johns Hopkins University. Returning to Wisconsin to teach in its state university, he made the study of frontier expansion his special interest, and in 1893 published his revolutionary essay, "The Significance of the Frontier in American History."

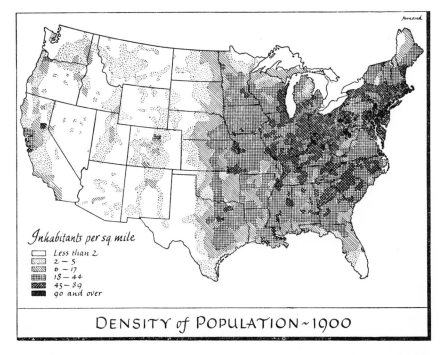

DENSITY of POPULATION ~ 1900

Inhabitants per sq. mile
- Less than 2
- 2 — 5
- 6 — 17
- 18 — 44
- 45 — 89
- 90 and over

In this he declared that not the inheritance from the East but the environment of the West determined the development of American democracy, individualism, and nationalism. At the successive stages of the frontier, defined as the "hither edge of free land," men discarded their civilized trappings and recapitulated the history of civilization from nomadry through stages of cattle droving, subsistence farming, market farming, and urbanism. The unique American fact of virtually free land for all comers, along with the rough equality of the settlers and their dependence on their own efforts, conditioned the uniquely American developments in human type and character, social customs, and political institutions. Turner's formulation of the frontier hypothesis was extreme, and it has been considerably modified by scholars in recent years, but it superseded the conservative Social Darwinist interpretation, opened up fruitful new fields of research, and gave new prestige to the men of the axe and the plow as makers of America.

More conventional American history was written by James Ford Rhodes, whose multivolume history of the United States since 1850 (1893-1906), though more understanding of the South than most previous Northern works, tended to prove that morality was on the Union side in the Civil War. John Bach McMaster in an equally detailed work paid little attention to philosophy or partisan claims but pioneered in the exploration of the social lives of the people as the most important stuff of history.

One of the most brilliant of all American historians, Henry Adams, was an evolutionist who could not sympathize with any variety of optimism. In 1889-1891 he published his great nine-volume *History of the United States During the Administrations of Jefferson and Madison.* Unable to reconcile himself to the fall of his family from political favor during the decades when a vulgar plutocracy displaced the old aristocracies of talent and genteel wealth, and shattered by the suicide of his wife, Adams gave up the conventional historian's career and occupied himself with study, observation, and speculation. He was one of the few great American examples of the intellectual who functions by virtue of inherited wealth without commitment to any faction or institution. Deeply impressed by the evolutionary hypothesis and also by current developments in physics, he tried to join the two in a comprehensive interpretation of history. The energy of coal and the machine symbolized by the electric dynamo seemed to him to control modern man as the energy of religious faith and the symbol of the Virgin Mary had controlled medieval man. He saw the American Republic as evolving towards the ruin of the Fathers' dream according to the second law of thermodynamics, the degradation of energy. His autobiography, *The Education of Henry Adams* (1907) was circulated during his lifetime only among a few friends, but it is now recognized as one of the notable productions of American thought and literature. He was the prototype of that talented group of modern American intellectuals whose criticism of their country has ended in despair.

A QUARTER-CENTURY OF LITERATURE

Henry Adams missed the main road of American cultural development. Most talented literary artists of the late nineteenth century rejected the exhausted genteelism of earlier decades, the optimistic determinism of the conservative Social Darwinists, and Adams's pessimistic determinism. Like the reformers in politics, they had a long struggle against formidable entrenched interests and were often defeated.

Regional Writers

The first attempt to escape the aridities of gentility in literature took the form of a modest regionalism. Emily Dickinson (1830-1886) spent her life in obscurity in Amherst, Massachusetts, and published only two of her poems. Dressed always in white, seemingly no more than a spinster touched with queerness like many others in New England, she cultivated her garden and avoided the society of the lively college town. But she left behind her a mass of lyric poems whose publication has won her a place among the great spirits and voices of New England. She combined the Puritan's intimacy with Divinity with sharpness of wit solidly founded on perception of inconsistencies between actualities and possibilites—her own and humanity's. At a time when most poetry was sodden with pseudo-romance, her lyrics were miracles of genuine emotion, observed by a superior intellect, and dealt out in eccentric verse forms and spare language full of the peculiar New England pith. Only that region could have produced her, but her genius transcended ordinary parochialisms. Almost as successful in avoiding the regionalist's danger of provincialism was Sarah Orne Jewett, who explored in short fiction the qualities of life and character in rural New England. Her *Country of the Pointed Firs* (1896) is a prose masterpiece of genre painting.

The South produced a group of writers who restored that section to its ancient standing alongside New England as the home of talent. Sidney Lanier was the greatest of them. He wrote accounts of critical explorations of the relations between poetry and music for which he may be remembered longer than for his own best verse, in which he celebrated the landscape of his native Georgia. In his poetry he also broached a theme which has since been central in Southern writing of world significance, the conflict between the ante-bellum ideal of a gentle agrarian civilization and the materialistic urban standards which were now invading the South in force. Lesser writers merely sentimentalized the Old South. Led by Thomas Nelson Page and gaining great popularity in the North, they fixed on the nation an enduring image of beneficent plantation life—of moonlight and magnolias, gallant masters, beautiful ladies, jolly mammies, and dancing pickaninnies. Joel Chandler Harris in his Uncle Remus stories conveyed a deeper reality in Negro fables, and George Washington Cable wrote effectively of the fascinating life of New Orleans in *The Grandissimes* (1880) and other novels.

Midwestern regionalism flowered somewhat later, but its future was foreshadowed in Edward Eggleston's *Hoosier Schoolmaster* (1871), E. W. Howe's *Story of a Country Town* (1883), and Joseph Kirkland's *Zury* (1887). Indianapolis was outstanding as a local center—cultivating the literary, theatrical, and forensic interests out of which a notable generation of writers and statesmen would grow. Chicago suddenly became aware that world preeminence in meat-packing was not enough to command the respect of outsiders or even maintain the loyalty of the women-folk and children of the first millionaires. In the eighties and nineties a determined group of Chicagoans set out to master literature and the arts. This "upward movement," besides furthering many mistaken and incongruous activities, had something to do with the emergence of Chicago as the cultural capital of the Middle West. San Francisco less self-consciously developed talents that brought it fame as the center of civilization in the Far West. Among the earliest of the literary men of this region were Bret Harte, whose *The Luck of Roaring Camp* (1870) exploited the picturesque crudities of the wild days scarcely gone, and Joaquin Miller, whose *Songs of the Sierras* (1871) romanticized the primitive in nature.

Mark Twain

Only one writer of this period was great enough to use regional materials for work of the first rank. Samuel Langhorne Clemens, who took the pen-name Mark Twain, was a product of frontier Missouri. As a young man he roamed the whole Union as a journeyman printer in the East, a pilot on steamboats down the Mississippi River to New Orleans, and a prospector and reporter in Nevada and California. Though he settled at Hartford, Connecticut, in 1871; he remained a Westerner whose most natural medium was the humorous exaggeration of the frontier. He developed a literary style that substituted for the prevailing code of genteel usage the vocabularies and rhythms of the daily speech of the Mississippi Valley. He transformed the tall tale of folklore into telling satire of humbug, and the spoken American variation of the English language into a magnificent written instrument.

After winning applause with a funny story, "The Celebrated Jumping Frog of Calaveras County" (1867), he made a national reputation with *The Innocents Abroad* (1869). This consisted of travel sketches of the Mediterranean countries, and its joke lay in the contrast between American practicality and modernity and Old World backwardness and superstition. This brash way of exorcising fear of cultural inferiority is not as attractive to readers today as it was in Mark Twain's time. He perpetrated the same joke again and again, most notably in the time-fantasy, *A Connecticut Yankee at King Arthur's Court* (1889). His best work dealt with the America he knew: small-town boyhood in *The Adventures of Tom Sawyer* (1876), his experiences as a pilot in *Life on the Mississippi* (1883), and *The Adventures of Huckleberry Finn* (1884). The last is a masterpiece of living prose, fascinating as a realistic narrative of rafting down the Mississippi and profound in its recognition of the honest values of the social outcasts—Huckleberry and his friend the escaped slave, Old Jim. The great river, flowing without beginning or end and giving them security, is a symbol of nature as the restorative of moral health. The life that transpires on its bank, marvellously satirized by Twain, becomes a series of symbols of fraud, as in the Fugitive Slave Act which made it an act of virtue to destroy a man's freedom. Aunt Sally pursued Huckleberry down the river with the sincere desire to rescue him for his own good. His last words were: "But I reckon I got to light out for the Territory ahead of the rest, because Aunt Sally she's going to adopt me and sivilize me, and I can't stand it. I been there before."

During his later years Mark Twain enjoyed perennial success as a lecturer, so well loved as a funny man that his mere step onto a stage loosed the laughter. Oxford University recognized his un-English genius with an honorary degree. But in his later writings, by giving open expression to his pessimism, attacking religion, organized society, and humanity itself as hopeless, Mark Twain yielded his power as an artist in favor of second-rate preaching. The aridity and despair of his last years have puzzled critics. Some have asserted that he traded Western strength for Eastern refinement because of his wife's demand for respectability, while others have declared that industrialism frustrated his frontier-agrarian spirit by making it irrelevant. Yet *Huckleberry Finn* is the only nineteenth-century book that Americans of all degrees of cultivation continue to read and love, and it is also an ancestor of the prevailing twentieth-century American prose style.

Henry James

It would be hard to imagine how a contemporary writer could differ from Mark Twain more than Henry James. The increasing diversity of American life was well exemplified by these two. The brother of William James remarked that he belonged to no country but the James family. He spent his boyhood chiefly in New York City and France but formed tenuous ties with New England and settled in London in 1876, finally becoming a British subject as a gesture of identification with the British cause in the First World War. He abandoned America, as he explained, because of its thinness of social texture. This he attributed to the lack of the military caste, diplomats, clergy, scholars, artists, and aristocracy which in an Old World society provided essential ore for the novelist. He elaborated his prose style steadily in the direction of obscurity. Few Americans of his time understood or appreciated him, but modern critics find in him the greatest explorer of the social, psychological, and moral significances of the American face to face with the European.

His earliest novels, *The Americans* (1877), *The Europeans* (1878), *Daisy Miller* (1879), portrayed in fairly simple terms the contrast between naïve but well-intentioned Americans and sophisticated but morally equivocal Europeans. *Daisy Miller* brought him some popularity. In a second group of novels—notably *The Princess Casamassima* (1886) and *The Sacred Fount* (1901)—he explored the English society whose aristocracy he admired extravagantly even though he came to believe it morally decadent. Americans thought of him as a social climber, but his only ambitions were to observe and understand the upper social and artistic circles he frequented. He tried to win an audience as a playwright but failed. In his third period he was generally neglected, although *The*

Wings of the Dove (1902), *The Ambassadors* (1903) and *The Golden Bowl* (1904) are today regarded as supreme examples of the art of fiction. In them he returned to the international theme.

Henry James wrote in the genteel tradition but he was also a psychological realist. He had some mannerisms of the aesthetic and social snob, and he was incapable of moving with his times towards the vulgarities of naturalism, but he understood better than many naturalists the ordinary human values of democracy. At the same time he rejected totally the identification of democracy with commercialism towards which so many Americans were drifting.

William Dean Howells

Mark Twain and Henry James marked extreme poles of the American spirit. Between their positions and performing something of the function of a mediator was William Dean Howells, an Ohioan who became an Easterner. Successfully acclimatized in Boston, he moved to New York in 1889 when it became the cultural capital of the nation. As editor of the *Atlantic* during the seventies and of other magazines afterward, he was a friend, admirer, and adviser of both Mark Twain and Henry James, and encouraged the rise of realism in fiction. Of this his own work was the best example. The America he pictured in his long series of novels, most famously in *The Rise of Silas Lapham* (1885), was the America of the middle class. His art had the moral integrity of that class, and also its prudishness. He believed that American writers should "concern themselves with the more smiling aspects of life, which are the more American." But this view, which led to fatuousness in the work of lesser writers, did not deter Howells himself from facing honestly the evils of American industrialism in his later years. Awakened to their importance by the Haymarket Riot, he used his position as literary arbiter to defend economic radicalism, and he himself prophesied socialism in *A Traveler from Altruria* (1894). He lived to be eighty-three years old, witnessed the birth of a strange new era before he died in 1920, and was adulated as a literary patriarch. He gave a helping hand even to young men who overthrew the moderations of his own realism and introduced the radical school of naturalism.

Naturalism

Most Americans were repelled by European naturalism as typified by Émile Zola's studies of vice. Naturalism was based on a determinist and pessimistic interpretation of Darwin that strongly influenced the outstanding American novelists of the new generation. The Naturalists viewed human life as a complex of biological forces without individual free will, spiritual significance, or hope. While conservative Social Darwinists viewed with complacency the emergence of the millionaire out of the biological struggle, the Naturalists contemplated the inadequacies and defeats of the mass of human beings in the same struggle and despaired. They cared little for the formal problems of art and rejected devices of plot in favor of detailed documentation of material realities as if they were scientists rather than artists. Hamlin Garland initiated the new movement in *Main-Travelled Roads* (1891) and other books that repudiated the traditional idealization of the farmer's life and stressed the grimness of existence among the latest generation of pioneers.

Perhaps the greatest of the American Naturalists was the shortest-lived—Stephen Crane, who died at twenty-nine in 1900 after a life of high tension, little recognition, and extraordinary achievement. In his style of personal behavior as well as his prose he was an innovator of the "tough" manner that removed all traces of sentiment from the surface but created an undertone of tragedy. His first novel, *Maggie: A Girl of the Streets* (1892), a Zolaesque study, had to be published at his own expense. He did not pity Maggie openly, but he showed her degradation and suicide to be inexorable consequences of New York slum environment. In this book Darwinian determinism took the place of divinely ordered fate with an effect not unlike Greek tragedy. Crane's most astonishing feat was *The Red Badge of Courage* (1895), which won him some immediate and great posthumous fame. It was a simple story of a Union soldier in a battle of the Civil War. Crane had never seen war, but veterans declared that he alone among writers told the truth about it. There was no glory in his picture. The first of the modern "debunking" treatments, it described cowardice and courage not in moral but in psychological terms. He served as a reporter in the Spanish-American and Greco-Turkish wars, went to England to escape difficulties in the United States, and in his fatal struggle with tuberculosis was befriended by Henry James. Some of his short stories, particularly "The Blue Hotel," are masterpieces. Crane's predilection for violence, "scientific" a-morality, taut prose style, and startling imagery were all portents of twentieth-century American fiction.

THE ARTS, TO THE CHICAGO EXPOSITION

These decades produced comparable movements of revolt against the genteel in the visual arts. A group of young American painters who went to Paris to study after the Civil War shared the excitements of the overthrow of prettiness and sentimentality by Manet, Monet, Pissarro, Dégas, Cézanne, and the other great Impressionists whom Zola wished to be called Naturalists. James McNeill Whistler, born in Lowell, Massachusetts, and in his youth expelled from the United States Military

Academy, developed a highly individual impressionism which he preferred to practice in London rather than in America. He became a spectacular figure, an aesthete with a murderous wit full of contempt for the mass· of insensitive humanity. He was a striking example of the American expatriate of the time. His *Portrait of the Artist's Mother* has been embraced by popular American taste as a tribute to motherhood, but Whistler himself originally called it *Arrangement in Black and Grey.*

Mary Cassatt, the daughter of a wealthy Philadelphian, was the only American to exhibit in Paris with the Impressionists. She did all her work in France, specializing in mother-and-child subjects which looked unsentimental to her own generation. Others returned to America and reproduced the European rebellion against the conservatism which was sponsored in New York by the National Academy of Design. In 1877, they founded the Society of American Artists, but the greatest of them, Thomas Eakins, broke even with this organization when it rejected one of his works. Eakins combined a faithfulness to visual fact with a penetration of spiritual realities which made his *The Gross Clinic, The Swimming Hole,* and other canvases more significant than any formula.

Winslow Homer never studied abroad but he was influenced by the new currents to abandon the illustrations for *Harper's Weekly* and the anecdotal paintings of his earlier years in favor of more profound studies—especially of sailors, boats, and the sea. His conventional work was featured at the Philadelphia Centennial Exposition, but in his later years at Prout's Neck in Maine he developed a personal vision which he powerfully transferred to paper and canvas. Still more subjective was Albert Ryder, whose strange paintings attracted almost no attention while he lived as a recluse in New York City. After his death in 1917, post-Impressionist taste caught up with his *Moonlight at Sea, Macbeth and the Witches,* and *Death on a Pale Horse.*

With these and lesser painters American art escaped bondage to middle-class respectability and substituted honesty in expressing the artist's own understanding of reality. The same movement occurred in architecture, but this most social of the arts could not be cultivated so easily by advanced spirits for the appreciation of a few, and the revolutionary momement in architecture suffered a severe defeat at the end of the century at the hands of a countermovement of traditional taste.

Chicago after its great fire of 1871 offered opportunity for fresh attempts to solve the problem of building design for an industrial democracy, and for a few decades it was the laboratory in which modern architecture was born. An Easterner and the greatest of the users of a traditional style, Henry Hobson Richardson, gave the Chicago school lessons in the treatment of a building as a mass of spaces rather than a set of walls to be ornamented. He used the style of southern French Romanesque, but in his Trinity Church in Boston (1877), the houses of John Hay and Henry Adams in Washington, his railroad stations in New England, and the Marshall Field warehouse in Chicago he was more a creator than a copyist. The Romanesque Revival in lesser hands became no more than another imitation of European forms. Richardson, however, was groping towards the concept of functionalism before he died. Louis Sullivan of Chicago formulated its doctrine that form follows function.

The technological requirements and the economic opportunity for the skyscraper were now at hand, and Sullivan was the first to see that this unprecedented class of building called for revolutionary design. His Chicago Auditorium and Wainwright Building in St. Louis were notable for honesty of form and simplicity of ornament. The latter building, begun in 1890, was the first to depend totally on steel for support and to express this interior character in its exterior walls, which were simply curtains of glass with masonry grids hung on the steel skeleton. John W. Root, in his Monadnock Building, and other Chicago architects explored the possibilities of the skyscraper before it was carried very far in New York, its greatest future home. In Sullivan's Chicago office a young draftsman was Frank Lloyd Wright, who began as early as 1892 to apply to domestic architecture an imaginative fusion of human needs, natural materials, and open planning. This he called organic architecture.

The future of architecture lay with the logic of the Chicago skyscraper builders and the genius of Wright, but in 1892 the social, economic, and cultural influences that combined to produce the Chicago Columbian Exposition were not favorable to logic or genius. Reminiscences of Greece, Rome, and the Renaissance seemed to most Americans the essence of taste. The plaster classicism the architects imposed on the lakeside exposition city had dignity but lacked creativeness. Only Sullivan's Transportation Building suggested that industrialism might give birth to its own architecture. The rest of the "White City" was a dazzling display of irrelevant grandeur. The classical buildings of Washington had accustomed Americans to associate that style with noble emotions, and the Columbian Exposition stirred Westerners with the hope that their section might surpass the East and the Old World in culture. The outstanding American sculptor, Augustus Saint-Gaudens, whose own work achieved great power within traditional limits, believed that the artists who painted and molded plaster for the Chicago buildings made up the greatest such gathering since the fifteenth century. But Henry Adams understood better that the great electric dynamo inside one of the plaster temples was the real symbol of the new America.

Sullivan's statement that the Exposition was the single most disastrous event in the history of American architecture was borne out when it gave a new lease on life to classical façades, of which banks were now the chief beneficiaries, while the "Queen Anne" taste for little pillars and wooden towers controlled domestic building. Symptomatic of the temporary defeat of modernism in American Architecture was the fact that Frank Lloyd Wright gained his first general recognition in Europe. When the skyscrapers grew tall in New York, prevailing taste required that they be topped by incongruous classical cornices and colonnades or medieval turrets. The contradiction between new materials and functions and old styles was symptomatic of the fear of most Americans that industrialism was the enemy of culture, the conviction of the genteel that democracy was incurably vulgar, and the self-assurance of new millionaires that culture was an Old-World commodity that New-World money could buy as readily as they secured titled bridegrooms for their daughters.

The era ended in an appearance of victory for the conservatism that opposed all agrarian, labor, intellectual, literary, and artistic innovations. Middle-class respectability seemed as firmly enthroned in 1896 as in 1876 it had been in fact. But these twenty years had produced vital new ideas that were capable of renovating all areas of American life.

Part III

IMPERIALISM AND PROGRESSIVISM
1896-1917

CHAPTER 11

The Emergence of
an Imperial Power

In the second year of the presidency of McKinley, American public affairs took a surprising direction. The United States fought a war with Spain and emerged from it as a world power. Whereas the presidential election of 1896 had hinged on the monetary question, that of 1900 was fought on the issue of imperialism. The major contestants were the same—McKinley and Bryan—but the presence of Theodore Roosevelt as vice-presidential candidate on the successful Republican ticket signalized the rise of new forces. These were propelling into world affairs a nation which had long been absorbed in domestic matters and prided itself on its political isolation. McKinley, whose protective policy verged on economic isolationism, and who wanted to hold his government in the conservative groove which Republican Presidents had worn smooth since the Civil War, did not shape these fateful events; events took command of him.

Before this time the industrial development of the United States, its wealth and potential military strength, had made it fully capable of supporting the role of a world power. Beginning with the first administration of Cleveland, the Navy had rebuilt in modern form, and during the late eighties and the nineties a new spirit of expansionism arose. This cannot be attributed to businessmen, for generally they were not interested in an adventurous foreign policy. The Spanish-American War and the extension of American rule into the Pacific cannot be adequately explained on economic grounds.

It seemed to some observers that the United States stumbled unwittingly into an overseas empire. But enthusiastic imperialists asserted the right and duty of the Republic to range outside its own boundaries, protecting the innocent and punishing wrongdoers; and the idea of a

195

national mission to extend the influence of American institutions to less fortunate peoples seized the imagination of many citizens. Many others adhered stubbornly to the belief that force was not the proper method of extending American influence in the world, and that the conquest and government of other peoples violated the fundamental principle of the Declaration of Independence and would corrupt the springs of freedom in the United States itself. Most of the imperialists were Republicans and most of the anti-imperialists were Democrats, but for a few years the doubts of the latter were overborne and the country seemed fairly united in support of a grandiose new experiment. Afterwards, when the results of the new policy proved disappointing, the arguments of the anti-imperialists gained credit. As a world power the United States has played a steadily enlarging role, but in later years the country gladly renounced territorial ambitions.

THE NEW EXPANSIONISM: HAWAII

Americans had believed ever since the Revolution that their institutions were the best on earth, and some publicists had drawn the conclusion that this belief entitled the United States to expand its territory indefinitely. The phrase "Manifest Destiny," which had been coined in the period of Texan annexation and war with Mexico, was revived late in the century. This time it signified not only faith in the inevitable expansion of American institutions by virtue of their merit, but also faith in the inevitable rise of the Anglo-Saxon race to power over lesser peoples by virtue of its biological superiority.

According to Josiah Strong, Congregationalist minister and Social Darwinist, the Anglo-Saxon was commissioned by God to be his brother's keeper. Americans were denominated Anglo-Saxons despite the presence of new and old immigrants of many other stocks. The idea that the "fittest" nation was entitled to rule also pervaded the contemporary imperialist thought of Germany and Great Britain. The German militarists came nearest to identifying fitness with naked power. British imperialists pointed to the superiority of British justice, which was extended by them to subject peoples. In the United States there was greatly increased interest in sending Christian missionaries to "heathen" lands.

The makers and supporters of the imperialist policy were fervent nationalists. In one generation the Union had been consolidated in the fire of a great civil war; transportation and industry had built a national economy second to none. Fears that the nation's success might be compromised by labor discontent, economic setbacks, or political panaceas had all been triumphantly surmounted in 1896. The young men who were inspired by these triumphs were unwilling to stand pat on the old formula of high tariff, sound money, and isolation. They were modern

Hamiltonians who dreamed of a national government active in seeking opportunities to increase its power, prestige, and good deeds in the world. At home they admired Big Business because it made the nation wealthy and strong, but they did not hesitate to side against it in certain contests. Abroad they sought places where the flag might be planted for the greater glory of the nation.

Henry Cabot Lodge of Massachusetts, Theodore Roosevelt of New York, and Albert J. Beveridge of Indiana were outstanding exponents of the new nationalist ideal. They used the arguments of the naval historian Alfred Thayer Mahan to bolster their cause. He urged a great modern navy, bases in the Caribbean Sea and Pacific Ocean, and an American-controlled canal at the Isthmus. He predicted contests among the great powers for commerce and control of the seas, and between the West and the Orient besides. The United States could be sure of playing a successful part in these impending struggles only if it hastened to organize the elements of sea power.

Hawaii

Events in Hawaii provided a first test of these new tendencies in the last days of the Harrison administration. New England missionaries had gone to the islands as early as 1820, and Americans had long used Pearl Harbor as a whaling and shipping base. The Kamehameha line of kings organized an effective central government. Finding American advice more trustworthy than that of English, French, or German nationals, they favored the United States in 1875 with a trade reciprocity treaty, and in 1887 with permission to build a naval base at Pearl Harbor. The descendants of the New England missionaries and traders developed the islands' agriculture by means of sugar plantations. In 1887, they led a movement to reduce the power of King Kamehameha IV and gained control of the government by constitutional reforms. Queen Liliuokalani succeeded to the throne in 1891. Early in 1893, fearful of American influence, she revoked the reforms of 1887 and made herself dictator of a native-oriented regime.

These actions led to the overthrow of the Queen and the establishment of a provisional government. The United States Minister to Hawaii, John L. Stevens, an ardent annexationist, co-operated with the revolting American planters. He recognized the provisional government and caused United States Marines to be landed to protect it. The Queen claimed that she yielded to American force. Stevens acted without instructions from Washington; but, far from repudiating him, Secretary of State Blaine eagerly signed a treaty of annexation and submitted it to the Senate.

This was the situation when President Cleveland was inaugurated on

March 4. His moral scruples against the methods used by Stevens to secure annexation, and the general reluctance of the Democratic Party to support foreign adventures, led him to take the drastic step of withdrawing the treaty from the Senate while he investigated the events that led to its negotiation. Convinced that Stevens had acted improperly, Cleveland tried to secure restoration of the monarchy, but the planters proclaimed an independent republic with Sanford B. Dole as president, and denied the right of the United States to interfere. In August 1894, President Cleveland recognized the independent Republic of Hawaii, and so matters were left until the Republican Party returned to power in Washington in 1897.

McKinley was not interested in the extension of American influence in the Pacific, but he was induced to reverse Cleveland's Hawaiian policy. The local government was eager for annexation. Mahan pointed to Pearl Harbor as a crucial position in a struggle between East and West, and the restless young Theodore Roosevelt, now Assistant Secretary of the Navy, told Mahan that if he had his way he would hoist the Stars and Stripes over the islands immediately and leave the details for later. McKinley agreed to the negotiation of a new treaty of annexation in the spring of 1897. Japan thereupon protested.

This newcomer on the stage of world politics had demonstrated her surprising success in imitating Western industrialism and organization by defeating China in a short war in 1895. Her own imperialists feared that the annexation of Hawaii by the United States would endanger the rights of Japanese immigrants in Hawaii, who outnumbered the natives as well as the whites, and would disturb the international balance in the Pacific. While the State Department assured the Japanese government that annexation would not injure private Japanese rights in Hawaii, secret instructions to United States naval commanders ordered them to protect the islands in case of a resort to force. The Japanese government expressed its satisfaction with American assurances, but annexation was delayed until July 1898, during the Spanish-American War. By that time the value of the Islands to naval operations in the Pacific had become a matter of common knowledge and national patriotism was at fever pitch.

LATIN AMERICA AND THE MONROE DOCTRINE, 1890-1897

Physical expansion into the remote Pacific and the establishment of farflung naval outposts in those waters represented the triumph of a new school of thought. On the other hand, the policy of asserting leadership in Latin America went back to the time of Henry Clay and John Quincy Adams.

James G. Blaine, when serving briefly as Secretary of State in the

Garfield-Arthur administration, had planned an Inter-American Conference. Assuming this office again under Harrison, Blaine was able to carry out his deferred plan. The First Inter-American Conference met at Washington for six months in 1889-1890 with Santo Domingo the only absentee. Blaine hoped for a customs union, which would give manufacturers of the United States a preferred position in the Latin-American market, in return for the free entrance into the United States of tropical foods and raw materials—most of which it bought in Latin America anyway. But the Latin-American delegates, besides being reluctant to weaken established trade relations with European countries, were suspicious that the United States would make political use of the economic dependence of their countries on the northern giant, and they refused. Nor would they agree to set up machinery for the arbitration of disputes.

The only concrete result of this first conference was the Pan-American Union, a permanent agency with headquarters in Washington for the exchange and dissemination of information. In the course of time this Union accomplished a great deal, especially in the area of medical and agricultural improvement for Latin America, but at the outset the United States insisted that an American must head the organization, giving the Latin Americans another reason to distrust this country's intentions. The emergence of an overt American imperialist policy at the end of the decade confirmed their suspicions. It was a long generation before the United States demonstrated that its policy was genuinely internationalist and finally won the confidence of the governments to the south. Meanwhile, the system inaugurated by Blaine gave the Latin Americans a forum where they could air their grievances against imperialism and appeal to American public opinion.

Cleveland, in his second administration, made an extreme application of the Monroe Doctrine against Great Britain and asserted the guardianship of the Western Hemisphere in unparalleled language. This he did on the advice of his Secretary of State, Richard Olney. The occasion was an old boundary dispute between Venezuela and British Guiana which became more heated when gold was discovered in the disputed patch of jungle. When Britain withdrew an old offer to compromise, Venezuela broke relations with her and appealed to the United States. In 1887, Cleveland tendered the good offices of the United States, but the British government refused to arbitrate. In 1894, he renewed the offer and was again turned down. Suddenly, in July 1895, a note to Britain raised this minor issue to crisis proportions. The famous Olney Note declared that British pressure on Venezuela would be regarded by the United States as a violation of the Monroe Doctrine, and that Britain must accept the United States policy of settlement by arbitration. Olney included a superfluous and provocative passage obviously directed to American emotions more than to British consciences:

Today the United States is practically sovereign on this continent, and its fiat is law upon the subjects to which it confines its interposition . . . because, in addition to all other grounds, its infinite resources combined with its isolated position render it master of the situation and practically invulnerable as against any or all other powers.

This is the high-water mark of verbal assertiveness in American official declarations to foreign governments. The crude appeal to might as the source of imperial right instilled fear in Latin Americans even though for the moment Venezuela stood to gain by it. The Olney Note opened a new era of jingoistic imperialism in the foreign policy of the United States. That is should have issued from the Cleveland administration was ironic, but it gained him temporary popularity at home and diplomatic victory over the greatest of maritime powers.

Lord Salisbury, the Prime Minister and Foreign Secretary, replied in November 1895 that the Monroe Doctrine was not international law or applicable to the dispute, and he rejected the proposal of arbitration. President Cleveland then asked Congress to authorize a commission to investigate the facts of the boundary dispute and determine an equitable solution. Upon acceptance of a solution by the United States this country should enforce it against any British interference. At this moment the dangerous rivalry of the Germans with the British was dramatized by the Kruger Telegram (January 3, 1896) wherein the Kaiser in effect offered aid to the South African Boers against Britain. British leaders, reflecting on their friendless situation in international affairs, concluded that a quarrel with the United States over the minor Venezuela affair would be highly inexpedient. While some publicists spoke of war against the impudent Yankees, the Colonial Secretary, Joseph Chamberlain, led a countermovement to consolidate friendship with the United States.

Consequently, when the commission authorized by Congress went to work, the British government co-operated with it. In February 1897, the affair was settled in a treaty between Venezuela and Great Britain, signed in Washington and providing for arbitration under the good offices of the United States. A reasonable compromise settlement resulted. Leaders in both Britain and the United States subsequently prevented any other dispute from degenerating into mutual defiance, and worked assiduously to organize Anglo-American friendship on the basis of co-operation for mutual benefits. Thus the Venezuela Boundary Dispute proved to be a turning point. It inaugurated the era in which Anglo-American friendship has been a most important fact in world affairs.

THE CUBAN CRISIS, 1895-1898

Perennial Cuban hatred of Spanish rule burst out in rebellion in 1895. The rebels destroyed sugar plantations and mills, some of which were owned by Americans, hoping to induce intervention. Spanish counter-measures were more important in creating interventionist sentiment. General Valeriano Weyler, called "Butcher" in the American press, unable to cope with guerrillas, used the desperate policy of corraling the population in *reconcentrados*. These were prototypes of the infamous concentration camps of more recent times.

The horrors of Spanish policy lost nothing in the accounts of them in the rising "yellow press" of the United States. William Randolph Hearst's *New York Journal* and Joseph Pulitzer's *New York World*, then engaged in a war of their own to win circulation, were inventing new methods of sensation-mongering. Many Americans helped the cause of *Cuba Libre* with money. Filibustering expeditions were organized by rebel *juntas* on American soil. The administration observed rectitude in blocking these. Congress in the spring of 1896 passed resolutions favoring recognition by the United States of the belligerent rights of the rebels. Cleveland disregarded these but offered mediation, which Spain refused.

McKinley's early conduct was also characterized by moderation. This was matched by Spanish concessions to the Cuban rebels and seemed at first to presage a peaceful solution. Late in 1897 a new liberal ministry in Spain recalled "Butcher" Weyler, reduced the evils of the *reconcentrados*, and granted a degree of self-government to the Cubans. But when the Spaniards did not make news, Hearst and Pulitzer manufactured stories of atrocities and urged the expulsion of the cruel dons from the country's doorstep. Extremist Protestant clergymen preached reform of Catholic Cuba, the victim of a "new Spanish Inquisition." John Hay, friend of Theodore Roosevelt and Ambassador to Great Britain, believed that a war to free Cuba was necessary and righteous. Still McKinley held fast until two incidents inflamed the country.

In February 1898, Hearst's *New York Journal* published a private letter of the Spanish Minister to the United States, Enrique Dupuy de Lôme, which had been stolen by Cuban rebels. Writing to a friend, he described the President as "weak and a bidder for the admiration of the crowd, besides being a common politician (*policastro*) who tries to leave a door open behind himself while keeping on good terms with the jingoes of his party." In the nationalistic hysteria with which the jingo press greeted this insult, all sense of proportion went by the board and the country demanded punishment. De Lôme immediately resigned, but this did not placate the press.

Then into the boiling cauldron, on February 15, was thrown the news of the sinking in Havana harbor of the *Maine*, one of the great new battleships of the United States, with the loss of 260 members of her crew. The automatic conclusion of the yellow newspapers was that the Spanish government had struck against the ship which was supposed to protect American life and property. Few reflected that such an act by the hard-pressed Spanish government was highly implausible, or that there could have been an accidental explosion of the ship's magazines, or that Cuban rebels might have used this method of bringing about intervention on their side. Years later, when these alternatives were faced by calm minds, it was thought that the question could be answered by determining whether the explosions had occurred inside or outside the hull. Accordingly, the ship was raised to the surface for examination, but no clear conclusions were reached.

The cry in screaming headlines, REMEMBER THE MAINE! drowned out the President's injunction that judgment of guilt be reserved. Congress unanimously appropriated $50 million for defense. A hastily convened court of naval inquiry reported that it could not find evidence fixing responsibility. Senator Redfield Proctor of Vermont made a calm report of conditions in Cuba after a personal investigation, but the press seized upon the details of suffering inflicted on the Cubans by the Spaniards and ignored his plea for careful consideration of American policy. The public demanded action.

Still McKinley sought to bring the horrors in Cuba to an end by peaceful means. Late in March, while informing the Spanish government that the United States did not want the island, he proposed the abolition of the *reconcentrados* and an armistice between Spanish forces and rebels until October 1 for the negotiation of peace through his good offices. The Spanish government desperately shopped around for aid among the European powers, but the British government and people sided strongly with the United States and the continental governments were not disposed to incur American displeasure. Spain appeared to give in. On April 5 she agreed to abolish the *reconcentrados* and on April 9 to an armistice in Cuba. The latter information was delivered to President McKinley on April 10. But he had already prepared a message to Congress asking it to authorize the use of the forces of the United States to terminate the hostilities in Cuba and establish a stable government there. On April 11 he sent it.

Why had the President abandoned his antiwar policy at the moment when it seemed to be approaching success? The best explanation seems to be that the President yielded to the belligerent mood of the nation because he had become convinced that the Spanish, while agreeing to concessions, would never grant Cuba independence of their own accord, and that nothing less than independence would satisfy American opinion or meet the actual needs of the situation. McKinley spoke in "the name of humanity, in the name of civilization, in behalf of the endangered American interests." Lest the last phrase be misinterpreted, Congress added to the joint resolution of April 20, authorizing the President to use force to expel Spain from Cuba, the Teller Amendment promising that the United States would not annex the island but accord independence to its people. The war which was formally declared on April 25 resulted in the annexation of all the other American and Asian possessions of Spain, with Hawaii thrown in, but it began as an idealistic campaign to serve the cause of human freedom in unhappy Cuba.

THE SPANISH-AMERICAN WAR, 1898

The actual fighting between the sailors and soldiers of the United States and those of Spain was short and decisive. The Americans won every engagement, and in three months the Spanish government asked for terms. This display of prowess signified that the United States had arrived at the Great-Power status which was warranted by the political strength and material wealth of the country.

The direction that government policy would take was largely fixed by Theodore Roosevelt, Assistant Secretary of the Navy. Keenly aware that a war with Spain would open an opportunity to carry out the naval strategy of his friend Mahan, Roosevelt busied himself during the months before the outbreak of war with plans for an expedition to Spain and an attack on the Philippine Islands. He would make it a war not merely to free Cuba but to destroy Spanish power on both sides of the world.

Most Americans, including the President, were scarcely aware that the Philippines existed, but Roosevelt sent secret orders on February 25 to Commodore George Dewey, in command of the Asiatic Squadron at Hong Kong, to prepare for an attack on the Spanish fleet in the Philippines in case of war. Roosevelt's superior, the elderly John D. Long, did not reverse these orders, and in the weeks before the declaration of war, Dewey made his ships ready. On the morning of May 1 he entered Manila Bay and destroyed the Spanish fleet without damage to his own ships. Only 8 American sailors were wounded, while 381 Spaniards were killed. The startling news sent a thrill of pride and joy through all Americans. The administration, equally surprised, hastily improvised an army to follow up the victory. Under Emilio Aguinaldo, Filipinos, who detested Spanish rule and looked upon the Americans as liberators, joined them and forced the Spanish garrison to surrender in August. The rush of spectacular victories left the policy-makers in Washington bewildered.

Roosevelt was unable to carry the war to Peninsular Spain but he had a conspicuous personal share in the military operations. Realizing that the greatest popular reputations would come out of the fighting, he resigned his post in the Navy Department and gave up battleships for horses. A sickly child of a wealthy New York Dutch family, "Teddy" had fought his way through his early youth to robust health and violent energy. Allied with the reform element of the Republican Party, he had served as United States Civil Service Commissioner and president of the board of police commissioners of New York City. He was an author of histories of the Navy and the West. Idealism and intellect and a Harvard accent did not ordinarily recommend a man for political preferment in late nineteenth-century America, but, as Henry Adams said, Theodore Roosevelt was "pure act," and his dynamism made him immensely attractive to the American people.

He now created a personification of the moralistic imperialism he believed in. As lieutenant-colonel of a privately-organized regiment of "Rough Riders," commanded by Leonard Wood, he led them in a charge against Spanish troops up San Juan Hill in Cuba on July 1. Reporters made this victory into a personal exploit of vast dimensions. Mr. Dooley, the Irish bartender and Democrat created as a character by the newspaper humorist Finley Peter Dunne, suggested that Roosevelt's own book, *The Rough Riders* (1899), should have been entitled, *Alone in Cubia.*

The American victory of San Juan Hill was matched that same day at El Caney at the eastern end of the island after hard fighting, with the result that American troops under General William R. Shafter controlled the land positions around Santiago de Cuba while the Navy under Commodore William T. Sampson blockaded the enemy warships in the harbor. Citizens of the eastern United States demanded that the American fleet be dispersed to protect them against the possibility of attack on the mainland by Spanish warships en route from Spain, but fortunately the administration paid no attention to this pressure. Admiral Cervera in command at Santiago, hopelessly outclassed, was under orders not to surrender, and with Spanish pride on July 3 he attempted to break out of the harbor. Sampson, who was conferring with General Shafter, was not in the main action and most of the popular glory for the American triumph went to Commodore William S. Schley. One after another the Spanish warships were destroyed or forced to run aground. The Spaniards had 474 killed to 1 American. An American commander enjoined his elated crew: "Don't cheer, boys; the poor fellows are dying."

The United States has never known a war so enjoyable for civilians to read about. The scandalous inefficiency of the War Department, the incredible disorder at Tampa, Florida, chief port of embarkation, the "embalmed beef" fed to the troops, the heavy winter uniforms and the poor rifles issued to soldiers bound for Cuba—these details were overlooked in favor of the glamorized narratives provided by Richard Harding Davis and swarms of other reporters. The country could take justifiable pride in the performance of its new steel navy, in the bravery of soldiers and sailors, and in the cementing of bonds between North and South that made genuine comrades out of the sons of former enemies. In the fighting the Americans actually accomplished what frontiersmen and "war hawks" had vainly boasted they would do in the War of 1812: in a frolic they demolished a European empire. The experience was heady.

The war opened a new era when Americans believed that benevolent imperialism would best express their new-found importance in the world.

This faith was fairly remote from the desire to make the Cubans independent which initiated the war, and the transition was as swift and surprising as the feats of the Army and Navy. On April 27, when war had been declared but no shot had yet been fired, Albert J. Beveridge of Indiana, a "young man in a hurry" who was rising to national fame on the strength of simplified and dynamic oratory that set a mode for the new century, made an electrifying speech in Boston. "We are a conquering race, and must obey our blood and occupy new markets, and, if necessary, new lands," he said.

> American factories are making more than the American people can use; American soil is producing more than they can consume. Fate has written our policy for us; the trade of the world must and shall be ours. And we will get it as our mother [England] has told us how. We will establish trading-posts throughout the world as distributing-points for American products. We will cover the ocean with our merchant marine. We will build a navy to the measure of our greatness. Great colonies governing themselves, flying our flag and trading with us, will grow about our posts of trade. Our institutions will follow our flag on the wings of our commerce. And American law, American order, American civilization, and the American flag will plant themselves on shores hitherto bloody and benighted, but by those agencies of God henceforth to be made beautiful and bright.

This doctrine seemed as brash and mistaken to some as it appeared wonderful and true to others. Beveridge sought election to the United States Senate on a platform he summed up as "The March of the Flag." This made a religious chant out of American history—interpreted preeminently as expansion. The chief argument of doubters who saw the ocean boundaries of the nation as final he derided:

> The ocean does not separate us from the lands of our duty and desire—the ocean joins us. Steam joins us, electricity joins us—the very elements are in league with our destiny. Cuba not contiguous? The Philippines not contiguous? Our navy will make them contiguous. Dewey and Sampson and Schley have made them contiguous, and American speed, American guns, American heart and brain and nerve will keep them contiguous forever.

Beveridge went to the Senate, and his ideas spread across the land. The people began to catch a vision that empire was in line with their progress from triumph to triumph, and that it meant freedom and prosperity for all. An important turning point was reached when businessmen gave up their opposition to a strong foreign policy and took to heart the imperialists' argument that the acquisition of the Philippines would carry American power to the door of China and the great untapped markets of the future. Following Japan's exposure of Chinese weakness, the European powers were engaged in chipping off portions of the ill-governed Celestial Kingdom. American chambers of commerce, a newly-organized American Asiatic Association, the *Wall Street Journal,* and similar agencies suddenly swelled the rising tide of American imperialism. It was not proposed that the United States should join in the carving up of China, but it was contended that undue greed by the other powers would be prevented, and a competitive opportunity to share the Chinese market would be enhanced, by building a position of American power at Manila. Some strategists doubted the wisdom of committing the United States Navy to defend the Philippines because this policy might compromise defense of the Samoa-Hawaii-Alaska screen of positions on which the safety of the Isthmus and the continental United States directly depended. Most Democrats and some "Mugwump" Republicans, furthermore, insisted that the United States brush aside all temptations to embark on an imperialistic policy for the sake of moral and material gains which they regarded as spurious.

It was President McKinley's responsibility to decide the momentous questions that crowded up to him from the swift events of the war and the rapid evolution of opinion. Well-meaning politician that he was, he went with the tide, and the tide was imperialistic while the opposition seemed timid, largely Democratic, and a minority. Later he told a delegation of clergymen how he reached his decision:

> I walked the floor of the White House night after night until midnight; and I am not ashamed to tell you, gentlemen, that I went down on my knees and prayed Almighty God for light and guidance more than one night. And one night late it came to me this way—I don't know how it was but it came; first, that we could not give [the Philippines] back to Spain—that would be cowardly and dishonorable; second, that we could not turn them over to France or Germany—our commercial rivals in the Orient—that would be bad business and discreditable; third, that we could not leave them to themselves—they were unfit for self-government, and they would soon have anarchy and misrule over there worse than Spain's was; and fourth, that there was nothing left for us to do but to take them all, and to educate the Filipinos, and uplift and civilize and Christianize them, and by God's grace do the very best we could by them, as our fellow-men for whom Christ also died. And then I went to bed, and went to sleep and slept soundly.

With Divine guidance pointing to a policy that united the requirements of courage, good business, benevolence, and religion, the problem was solved. The President correctly interpreted the desire of most Americans to launch a new era of expansion.

THE TRIUMPH OF IMPERIALISM

Before the brief war with Spain was over, hesitations over expansion suddenly disappeared and the United States took territories unrelated to

Spain but highly significant for the strategy of navalists and the burgeoning ideal of imperialism. The Navy made excellent use of the Hawaiian Islands on the route to the Philippines during the war, and annexationists in the Senate determined to overcome the opposition. Following the exact procedure of the Texas annexationists in 1846, they avoided the two-thirds rule governing treaties in the Senate by putting through the houses of Congress a joint resolution which required only simple majorities. The President signed it on July 7, 1898. Three days earlier, uninhabited Wake Island was occupied by American forces on their way to the Philippines. Midway, another stepping-stone from Hawaii to the Orient had been acquired in 1867. At the other extreme of strategic geography, the Spanish island of Puerto Rico was occupied by General Nelson A. Miles on July 25 virtually without opposition. Thus events filled out the strategic pattern which Captain Mahan had perceived, and when President McKinley decided in favor of Philippine annexation, American diplomats were instructed to negotiate with Spain not merely for Cuban independence but for an American empire.

The Settlement with Spain

Commissioners of the two countries met in Paris on October 1. The Spaniards strongly opposed turning over the Philippines. The Americans, in effect admitting that the demand for them was not justified by the American purposes in the war, offered to pay $20 million for the cession, and the Spaniards accepted. Spain ceded to the United States as indemnity Puerto Rico and Guam; and she gave up all title to Cuba in recognition of the island's successful revolution. On December 10, a treaty was signed incorporating these arrangements. For this treaty of peace, which was also one of annexation, the administration could not avoid the necessity to gain a two-thirds vote in the Senate. A major debate in that body thoroughly aired the great issues involved, and in this the public joined.

Anti-imperialists, who were recovering from the emotional excitement of the war months, assembled powerful arguments. Populists, Democrats, and some influential Republicans, chiefly New Englanders, joined together to check imperialism. Such important persons as ex-Presidents Cleveland and Harrison, Charles Francis Adams, Jr., President Charles W. Eliot of Harvard, Andrew Carnegie, William Dean Howells, and Mark Twain protested against denial to others of that liberty and self-government which Americans claimed for themselves and regarded as universal human rights. The anti-imperialists stressed the insignificance of American trade with the Far East and the dangers of engaging in political and economic competition with other empires. How, they asked, could the United States argue the rightness of the Monroe Doctrine in the

American hemisphere while violating the same principle in the Far East?

The anti-imperialists in the Senate gained enough support to vote down the treaty. But the leader of the Democratic party, William Jennings Bryan, although a staunch anti-imperialist, decided that it would be a mistake to defeat a treaty providing for peace with Spain, and he believed that the Democrats could appeal successfully to voters in the next elections on a platform of anti-imperialism in general and Philippine independence in particular. He advised Democratic opponents of the treaty to vote for it on these grounds, and on February 6, 1899, enough of them followed his advice to provide a two-vote margin in favor of ratification. Two days earlier, in the Philippines, Aguinaldo and his followers broke out in rebellion against American rule. An army of 70,000 United States soldiers ended the formal war within a year, but rebel guerrillas continued to resist. Bryan's strategy went down in Democratic defeat in the election of 1900, while ruthless measures typical of imperialist armies were used against the Filipinos.

The Empire and Traditional Liberties

In the first excitement, Americans gave little thought to the crucial question of how the new empire was to be reconciled with the federal Constitution and the Bill of Rights. The established tradition was that territories should be admitted to the Union as equal states as soon as they acquired a sufficient population. This had differentiated American expansion from European imperialism and prevented the continental United States from becoming an empire for exploitation. Now as a result of ill-defined purposes and precipitate action the nation faced a great test of its commitment to self-government and individual rights.

The imperialists assured the American people that the annexations would greatly benefit the island populations in diverse economic, social, political, and cultural ways. But they assumed American racial superiority and the inferiority of the island peoples. It seemed to follow, therefore, that the benefits of American rule in the new empire would come not as matters of right and self-determination on the part of the natives but as a voluntary gift from superiors to inferiors, from rulers to subjects. Many lovers of liberty were convinced that no people could maintain voluntary benevolence towards subject peoples, and that the worst consequence of imperialism was the corruption of the rulers themselves. Having failed to defeat the measures of annexation in Congress, they organized the Anti-Imperialist League for a long campaign.

The Supreme Court made the imperialist doctrines official in the Insular Cases of 1901. Clothed in verbiage whose confusion suggests the intellectual difficulties of the justices, these decisions in effect denied that the Constitution necessarily follows the flag, and allowed Congress and the Executive to govern the islands in ways which would be unconstitutional even under territorial government in the continental United States. Drawing a distinction between incorporated and unincorporated territories, the Court held that Congress and the Executive might establish government in the islands in violation of constitutional requirements so long as they did not "incorporate" them in the United States. The Insular Decisions, along with the contemporaneous support of business interests by the federal courts against the government and the people, marked the high point of judicial conservatism in American history.

The most substantial practical effects of the decisions were that Congress and the Executive were absolved from the necessity to extend the protection of the tariff laws to those island products which competed with mainland interests and were able to suppress at will the civil liberties of islanders. Federal authorities were entitled to dispose of public privileges such as utility franchises, and this they did with a will—generally in favor of promoters from the mainland. But in the new possessions the federal authorities also did much constructive work which genuinely expressed the original idealistic hopes of the American people. American rule brought material benefits, and in the long run American ideas of liberty could not be prevented by any quarantine from invading the islands.

THE COLONIAL EXPERIMENT

Cuba

Cuba was the first scene of American experiments in colonialism. Despite the Teller Amendment, the United States Army occupied the island for four years. Major General Leonard Wood, whom Colonel Roosevelt succeeded as commander of the Rough Riders after San Juan Hill, commanded the American occupation troops and as the ruler of Cuba he did much to "Americanize" the island. Its governmental machinery and finances were modernized. Education on the model of American public schools was supported. Transportation and public health measures were vigorously developed. Most dramatic was the famous victory over yellow fever, a scourge to the island. Walter Reed and a corps of American doctors tested the hypothesis of a Cuban, Dr. Carlos J. Finlay, that the dread disease was carried by the stegomyia mosquito. They allowed themselves to be infected to prove their case. Then the Army cleaned up the breeding places of the insect and the battle was won. This boon was typical of American success in practical benevolence.

Senator Beveridge and other extreme imperialists believed that the United States should ignore the Teller Amendment and keep Cuba. Democrats made political capital of the division of Republican opinion on the issue in the election of 1900 and put the administration on notice against the betrayal of the Teller Amendment. General Wood was ordered to authorize the Cubans to organize a constitutional convention. This met in November 1900, drew up a constitution modeled on that of the United States, and refused to include any acknowledgment of American authority. Before withdrawing its troops, however, the United States government required certain promises. Since these were originally provisions attached to an army appropriation bill (March 2, 1901) and introduced by Senator Orville H. Platt of Connecticut, they go by the name of the Platt Amendment, though they were chiefly the work of the Secretary of War, Elihu Root. The stipulation was that their provisions must be included in or appended to the Cuban constitution, and that for further assurance they should be embodied in a permanent treaty between the two countries.

The chief provisions were: (1) that Cuba should enter into no treaty or compact with a third country which would impair her independence; (2) that the Cuban government should make no debt to the carrying of which its ordinary revenues were inadequate; (3) that the United States should have the right to intervene to preserve the independence of Cuba or maintain her government; (4) that lands for coaling or naval stations be leased to the United States. As a result of this last provision the naval station at Guantánamo Bay was established. Imperialists were particularly anxious to retain naval control over the passage to the Isthmus of Panama south of the island. It was under authority of the third provision that United States troops again occupied Cuba in the administration of Theodore Roosevelt. When they left the island in 1902 it was nominally independent but effectively a protectorate, and so it remained until the Platt Amendment was abrogated in 1934.

Puerto Rico

Puerto Rico suffered more from American inattention than willful exploitation. The Foraker Act of 1900 established a government like that of the British crown colonies. A governor and executive council were appointed by the President of the United States, and the governor could veto acts of the popularly-elected House of Delegates. Cane-growing and sugar refining dominated the island's economy. A good share of the land and the mills came under the ownership of absentee Americans while most Puerto Ricans lived in extreme poverty. The American authorities did something to reduce disease and illiteracy, but underourishment remained prevalent until very recently.

In 1917, the Jones Act made Puerto Ricans citizens of the United States. In later years many were able to take advantage of their new status by migrating to the mainland, chiefly New York City, but not enough to solve the island's problem of overpopulation. Little attention was paid the island "stepchild" by the United States government until the presidency of Franklin D. Roosevelt. After the Second World War, the Puerto Ricans were given (1947) the right to elect their own governor and really began to share the American heritage of liberty and opportunity. They showed little desire for independence and, despite the decades of neglect, developed great loyalty to the United States.

The Philippines

The Philippines gave the United States the most perplexing of all its new imperial problems. Americans wished to demonstrate their talents for administration in this above all the other island possessions, but Aguinaldo and his tough fighters would accept no substitute for independence. The Senate on February 14, 1899, resolved that annexation of the islands by the United States was not intended to be permanent. This did not lead the Filipinos to submit. United States troops had little trouble in driving the rebels out of the settled districts, but two more years of campaigning in jungles and mountains were required to end guerrilla resistance, and later investigations showed that the disheartening work led some American soldiers to torture and murder prisoners. Public revelations of this kind disillusioned many Americans with the whole experiment in imperialism. The Philippine Insurrection was declared at an end in 1901.

In 1900, President McKinley sent a civil commission headed by William Howard Taft of Ohio to take over the functions of government from the military. The instructions to the commission defined American policy for the next sixteen years. They called for taking the vast landholdings of the Catholic religious orders in return for payment, and the distribution of these lands to farmers. They provided for the promotion of education, a grant of traditional American civil rights with the exceptions of trial by jury and the right to bear arms; popular election of local officials; and preference to Filipinos for appointment to higher offices. Taft became Governor in 1901. Other members of the commission, along with a few Filipinos, substituted for a legislature until 1907. Then the Filipinos were allowed to elect their own assembly while the United States continued to appoint the governor and members of the upper house. Governor Taft by his genuine devotion to the welfare of the Filipinos and his genial friendship for them did much to create loyalty to the United States. He set up a landmark in colonial administration.

Americans became dominant in the Philippine economy and the United States bought almost all the exports of sugar, cocoanut oil, and cordage, but neither the Philippines nor the China trade ever fulfilled the predictions of the imperialists.

Hawaii and Alaska

The case of Hawaii was different from that of the Philippines because of the existence before annexation of strong American influence in the local life, and also because of the extreme importance of Pearl Harbor for the naval defense of the American hemisphere. These two factors ruled out independence as a likely goal for Hawaii and made statehood within the Union the ultimate political aspiration of her people. Alaska was also a candidate for eventual statehood. The region had been organized as a "civil and judicial district"—a status lower than territorial—in 1884, and from time to time Congress elaborated its governmental machinery. In 1900, the Organic Act for Hawaii created a territorial government and extended the Constitution to it. The Supreme Court decided in the Insular Cases that Congress had converted Alaska and Hawaii into incorporated territories. No other extracontinental possessions of the United States have been so recognized.

Samoa

Solution of the Samoan question was the last imperialist action of the McKinley administration. The strategic importance of Pago Pago, a natural site for a naval base on the island of Tutuila, is almost comparable for the South Pacific to that of Pearl Harbor in the central area. With Alaska, the three positions are a screen covering all the western approaches to the Hemisphere.

The American-British-German Condominium of 1889 over all of the Samoan Islands proved unworkable, not because the Samoans objected— they were remarkably amiable—but because the political agents of the Great Powers on the scene squabbled incessantly. President Cleveland wanted to withdraw, but the public paid little attention. The German government sought a partition in 1899 and got Britain to withdraw by compensating her elsewhere. Then the United States and Germany signed a treaty giving the latter the largest islands, which had commercial importance in the copra trade, while this country received Tutuila and some smaller islands. Subsequently the Samoan chiefs ceded these islands to the United States.

When McKinley was assassinated in 1901, only at the Isthmus of Panama was there a gap in the string of positions encircling half the globe which made up the new American Empire. But the Isthmus was the central link. It was a strange circumstance that brought to the White House in McKinley's place the man of all Americans who was most eager to close the gap, and "T.R." did it with gusto.

CHINA AND THE "OPEN DOOR"

The annexation of the Philippines had not been justified for defensive purposes but represented an American bid for influence in the Far East in general and China in particular. Japan, Great Britain, France, Germany, and Russia were busily carving out spheres of influence in China. They manipulated railroad and trade concessions and leaseholds to support claims to political authority over pieces of the vast country. Great Britain had the largest investment and trade in China, but she was without allies, and the other powers formed combinations to displace her. This placed British policy on the side of equality of economic opportunity for all the powers in China. The United States had committed itself to the same policy as early as 1844 in the Sino-American Treaty of Wanghia.

In 1898, British officials tried to develop some form of co-operative policy to carry out the Anglo-American coincidence of interests. Both countries were confident they could profit in free competition in the China market, and both were unwilling to undertake further annexations in the Far East. Sir Julian Pauncefote, British Ambassador to the United States, proposed to Secretary of State John Sherman a joint guaranty of equal commercial opportunity for all nations in China, but Sherman refused. John Hay, the former private secretary of President Lincoln and an intimate friend of Theodore Roosevelt, became Secretary of State in September 1898. He was one of the intellectual nationalists who were the chief architects of the American imperialist adventure. He accepted advice on the Far East from W. W. Rockhill, an American who had spent many years in China, and Rockhill in turn accepted from Alfred Hippisley, a British subject, a suggestion for American policy in China. Rockhill gave the Hippisley plan to Secretary Hay who with slight changes sent it to all the governments interested in China.

This origin of the First "Open Door" Note of 1899 has led some historians to regard it as a British imposition leading the United States to make an ill-considered gesture going beyond what it would support with force. Thus it can be regarded as idealistic but impractical, and even dangerous. But the dissolution of China may have been impeded by the American use of moral influences, and this delay served the material and strategic as well as idealistic interests of the United States. The first note asked Germany, Japan, Italy, Russia, France, and Great Britain to promise not to interfere with the commercial rights of citizens of other countries in their own spheres of influence. Russia virtually declined and the other powers hedged their acceptances with qualifications, but Hay announced that all the powers had accepted the principle of commercial equality in China. The episode amounted to no more than an announcement of American policy.

A stronger action resulted from an uprising of Chinese nationalists against "foreign devils" and against their own government for not expelling them. Calling themselves the Fist of Righteous Harmony (hence "Boxers"), the rebels committed some crimes against foreigners and besieged whites, including diplomatic officials, in Peking. All the powers, including the United States, contributed troops to a successful rescue expedition.

Hay feared that the other powers would exploit their victory by dismembering China. He used his influence to quiet the Boxers and addressed the Second Open Door Note of July 3, 1900, to the Powers. It called for no answer but declared it to be the policy of the United States to "preserve Chinese territorial and administrative entity" and to safeguard the principle of commercial equality in all China. Hay's note may have played a part in restraining the Powers from demanding territorial cessions. They did demand an indemnity of the Chinese government, and this might have been larger but for the American action. The share of the United States was $25 million, but $18 million of this was returned to the Chinese government, which used it to pay for the education of young Chinese in the United States.

Hay himself secretly contradicted his own policy by attempting late in 1900 to gain a naval base at Samsah Bay in southern China, but Japan frustrated him. This was perhaps evidence that he regarded the Open Door as a lost hope. Nevertheless his notes had attracted a great deal of attention in the world, and subsequent American administrations felt bound to support the Open Door by diplomatic means. Hay as Secretary of State experimented with the formation of a foreign policy to express the new status of the United States—by trying to influence international affairs beyond the old limits of the Monroe Doctrine and beyond the new limits of the American Empire. After his friend Theodore Roosevelt became President, he remained in office and had much more of the same work to do.

The Open Door Notes seemed to please most Americans. They enjoyed hearing their government read moral lessons to the other Powers. In the election of 1900 McKinley was triumphantly vindicated against the criticisms of Bryan and the anti-imperialists. The Republicans attributed prosperity at home to their gold standard and high tariff policies, and workingmen mostly accepted the Republicans' claim that theirs was the party of "the full dinner pail." They also pointed with pride to expansion abroad, and most voters saw nothing to darken the shining victories in war and diplomacy. Bryan as the Democratic candidate made imperialism the chief issue, but other Democratic orators revived demands for free silver and the reform planks of the 1896 platform. McKinley had a larger popular majority than in 1896, gaining the electoral vote of every state except the Solid South and the four silver states of Colorado, Montana, Nevada, and Idaho.

But the Republican managers had given the vice-presidential nomination to Governor Theodore Roosevelt of New York, whose popularity could not be overlooked. Boss Platt of his state thought the naming of him for the second place an excellent device to end the political career of an obstreperous public man. Mark Hanna warned to no avail that only one life stood between "this madman" and the White House. His fears were realized when an anarchist shot President McKinley on September 6, 1901, six months after the beginning of his second term. It is said that certain financiers went into a faint not in sorrow at the assassination but, as Hanna put it, because that "damned cowboy" was now President.

CHAPTER 12

Theodore Roosevelt's Square Deal, 1901-1909

IN FOREIGN AFFAIRS THEODORE ROOSEVELT WAS A vigorous imperialist throughout his national career, and as President he gained the name of domestic reformer. At the outset, however, he issued his challenge to the dominant business groups in carefully guarded terms, and he was too much of a political realist to break with the conservative leaders of Congress. Indeed, some historians deny that his reform impulse was ever very strong or that he cut very deeply into the domestic ills of the country at any time.

Roosevelt regarded himself as a practical man, not a theorist or visionary, and he stated in his autobiography that as a young man he was repelled by the personal unattractiveness of so many of the reformers of that day. More significant in history than the specific domestic reforms he achieved is the fact that, more than anyone else in his era, he made reform respectable. Now, for the first time, the federal government successfully prohibited *some* abuses by business and actually regulated *some* industries in the public interest. There never was any doubt in his mind that the seat of power ought to be in the White House rather than in J. Pierpont Morgan's office; and under him the federal government showed itself more powerful than Big Business in those areas which he chose for tests.

In later years predominant public opinion repudiated his imperialism but the most significant reform administrations built upon his domestic foundations. He pointed the way between socialism on the left and reaction on the right. If Roosevelt, gentleman-adventurer and shrewd politician that he was, did not himself proceed far along this middle course, he greatly facilitated the pursuit of it by later leaders of the nation.

ROOSEVELT AND THE PRESIDENCY

Theodore Roosevelt enlarged the office of President of the United States to proportions unimagined by any previous national leader, except perhaps Alexander Hamilton. Most Presidents before him, and especially those following Lincoln, had been timid in exploring the possibilities of their office as if they feared to use their power. Roosevelt gloried in the exercise of power. He regarded courage as the greatest of virtues, and he tended to overestimate the value of activity. Some observers were disdainful of his furious activism. John Morley called him an "interesting combination of St. Vitus and St. Paul." Conservatives naturally feared his propensity to embark on new ways. But to most Americans he communicated a spirit of joy in life combined with moral aspiration, and they reveled in his glorification of his office.

He was projected into it under extraordinarily dramatic circumstances. This vigorous outdoor man was tramping in the Adirondacks when he learned that McKinley's condition had become grave. He drove all night in a wagon to the nearest railroad station, where he was informed of the President's death. Proceeding then by special train to Buffalo, he took the oath of office there. Not yet forty-three, he was the youngest man ever to do so. He promptly announced that he would continue the policies and retain the Cabinet of his predecessor, but he soon left no doubt that he was a very different kind of President.

Ever thereafter he kept himself in the center of the stage, to the delight of his nationwide audience. Roosevelt was the first President to realize upon the immense opportunities for publicity afforded by his office, and he proved to be an incomparable showman. Far from shunning reporters, he talked with them eagerly, making it a custom to provide them with a good story on Mondays when their columns were hard to fill. Even his critics made him interesting to the public, and indifference was the one response he did not evoke. He dramatized and personalized government and politics. Such talent can be prostituted to demagoguery, but Roosevelt's domestic accomplishments—especially in his second term, when his position was more assured—proved his desire to use his popularity and power for the public welfare.

He conceived of himself as the "steward" of the whole people—in a sense that Congress, which represents states and lesser geographical districts, can never be—and he regarded himself as responsible only to the people. In interpreting his constitutional powers he was a liberal not a strict constructionist. He believed that, acting in the public interest, he could do whatever was not expressly prohibited by the Constitution or the laws. The practical consequence was that he made things happen in the Executive sphere, including foreign affairs, and ignored charges that he was highhanded. He was much less successful in matters requiring Congressional action, and the legislative record of his presidency is much less impressive than that of certain later administrations. Defeated by Congress, where conservatives were in the ascendant, he either bided his time or went to the people, seeking to popularize his proposals. In many respects, therefore, this was more a period of agitation than one of accomplishment.

The President did not confine himself to political matters. He saw nothing incongruous in using his great prestige to urge the reform of English spelling, or to pillory the "nature fakers" who wrote stories humanizing animals. He delivered exhortations on the necessity for women of the upper classes to bear more children and for everyone to live strenuously according to his creed of "Muscular Christianity." When his incidental crusades brought unfavorable reactions he was quite willing to abandon them. He knew that without public support he could accomplish very little. His exuberance made him yearn to ride off in many directions at once, but he was generally careful to yield to such temptations only in minor matters while exercising superb strategic caution in pursuing major political objectives.

This caution was very much in evidence in his domestic policy during his first years as President. The youngest man who had entered the White House knew that the party leaders generally distrusted him, and he made election in his own right in 1904, which would require a united party, his objective. He moderated his reformist principles accordingly.

The Cabinet he inherited from McKinley contained unusually able men. The Secretary of State, John Hay, and the Secretary of War, Elihu Root, were specially compatible with Roosevelt though both were more conservative than he. He had served his apprenticeship as Civil Service Commissioner, and he brought to his high task an emphasis not merely on clean but also on efficient government. It may be doubted if the affairs of the Executive branch had been conducted so effectively since the first generation of government under the Constitution, when the administrative ideals of George Washington were maintained. At the end of Roosevelt's presidency the British Ambassador, James Bryce, who was widely acquainted with the governments of the world, said that he had never seen anywhere "a more eager, high-minded, and efficient set of public servants." Included among them were an energetic little group known as the "tennis Cabinet." "T.R." set a grueling pace in work and play, and made life in the White House more interesting than it had been within the memory of anyone then living. Not since John Quincy Adams had there been so well-educated a President, and not since Thomas Jefferson had there been one with such an enormous variety of interests. Before he was through he engaged in many unseemly altercations, but quite clearly he enhanced the presidency.

GOVERNMENT AND BUSINESS IN ROOSEVELT'S FIRST TERM

In his first annual message to Congress (December 3, 1901), Roosevelt showed his belief that the growth and vast power of Big Business posed problems with which only the national government could grapple. He favored regulation of all firms engaged in interstate business, but at this stage his specific proposals were more moderate. By the middle of his first term he won some response from Congress. He got a Department of Commerce, with a Bureau of Corporations to procure information; the Elkins Act of 1903 forbidding railroads to grant rebates to favored shippers; and a law designed to expedite prosecutions under the Sherman Anti-Trust Act. Considering the conservatism of the legislative body, these laws represented real gains for the general interest, but they did not get at the root of the problem. He rendered his greatest service by publicizing the inadequacy of existing laws and old customs.

On the trust question he took a position between extremes, both of which he regarded as foolish. On the one hand, the giant corporations, with their spokesmen in the press and public life, demanded that they remain immune from governmental action. On the other, certain reformers demanded that business consolidation be prohibited and free competition be fully restored. To Roosevelt it was folly either to allow the corporations unbridled power or to oppose combination as such; he recognized the many economic advantages of consolidation and had no fear of bigness; his concern was to prohibit and prevent abuses. He called his policy the "Square Deal" for both capital and labor, and he sought to associate the "Big Stick" with it by gaining clear recognition of the power of the national government.

The year of his inauguration was also the year of the formation of the United States Steel Corporation, the first billion-dollar corporation. This giant, the creation of financiers headed by J. Pierpont Morgan, owned iron and coal mines, transportation facilities, and mills and factories that turned out finished products from nails to armor plate. The public was appalled by the sheer bigness and power of the United States Steel Corporation, but in terms of efficiency, production, and profits, although not its harsh labor policy, the consolidation was richly justified by its fruits.

Roosevelt believed that bigness in industry had come to stay, but he soon perceived that Congress would not go far in the matter of regulatory legislation. Nothing if not a fighter, he made impressive use of such weapons as he could command. In March 1902, he directed Attorney General Philander C. Knox to file suit against the Northern Securities Company, another of Morgan's holding companies. It controlled the

Northern Pacific and Great Northern railroads and threatened to control others west of the Mississippi River. Following the decision in the Knight case in 1895, which removed the teeth from the Sherman Anti-Trust Act, there had been no government prosecutions of industrial combination. To the surprise and shock of the corporate world, the government won its case in 1904, when the Supreme Court by a 5 to 4 vote decided that this holding company was an unlawful combination. Justice Oliver Wendell Holmes, Jr., who had been appointed to the Court by Roosevelt, in a dissenting opinion argued for a "rule of reason" which would differentiate between reasonable and unreasonable restraint of trade.

This was what Roosevelt himself wanted in the long run, though he was much annoyed with Holmes at the time, when his fighting blood was up. He interpreted the decision as restoring to the government the power to suppress monopoly and to control and regulate combinations. Afterwards he said: "When I became President, the question of the *method* by which the United States Government was to control the corporations was not yet important. The absolutely vital question was whether the Government had power to control them at all." If this decision did not quite reverse the one in the Knight case, as he believed it did, unquestionably it vitalized the Sherman Anti-Trust Act. It gave "T.R." a Big Stick to brandish. He afterwards attacked the Tobacco Trust and Standard Oil, but in general he made sparing use of his power to initiate antitrust suits, once that power was established.

What the Square Deal might mean for labor he demonstrated in the fall of 1902 when a strike of anthracite miners threatened the country with a winter coal shortage. The union was willing to arbitrate questions in dispute with employers, but the latter refused. Roosevelt, acting on his enlarged conception of the proper role of the President, called union leaders and employers to Washington and proposed a commission to be appointed by himself to mediate the dispute. Fearful that this would entail recognition of the union, the employers refused until Roosevelt bore them down by sheer insistence. The strike ended and the commission awarded a small wage increase to the miners without granting recognition to the union. This was the first time that a President of the United States intervened in a strike not by using force against the workers but to secure a negotiated settlement. The action, therefore, was one of historic significance.

CONSERVATION

In the conservation of natural resources Theodore Roosevelt found a policy which he could pursue vigorously without directly challenging Big Business, though in exalting the public interest he antagonized certain private interests in the region most affected—the Far West. Conservation meant the safeguarding of forests, mineral resources, and the country's streams against reckless exploitation for immediate private gain, and it was associated with the reclamation of arid lands. In the fullest sense this was a national policy and in the truest sense conservative, but it marked a reversal of time-honored practices of both federal and state governments. For decades they had been disposing of natural resources to corporations and individuals with lavish hands.

The reversal of the policy of largesse and laissez faire began with the passage in 1891 of the Forest Reserve Act, which permitted the President to withdraw timber tracts in the public domain from settlement. Under this law President Harrison set aside 13 million acres. Before Roosevelt's administration the science of forestry had been introduced from Europe to the United States. The most noted professional in this field was Gifford Pinchot, head of the Forestry Bureau in the Department of Agriculture. But the forest reserves were under the Department of the Interior. "Forests and foresters had nothing whatever to do with each other," as Roosevelt noted ironically. Thousands of acres in the federal domain were arid and required elaborate irrigation works to make them productive. The Carey Act of 1894 authorized the President to turn over such tracts to state governments for development. But the rivers were no respecters of state boundaries, and little was accomplished.

Roosevelt did not start the conservation movement but he vitalized it and greatly increased its momentum. His personal knowledge and love of the West, combined with his bold nationalism, led him to press this cause. In his first annual message he called attention to the forest and water problems as perhaps the most vital internal problems of the country. Nowhere else in the domestic sphere, perhaps, was he so successful. The earliest achievements were in the relatively uncontroversial field of reclamation. In 1902, with his support, Congress passed the Newlands Act, named for Senator Francis G. Newlands of Nevada, a major champion of reclamation. This measure provided for the setting aside of proceeds from federal land sales in sixteen western states for the construction and support of irrigation works in arid districts. Payments from water-users and proceeds from the sale of reclaimed lands were to go back into the fund. The Act was designed to aid small landholders, sales of water rights to private proprietors being restricted to owners of 160 acres or less who were actual residents. Within four years, projects were begun by means of which 3 million acres were to be irrigated. Certain practical difficulties arose in the administration of the Act, for the costs of these projects were very great and purchasers of reclaimed lands were often undisposed or unable to pay for them, but the reclamation policy aroused little direct opposition. Appropriately, the dam on Salt River, Arizona, was named for Roosevelt and in 1911 the reservoir was formally opened by him.

In 1905, Congress at length accepted the President's recommendation to transfer the forest reserves to the Department of Agriculture and set up the United States Forest Service. Roosevelt promptly appointed Gifford Pinchot to head this, and from that time on the national forests were administered according to scientific principles and served as models of conservation. Thus traditional American practices of devastating exploitation gave way to principles of sustained yield, reforestation, and continual improvement. Private lumber and paper companies eventually learned the lesson.

The regulatory measures of the Forest Service aroused the resentment of large stockowners, whose herds had previously grazed in the public domain; and the President, by withdrawing millions of acres of forest and mineral lands, aroused the hostility of certain other private interests in his second term. Altogether he quadrupled the size of the national forests, and he guarded the mineral resources of the country by withdrawing millions of acres of coal lands. The latter were under the jurisdiction of the Department of the Interior, which was ably administered from 1907 onward by James R. Garfield. There could be no doubt that the President and the officials associated with him zealously guarded the natural resources of the country in the public interest, but they were prone to interpret the laws freely. When cattle barons secured from Congress in 1907 a rider to an appropriation bill forbidding the President to set aside any further forest lands in the six northwestern states, Roosevelt faced a problem since he did not want to veto the whole measure. He met the situation by quickly withdrawing some 16 million acres which had already been designated by the Forest Service, and then signed the bill. He himself told this story afterwards with glee.

Valuable as his direct services to the conservation movement were, the publicity he gave it was probably of even greater value. Following his appointment of the Inland Waterways Commission in 1907, he called in 1908 a conference of state governors in the White House. Among the results of this was the organization of thirty-six state conservation commissions and the National Conservation Commission. The report of the latter, submitted that year, comprised the first inventory of the physical resources of the nation. Submitting it to Congress in January 1909, Roosevelt described it as "one of the most fundamentally important documents ever laid before the American people." When he left office that year, much needed to be done to end the dangerous exploitation of resources in the United States, but the federal government was finally started on the road of conservation. Thenceforth there would be betrayals of the public interest by particular officials and indifference by a few administrations, but there would be no turning back. The nation had arrived at maturity in the fundamental matter of dealing with the material environment of its civilization. This was one of the best accomplishments under the new governmental philosophy which came to be called "progressive nationalism." The era of individualistic frontier development ended and a new era of social control began.

THE "MUCKRAKERS"

Conservation at first seemed to most Americans a rather romantic matter of saving a little wildness for future generations. The evils of unrestricted logging, grazing, and erosion in the West seemed far less important than the sins of industrialists, financiers, and politicians in the East. As if to encourage Roosevelt to greater boldness in attacking the most powerful fortresses of privilege in the nation, there began suddenly in 1902 an agitation which made even the abolitionist crusade against slavery seem mild. The date suggested that after a year many were disappointed by the contrast between Roosevelt's vigorous words and cautious actions. That he was not altogether pleased by the agitators' work is clear from his public condemnation of them as "muckrakers," who, like the character in *Pilgrim's Progress*, forever looked downward and stirred the filth.

Muckraking had begun at least as early as 1894 in Henry Demarest Lloyd's *Wealth Against Commonwealth*, an exposure of trust evils, but the muckraking era proper began with the publication of Ida M. Tarbell's *History of the Standard Oil Company* by S. S. McClure in his magazine, and his discovery that it appealed to a mass appetite. The era lasted for scarcely ten years, but during this time respectable general magazines —*McClure's, Collier's, Munsey's,* and others—found that detailed and indignant exposure of economic, social, and political evils brought them vast circulations. Muckraking books, and newspapers from the crude Hearst chain to the intellectual peak of the *New York Evening Post* under Oswald Garrison Villard, greatly accentuated dissatisfaction with the status quo and increased the demand for reform. Ida Tarbell's series of articles, later published as a book, made the Standard Oil the archetype of American monopolies and John D. Rockefeller—who was portrayed as a cold, ruthless monster—the most unpopular man in the United States. Lincoln Steffens in *The Shame of the Cities* (1904), not only detailed the corruption of political bosses in many cities, but blamed businessmen for corrupting politicians and citizens for inertia. David Graham Phillips, in *The Treason of the Senate* (1906), described the corrupt affiliations with Big Business of United States Senators and the state legislatures that elected them. Thomas W. Lawson, himself a banker, in *Frenzied Finance* (1902) provided an inside view of practices which he finally decided he could no longer endure in silence. Gustavus Myers' laborious *History of the Great American Fortunes* (1910) traced the rise to wealth of one family after another, and poured pitiless light on innumerable family skeletons. Charles Edward Russell's *The Greatest Trust in the World* (1905) explained operations of the beef trust and Upton Sinclair's novel *The Jungle* (1906) horrified consumers of meat by describing conditions in the Chicago stockyards.

The best muckrakers were careful to authenticate their material and let the facts speak for themselves, but the popularity of the movement invited sensationalism. The shallowness of journalistic treatment dissatisfied serious students who wished to discover causes, and the inflammation of public opinion frightened conservatives. Relying frequently for advertising revenue on the very corporations they attacked, the magazines soon abandoned the campaign or went under, while more profound studies of American economics, politics, sociology, and history were initiated by scholars whose books rarely caused scandal but had a far more important effect in the long run. Some of these scholars, along with a few of the original muckrakers like Upton Sinclair and Lincoln Steffens, decided they had been uncovering only the symptoms of pervasive capitalist disease, and turned to socialism.

THE ELECTION OF 1904

In approaching the presidential election, Roosevelt presented himself and his moderate reformism as the only alternative to demagogy and radicalism. This argument did much to hold businessmen in line for him. He had kept his hands off the tariff and monetary questions, and economic prosperity had proceeded apace. Also, at the moment his foreign policy seemed brilliantly successful, and favorable to the extension of American business in the world. Some conservative Republicans had favored Mark Hanna for the presidential nomination in 1904, but he died in February, and conservatives in the Cabinet, like Elihu Root, reassured the "Old Guard" that Roosevelt was "safe" enough. Nominated by acclamation, he made effective campaign speeches elaborating on his Square Deal promises. He paid court to protectionists and stand-patters like Senators Aldrich, Spooner, Lodge, and Penrose while rebuffing progressive rivals, particularly the fiery Senator La Follette of Wisconsin. He sought to give the impression that he was following a safe course.

Actually, the Rough Rider who had showed such wonderful talent for entertaining the public and delivering moral homilies had not moved very far to the left as yet, but the Democrats acted on the belief that he had taken over Bryan's role and was bound to lose votes among conservatives. They nominated for the presidency Judge Alton B. Parker of New York, an able man whose attitude toward vital public questions was little known. He promptly declared his unequivocal support of the gold standard, which had not been approved in the party platform, and in the campaign he was presented as even more conservative than he really was. Events proved that this was mistaken strategy and Parker, a colorless candidate when compared with Roosevelt, was more roundly defeated than Bryan had ever been.

A last-ditch faction of Populists, refusing to support either major presidential candidate, nominated Thomas E. Watson, who got a tiny vote. More significant now as a radical organization was the Socialist Party, most of whose leaders were for the first time native-born Americans with the earnest and effective Eugene V. Debs at their head. This party, like all Marxist parties that have tried to function democratically, was torn by internal dissensions between those who wanted to follow a policy of immediate revolution, which would scare away most followers, and those favoring a strategy of indirection whereby reforms of capitalism would be advocated to attract support and revolution indefinitely postponed. Debs had a remarkable talent for holding both factions together. As candidate for President in 1904 he received more than 400,000 votes.

Roosevelt got 7,600,000 popular votes to Parker's 5,000,000, and the electoral count was 336 to 140. Roosevelt was so *"dee-lighted"* on election night that he promised "under no circumstances" to be a candidate for or accept another nomination. When he ran again in 1912, it took more ingenuity than he possessed to convince others that this statement had referred only to nomination in 1908.

Though his tactical mistake in limiting himself to four more years weakened his position toward the end of his term, as President "in his own right" he was now at the peak of his career. His children romped through the White House and he would keep an ambassador waiting if he had promised to romp with them at a certain hour. His country home at Oyster Bay, Long Island, was enlarged to accommodate the extraordinary procession of important and fascinating persons whom he loved to entertain there. His zest was typified on a day when naval officers gingerly navigated an experimental submarine to the shore near his lawn, invited him aboard to inspect the strange craft, and to their consternation heard him as Commander-in-Chief of the Navy ordering them to batten down the hatches so he could command the vessel in a trial dive. Now during his second term, in all save a few of the most dangerous areas, he abandoned the caution he had hitherto shown in pursuing domestic reforms. This was partly because of his consciousness of popular support which probably exceeded that given any President since Andrew Jackson; it was partly because he sensed and responded to the growing progressive trends.

THE BEGINNINGS OF EFFECTIVE REGULATION

Shortly after the election, antitrust suits were started against a number of great corporations, the most notorious of them the beef, oil, and tobacco trusts. These suits dragged on interminably, the courts often decided against the government, and even the successful actions against the Standard Oil Company and the American Tobacco Company resulted in dissolutions into smaller units without affecting the ability of these to co-operate for monopolistic ends. The alternative procedure of subjecting Big Business to governmental regulation was more promising.

Railroad Regulation

The Hepburn Act of 1906 was the most important reform law of Roosevelt's administration. The Interstate Commerce Commission had waited until after the election to start a genuine effort to enforce the prohibition of railroad rebates in the Elkins Act. Roosevelt had urged Congress in 1904 to give the ICC much more authority but the Senate had marked time. The Hepburn Act gave the Commission authority not only over the railroads but over all forms of transportation, including pipelines, the Pullman Company, express companies, storage companies, and auxiliary services.

The crucial matter of rate-fixing powers was compromised. Robert M. La Follette and other advanced Progressives fought for the vesting of maximum authority in the ICC. They advocated a physical valuation of the railroads as a basis for calculating rates instead of allowing rates to be based on the well-watered stock issues, and they wanted the companies' right of appeal from decisions of the ICC to the regular federal courts to be reduced to a minimum. The powerful Old Guard Republicans in Congress fought to avoid any effective regulation whatever. The President withdrew his support of the provision for limited judicial review when he learned that the conservative Republicans would probably defeat it. La Follette never forgave Roosevelt for his willingness to accept half a loaf. Physical valuation was also defeated but all transportation companies were required to adopt uniform accounting practices to facilitate the work of the ICC. The railroads' practice of distributing passes to make political friends was prohibited. The Act forbade railroads to change rates suddenly, thus eliminating the "midnight tariff" evil. Most important, the ICC was authorized to fix a lower freight rate if it found shippers' complaints of "unreasonable" rates justified, and the burden of proof that a rate was too low was placed on the railroads.

This provision put the first strong teeth in the Interstate Commerce Act of 1887. Within two years shippers filed almost twice as many complaints of unfair rates as the ICC had received during all the preceding eighteen years. Conservative federal judges often overruled decisions of the ICC, the latter had no authority to fix rates unless shippers complained, and the companies continued to pay dividends on watered stock. Nevertheless, the Hepburn Act marks the beginning of effective federal regulation of a great business. The constitutional justification for giving this great power to the federal government was its authority over interstate commerce. The philosophic justification of it was the clear status of the railroads as a "natural monopoly," in which the self-regulatory processes of free competition envisaged by classical political economy did not really operate. Where monopoly was inevitable and even desirable, only the government representing the whole people could prevent the monopolists from abusing their power.

The Regulation of Food and Drug Industries

The next great regulatory enactments were directed against private food and drug industries. In English and American tradition, measures of public health were always within the authority of government. In the United States this authority had been inherited by the state governments, but the federal government had occasionally used its constitutional power over commerce to impose health regulations, particularly against the danger of diseases brought into the country from abroad. Formerly, local regulations of food supplies had been regarded as sufficient to protect the public. But mechanization and the nationalization of the market had steadily centralized food industries in great plants, the most impressive and dangerous of which were those devoted to meat-packing in Chicago.

The Chicago stockyards bought cattle from many states and shipped meat to the whole nation. The governments of Chicago and the state of Illinois were notoriously under the influence of the great packing companies. Other state governments, if they attempted to regulate food coming inside their borders, were frustrated by the "original package" doctrine of the Supreme Court (Leisy vs. Hardin, 1890, and Rhodes vs. Iowa, 1898). This forbade state interference with goods if they had not yet been taken out of their original package by local distributors before they crossed the boundary. The strict reservation of power over interstate commerce to the federal government made federal regulation the only alternative to hideous abuse of consumers' health.

Besides meat, more and more other foods, notably canned goods, dairy products, and milled cereals, were coming under the control of centralized processing industries. Furthermore, drugs were purveyed to the public with growing disregard of honest standards. Patent medicines and un-mixed drugs, far from performing the miracles claimed in advertisements, were frequently useless or adulterated or a positive menace to the healthiest organism. Free enterprise in these industries was becoming a system of poisoning the public for profit.

Public agitation in favor of federal pure food and drug regulation began to crystallize at the end of the century. Dr. Harvey W. Wiley, chief chemist of the Department of Agriculture, was a lifelong crusader in this cause and the most important single figure in this reform movement. Muckrakers increased public concern by exposing numerous cases of filth and adulteration with consequent disease and death. The House of Representatives soon showed its willingness to enact regulations, but the Senate refused until President Roosevelt in 1905 threw his weight into the struggle against the Senate stalwarts. Early in 1906, Upton Sinclair's book, *The Jungle,* created concern by its gruesome picture of the stockyards. Roosevelt sent personal agents to the Chicago packing houses to investigate, and they reported that Sinclair had understated the truth. Roosevelt made part of their report public in order to help Senator Albert J. Beveridge put through a bill. As Mr. Dooley described it, the President was eating his breakfast sausages one morning and glancing through Sinclair's novel. Then Senator Beveridge, happening to pass outside the window, got hit on the head with the book.

Roosevelt signed two measures on June 30, 1906. The Meat Inspection Act required that federal officials inspect all packing houses engaged in interstate and foreign commerce and enforce sanitary regulations. The Pure Food and Drug Act covered such a vast number of businesses that inspection of all of them would require an army of officials. To avoid this, an ingenious system of self-regulation was devised. The Department of Agriculture was required to fix standards of purity for foods, and manufacturers of both drugs and foods were required to state contents on the labels of cans or packages. The law forbade the passage in interstate commerce of adulterated or mislabeled foods and drugs. A relatively small number of federal officials could make spot checks of shipments and investigate complaints. An amendment in 1910 forbade unprovable claims of the curative powers of drugs.

The courts for many years interpreted these laws favorably to businessmen who wished to avoid their intent, and the government was unable to exact a high level of obedience to them because of the lack of funds and the lightness of penalties. But for the ancient laissez-faire principle, "Let the buyer beware!" in these vital industries the federal government had now substituted the maxim, "Let the seller beware!" The improvement in consumers' safety was enormous. Upton Sinclair had intended to prove the necessity of socialism by exposing evils of capitalism. But Roosevelt and the progressives sought to preserve the values of free enterprise from both its presumed friends and its avowed enemies.

The Panic of 1907 and What Followed

Such an ambivalent policy required pragmatic skill of a high order. It required a technique of experiment painstakingly applied to one problem after another and abstention from doctrinaire solutions. That

Roosevelt was just as willing to give support to business, when that seemed required by circumstances, as to attack it when the moment seemed ripe for reform, he demonstrated during the Panic of 1907.

In the fall of that year a number of great New York banks failed, some railroads went bankrupt, and widening fear quickly spread to manufacturers who cut wages and dismissed workingmen. Some business-men blamed Roosevelt's trust-busting campaign for the failure of con-fidence in continuing prosperity. Actually, the effects of the National Banking Act of 1863, which made the quantity of paper money issued by national banks dependent on the price of government bonds held by them, intensified the movement of the business cycle—both upwards, when rising bond prices caused expansion of paper-money issues, and downwards, when sinking bond prices caused contraction of these issues. The contraction of paper money during prosperity and expansion during depression would have compensated for the swings of the cycle and helped to avoid the extremes of boom and bust. Furthermore, the exist-ing system provided no machinery whereby a particular bank might quickly realize cash on its loans in order to reassure depositors that the bank was sound. False rumors of a bank's condition could destroy it. These were weaknesses in the nation's credit and banking structure which the Panic dramatized and Congress presently sought to correct.

Meanwhile, Roosevelt was stung by the charge that he was responsible for the Panic and co-operated with the lords of finance and industry in the effort to check it. He was informed by Judge Elbert H. Gary and H. C. Frick that an important firm on the point of failure had among its assets a majority of the stock of the Tennessee Coal and Iron Com-pany which was virtually unmarketable. The United States Steel Cor-poration was willing to save the situation by buying this stock, but its officials feared they would be prosecuted under the antitrust laws, and refused to act without prior assurances from the President. Roosevelt gave the promise they desired and the deal was effected in the library of J. Pierpont Morgan. Morgan and his associates bought the Tennessee Company's important mines and mills for a small fraction of their value. The merger reduced to a legal token the element of competition in the steel industry, and thoroughly subordinated the promising iron and steel business of the South to Eastern interests. Extreme progressives regarded Roosevelt's concession as a betrayal of his antitrust policy, and at a later time a Senate committee charged him with exceeding his authority, but he always claimed that he helped allay the Panic by taking this conservative tack.

The government also had recourse to emergency banking regulation. For immediate relief, the Aldrich-Vreeland Act of May 1908 permitted national banks to issue paper money not only on federal bonds but also on certain commercial loans and municipal, county, and state bonds.

To prevent inflationary abuse of this power in prosperous times, such paper money was subjected to federal taxation which would discourage its issuance except in temporary emergencies when panic or depression made expansion of the currency a sound national policy. For long-range purposes, the Act established the National Monetary Commission. This was to undertake a fundamental study of the banking system in the United States in comparison with that of the other industrial nations, all of which had central banks. Senator Aldrich was chairman of the Commission. This assured that its report, issued four years later in forty volumes, would recommend only such a system as leading bankers approved.

During his final months in office, President Roosevelt seemed to wish to change his tack again and join the more advanced progressives. Consolidation of industry in many lines was proceeding apace. There were many more trusts in existence when he left the White House than when he arrived. While he was proud of "my policies," he bitterly attacked the conservatism of the Supreme Court, exhorted the public to support the progressivism whose leaders he distrusted, and made up in words for the compromises he had found expedient in action.

Perhaps his most important compromise was his choice of Secretary of War William Howard Taft as his successor. Roosevelt's popularity was so great that his preference would be heeded by most party leaders. But like other "strong" Presidents, he did not care for too much political strength in his closest associates. Nor was he able to develop any enthusiasm for Governor Charles Evans Hughes of New York, who was building a reputation as a brilliant and sound progressive. Roosevelt's relation to Taft was that of affectionate friend. He had found Taft to be an admirable administrator in a series of important positions. He admired Taft's jovial good nature and sometimes envied the rotund Ohioan's inability to offend anyone. Taft wished to be utterly loyal to Roosevelt's policies, and he had no disturbing habits of independent thought. The people at large accepted Taft as if they saw him with Roosevelt's eyes. Unhappily for him, however, the forces of progressivism and conservatism had grown so antagonistic that they could no longer be held in balance. Roosevelt was actually escaping from a very difficult political situation when, immediately after his term ended, he went to Africa as a big-game hunter. The American people were more interested in his exploits there than in his successor's problems at home. Never dull, he had often been spectacular, but his boldest and most striking actions were not in the domestic field, where he tried most of the time to follow a middle course. They were in foreign affairs, where he suffered from virtually no inhibitions.

CHAPTER 13

Imperialism and Dollar Diplomacy, 1901-1913

IT WAS IN THE FIELD OF FOREIGN RELATIONS THAT Theodore Roosevelt gained his greatest popularity. Imperialism was still a glowing vision during his presidency, and he won acclaim as a prophet and promoter of American destiny in the world. Though he declared himself a man of peace, he wielded the Big Stick more menacingly in the international arena than ever he did at home. No other political leader did so much to establish the United States as a world power. He set his country on a relatively benign imperialist course in the heyday of European imperialism. He had distinct limitations as a long-range prophet, but no President before him played so conspicuous a part in world affairs.

THE PANAMA CANAL

Not even in his first term did Roosevelt's political instincts dictate caution in external affairs. Indeed, he carried out his boldest enterprise in 1903. This was the acquisition of the Panama Canal Zone. Roosevelt was acutely aware that there was a missing link in the chain of outlying naval positions the nation held. A friend and ardent student of Mahan, he agreed with the navalist's metaphor that a canal at the Isthmus was "part of the coastline of the United States." It was the new status of the United States as a great power that made the Canal important. The frantic voyage of the *U.S.S. Oregon* from Puget Sound around the Horn in order to beat Spanish warships to Cuba in 1898 had demonstrated the strategic need of a short cut.

Merchant ships would of course use a canal, and Great Britain had a larger merchant fleet and more extensive trade with the Far East than

231

the United States. Furthermore, Britain had a naval interest in any Isthmian canal. This arose from her concern that it should not be used to lessen her supremacy on the seas when she was at war and the United States was neutral. These British interests were recognized by the United States in the Clayton-Bulwer Treaty of 1850, which provided for joint action to build a canal and prohibited its fortification.

Several times after the Civil War the United States had shown impatience over its Isthmian obligations to Britain. An effort of a private French company to dig a passage at Panama ended in failure by 1890. After 1896, it became British policy to placate the United States in disputes over detail in order to build up friendship. Secretary Hay and Sir Julian Pauncefote in 1899 negotiated a treaty which abrogated the Clayton-Bulwer Treaty by giving the United States exclusive right to build and own a canal. But the new arrangement still forbade the fortification of the passage. In the election campaign of 1900 the Democrats, not unmindful of the Irish vote, attacked this "surrender" to Great Britain, and the Senate subsequently amended the treaty to give the United States the right to fortify.

Hay was disgusted and the British were annoyed. But the discouragements of the Boer War and ominous motions by Germany led the British government to gamble on friendship with the United States. A second Hay-Pauncefote Treaty, giving the United States the right to fortify as well as build and own a canal, was promptly approved by the Senate in December 1901. A few years later the British withdrew their traditional West Indian naval squadron, leaving the United States in exclusive control of the eastern as well as the western approaches to the Isthmus.

The way was now clear for Roosevelt to concentrate on unsolved local problems of the canal, and he probably never found a troublesome task more congenial. The first question at issue was the location. Nicaragua and Panama both offered feasible routes, and the former had been designated in a bill passed by the Senate in 1899 at the instance of Senator John T. Morgan of Alabama. But representatives of the New Panama Canal Company, successor to the French firm, now set to work. Anxious to dispose of its rights and properties, which they valued at over $100 million, they urged the advantages of the shorter Panama route, where considerable work had been done already. A governmental commission of engineers (the Walker Commission) reported in favor of the Nicaraguan route as the more practicable, saying that the holdings of the new Panama Company were worth only $40 million. The Company hastily lowered its price to that figure, whereupon Roosevelt influenced the Commission to recommend the Panama route. To influence Congress and public opinion the Company distributed lurid propagandist literature stressing Nicaraguan volcanoes. The eruption of Mt. Pelé on the island of Martinique in May 1902 was timely. In June, Congress passed the

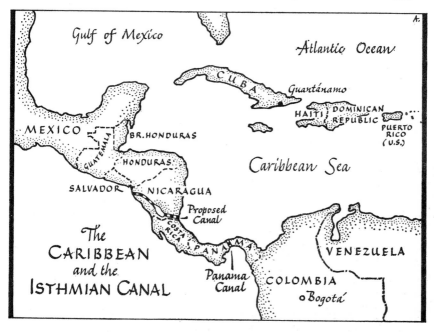

The Caribbean and the Isthmian Canal

Spooner Act, authorizing the President to proceed at Panama. It appropriated the amount now asked for the New Panama Company's concession and directed that a perpetual right-of-way under United States sovereignty be obtained from Colombia. If negotiations failed, the United States should turn to Nicaragua.

Colombia proved difficult. Secretary Hay negotiated a convention whereby the United States would pay her $10 million and an annual rental of $250,000 in return for a 99-year lease with renewal option on a canal zone six miles wide. The Senate approved this Hay-Herran Convention in 1903, but the Colombian legislature wanted a higher price and turned it down. This "impudence" by a small country brought out the unlovely side of Roosevelt's nature. He was very angry, in private he called the Colombians "homicidal corruptionists," and he thought of seizing Panama. While his specific part in the ensuing events is not fully known, the evidence strongly suggests that he gave up the idea of seizure in favor of a plan of the Panama Canal Company, particularly its New York attorney, William N. Cromwell, and the mysterious Philippe Bunau-Varilla.

In October 1903, American warships were ordered to steam to Panama. Bunau-Varilla then cabled to his collaborators in Panama to start a revolution against Colombia. The revolt commenced November 3, and, while American warships prevented Colombian troops from landing, the United States recognized the independence of the Republic of

Panama on November 6. This was probably the world's record for prompt-
ness in such a matter. Bunau-Varilla, although a citizen of France, was
now received as Minister to the United States from the new Republic,
and on November 18 he signed a Convention with Hay giving Panama
the financial terms Colombia had refused and granting the United States
better terms—a canal zone in perpetuity and ten miles wide. The
United States guaranteed the independence of Panama and made the
little country a virtual protectorate. Enough of the inside story of these
events was known at the time to cause an outburst of opposition from
anti-imperialists against what they called Roosevelt's "piracy." But this
did not prevent the Senate from giving its approval to the Hay-Bunau-
Varilla Convention in February 1904.

After so many dreams and plans and failures, United States Army
engineers under Colonel George W. Goethals, ably abetted by sanitation
experts under Colonel William C. Gorgas, completed the waterway in
ten years. Still many Americans were troubled by the treatment of
Colombia and the Harding administration in 1921 paid it $25 million
"conscience money." Various American historians of the Panama Revolution have taken the position that Roosevelt and Hay, by exercising a
little patience and conceding the Colombians' right to bargain, could
have gained the result without resorting to high-handed methods. Roosevelt, who claimed that speed was imperative, was far from penitent.
He publicly boasted in 1911: "I *took* the Canal Zone."

The criticism by Americans was temporarily drowned in his victory in
the election of 1904. Obviously he had not hurt his candidacy, and many
voters were positively entranced by "cowboy diplomacy." European
criticism of him could be disregarded, because all the important European
powers were guilty of similar or worse treatment of weak countries. But
the distrust of Latin Americans was a severe misfortune for the United
States—if for no higher reason because it tempted them to "balance off"
the United States by making concessions to its potential enemies, particularly Germany and Japan. In the thinking of Roosevelt, the naked exercise
of superior power was the best guarantee of the hegemony of the United
States over the whole Caribbean area, and he regarded this hegemony as
a strategic necessity in a world of intensifying naval competition. But
the governments of the Caribbean area often showed the same extreme
irresponsibility in dealing with powerful foreign governments as in their
domestic habits of "dictatorship tempered by revolution." Events in Venezuela and Santo Domingo led Roosevelt to formulate a general policy.

THE ROOSEVELT COROLLARY OF THE MONROE DOCTRINE

The dictator Castro had put Venezuela in heavy debt to private European investors and then refused to pay interest as promised. Great Britain

proposed to Germany and Italy a combined naval demonstration to collect the money. Roosevelt's contempt for the habits of the Latin Americans led him to observe in his first annual message to Congress that under the Monroe Doctrine the United States does not guarantee any state against "punishment" if it "misconducts" itself, so long as the punishment does not include annexations of territory. But when the warships of three European nations in 1902 commenced operations along the Venezuelan coast, blockading it and seizing gunboats, Roosevelt was troubled. He solved the immediate problem by urging arbitration. The European warships departed and the debt dispute was referred to a commission set up by the Hague Tribunal. A similar situation developed in the Dominican Republic. There the United States undertook to supervise administration of the customs and distribution of the proceeds to American and European creditors. When the administrators favored the American creditors, European powers planned a forceful intervention.

In the new era of finance imperialism, when investors were eager to find opportunities in "backward" areas of the world, and the Great Powers were eager to exploit financial irresponsibility by local authorities to gain strategic political positions, Latin America seemed destined to go the way of Africa and Asia. Roosevelt sympathized heartily with the claims of superior civilization and morality which the Powers made to justify their imperialism, but he was determined that in Latin America, and especially in the Caribbean area, the United States should have no rival. Therefore he formulated the "Roosevelt Corollary of the Monroe Doctrine" to make the United States the sole teacher of civilized behavior in the New World, the sole collector of debts, and the sole beneficiary of the political and military advantages that accrue to the guardians of weaker countries. He announced this policy in his annual message of December 1904, as a warning to the European powers to attempt no use of force in the Dominican Republic or anywhere else in the American Hemisphere. He said:

> Chronic wrongdoing, or an impotence which results in a general loosening of the ties of civilized society, may in America, as elsewhere, ultimately require intervention by some civilized nation, and in the Western Hemisphere the adherence of the United States to the Monroe Doctrine may force the United States, however reluctantly, in flagrant cases of such wrongdoing or impotence, to the exercise of an international police power.

This pronouncement officially converted the Monroe Doctrine from a warning against European intervention in Latin America to an arrogation of a right of intervention by the United States. It brought the Monroe Doctrine, originally an expression of the era of libertarian political revolution, into conformity with the new imperialism which made industrial and financial modernity synonymous with civilization, and superior morality indistinguishable from superior power. As the original Monroe Doctrine was the capstone of the libertarian expansion of the United States, the Roosevelt Corollary was the capstone of its imperialist expansion. Until it began to be repudiated a quarter of a century later, this policy and the actions undertaken to effectuate it justified Latin-American fears of the "Yankee Colossus."

At the moment, Latin-American objection was surprisingly mild, perhaps because Roosevelt applied the new principle only in the admittedly bad Dominican situation. Britishers expressed satisfaction that the United States was exercising authority in the Caribbean area from which British naval power had been withdrawn. The United States landed marines in Santo Domingo and stationed warships there. In January 1905, the Dominican government signed a protocol with the United States under which American administrators of the customs offices allocated 45 per cent of receipts to the local government and 55 per cent to service of its external debt. The Senate refused to approve this protocol, Democrats taking the lead in condemning it as a device of imperialism. Roosevelt proceeded under an Executive Agreement without Senate approval until 1907, when the Senate consented to a permanent treaty and United States forces were withdrawn.

In Cuba the Platt Amendment tempted political leaders who lost elections to threaten violence in order to bring about United States intervention which would give them another chance to win power. Estrada Palma followed this procedure in 1906. Secretary of War William H. Taft visited Cuba and advised Roosevelt to act. The President sent troops and appointed a civil governor. This second occupation of Cuba lasted until 1909. In Central America, conflicts among the small republics led the United States, with Mexico, to call a peace conference in Washington in 1907. This succeeded in making peace but the machinery it set up to prevent future conflicts was a failure.

ROOSEVELT AND THE FAR EAST

In the Far East the United States had no interest in hegemony, nor would the public support overt imperialism beyond the Philippines with all the attendant dangers of conflict with the other Great Powers. But Roosevelt was determined to develop American influence in the Far East for strategic and commercial purposes and to fulfill the imperialist conception of the civilizing mission of the United States. Second in significance only to the Corollary, Roosevelt's Far Eastern policy illustrated his understanding of how the United States should use its power in international affairs.

On February 1, 1902, Secretary of State Hay addressed a third Open Door Note to the powers. This extended to industrial opportunities in

China the principle of equality among the powers. Russia had expansive plans in Manchuria, which was part of China, and in the independent kingdom of Korea. In both places Japan was Russia's chief rival, and American opinion favored Japan. The Czarist government, with its Siberian exile of political prisoners and its persecution of Jews, was very unpopular, while "little Japan" was looked upon as a protegé of the United States, charming in her culture and deserving of encouragement in her progress towards Westernization.

In February 1904, after the Russo-Japanese War began, Secretary Hay, sent a note to both belligerents asking them to respect the neutrality and administrative entity of China. Japan made her answer conditional upon Russia's, and Russia rejected the neutralization of Manchuria. Roosevelt decided that a complete victory by either country would injure American interests, which would best be served by a balance of power in the Far East. To the astonishment of the world, Japan showed herself a military and naval match for the Russian giant. After her victory over the Russian fleet in the Battle of Tsushima (May 1905), her government asked Roosevelt to mediate for peace. Rumbles of internal revolution in Russia and fear that "little Japan" might entirely destroy Russian power in the Orient, as well as Roosevelt's penchant for playing a spectacular role among the rulers of the earth, made him agree. Russia consented, and there followed in August 1905 the Russo-Japanese Peace Conference at Portsmouth, New Hampshire, a vivid emblem of the emergence of the United States as a world power.

Roosevelt at the same time made a deal in which he promised that the United States would not interfere with Japanese ambitions in Korea, in exchange for a Japanese promise to respect United States ownership of the Philippines. First written down secretly as the Taft-Katsura Memorandum, the arrangement was later given the public status of an Executive Agreement. It has been called a confession by the United States that the Open Door policy was a failure, but, coupled with Roosevelt's efforts to prevent Japan from achieving hegemony in the Far East, which would have brought all China under her control, it may better be called a partial retreat to a stronger position. At Portsmouth, Roosevelt was partly responsible for Japan's failure to obtain a cash indemnity from Russia and her restriction to southern Sakhalin. Japanese rights in Korea and Manchuria were recognized. For his mediating work, Roosevelt was awarded the Nobel Peace Prize in 1906, but the Japanese cherished resentment against the United States for narrowing the spoils of their victory. Roosevelt, on the other hand, along with many other Americans, acquired a fear of Japan that was cast in the virulent racist terms of "The Yellow Peril."

On the West Coast this hatred burst into action against Japanese and Korean immigrants. The Japanese government had restricted emigration to the United States in 1900, but Japanese continued to come by way of Hawaii, Canada, and Mexico. Justifying racial antipathy by charging unfair competition of Orientals willing to live chiefly on rice, California workmen and farmers organized to impose on the Japanese in their midst a system of segregation. In 1906, the San Francisco School Board ordered Oriental children into segregated schools. The Japanese government charged that this was a violation of a Treaty of 1894 with the United States. Roosevelt vigorously moved to prevent local authorities from disturbing national foreign relations. He persuaded the School Board to withdraw its order in return for a promise that he would act to stop Japanese immigration. Congress obliged by giving the President authority to restrict immigration that was injurious to American "labor conditions," and to use a passport system to gain federal control over immigrants. Roosevelt then made a "Gentlemen's Agreement" (1906) which saved Japanese sensibilities by imposing no racial bar in American law. But it secured the same end by obtaining the co-operation of the Japanese government in refusing to issue passports to laborers intending to emigrate to the United States and its consent to American enforcement of the passport system against illegal entry. This was a statesmanlike solution of a delicate problem, but Roosevelt was stung by the accusations of jingoes that he had truckled to Japan.

It was in part to refute such charges that he ordered the "Great White Fleet" of the United States Navy on its famous cruise around the world (1907-1909). This dramatized, for the benefit of Japan especially, the fact that the United States now ranked second only to Great Britain in naval power. It was a bit of bravura that almost ended in debacle when Congressmen who objected to the "vainglorious gesture" threatened to withhold appropriations necessary to bring the fleet home again. Roosevelt defied them to carry out their threat, and they gave in. The fleet actually met with very friendly demonstrations in Japan and everywhere. Roosevelt claimed that the cruise was his most important service to peace.

His efforts to secure equilibrium in the Far East were climaxed in the Root-Takahira Agreement of 1908. This broadened out the Taft-Katsura Agreement by extending to all territories in the Pacific area the mutual promise to respect each other's possessions and to maintain the status quo there while upholding the Open Door in China and supporting Chinese independence and integrity. It seemed to be a great diplomatic victory for the United States, but Japan took full advantage of her interpretation that the United States had now recognized as part of the status quo Japanese predominance in Manchuria. Since Americans were unwilling to use force, the practice of obtaining diplomatic promises was probably the most effective means available to the United States to save the Philippines and China. The United States under Roosevelt undertook to maintain a balance of power in Asia.

THE UNITED STATES AND THE EUROPEAN POWERS, 1901-1909

Europe was less important than Latin America and Asia as an area for Roosevelt's operations to strengthen the security of the United States. This was because British policy and the British Navy in effect served American interests. British statesmen now saw the industrial, naval, and military strength of the United States as an important aid to Britain if she ever had to fight against a German threat to dominate the Continent. Few American statesmen had an equal understanding that American security would suffer from the destruction of the balance of power in Europe. Even Roosevelt was sometimes confused into thinking that because Germany, Great Britain, and the United States were all "Teutonic" nations, their racial interests must draw them together against threats by nations of "inferior" stock. But the erratic character of Kaiser Wilhelm II, the unpopularity of the Junker officer caste of the German Army, and the menacing techniques of the German government in seeking imperialist advantages everywhere in the world steadily overcame assumptions that race determines international alignments. American suspicion of Germany was particularly aroused by the appearance of a German fleet in Manila Bay during the Spanish-American War, by German aggressiveness in bombarding Venezuela during the debt-collecting demonstration of 1903, and by endemic rumors of German maneuvres to gain a naval position near the Isthmus.

Statesmen and publicists of both Great Britain and the United States encouraged with words the growth of Anglo-American amity, but it was chiefly the British government that acted to eliminate possible sources of friction and open the way for positive co-operation. The Second Hay-Pauncefote Treaty was one such action, and in 1903 Britain sacrificed Canadian interests for the sake of satisfying American claims in the Alaska Boundary Dispute. At stake were the coastal areas around the inlets of the Alaska Panhandle. Control of these became important when the Klondike Gold Rush of 1897 revealed the inlets to be the best means of access to the gold fields of the interior. In January 1903, the United States and Great Britain signed a convention providing for a joint commission to settle the dispute by arbitration. The commission was to be composed of three British and three American "impartial jurists of repute." Roosevelt nevertheless appointed Secretary of War Elihu Root, a reputable jurist but also a member of the administration, and Senators George Turner of Washington and Henry Cabot Lodge of Massachusetts, neither of them jurists nor likely to be impartial. King Edward VII appointed two Canadians and Lord Alverstone, the Lord Chief Justice of England. While the commission met, Roosevelt let it be known that if the decisions went against the United States claims, he would occupy the area with troops and fix the line. The American commissioners voted unanimously in favor of American contentions, and the two Canadians voted against them, but Lord Alverstone, in a remarkable display of Britain's determination to avoid trouble with the United States, sided with its representatives. The line was drawn so that Canada was excluded from all the inlets.

Some Englishmen and Americans advocated an Anglo-American alliance, but American fear of European entanglement was not easy to down, and wiser counsel had it that an "unwritten alliance" was coming into being and would actually be firmer than a written one because it would rest upon voluntary decisions based on common interest rather than a reluctant agreement. In 1904, Britain gained an ally in France. Then it seemed for a time that the United States would enter into European diplomacy actively in favor of the Anglo-French Entente. The occasion was the Moroccan Crisis of 1905.

The Algeciras Conference

Roosevelt had shown his willingness to follow a bold policy in Morocco in 1904 by sending warships to Tangier to back his demand that a Greek who claimed United States citizenship be released from captivity by the Moroccan chieftain Raisuli. Roosevelt shared the inflamed nationalism of the period which sanctioned a risk of war for the sake of protecting even the most dubious of citizens in foreign misadventures. The political significance of such nationalism is suggested by Roosevelt's timing: his challenge to Raisuli was read to the Republican National Convention then meeting in Chicago. Raisuli gave in.

The important question about Morocco was whether Germany would allow France to develop control over this weak but rich country. In March 1905, the Kaiser arrived at Tangier on a warship and made a provocative anti-French speech. A general European war seemed possible. Germany was not ready for this, however, and the Kaiser asked Roosevelt to call an international conference to settle the Moroccan question. Roosevelt agreed and convinced Britain and France that they should attend the meeting at Algeciras, Spain, in January 1906. Americans were startled to find that two delegates represented the United States in this conference which seemed to concern European rivalries exclusively. But Roosevelt could point to United States treaty relations with Morocco, the Open Door principles, and general interest in peace, as reasons for American participation. Such considerations had never before been urged to justify American participation in European politics.

The United States delegates sided with the British and French at Algeciras. A convention was drawn up that affirmed for Morocco the Open Door principles of territorial integrity and trade equality, but

France and Spain were given control over local police forces. Roosevelt helped persuade the German government to accept this settlement. To increase its prestige, Roosevelt submitted the Algeciras Convention to the United States Senate for approval as a treaty. This action frightened isolationists, particularly Democrats, with the prospect of American enforcement of the Convention if the Kaiser should violate it. Opposition was vociferous, but approval was secured by a small margin after a reservation had been attached specifying that ratification was not to be interpreted as a departure from the traditional refusal of the United States to take part in European affairs.

Roosevelt believed that he had been the chief engineer of a peaceful resolution of the Moroccan Crisis and was prone to exaggerate his role. The fundamental rivalries leading the European Powers towards war had not been dissolved, and a tendency of the United States to make common cause with the Atlantic Powers against the Central Powers had become visible. An armaments race was now under way, and the United States was a leading contender in the naval race. The United States Navy was intended for defense, but its building policy was based on the doctrine of Mahan that the best naval defense is achieved by a force that can seek out an enemy in its own waters and destroy it. This required chief emphasis on battleships, and it made the United States Navy indistinguishable from navies built for aggressive imperialist purposes.

The Peace Movement

The armaments race and the periodic international crises made anti-imperialists and pacifists in the United States and other countries intensify their campaigns for peace. In 1899, at the invitation of Czar Nicholas II of Russia, delegates of 26 nations, including the United States, met at The Hague to consider disarmament and peaceful methods of settling international disputes. This First Hague Conference may be regarded as the ancestor of the League of Nations and the United Nations. Efforts to achieve an agreement on disarmament were a failure, partially because the Czar was suspected of wishing to compensate for the loss of position by Russia in the race for armed strength, and possibly because the powers were careful to send generals and admirals as members of their delegations.

The Conference did establish the Permanent Court of International Arbitration. When the United States ratified the Convention, however, it stipulated that it would not resort to arbitration in any case involving national honor or integrity, and by a special reservation excluded from arbitration any dispute involving the Monroe Doctrine. So the United States was partly to blame for the meagerness of the results of this first modern effort to organize world peace.

President Roosevelt in 1904 suggested another effort, and after the Russo-Japanese War the Czar called the nations to the Second Hague Conference in 1907. Again efforts to halt the arms race failed. Secretary of State Elihu Root proposed a court of international justice with genuine powers, but he received slight support. An international prize court to adjudicate cases involving neutral rights at sea was established. The United States pleased Latin Americans by proposing a modified version of the "Drago Doctrine" in which an Argentinian had proposed the prohibition of debt-collecting expeditions. The American proposal was that force should not be used to collect debts until after an attempt at arbitration or refusal of the debtor to abide by an arbitral decision. This was adopted by the Conference. The Roosevelt administration tried to negotiate bilateral treaties of arbitration with many nations but it offended the Senate by defining the instruments which would settle specific disputes as "agreements" over which the Executive would have exclusive authority, and refusing to accept the substitution of the word "treaties." So it was left for the Taft and Wilson administrations to attempt to carry forward the building of machinery for peace.

The Hague Conferences deluded almost no one into thinking that rising world tensions would be reduced by the very governments which produced them. The great remaining hope was that public opinion could be mobilized in sufficient strength to force legislative bodies to prevent war. In Europe the Social Democratic parties, growing in strength almost everywhere, were looked to as the chief hope for peace. In the United States the chief strength of the antiwar movement, closely linked as it was to anti-imperialism, lay in the Democratic Party. For all Roosevelt's skill in exploiting American power and influence in the world, he was widely distrusted as an adventurer who treated international politics as a game and played it too recklessly.

"Dollar Diplomacy," 1909-1913

When Taft succeeded Roosevelt in 1909, he appointed as Secretary of State Philander C. Knox, an able corporation lawyer who had served as Attorney General under McKinley and Roosevelt. The President, taking no particular interest in foreign affairs, allowed Knox to develop the system of "Dollar Diplomacy" which was his administration's only important contribution to the effort to use the power of the United States to national advantage.

To Knox the most important aspect of foreign relations was commercial intercourse. The United States now produced not only surplus food and manufactures but also surplus capital whose owners eagerly sought opportunities for profitable investment abroad. Investments in European countries presented the government with no great problem, and most of the surplus American capital went into them. But investments in countries with undeveloped economies and unstable governments raised important questions of governmental policy. Knox conceived it to be the duty of his department to promote and support investments in "backward" countries. This seemed to him a way to bring material improvements to them, to open doors for exports of American surplus capital, and to increase the political influence of the United States. The risks to which such investments were subject made high profits imperative, but such profits were possible by virtue of low wage scales. If the United States government supported the investments, the whole system would become workable and beneficial to all concerned. This was the reasoning behind the experiment in Dollar Diplomacy. It was tested most fully in China and in Latin America.

China

Willard Straight, the United States consul in Manchuria, became alarmed by the growth of Japanese influence. He decided that the United States could maintain the Open Door much more successfully by increasing its financial stake and consequently its political influence in China than by confining itself to moral exhortations. Straight, who became in 1908 acting chief of the Division of Far Eastern Affairs in Washington, convinced Secretary Knox that the financing of the Hukuang Railroad in central and southern China offered an opportunity to gain for "the voice of the United States more authority in political controversies in that country which will go far toward guaranteeing the preservation of the administrative entity of China." Knox induced J. P. Morgan and other investment bankers to provide the capital, and the administration insisted that the British, French, and German financiers of the Hukuang project allow the Americans to participate. Without American participation the Hukuang consortium might have tried to exploit ownership of the railroad more disadvantageously for China. But American anti-imperialists saw little or no difference between Dollar Diplomacy and the imperialism of other powers in China.

In Manchuria, Knox tried another scheme, whereby bankers of all the powers would create a pool of capital so that the government of China could buy the Manchurian railroads and fend off the political dangers of Japanese and Russian ownership. But the proposal only turned the rival Japanese and Russian governments into allies long enough to defeat the scheme. Knox induced the Chinese government to borrow a large sum of money from foreign bankers in order to strengthen Chinese currency and finance industries in Manchuria. Although the United States joined a six-power consortium agreement to make the loan, the bankers, who had been reluctant from the beginning, informed President Wilson the day after he was inaugurated in 1913 that they wished to withdraw. Wilson, who represented the critical anti-imperialist view of Dollar Diplomacy, withdrew the United States from the consortium on the ground that this was itself a threat to China's independence.

Dollar Diplomacy in the Far East was a failure, and perhaps worse than no policy at all. Knox's activities precipitated the Russo-Japanese Agreement of 1911 dividing Manchuria into spheres of influence. Theodore Roosevelt told Taft that the policy in the Far East amounted to a dangerous bluffing game, since the United States was not prepared to go to war in defense of the Open Door. Japan was clearly driving for hegemony in Asia. Great Britain, no more willing to war against such a threat than the United States, tried to contain it; and, by means of the Anglo-Japanese Alliance of 1911, she sought to prevent Japan from joining enemies of Britain in case of a European war. China fell into chronic civil war when republicans under Dr. Sun Yat-Sen rebelled against the Manchu dynasty. The British policy and the Chinese Revolution played into the hands of Japanese imperialists when the World War began, and the Wilson administration in a greatly aggravated situation had to search once more for a sound policy towards Asia.

Latin America

Dollar Diplomacy was pursued most aggressively in Latin America. Realizing that the Panama Canal would be endangered if some other power should gain influence in one or another of the neighboring republics, Knox sought security by making the United States their sole guardian. If the dollar should push investors of all the other powers out of the region, no excuse for intervention by them would remain. The Roosevelt Corollary had asserted the authority of the United States to intervene in Latin America to collect debts owed to European investors; Knox extended the Corollary to eliminate European creditors from the scene. In the Far East, Dollar Diplomacy was an attempt to buy some chips in order to win a seat for the United States among the powers at the political poker table; in Latin America it was an attempt to end the game entirely by declaring the United States the sole winner. In 1909, Knox feared that British holders of Honduras bonds would induce their government to help them collect payments, so he urged American bankers to buy the bonds. In 1910, he persuaded four American bankers to put capital into the National Bank of Haiti. But Nicaragua and Mexico turned out to be the crucial Latin-American arenas for the experiment in Dollar Diplomacy.

Since Nicaragua offered an alternate canal route, the United States government was especially sensitive to foreign influences there. Periodic revolution made a hunting ground for foreign diplomats, and American agents were active. In 1911, Adolfo Díaz, who was friendly to the United

States, became president. Secretary Knox obtained from him the Knox-Castrillo Convention granting to the United States rights of intervention and turning over administration of the customs to an American official. Immediately, Nicaragua defaulted on payments to British creditors. Knox, without waiting for the Senate to approve the Convention, persuaded American bankers to lend Nicaragua $1.5 million, customs receipts being pledged for repayment. The bankers were also given control of the National bank of Nicaragua and of the government-owned railroads.

This arrangement was so bald that anti-imperialists in the Senate prevented approval of the Knox-Castrillo Convention and of a similar arrangement with Honduras. Nicaraguans also objected to their government's selling their country to American banks and revolted in 1912. President Taft ordered United States Marines to land in order to protect American interests. Knox negotiated a new treaty with the Díaz government, giving Nicaragua $3 million in return for exclusive right to build a canal, a ninety-year lease on Great Corn and Little Corn Islands on the Caribbean side and a naval base in the Gulf of Fonseca on the Pacific side. The Senate refused to act. Marines were nevertheless maintained in Nicaragua for twenty years and they prevented any change to a governmental policy unfriendly to the United States.

When a syndicate of Japanese businessmen began to negotiate the purchase of a huge tract of Mexican land near Magdalena Bay in Lower California, an inviting site for a naval base from which both the Panama Canal and the Pacific Coast of the United States could be menaced, Secretary Knox conveyed the disapproval of his government and they dropped the project. Senator Lodge seized the occasion to introduce a resolution declaring United States opposition to the transfer of strategic sites in the Americas to non-American private companies which might be acting as agents for a foreign government. The Senate, in August 1912, overwhelmingly approved this. The Lodge Corollary to the Monroe Doctrine extended the no-transfer principle to private groups as well as governments and to Asian as well as European countries. It was invoked several times in later years to prevent the sale to Japanese of Mexican properties owned by Americans.

Dollar Diplomacy was temporarily more successful in Latin America than in Asia. But the United States virtually denied independence to the Caribbean and Central American republics, and openly denied the right of revolution and the right of these small countries to conduct their own foreign and financial affairs. All Latin America watched this assertion of American might with growing apprehension.

Canadian Reciprocity and International Arbitration

The basic goodwill of Taft's foreign policy was demonstrated in several actions which unfortunately attracted little attention and most of which proved futile. In 1912, an Anglo-American Convention accepted a decision of the Hague Tribunal which compromised disputed American claims to rights in the fisheries around Newfoundland. This finally solved the old fisheries question.

Exploitive hunting of seals in the North Pacific by citizens of several countries threatened the herds with extinction. To institute reasonable regulations, a conference of the United States, Great Britain, Russia, and Japan was held in Washington in 1911. It drew up a convention which forbade pelagic (oceanic) sealing north of the 30th parallel for fifteen years, gave the United States exclusive authority to hunt the animals, and required that profits be shared with Great Britain and Japan. This agreement remained in force until 1940, when Japan abrogated it.

The United States tried to re-establish trade reciprocity with Canada, which had been ruptured by the Civil War. Canadian exports to the United States were severely injured by the Payne-Aldrich Tariff Act of 1909. The Canadian Reciprocity Agreement of 1911 exchanged tariff reductions on Canadian agricultural products for reductions on United States manufactures. The House and Senate approved the Agreement, but unfortunate references by President Taft and some Congressmen to reciprocity as a prelude to annexation deeply offended Canadians. In the Canadian elections of 1911 the Conservative party opposed reciprocity as a matter of patriotism and carried the election.

President Taft, because of his deep respect for the judicial function, believed that the way to secure world peace was to strengthen Secretary Root's arbitration treaties. A special motive for reopening the question appeared when a renewal of the Anglo-Japanese Alliance in 1911 provided that neither party would be bound by the alliance to go to war with a third country with which it had a treaty of general arbitration. Great Britain had secured the insertion of this clause to reassure Americans. A strong arbitration agreement was promptly signed with Britain and another with France.

These agreements did not exempt from arbitration questions involving vital interests or national honor, and they provided that if one of the parties still denied that a dispute was "justiciable," a high commission should decide whether it must nevertheless be submitted to arbitration. The latter provision seemed to some Senators, especially Henry Cabot Lodge, to leave the United States Senate out of consideration, although that body would still have opportunity to reject a final treaty incorporating an agreement reached by arbitration. President Taft vigorously appealed to the public to support the treaties, but the Senate amended them to exempt from arbitration questions involving the Monroe Doctrine, Oriental immigration, and national debts, and to assure the right of the Senate to determine whether a dispute might be arbitrated. These with other reservations left the treaties mere shadows. President Taft, deeply disappointed, refused to ratify them. Senator Lodge employed in the arbitration fight the technique of weakening an internationalist project by means of Senate reservations. He was to do this again in the presidency of Woodrow Wilson.

CHAPTER 14

The Progressives and President Taft

During the administration of Theodore Roosevelt a movement got under way to which his successor was unable to adjust himself. As consequences the Republican Party split in 1912, a new national party bearing the name "Progressive" offered candidates at the polls, and a Democrat, Woodrow Wilson, was elected President. The Progressive movement was more than the Progressive Party. Represented in both major parties considerably before 1912, it owed much to the political evangelism of William Jennings Bryan, whose monetary policies were repudiated but whose eloquent advocacy of popular rule and spirited attacks on the abuses of wealth were well remembered. Its origins may be seen in the beginnings of the governorship of Robert M. La Follette in Wisconsin in 1901, in the work of muckrakers soon thereafter, and in the Square Deal of Theodore Roosevelt. Its end result was the reform program of Woodrow Wilson. The Progressive Party was short-lived, but in the domestic sphere the entire period between the turn of the century and the outbreak of the First World War may be designated as the Progressive Era.

The Progressive Movement

Progressivism differed from Populism in that it added to Western and Southern radicalism elements of the Eastern labor movement and a strong middle-class representation. It drew leaders from all these groups and from descendants of the old merchant and landed aristocracies, many of them ill at ease in the new age of industrialism and finance capitalism. An emerging class of intellectuals—including journalists, editors, clergymen, novelists, sociologists, economists, historians, poets, and artists—

directly or indirectly worked for Progressivism. Even the philanthropy of Andrew Carnegie tended to support the cause—in its social aspirations if not in its political purposes.

Progressivism was an effort to restore the individual human being to his position as the chief beneficiary of American life and institutions, under conditions of maximum liberty. In this it did not differ from Populism or any of the earlier great reform movements of American history. But Populism had tried to reverse the course of economic and political development and restore the old agrarian and small-business foundations of individual liberty. Progressivism accepted urbanism and large-scale business as inevitable. It tried to find ways to reduce their injurious effects on individual freedom and to make them serve the welfare of the many instead of the profits of the few. The Populists were belated Jeffersonians who wished to restore the individual to supremacy by weakening the economic and political centers of power that threatened to dominate him. Progressives tried to accomplish the same thing by making government stronger than Big Business; they sought to use Hamiltonian power in the popular interest. The Democratic Party retained the Populist and Jeffersonian affection for smallness in industry and state-rights in politics longer than the Insurgent Republicans, but when its leaders assumed responsibility for administering the national government, first under Woodrow Wilson and later under Franklin D. Roosevelt, they, too, without hesitation used Hamiltonian means to secure Jeffersonian ends.

The first generation that witnessed the triumph of industry after the Civil War defined progress as advance in the production of wealth. The uneven distribution of this wealth led the second generation to redefine progress as advance in the welfare of the many—intellectual, spiritual, and social as well as economic and political welfare—and this was the definition understood by those who called themselves Progressives. Theirs was a movement to make human values supreme over material values despite the prestige of unparalleled material achievements. Socialists declared that the mere existence of private ownership of industry made it impossible to avoid the political dictatorship of capitalists, and that socialized ownership of the means of production was a precondition of political democracy. But the Progressives believed that socialized ownership would require a governmental apparatus for economic administration so powerful that the cure would be worse than the disease. They believed that the forms of American government were not inevitably and exclusively instruments of capitalism; rather, they could be used by the people for their own benefit. Accordingly, the Progressives had as one of their great aims the restoration to the people of control over government—federal, state, and local. In all fields they sought to popularize political processes.

Extension of Popular Government

The United States Senate had been designed to withstand vagaries of the more democratic lower house; now this caution of the Fathers had eventuated in wholesale bribery of state legislatures by regional economic interests to elect Senators. It was a notorious fact that there were coal, lumber, steel, meat, oil, railroad, silver, and copper Senators. Time after time the House passed reform bills and the Senate defeated them. The Progressives' cure for this situation was the Seventeenth Amendment to the Constitution, adopted in 1912, which required that the people vote directly for their Senators.

The Progressive criticism of the political process cut still deeper. Even when the people voted directly for officials, often their only choice was between candidates nominated by party bosses. The cure advocated for this was the direct primary, that is, the nomination of party candidates by ballot of all party members. This technique was not widely advocated for nominations for the presidency. That task was left to national party conventions, but the Progressives demanded that the delegates to these be elected by party members rather than appointed by party officials. They also devised the presidential preference primary in which party members could instruct their delegates whom to support in the national conventions.

Not content with giving voters more control over the election of officials, the Progressives worked in various states to give them control over the conduct of officials. The ancient American suspicion that power corrupts found new expression in the initiative, whereby voters themselves could force the legislature to consider a bill; the referendum, whereby a bill before becoming law would be referred to voters for approval; and recall, whereby officials duly elected or appointed could be removed from office on demand of the voters. All these devices were designed to increase the power and participation of the people in government and to make office-holders more responsive to them.

In some respects the political reforms of the Progressives favored pure democracy and violated the theory of representative government. That theory assumed that public officials should be chosen for special governmental skills, knowledge, and experience which the ordinary voter could not be expected to match, and that authority to use his judgment should therefore be allowed an official. Impeachment would serve as a safeguard against crime, while periodic elections would give the voters power to approve or disapprove the broad course of an official's work. Most controversial were the Progressive demands that judges be subject to recall —even that their decisions be reversible—by popular vote. To make the work of judges, which requires highly specialized training in law, subject to direct popular control would end the independence of the judiciary and place the ultimate guarantees of individual and minority rights at the disposal of majorities no matter how temporary or impassioned. But Progressives were so intent on abolishing the evils resulting from business-men's abuses of constitutional guarantees that they were blinded to the fact that civil liberties also depend on those guarantees. In 1911, President Taft vetoed a joint resolution of Congress admitting Arizona as a state because the proposed constitution included recall of judges. Arizona removed the clause in 1912, was admitted, and then restored it. Roose-velt's pronouncement, early in that year, in favor of recall of judicial decisions marked his defiance of conservative Republicans.

The western states were generally most militant in advancing Pro-gressive political reforms, and the southern states most hesitant. But even states like Wisconsin and Oregon, which adopted virtually all of the Progressive political devices, did not use them very often. Results did not come up to expectations. It proved to be as difficult to arouse voters to action under the new machinery as under the old. The most effective procedure in the Progressive as in every other reformist era was that of electing officials of integrity and ability who were committed to reform.

The woman suffrage movement aroused more enthusiasm than any other political reform. It gained success first in the western states and then in the nation. The winning arguments were that women were show-ing devotion to public welfare equal or superior to that of men, par-ticularly in humanitarian endeavors, and that, because of their idealistic natures, women would be less subject than men to political machines and corruption, more likely to vote for reform and reform candidates. Colorado, Wyoming, Idaho, and Utah had granted women full voting rights by 1900. Progressivism gave the movement new impetus. Five more states granted women suffrage between 1910 and 1912. Eastern women of wealth and social position joined the movement after aristocratic Englishwomen had given them an example of militancy. The demand for an amendment to the federal Constitution was espoused by Roosevelt early in 1912; Wilson and the Democrats were more reluctant.

The Struggle against Boss Rule

Reformers looked to the overthrow of political bosses and machines as an indispensable first step in any Progressive program. The struggle against boss rule illustrated the evolution of reform from agrarian Populism to urban Progressivism. A link between them was Henry George. His Single Tax program derived from the agrarian belief that land is the source of all wealth, but its most dramatic implications were manifest in the cities— with their slums, their extremes of wealth, their corrupt political machines, their real-estate speculators, and their gouging landlords.

A whole corps of municipal reform leaders were inspired by George's *Progress and Poverty*. An early one was Samuel ("Golden Rule") Jones, the mayor of Toledo, Ohio, from 1897 to 1904. The granting of city franchises to private companies for the operation of electric street railways and other utilities was a chief source of graft for the machine bosses of the era, and Mayor Jones fought to a standstill both major party organizations by appealing to the people for a nonpartisan vote in favor of municipal ownership of utilities. His successor was Brand Whitlock, who carried on the reform administration for some years. Tom Johnson, himself a traction magnate who was converted to reform by reading George's book, was elected mayor of Cleveland on a municipal ownership platform in 1901. For eight years his fight against bosses and businessmen won national attention, and he greatly improved the city's schools, parks, and prisons, while gaining lower street-car fares and more honest tax assessments.

In 1910, Emil Seidel was elected mayor of Milwaukee on the Socialist ticket but his program was essentially reformist rather than Socialist. The great cities of the East were most difficult to reform. The Republican machine in Philadelphia, the Democratic machine in Boston, and, most infamous, the Tammany Democratic machine of New York were scarcely affected by spasmodic uprisings of good-government leaders whom they called "Goo-Goos." Municipal reformers were mostly political amateurs, driven to act by indignation. Over the long pull, they were no match for professionals who worked at politics calmly and methodically all their lives. The larger the city the more important was the immigrant vote, and the machine politicians knew how to appeal to the slum-dwellers with occasional favors, picincs, and a friendliness that gave strangers a sense that they "belonged," that they had a contact with power. The reformers were often righteous in manner and so high-toned in their appeal to idealism that near-illiterate voters were unmoved by them. The standard pattern of the struggle between the Progressives and the bosses was one of temporary successes for reform, giving way to apathy and the return of the machine. But the machine bosses themselves perceived that blatant abuses would bring on a revolt of the Good Government groups and leaders. An occasional leader like Al Smith of New York emerged with a talent for combining the methods of machine politics with the aims of the reformers.

A permanent gain of the Progressive Era was the city-manager form of government. It was invented by the city council of Dayton, Ohio, in 1914, when a great flood caused the legislators to appoint an emergency administrator with power to conduct municipal affairs as a business manager would rule a corporation. A city manager was relatively free of political pressure because he held his job so long as he rendered satisfactory service. The plan was adopted by other cities, particularly in the Middle West. But it was rarely adopted by large cities precisely because in them the machine bosses were most powerful. The only hope for urban political salvation lay in a growth of the individual citizen's sense of responsibility for the proper conduct of public affairs. A sign that such growth had begun in the Progressive Era was the increase in permanent, organized citizens' groups which watched the details of governmental activity and kept officials in a wholesome state of respect for their influence on voters.

The war against boss rule was waged also on the state level. The states were the seed-ground of national Progressivism. Reputations made by governors could lead to the Senate and even to the White House. The states proved to be laboratories in which new types of legislation and administration were tried out and advocated for national adoption.

As early as 1880, Robert M. La Follette of Wisconsin began his struggle against local Republican bosses and found he could win office by going personally to farmers and convincing them that he would honestly support their interests. After three terms in Congress he broke with his state's "Lumber Senator," Philetus Sawyer, returned to Wisconsin, and fought the Republican bosses for the governorship. He learned from his defeats to strengthen his ties with the voters and to develop a sweeping program of reforms needed by the people of his state. An important innovation was his use of scholars on the faculty of the state university as experts to advise him. Common sense perhaps sufficed for a governmental administrator in Jackson's time; specialized knowledge of economics, sociology, and political science were now essential. In 1900, La Follette overturned boss control of the Republican state convention, gained the nomination for governor by acclamation, and then won the election. In his three terms he installed the Progressive system which became nationally famous as the "Wisconsin Idea." He appointed academic and technical experts to office, particularly in new agencies for business regulation.

In 1906, he carried a national version of his program to the United States Senate and began his dynamic bid for the leadership of all Progressive elements. Hiram W. Johnson of California, Albert B. Cummins of Iowa, Charles Evans Hughes of New York, "Alfalfa Bill" Murray of Oklahoma, Charles B. Aycock of North Carolina, Robert Bass of New Hampshire, James M. Cox of Ohio, and Woodrow Wilson of New Jersey were some of the other most successful leaders of state Progressivism. Everywhere the bosses of one or both major parties were allied with business interests, and everywhere the Progressives fought for the liberation of their states from this alliance and for a restoration of government to the people.

Social and Labor Legislation

It was on the state level that Progressivism added to its reforms a significant new program of social and labor legislation. This was designed to raise the status of the people who had lost position in the new economic order. Progressive state administrations adopted workmen's compensation laws to force employers to assist those who were maimed in their service. One interesting result was a new regard for the value of the human being on the part of employers as expressed in safety practices in industry, although these had to be made statutory to bring backward employers into line. State health codes were modernized to force employers to observe elementary precautions and install sanitary facilities in factories.

Agitators like Jacob Riis of New York showed that urban slums were breeders of disease and crime. Interference with the traditional freedom of landlords to offer what they pleased to tenants on a take-it-or-leave-it basis was necessitated by the extremes of exploitation. New York in 1900 adopted a state law establishing minimum standards of ventilation, safety, and health for housing in cities. Most of the states containing large cities adopted tenement laws and strengthened the codes as years passed, but enforcement was perhaps less sucessful in this than any other area. Overcrowding, filth, disease, and crime remained the common lot of slum dwellers. The venality of petty officials who winked at landlords' violations of law, and the unwillingness even of Progressives to deal radically with private-property rights, allowed the slums to survive in almost undiminished horror. Some aid to the most helpless victims came from state laws to safeguard women workers in industry, to prohibit child labor, to give aid to mothers with dependent children who lacked other means of support, and to provide pensions for the aged. American experiments with social security laws were still insignificant compared to the advances in other industrial nations.

Most of these laws dealt with the symptoms of poverty. But a group of labor laws attempted to relieve poverty itself by putting an end to the freedom of employers to offer what wages they pleased. Maximum-hours laws were first passed to protect children and women, and women were the first beneficiaries of minimum-wage laws. Trades particularly dangerous to health were sometimes regulated by maximum-hours laws, and such a law of New York, limiting bakers to ten hours a day, raised the constitutional question of freedom of contract. Employers argued that if an employee wished to make a contract to work more than the statutory ten hours, his freedom as well as the employer's was violated by a state prohibition. In 1905, the Supreme Court supported this view and declared the New York law invalid (Lochner vs. New York). In 1908, however, the Court upheld an Oregon law limiting women to ten hours' work per day (Muller vs. Oregon). Many states subsequently passed hours laws while a few adopted wage laws for women and prohibited child labor.

Enforcement of these laws was not rigorous and the federal courts presently interposed new constitutional barriers against them. The most serious weakness of state Progressivism was that it placed any state that adopted advanced laws in an unfavorable competitive position. When New York outlawed child labor or sweatshops, employers simply moved across the Hudson River to New Jersey. Some states, particularly in the South, eagerly invited "runaway" companies to escape the social legislation, the taxes, the militant labor unions, and the higher labor costs of Progressive states. This was a leading reason why many Progressives who had won some success in their own states turned to the national government for national legislation.

ELECTION OF 1908: TAFT AS PRESIDENT

Long before the election of 1908, the public understood that Roosevelt wanted his Secretary of War, William Howard Taft, to succeed him. The caution of Roosevelt in driving for Progressive legislation during his first years in the White House was forgotten in the establishment of federal regulation of the transportation, food, and drug industries; and Roosevelt's failure to push other Progressive reforms through Congress during his last two years in office was not remarked as much as the increasing militancy of his speeches. The total absence from Taft's personal record of any initiative in favor of any Progressive idea was ignored in the face of Roosevelt's obvious affection for him. All this, coupled with the steady growth of Progressivism in the Republican Party, resulted in serious misunderstanding that was exposed but not resolved at the Republican National Convention of June 1908 in Chicago.

Senator La Follette was able to gain only minority support, mostly from westerners, for a proposed platform that advocated a physical valuation of railroads as a basis for rate regulation, reduction of the tariff, popular election of Senators, and other reforms. The majority, under the guidance of Senator Henry Cabot Lodge as chairman, called the La Follette proposals "Socialistic and Democratic." The platform they adopted nevertheless pledged continuance of Roosevelt's policies and specifically called for tariff revision and the strengthening of the Sherman Anti-Trust Act and the Interstate Commerce Act. The Lodge forces, essentially constituting the Old Guard, sought by these concessions to avoid a party split, to win the election, and to hold the westerners in check. Taft gained the presidential nomination on the first ballot and James S. Sherman of New York, a recognized conservative, was named for Vice-President.

The Democrats met in Denver in July. Repenting of their abandonment of the party's most noted leader in 1904, the National Convention for the third time nominated William Jennings Bryan for President. The party platform was a thoroughly Progressive document, promising reduction of the tariff with free entry for products which would compete with those of American monopoly industries, vigorous enforcement of the antitrust law, and prohibition of injunctions in labor disputes. Eugene V. Debs was nominated again by the Socialist Party. In this contest the positions of the two major parties in 1904 seemed to be reversed, as the Republican nominee was more conservative and the Democratic more Progressive; but the mantle of Roosevelt meant more than shadings of political philosophy. Taft got almost exactly the same popular vote that Roosevelt had received, Bryan got a larger vote than Parker, and Debs held his own. The electoral vote was 321 for Taft, and 162 for Bryan.

During the winter the first shadow fell on the Taft-Roosevelt friendship when the President-elect failed to follow all of Roosevelt's preferences in appointments. But Taft continued to want the counsel of his predecessor. Indeed, during Roosevelt's hunting expedition in Africa and grand tour of the European capitals, Taft often seemed at a loss without it. He was bound to administer his office in accordance with his nature. He did not know how to take the limelight away from Roosevelt. He liked to mingle with people, to make pleasant ceremonial speeches around the country, and to radiate good cheer. But he did not believe in Roosevelt's enlarged conception of presidential leadership. He left Congress largely to its own devices, he allowed the rather mediocre members of his Cabinet to make policy for their departments, and he himself offered no important ideas to the public. The consequence was that his administration, when compared with Roosevelt's, seemed like a play without a hero.

Taft was one of those unhappy Presidents with little political skill, although this large and genial man was otherwise highly qualified for the office. He was an excellent administrator but he was not a maker of policy, at a time when the Progressives were gaining control in both parties and a negative position was becoming unacceptable. The office that really comprised all his ambition was a Supreme Court justiceship, and he was miscast in the presidency. His successes seemed at the time few and insignificant, his mistakes disastrous and overwhelming. That in four years so admirable a man should have wrecked his party, lost his friendship with Roosevelt, and suffered rejection by the public was one of the great personal tragedies of American political history. The office of Chief Executive had now grown so important that nothing less than a high order of political talent was adequate for success in it.

DOMESTIC AFFAIRS UNDER TAFT

President Taft wanted to pursue the domestic policies of his friend Theodore, and to a fair extent he did. On certain critical issues, however, he aligned himself with the "stand-pat" wing of his party, while stubbornly refusing to recognize that fact. He got himself into a position where he was impelled to condone, and at length even to extol, measures which he probably did not wholly approve and which Progressives thought indefensible.

Payne-Aldrich Tariff

Nothing except appallingly bad judgment can explain Taft's actions on the tariff. Roosevelt had shown great astuteness in avoiding any action whatever on this divisive issue. No forthright policy on the tariff could please both of the major factions of the Republican Party, and Taft made a bad choice unnecessarily worse. For years the Western Progressive and Eastern reformist elements in both parties had clamored for reduction of the superprotective rates of the Dingley Act of 1897. The cost of living had been rising since that time, and consumers generally blamed the tariff. The Republican Party in its 1908 platform finally advocated a "revision" of the rates. In common political usage this meant revision *downwards*, and during the campaign Taft himself thus defined the word.

To carry out his and the party's promise he called Congress into special session after he was inaugurated. On April 9, 1909, the Payne Bill passed the House. It placed a number of raw materials on the free list and reduced rates on some items of interest to great trusts, such as iron, steel and lumber, while raising duties on some finished textiles, fruits, and plate glass. On average it was a moderate downward revision. In the upper house the Payne Bill was committed to Senator Aldrich's fortress of the Old Guard. In secret session the Committee on Finance added 600 amendments, most of them raising rates for favored industries, notably those controlled by great Eastern corporations and Wall Street banks. Rates were meaninglessly raised for a few industries that faced no foreign competition. The notorious "Schedule K," dealing with wool and woolens, actually represented little change from the high rates of the Dingley Tariff, but in all significant respects the bill now amounted to a revision *upwards*. A House provision for an inheritance tax was eliminated. On the Senate floor the Bill was subjected to scathing attack by the Progressives led by La Follette, Dolliver of Iowa, and Beveridge. Democrats joined in the assault while newspapers excoriated the Bill, which raised the rate on newsprint.

The Old Guard did not bother to answer the elaborate statistical and sociological arguments of the Progressive orators. President Taft remained strangely silent, as did the party's elder statesman, Senator Elihu Root, and others who had declared at election time that tariff rates should be lowered. The Payne-Aldrich Tariff was put through both houses and the President signed it on August 5, 1909. It was a clear proof that, while the Republican Party officially admitted that justification for such high protective rates no longer existed, its legislative leaders were more interested in helping the large corporations to avoid competition than in relieving the consuming public. President Taft made his surrender to the Old Guard seem much worse to aroused Westerners by stating in a speech at Winona, Minnesota, that the law was the best tariff act ever adopted under the aegis of the Republican Party. It did more than any other single measure to convince voters that government must be returned to the people.

Taft's ineptitude, which was so strikingly manifested here, tempted Roosevelt to recover for himself the office his successor could not manage, and Taft's support of the Old Guard made the Progressives willing to split the party to ensure his defeat. Yet the outcome of his domestic policy —the shattering of his friendship with Roosevelt and the splitting of the Republican Party—made him seem a more thorough conservative and opponent of Progressivism than he really was.

Antitrust Actions and Reforms

He was more active than Roosevelt in prosecuting trusts for violation of the Sherman Act. In Roosevelt's seven years, 44 antitrust suits were initiated; in Taft's four years, Attorney General George W. Wickersham initiated 90 suits. One of these took on an anti-Roosevelt aspect when the government charged that the Steel Trust had evidenced its monopolistic character in the purchase of the Tennessee Coal and Iron Company which Roosevelt had approved during the Panic of 1907. Roosevelt and his followers resented the implication of this suit that he had been a cat's-paw of Morgan and the United States Steel Corporation.

Taft's most far-reaching program for reducing the power of Big Business was a proposal to require all business corporations engaged in interstate commerce to obtain federal charters. Such charters would give the federal government a powerful regulatory weapon, and Taft proposed that the weapon be used by a Federal Corporation Commission with the threat of cancellation of a corporation's charter as a sanction to secure obedience to federal rules of business conduct. Congress failed to act on this proposal and Taft lacked influence enough to persuade the legislative branch. To this day the federal government has not developed any such planned program of over-all supervision of business as President Taft advocated.

Congress went farther than his recommendations in the Mann-Elkins Act of 1910. This placed telephone, telegraph, cable, and wireless companies under the jurisdiction of the Interstate Commerce Commission, and increased the powers of that body by giving it complete authority over rates. It could now take the initiative in proceedings against any carrier. The law also created a federal Court of Commerce. This might have obviated obstructive tactics of companies appealing decisions of the ICC to the federal courts, but it was abolished by Congress in 1912. La Follette opposed it on the ground that in practice it increased litigation.

In 1913, Taft signed a bill much more to the Senator's liking, the Valuation Act, requiring a report by the ICC in five years on the cost of reproduction of all the property of common carriers. After this valuation was made in the 1920's, the courts accepted the judgment of the ICC in matters of fact.

The federal government entered into direct competition with private savings banks upon Taft's recommendation when Congress, in 1910, provided that the post offices should receive money on deposit and pay 2 per cent interest. This action stimulated the states to strengthen their laws governing private savings banks in order to increase public confidence in them. It was an early example of the federal government's providing services competitive with private business as a means of encouraging the latter to develop a higher standard of public service.

The Publicity Act of 1910 required the filing of statements of campaign contributions to candidates for the House of Representatives and inaugurated a long series of efforts to reduce the possibility that moneyed individuals and corporations would buy elections. The Mann Act of the same year responded to a muckraking campaign by prohibiting the interstate transportation of women for immoral purposes. In 1911, Taft secured a Commission on Efficiency and Economy which reported, among other reforms of antiquated methods of governmental administration, in favor of a national budget to replace the chaotic system of piecemeal requests and appropriations. This program was a casualty of Taft's break with Roosevelt, and Congress ignored a national budget that he transmitted in his last year.

The Insurgents

Progressivism became Insurgency during the Taft administration. Anger and fervor mounted to crusade pitch. Revolt first flared up in the House of Representatives against "Uncle Joe" Cannon, long the dictator of the body as its Speaker with power to appoint the Committee on Rules, which could determine the fate of any bill. Cannon was personally likeable and used his power amiably enough but with a special regard for conservative interests. In 1908, Republican Progressives, led by George Norris of Nebraska, concluded that his power must be reduced as a precondition of any other reform. In March 1910, Norris won a majority vote for a resolution that the membership of the Committee on Rules be elective. In 1911, the Democratic majority of the House took away the remainder of the Speaker's authority to appoint members of committees. The overthrow of "Cannonism" was a first and heady victory of the Insurgent movement against the official Republican leadership.

In June 1910, Roosevelt, returning from Africa and Europe, was met by a spectacular outpouring of public affection. He went through the motions of settling down at Oyster Bay to private life mitigated by some writing for publication and some speaking. Even if he sincerely wished to avoid re-entry into national politics, Progressives who turned to him, newspaper reporters and an endless stream of important visitors urged him to take leadership of the Republican Party away from Taft as the only practical alternative to Democratic victory in the presidential election. His own love of action goaded him to the same purpose. In August, he made a speech at Osawatomie, Kansas, on "The New Nationalism." A logical development of his own unheeded recommendations during his last months as President, it seemed to provide a platform of forthright Progressivism on which he could stand again as presidential candidate. The warm friendship between him and Taft gave way to coolness and this in turn gave way to enmity, a transformation made pathetic on Taft's side by his clinging too long to hopes that Theodore would advise him how to be a more successful President, and protestations that their differences were due only to misunderstanding.

Ballinger-Pinchot Controversy

A crisis in conservation affairs hardened hearts on both sides. Conservation was pre-eminently a Roosevelt policy which Taft was pledged to maintain, and the continuation in office of Gifford Pinchot as Chief Forester was a guaranty of Taft's faithfulness. But Taft named as Secretary of the Interior Richard A. Ballinger, who excited the suspicions of some conservationists when he confirmed doubtful claims to Alaskan coal lands of the Guggenheim interests which he had formerly served as attorney. *Collier's* magazine published, in November 1909, an exposé written by Louis P. Glavis, a minor official of the Interior Department. Ballinger furthermore restored to sale some Wyoming and Montana water-power sites which had been reserved under Roosevelt for public ownership. For this Pinchot publicly accused Ballinger of betraying the policy of conservation, and he defiantly championed Glavis. While excitement among the public and in Congress mounted, Taft sided with Ballinger and removed both Glavis and Pinchot from office. The latter hastened to Roosevelt.

The ordinary rule that subordinates in office must not publicly attack their superiors seemed to the Progressives insignificant when conservation was at stake. Congressional investigation of the affair sustained the excitement, and Taft was placed in the position of a tool of predatory interests. Public indignation led Ballinger to resign in 1911. Actually Taft supported new laws to strengthen conservation policies. It was his sense of administrative propriety that made him support Ballinger against the rebels. He appointed a thorough conservationist, Walter Fisher of Chicago, in Ballinger's place. But Taft's lack of skill in handling his subordinates, his inability to make the public side with him emotionally, and his preference for consistency in uninspiring issues over militancy in great ones made the Ballinger-Pinchot controversy a disaster for his administration and a boon to the Insurgents.

The Congressional elections of 1910 marked the turn of opinion against Taft. Only the Eastern conservative Republicans remained loyal to him. The Democrats won a majority in the House, and an alliance between Democrats and Insurgent Republicans nullified the nominal Republican majority in the Senate. At the same time, Democratic candidates won gubernatorial elections in more than half the states. One of them was Woodrow Wilson of New Jersey. In January 1911, Republican Insurgents organized the National Republican Progressive League to make sure that one of their leaders would be the Republican nominee for President in 1912. It was a question whether the victor would be the uncompromising La Follette or Theodore Roosevelt, whose public utterances seemed to mean that he had declared war against the Old Guard as well as Taft. The latter, aggrieved in his isolation, was unable to accomplish anything further. Public enthusiasm centered on the dramatic personalities of Roosevelt and La Follette and Wilson.

ELECTION OF 1912

Theodore Roosevelt's New Nationalism speech at Osawatomie in 1910 offered a complete program of national Progressive reform. He proposed tariff revision, new conservation measures, income and inheritance taxes, publicity for the affairs of private corporations, government regulation of capitalization, and government supervision of corporations dealing in food, medicines, clothing, housing, and the necessities of life. He presented also a detailed program of national labor legislation, including workmen's compensation, laws setting minimum wages and maximum hours, and the prohibition of child labor. He showed a willingness to use the powers of the national government in new ways and well beyond the limits formerly recognized. Roosevelt exulted in such an expansion of federal power and frankly called for more governmental intervention in the economic and social systems. As for the ultimate purpose of his program, he said:

> I stand for the square deal. But when I say I am for the square deal I mean not merely that I stand for fair play under the present rules of the game but that I stand for having those rules changed so as to work for a more substantial equality of opportunity and of reward for equally good service.

La Follette made great efforts to secure the Republican presidential nomination. Progressives became convinced that they could recapture the party from Taft and the Old Guard, but many of them distrusted

La Follette because his refusal to enter into the traditional give-and-take of politics made him seem too fanatical for a Chief Executive. On February 10, 1912, a group of Progressive Republican governors and other party leaders publicly called upon Roosevelt to run. La Follette claimed that Roosevelt had used him as a stalking horse. On February 12, while attacking the "Money Trust" before an audience of publishers in Philadelphia, he suffered a temporary breakdown. Within two weeks Roosevelt announced that his hat was in the ring. Progressive Republicans were overjoyed. They were untroubled by jibes at Roosevelt's explanation that in 1904 he had meant only *consecutive* terms when he had promised never again to run for the presidency. They worked to send a majority of pro-Roosevelt delegates to the Republican National Convention in Chicago in June.

But the Old Guard controlled the convention machinery and were determined not to yield control of the party to the Progressives even at the cost of defeat in the election. Under Elihu Root as chairman, they settled a number of cases of disputed seats in their own favor. Taft was then renominated on the first ballot. Few paid much attention to the platform his supporters adopted. Like his record, it was far from conservative, but he was nevertheless damned in the eyes of the great majority of voters as the candidate of the Old Guard and Big Business.

Having failed to gain control of the Republican machinery, Roosevelt seemed unconcerned by the virtual certainty that the Democrats would win the election if he split the Republican Party. He completed his break with Taft by announcing that acceptance of the Old Guard nomination made his former friend the beneficiary of fraud, and he prepared for a third-party convention to nominate himself.

Before that convention met, the Democrats, who had watched the Republicans fall into civil war with growing hope, met at Baltimore. Bryan was at last considered ineligible, but his influence was important. The chief contenders were Champ Clark of Missouri, Speaker of the House, Governor Woodrow Wilson of New Jersey, and Congressman Oscar W. Underwood of Alabama. Clark led on early ballots but could not gain the necessary two-thirds majority, even when Tammany men shifted the vote of New York to him on the tenth ballot. Soon Bryan threw his personal support to Wilson, who was finally nominated on the forty-sixth ballot after the conservative Underwood bloc swung to him.

The Democratic platform contained the standard Progressive proposals but laid more emphasis on the enforcement of the antitrust laws than on regulation of business, and less emphasis on social and labor legislation than on aid to farmers. Governor Thomas R. Marshall of Indiana was nominated for Vice-President. Wilson, formerly president of Princeton University, had been a late convert to reform. But Democratic leaders were impressed by the extraordinary political talents he had shown in

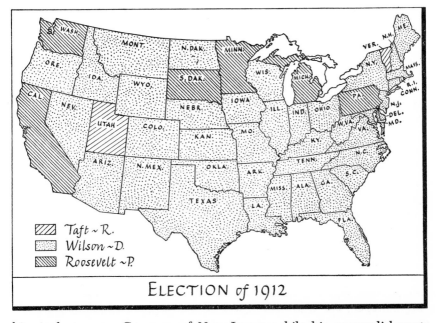

Taft ~ R.
Wilson ~ D.
Roosevelt ~ P.

ELECTION of 1912

his single term as Governor of New Jersey, while his accomplishments against great odds encouraged reformers to believe that the noble idealism of his public utterances would be matched by effective action. The Democrats knew that Roosevelt was the man they had to beat and believed that Wilson would enjoy the support of a united party. He would hold reform Democrats against the appeal of Roosevelt, as well as the conservative Democrats, who longed for victory.

In August, the supporters of Roosevelt met in Chicago and organized the Progressive Party. It was a gathering of enthusiasts. Professional reformers as well as cranks and purveyors of nostrums responded to the Roosevelt magic much more readily than to the chilly scholar whom the Democrats had nominated. In the exalted spirit that periodically lifts American politics, some 2000 delegates—for no one was refused a seat—sang "Onward, Christian Soldiers" and nominated Roosevelt in a frenzy of unanimity. They named Hiram W. Johnson of California as his running-mate. The platform was a resumé of Roosevelt's New Nationalism and Square Deal. He told people he felt like a "bull moose," and made a long speech pledging himself to the regeneration of the Republic. The delegates dispersed to wage a fight for his election which many of them would remember as the high point of their lives.

But Bull Moose enthusiasm was no match for Democratic unity. Taft privately conceded defeat and hardly entered the struggle. It was a battle between two varieties of Progressivism which were scarcely distinguishable to most voters. Roosevelt welcomed the prospect of enlarging governmental functions in order to effect reforms, while Wilson regretted it and hoped that a reversal of the trend towards economic consolidation would reduce the necessity for enlarging governmental power. Roosevelt proposed to use American power in international relations to strengthen American security, while Wilson proposed to use it to strengthen freedom and justice in the world. These distinctions were less important to voters than personalities, local party situations, and traditional party loyalties. The great significance of the election lay in the defeat of Taft and conservatism twice over: by the Democrats and also by the majority of Republicans.

The country wanted an end to the rule of Big Business. Eugene V. Debs, the Socialist candidate, might have been at a disadvantage in running for President when two major-party leaders spoke for most of the reforms short of socialism which his own party customarily put forward at election time. But he received 900,000 votes, more than twice his total in 1908. Wilson got 6,300,000, Roosevelt 4,100,000 and Taft 3,500,000. This was a vote of more than three to one for reform, a startling result that outweighed the technicality of Wilson's failure to win a majority of the popular vote. His strength was so well distributed through all sections of the country that he won the greatest victory in the electoral college since Monroe's uncontested election in 1820. Taft carried Vermont and Utah; Roosevelt took Pennsylvania, Michigan, Minnesota, South Dakota, California, and Washington; Wilson received the 435 votes of the remaining 40 states. In the new Congress, Progressivism and reform would not be as strong as the combined Roosevelt and Wilson votes; but they would be strong enough to give Wilson an opportunity to carry out a legislative program such as no President had had since the departure of the Southerners in 1861 gave Lincoln and the Republicans a free hand. Wilson's opportunity came not from sectional division but from the reconstitution of the great sectional alliances of Jefferson and Jackson joining the South with Western farmers, Eastern laborers, and idealistic reformers.

CHAPTER 15

Economic and Social Life in the New Century

THE PROGRESSIVE ERA BROUGHT A CHANGE IN THE direction of American economic and social purpose. Dissatisfaction with the consequences of industrialism for the majority of people was apparent in the growth of radical and reformist political activity. But in the long run the accomplishments of Progressivism may have been less responsible for moderating the ill effects of industrialism than the shift in direction by industry itself towards a new emphasis on the mass of consumers. Henry Ford was the first manufacturer to combine production of a "luxury" article for a mass market with a high-wage policy that helped to create such a market. Other businessmen as well as labor leaders were suspicious of Ford, but his assembly-line and $5 day pointed to the American economy of the future and contained the possibility of a social as well as economic revolution. Underlying the political efforts of these years to recover popular control over government were economic and social developments which weakened the control of the economy by monopolists and the leadership of society by the new caste of plutocrats.

MASS PRODUCTION FOR THE MASS MARKET

The production of consumers' machines had distinguished the industrial revolution in America from the beginning. But the ending of frontier development, the flooding of the labor market by the New Immigration, and the decline in the real wages of labor even during years of general prosperity, threatened in the early twentieth century to restrict the ability of the mass of consumers to provide a market for advanced products of industry. The ultimate test of the wisdom of the industrial and financial titans who controlled the American economy was whether they would use their power short-sightedly for maximum immediate profits by raising prices and lowering wages, and thereby reduce their markets, or whether they would use their power far-sightedly to maximize their markets.

Steel and Electricity

Steel production rose phenomenally during the first decade of the twentieth century from approximately 10 to 25 million tons. Wages in the industry were notoriously low, but the great new United States Steel Corporation exercised its "price leadership" wisely to secure an enormous expansion in the use of steel. Since dividends were high, it was efficiency and economy of operations that explained the industry's success in building up its markets. The open-hearth process, which permits the use of lower-grade ores and scrap, superseded Bessemer converters. The fabulous ore deposits of the Mesabi Range in Minnesota became the chief American source. Coke displaced coal as the chief fuel. Metallurgists elaborated mixtures of other metals with steel for specialized uses. Structural steel displaced rails as the main finished product. Steel for ships, armor plate for the Navy, and thousands of lesser uses of steel added to its importance as the backbone of the economy.

Similarly, the rapid expansion of the use of electricity demonstrated a reasonable price policy. The electrolytic process of copper-refining came into general use and the Anaconda Copper Company won a position in control of this metal, used chiefly for the transmission of electricity, comparable to that of the United States Steel Corporation. Its low wage policy was even more extreme. Most electricity continued to be manufactured by dynamos turned by steam engines. Manufacturers adopted the electric motor to the extent of 17 per cent of their primary power sources by 1914. The electric motor car lost in competition with gasoline automobiles, but electricity for illumination defeated gas and became general in towns and cities throughout the nation. Farms generally lacked electric power until another generation, but a few of them installed their own gasoline-driven power plants. Plumbing of the modern variety now became standard in town or city houses except for slum districts, but not yet in the country. Thus important new consumer's goods were being produced at prices low enough for all but the rural and the poorest city classes to obtain them.

Henry Ford and the Automobile

The greatest of all consumers' machines, the automobile driven by an internal combustion engine, gave rise to the most significant modern American manufacturing industry. Automobiles were not even listed in the census of 1900, when there were 8000 vehicles in use and 144 miles of paved roads. The state of Tennessee at this time required anyone intending to drive an automobile on a public road to advertise the fact a week in advance as a fair warning to potential victims. During the first years, more and better automobiles were manufactured in England and France than in the United States. In both Europe and America the automobile was initially used for pleasure by the wealthy. The American contribution was the conversion of this expensive plaything into an instrument of utility for the mass of people. The first steps were taken by a group of young American mechanics, including Charles E. Duryea, Ransom E. Olds, and Henry Ford, who began in the 1890's to simplify and standardize the mechanism. Many small manufacturers increased total production 3500 per cent during the first decade of the new century, and by 1912 the United States had far outdistanced Europe.

Mass production methods were climaxed by Henry Ford's assembly-line, a continuous-flow system of putting together the machine. Among all the commanding figures in the industry, Ford emerged as the prophet of the Motor Age because he combined talent as a mechanic and genius for production and management with the ability to comprehend some of the consequences of the automobile as a necessity of life. He reduced the skill needed by his workers by breaking up the manufacturing process into petty tasks which were endlessly repeated by single workers. But he then began to convert this unimportant producer into a very important consumer. On January 5, 1914, he announced that he would pay a minimum wage of $5 for an eight-hour day. This was about double the going rate.

Ford's policy, which astonished the world, contradicted the presumed "natural law" of economics according to which labor is a commodity whose price is dictated by impersonal forces of supply and demand. It was the most dramatic event in the development of American "welfare capitalism." Critics pointed out that Ford's Service Agency policed the private lives of his employees with dangerous implications of paternalism if not tyranny, and that his control over the assembly-line permitted him to wear out his workers by inhuman speed-ups. For several decades he successfully fought off both unionization of his employees and dependence on bankers or the stock exchange for his capital. In 1911, he won an eight-year patent suit against an association of manufacturers who had held up progress. In the "Model T" he created a vehicle for the millions. The "flivver" was not a beautiful car but it gained the affection of millions of owners because of its homely, wiry toughness.

The greatest significance of Ford as an industrialist was that he combined with high wages the policy of low price for his product. He cut the price of the Model T from $950 in 1909 to $290 in 1924. This seemingly impossible combination of policies he effected by quantity production, reaching 1000 cars per day soon after the assembly-line was organized in

1913, and low unit profits, almost all of which he used for capital expansion of his great plant on the River Rouge near Detroit. This was the hard way to make money, and it took time for other American industrialists to adopt it. "Fordism" was a marvel that attracted heated debate and learned study by Europeans as well as Americans. It was a portent of the transformation of capitalism from a system of exploitation and contrived shortages to a system of increasing mass purchasing power and mass consumption: from the economic policies of scarcity to those of plenty. Marxists thundered that this transformation could be effected only by destroying capitalism and establishing socialism, and Ford was attacked at first even by businessmen as a species of dangerous radical, while radicals attacked him as a fraud. But in time, after another great Depression had produced governmental and labor union activity to enforce the lesson, his policies were accepted by American industry generally. They became the distinctive characteristic of the American economy in the new century.

The automobile was now the center of a galaxy of new industries. Machine tools—turret lathes, planers, presses, gear-cutters and drills—were suddenly in tremendous demand to "tool-up" automobile factories. The pneumatic tire and tube required latex from forests in distant lands, great factories came to center in Akron, Ohio, and thousands of little repair shops spread across the country. Just when gas and electricity were reducing demand for kerosene, the automobile magnified demand for grease, oil, and gasoline. The production of fuel oil rose from 300 million gallons in 1901 to more than 1700 in 1910, and new oil fields were opened in Texas, Oklahoma, California, Venezuela, Mexico, and the Near East. The new demands and the new supplies put an end to Standard Oil control: they were simply too vast for one company, although the oil industry continued to display a tendency towards centralized control by a few international companies.

For speed and traction the automobile needed a very hard pavement. This resulted in a revolution in road-building that gave birth to another industry using new armies of workers. The first great effort to construct hard, all-weather roads took place during the first fifteen years of the century. These roads were subject to rapid obsolescence and were superseded by improved construction like the automobile itself. The social effects of the introduction of the automobile into American life were incalculable. Perhaps the most profound transformation occurred in the lives of farmers. The first improvements in roads were designed to permit city people to drive through the countryside; the next stage, which began about 1910, was designed to permit the farmer to go to town and city. Riding on a train had been a rare experience for most farmers; driving his own Ford became a daily affair and decisively broke down his isolation. Joined with telephones and rural-free-delivery mail, the automobile transformed the "hick" farmer of 1900 into a citizen scarcely distinguishable from the city person. Indeed, he came to be admired and envied as a superior type of humanity, and city people began to try in various ways to regain the values of country living.

Suburbanism, and its later stage of "exurbanism," were effects of the automobile. Among city and suburban people the chief effects of the new machine occurred in the domain of public manners and mores. The stateliness of the upper classes which had provided the model for all in former times was attuned to the pace of the horse and the sedateness of the carriage. The automobile was perhaps the chief impeller of the revolution in manners which started during the last years before the First World War. It ushered in an era of informality. At first automobiles were manufactured in extreme variety from the luxury of town cars with chauffeurs and footmen to the unpretentious "runabout" and the ultimate simplicity of the Model T; but the tendency of automobile design and the manners it encouraged was to erase distinctions of class.

The Airplane and Radio

No sooner had the internal combustion engine initiated the revolution in surface travel—and life in general—than it was applied to the realization of man's ancient dream of flying. The airplane was an American invention and its pioneers were more experimental than theoretical in their approach to a problem. The brothers Orville and Wilbur Wright of Ohio, sons of a bishop of the United Brethren in Christ, began with bicycles and graduated by 1900 to gliders. They built a wind tunnel to try the effects of different wing designs and in 1902 began to build a heavier-than-air machine with a 12-horsepower engine. Others were working towards the same goal. Samuel P. Langley failed in an attempt to fly his own machine just a few days before December 17, 1903, when the Wright brothers flew above the sands at Kitty Hawk, North Carolina, distances up to not quite 1000 feet. They maintained their superiority over European as well as American inventors for some years and sold their machine to the United States Army in 1909. Then they organized a factory for improved models. Until the First World War the airplane was used chiefly for "stunt flying" by daredevil "barnstormers" at country fairs. It had not demonstrated its usefulness as yet, but it fascinated humanity and stimulated the burst of optimism that man was in the process of definitively conquering nature.

Similarly stimulating was the invention of radio. It depended upon theoretical research in electricity by Heinrich Hertz of Germany, and the development by Marconi of Italy of devices for the transmission of voice without wires. Thomas A. Edison received the first American patent in 1891 and American developments were climaxed by Lee DeForest's invention of the 3-electrode vacuum tube in 1906. The United States Navy was the first important patron of radio; during the first decade of the century it established high-powered shore stations for the transmission of orders to ships at sea. Later, radio's greatest importance turned out to be the broadcasting of news, entertainment, and advertising by commercial stations to home receivers as one of many new instrumentalities of mass culture.

Motion Pictures and Mass Entertainment

The motion picture was the first in the modern series of these instruments. Edison in 1893 invented the kinetoscope which permitted a single viewer to obtain the illusion of movement by the display of photographs taken at short intervals on a continuous roll of film. The Lumières of France and various Americans contributed to the development of projection on a large screen. The dramatic potentialities of the device were immediately apparent, and a new "industry," as its leaders significantly called it, was soon on its way to immense popularity.

The purveying of inexpensive entertainment to mass audiences became the purpose of old as well as new industries. Five- and ten-cent magazines, headed by the *Saturday Evening Post*, were edited with a new skill in popular appeal and gained vast circulations. These magazines became industries. Similarly, the production of books that would be "best sellers" was encouraged by publishers, many of whom now saw their profession less as a department of intellectual and literary life than as a branch of business.

The trend away from individual participation in the making of entertainment was visible in the popularity of the phonograph, invented by Edison in 1878 and by this time manufactured on a mass scale. Records of musical performances and comic readings sold by the millions. The most grotesque application of industrial methods to cultural activity was the mechanical piano. At home or for five cents in a public resort, a perforated roll of paper could be made to sound the keys of the instrument in a parody of music which reached a kind of grandeur in those machines which orchestrated machine-driven drums, violins, and banjos with the piano. Americans for a time seemed to delight in the mechanical quality of the results. If pulling a lever was all that was required now to make music, it became possible also to make a picture by pressing a button. Photography had been invented decades earlier, but George Eastman developed during the 1880's roll film and the cheap hand camera. He named it the "kodak," and put it into mass production at Rochester, New York, in subsequent years.

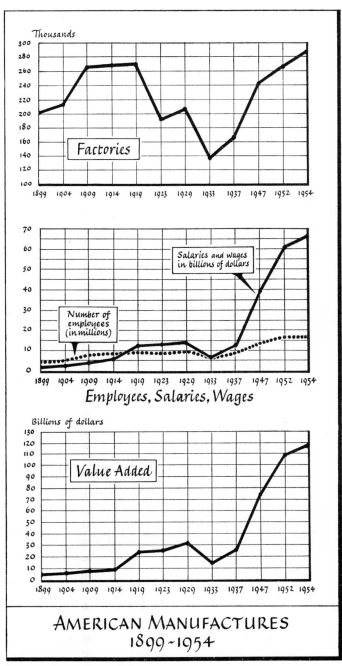

AMERICAN MANUFACTURES
1899~1954

SOURCE: Department of Commerce

Prosperity

A thousand minor devices marked the orientation of industry towards new mass markets. Consumers eagerly patronized the new industries and they also had the means to raise their standard of living importantly as measured in terms of food, housing, and clothing. The years from 1897 to 1913 witnessed one of the most prolonged and substantial eras of prosperity in peacetime. An index of commodity prices rose from 46.6 to 75.5. The farmers who had suffered so severely during the post-Civil War decades now enjoyed an improvement which made these years a standard used after the First World War to define sound relations between the prices farmers received and those they paid. Labor benefitted least among the major groups of the people. The small businessman prospered even while Big Business achieved greater centralization than ever. Big Business itself became an increasingly important employer of skilled office personnel, including that newcomer on the economic scene, the young woman typist and stenographer, and of administrators, lawyers, engineers, and scientists.

The only important break in this sixteen-year wave of prosperity occurred in 1907 when panic struck the money markets. But this disaster did not deepen into a depression. After a series of bankruptcies and a fall in values and prices, recovery began within a year. The irony of a sudden shortage of gold, as banks and individuals hoarded it in fear of falling prices of securities and commodities, in the country with the largest quantity of gold in the world, brought home the necessity for reform in the banking system. It also intensified public fear of the "Money Trust" as the most dangerous of all the burgeoning powers over the market.

THE CLIMAX OF LABOR RADICALISM

During the years after 1896, laborers succeeded farmers as the most disadvantaged group of American people. The real wages of industrial workers actually declined because the growth of centralized control over the economy permitted businessmen to increase their profits while labor failed to gain corresponding increases in wages. Fordism was a new idea without measurable effect as yet on the economy as a whole. A heavy influx of immigrants and the increasing use of labor-saving machinery resulted in a surplus labor market which was advantageous to employers. The failure of industrial workers to share in the brilliant economic progress of the nation was the fundamental cause of mounting labor unrest and a climax of radicalism in 1912.

At first it had seemed that the new era of prosperity would be one of labor gains and industrial peace. The American Federation of Labor with its conservative policy dominated organized labor, while business-men seemed determined to avoid clashes like those of earlier decades. The National Civic Federation was an expression of this hopeful mood. It was a private organization devoted to the establishment of "right relations between employers and workers." Its policy was to support unionization and bargaining agreements. Its leadership could hardly have been more influential: Samuel Gompers, Mark Hanna, Grover Cleveland, President Charles W. Eliot of Harvard, John D. Rockefeller, Jr., Charles M. Schwab, Archbishop Ireland, President John Mitchell of the United Mine Workers, and others. An attempt by the Amalgamated Iron and Steel Workers union to organize the steel industry and a great steel strike in 1901 both failed, but after that AFL unions achieved recognition and agreements in a number of trades.

Repression and Retreat

It was in the new mass production industries and among the unskilled who formed the bulk of their labor force that this "honeymoon period" of capital and labor broke down. Union membership rose from less than 900,000 in 1900 to 2,000,000 in 1904, and this alarmed businessmen. Many who had supported the program of the National Civic Federation, as the best alternative to violence and radicalism, abandoned it after 1904 and joined a counterattack against unionism. A leader in this was a new organization of employers' associations called the Citizens' Industrial As-sociation. Speakers at a convention of this body in 1906 pointed proudly to the growing success of its lobbying and propaganda activities against the "Labor Trust." The National Association of Manufacturers was ex-tremely active in the same cause of the open shop. Gompers was classed with the Socialist leader Eugene V. Debs as equally dangerous.

In the struggle for public favor the employers' associations were much more successful than the labor unions. Muckraking and prolabor views died out in the newspapers and popular magazines. The large corpora-tions adopted antiunion devices such as the "yellow-dog contract" and the "iron-clad oath," both of which bound employees not to join unions; they set labor spies to inform on union leaders so they could be dis-charged; they encouraged immigrant groups to perpetuate their Euro-pean hatreds; and they waged legal compaigns for indictments and injunctions against union activity.

Some labor leaders played into the hands of the employers by resort-ing to violence. Workers in the structural steel trade, men accustomed to ride girders on bridges and skyscrapers, used dynamite to show their hatred of the United States Steel Corporation. Western workers, accus-tomed to gunplay, were most intractable of all. By their tactics they supplied evidence which was used by the employers' associations to turn the public against unionism.

The most sensational of many incidents of violence was the dynamiting of the *Los Angeles Times* building on October 1, 1910, in which 21 persons were killed. The editor of the paper, General Harrison Gray Otis, who was bitterly hostile to organized labor, was fighting the Typographical Union in his own plant as well as a structural iron workers' strike in the city. The private detective William J. Burns after six months' work claimed he had unearthed a conspiracy by the Bridge and Structural Iron Workers Union that lay behind this and dozens of explosions. John J. McNamara, secretary-treasurer of the union, and his brother James, a union printer, were arrested. Labor leaders, including Samuel Gompers, who testified that McNamara was a "conservative" official, were certain that the affair was a frame-up by the employers' National Erectors' Association. The brilliant young radical attorney, Clarence Darrow, defended the brothers, but the trial ended when the muckraker Lincoln Steffens gained their confidence and persuaded them to confess their guilt. This was a blow to the morale of law-abiding supporters of labor; but some others blamed Steffens for an error of strategy. Acceptance of violence as a policy and of revolution as their goal was spreading among partisans of labor.

The federal courts ranged themselves on the employers' side against peaceful as well as violent tactics of organized labor. The Erdman Act of 1898 had prohibited the yellow-dog contract for railroad labor. In 1908, the Supreme Court (Adair *vs.* U. S.) found this law unconstitutional as an unreasonable violation of the freedom of contract and property rights guaranteed by the Fifth Amendment. A similar state law was invalidated in 1915. The most celebrated antiunion decision of the period came in the Danbury Hatters Case (Loewe *vs.* Lawler, 1908). The American Federation of Labor in devising means short of strikes to influence employers had hit upon the "union label." It was fixed on products so that all union members and sympathizers could use these and boycott products displaying no union label. In the printing trade and some others this procedure was quite effective in influencing all employers to recognize the union. Employers feared the spread of the tactic and organized the American Anti-Boycott Association, which among other activities helped nonunion employers to obtain court injunctions against boycott drives. A case involving the Hatters Union against the Loewe Company of Danbury, Connecticut, was decided on the ground that the union-label boycott constituted a conspiracy in restraint of trade and therefore violated the Sherman Anti-Trust Act. Triple damages of a quarter of a million dollars under that law were awarded the manufacturer, and the homes of union members were attached to pay it.

Among many similar cases, one involving Buck's Stove and Range Company, whose president, J. W. Van Cleave, was also president of the National Association of Manufacturers, resulted in a sentence of a year in prison for Samuel Gompers for speaking publicly in seeming violation of an antiboycott court injunction.

Gompers never served the sentence because the other principals in the case died. He and most of the AFL leaders patiently worked to obtain from Congress exemptions of labor unions from the interpretive restrictions of the courts. It seemed to ardent advocates of labor's cause that his policies of "business unionism" converted union leaders into virtual businessmen, chiefly interested in holding their remunerative offices and retreating towards co-operation with employers in every crisis. The antiunion campaign of businessmen seemed to immobilize the AFL and henceforth it failed to command the support of militant labor idealists. Its membership declined in 1905 and failed to recover until after the outbreak of the First World War.

The Garment Workers Organize

An important exception to the general retreat of organized labor occurred in the garment industry. This was one of the most exploitative industries in the country, divided into many small sweatshops employing women and children under medieval working conditions. In its headquarters in New York City, many of its employees as well as employers were Jewish immigrants, and the former proved to be an exception to the general rule that immigrants were backward in union activity. In 1909, the shirtwaist makers of New York City won a strike under the leadership of the International Ladies' Garment Workers Union and with the support of public opinion. Workers in the cloak and suit trade struck in 1910. Louis D. Brandeis served as mediator and worked out terms favorable to the strikers, including a protocol of arbitration which led to a permanent "impartial chairman" to mediate future disputes. In March 1911, the country was shocked by a fire in the Triangle Shirtwaist factory in New York City in which 146 workers were killed, evidently as a result of the employers' negligence. This led to indictments of the owners, stringent new labor and factory laws in New York State, and further growth of the ILGWU. This union was thoroughly devoted to the welfare of its members and it pioneered in many progressive union activities. The strongest union in the garment industry turned out to be the United Garment Workers, whose brilliant leader was Sidney Hillman. In 1914, this group broke away from the AFL and formed the powerful Amalgamated Clothing Workers Union. Under Hillman the machinery of impartial chairman was perfected.

The IWW and Violence

The Amalgamated like the ILGWU was an industrial union, covering an industry rather than a craft, but unskilled labor was not as important in the garment trade as in new industries like automobiles, which remained virtually untouched by unionism. Industrial unionism in these circumstances became the doctrine of the most important radical labor organization the United States has known: the Industrial Workers of the World. It originated in the Western Federation of Miners, an industrial union that broke away from the AFL in 1897 because it was too moderate, and conducted a series of strikes in the silver, copper, gold, and lead mines culminating in the Cripple Creek, Colorado, strike of 1903-1904. Both sides resorted to violence as a matter of course. The miners organized rifle teams and dynamite squads, while the owners used the state militia, armed strikebreakers, and vigilantes. Mine explosions, train wrecks, and assassinations on the one side, and machine-gunning of miners' meetings on the other, made the doctrine that capitalism is a system of class warfare seem obvious truth to the miners. After more than a year, they lost the strike by sheer defeat in warfare.

The Western Federation leaders decided that they needed allies. "Big Bill" Haywood, a tough, one-eyed giant, was their chief. Formerly a cowboy, a homesteader, and a miner, he became the most militant leader of anticapitalist revolutionaries this country has produced. The IWW was organized in Chicago in 1905 by a convention of delegates of the Western Miners, Daniel De Leon's left-wing Socialist Labor Party, Debs's more moderate Socialist Party, and sundry radical unions, journalists, and agitators. It was essentially a syndicalist organization advocating the organization of the working class in "One Big Union." It sought, not collective bargaining agreements, but "direct action" leading to a revolution by a general strike which should overthrow both capitalism and the government and substitute labor union administration as the sole economic and political institution of society. Debs, De Leon, and other Socialists soon abandoned the IWW, and it never gained more than about 60,000 members, but Haywood and the Westerners succeeded in winning lumberjacks and migratory harvest hands, who, along with the miners, made the IWW a force to contend with in the West for about a decade.

The "Wobblies," as they were called, had little stake in society; few even had families. Exploitation of their labor was severe, and the IWW gave them a romantic solidarity. Haywood described them affectionately as "red-blooded working stiffs" whom he found "down in the gutter." Their speakers and their songs—"Dump the Bosses Off Your Back," "Paint 'Er Red," "Hallelujah! I'm a Bum!", "Pie in the Sky"—were frankly revolutionary. They invented a dramatic form of demonstration called a "free-speech fight" when a sheriff dared to act vigorously against any of their comrades. Wobblies would flood into the offending town and hold provocative meetings until the frantic sherriff could find no more room in his jail and had to surrender.

But successes in western states were ephemeral because the workers themselves were too individualistic to accept even the IWW brand of discipline. They quit the organization as casually as they joined it. The leaders realized that they must invade the East if the IWW was to become One Big Union. Their opportunity came early in 1912. Some Wobblies who were involved in a textile strike against the American Woolen Company in Lawrence, Massachusetts, called Haywood to take charge. The authorities alienated public sympathy by police attacks on women and children while the Wobblies established excellent strike organization and, in a gesture of respect for Eastern sensibilities, avoided violence. The strikers won and the IWW gained sudden prestige. The next year the IWW led a strike in the silk mills of Paterson, New Jersey, but after a prolonged and bitter struggle they lost it. Thereafter the IWW declined into a minor organizer of labor violence and was permanently defeated, by government and mob action bolstered by public opinion, when it took a strong stand against United States participation in the First World War. Haywood escaped to Soviet Russia while he was under indictment.

Socialism

The IWW revealed dangerous potentialities if progress in economic and social welfare were frustrated. The rise of the Socialist Party during these years demonstrated the same truth with respect to Eastern laboring groups who got their inspiration not from the frontier heritage but from the doctrines of Karl Marx. These doctrines were winning mass support in every other industrial nation of the world and came closer to winning such support in the United States at this time than at any other before or since.

Marxist socialism stands for political as well as economic action against capitalism, and for political as well as economic organization of a new society. Marx's economic theory and historical and dialectical materialism constitute a far more impressive doctrine than any other which had appeared in opposition to the traditional American doctrine of liberty, including the right to own productive property. Until the destruction of all human liberties was demonstrated and admitted by the Soviet Russian government to be a consequence of the establishment of a Marxist system, Marxist doctrine won influence even in countries deeply committed to liberty such as Great Britain and the United States. During the later half of the nineteenth century it was represented in this country only by tiny groups in the cities who were mostly neither native-born nor workers. But Eugene V. Debs of Indiana, who had been converted to Marxist socialism while serving a prison sentence for his part in the Pullman Strike of 1894, led in the founding of the Socialist Party of America in 1901, and it was predominantly American in its leadership.

Debs was a sincere and talented man who ran for President of the United States many times. His vote increased from 90,000 in 1900 to 900,000 in 1912, and the membership of the Party reached about 125,000 by 1910. This growth paralleled the rise of Socialist parties elsewhere in the world, and many observers expected it to continue until the Party could take over the national government. Debs and most of the Socialist leaders advocated "revolution by ballot." Inner-party struggles occurred, as in other countries, chiefly over the question of relative emphasis on socialization of the means of production as compared with reforms under the capitalist system. Doctrinaire Socialists sneered at reformism; but Debs tried to use reformist appeals to win support which would, he hoped, gradually turn to all-out socialism. The party's schools and press were developed into a network of propaganda with headquarters in New York and Chicago.

Some of the leading authors of the period, including Jack London, Theodore Dreiser, and Upton Sinclair, as well as talented younger men like Sinclair Lewis, Walter Lippmann, and John Reed, identified themselves with the Socialist Party in varying degree. A number of wealthy persons, such as the repentant Los Angeles billboard magnate William Wilshire, poured their money into the Party's treasury. For a few years it was fashionable for idealistic college students to join the Intercollegiate Socialist Society. The chief electoral successes of the Party occurred on the municipal level. Milwaukee, Schenectady, Bridgeport, Connecticut, and other communities sometimes had Socialist mayors. Their administrations were scarcely dangerous to capitalism.

A few labor unions were led by Socialist officials, but Gompers castigated the Party as bitterly as he did the IWW. In the United States alone of all modern industrial nations, organized labor in general refused to affiliate with any radical political party. The greatest effect of the rise of the Socialist Party of America was to warn the public that reasonable reform might be the only alternative to drastic revolution. Theodore Roosevelt and other Progressives constantly harped on the theme, and in the end they convinced more voters than did the conservatives who accused Progressives of promoting socialism. Considering the abuses of American Big Business, the rise of socialism in America is not so surprising as its decline after 1912. The refusal of the American workingman to develop Marxian class-consciousness can be explained in large part by the vigor and the successes of the Progressive movement.

Position of the New Immigrants

This refusal was all the more striking in view of the climactic influx of immigrants, most of whom had acquired in Europe instinctive hatred for all governmental authority and experienced in America a considerable initial disillusionment of their hope that here "things would be better." During half of the years of the twentieth century before the First World War, immigrants numbered more than a million per year. About three-fourths of them were of the New Immigration from southern and eastern Europe. Seemingly unassimilable blocs of Italians and Jews congregated in New York, as did Poles, Bohemians, and Hungarians in Chicago, and similar groups in smaller cities. While most lacked education, a few of those who had some tended towards Marxism, and there were sprinklings of syndicalists and anarchists among them. To their own handicaps were added racial contempt and fear overtly directed against them by older Americans. This drove the newcomers to cling together for mutual support and made assimilation all the more difficult.

Fear of radicalism was apparent in a law of 1903 which added anarchists to the list of persons excluded from entry to the United States along with prostitutes, criminals, and the insane as undesirables. This law had a humane clause providing for the examination in foreign ports of applicants for immigration. It also granted authority to deport illegal entrants. In 1906, the Bureau of Immigration was established. Tighter regulations did not prevent determined persons, including a few genuinely dangerous anarchists and criminals, from slipping into the country. On the other hand, the world was now treated to the spectacle of American officials requiring all visitors to declare that they were not guilty of moral turpitude or anarchistic intentions.

Sensible and effective regulation seemed beyond the capacity of Congress to legislate or officials to enforce. Public sentiment divided into a resurgence of nativism, which advocated the suppression of Asian, southern and eastern European, and even all immigration whatever, and a growing sympathy for the problems of the immigrants fostered by sociological and anthropological studies. This conflict was decided temporarily in favor of nativism when the First World War magnified fear of "hyphenated Americans" as well as radicals.

THE FAILURE OF THE PLUTOCRACY

At the turn of the century American Society, considered as aristocratic pageantry, entered its Golden Age, if expenditure and effort be the criteria. The problem of income had become in its way as difficult for the owners as for the worker in industry. The Vanderbilts, Morgans, Rockefellers, Astors, Goelets, Belmonts, and their like could not easily continue the traditional practice of "plowing back" profits into their businesses. On the other hand, they certainly did not have to dip into capital for expenditures which made the scale of living of most royal families look penurious.

Attempts to Establish an Aristocracy

A major experiment to solve the problem was an attempt to make a true aristocracy for the United States out of its existing plutocracy. The English aristocracy provided the model. The editor of *Town and Country*, like many other publicists, advised young Americans of wealth to adopt the English ideal of a responsible aristocracy by entering politics and cultivating the arts and scholarship. If American domestic politics were too vulgar, they should man the diplomatic service where their wealth and, he hoped, their intelligence, would fit them to compete with Old World diplomats. Architecture, painting, and sculpture were peculiarly suited to expenditure on the requisitely colossal scale and would create an American civilization worthy of comparison with that of England. If no other imitation succeeded, Americans should at least take up the country life and outdoor sports which accounted for the good looks of their English cousins. But English standards could not be bought as easily as English titles could be acquired by marriage, and the reputed sense of responsibility of the English aristocracy seemed rather dull to the tastes of most American millionaires.

It was the material and symbolic externals of Old World aristocracy that the American plutocracy acquired. Mansions were truly princely in cost. Richard Morris Hunt became the favorite architect of the rich. He designed fifteenth-century French châteaux complete with moats, convincing the Vanderbilts and other patrons that such styles were appropriate to Fifth Avenue. As they competed for ultimate authority over the nation's economy, so the multimillionaires competed in architectural expenditure. At Newport, Cornelius Vanderbilt's "The Breakers" and William K. Vanderbilt's "Marble House" set the new scale for fabulous seaside "cottages." At Asheville, North Carolina, Hunt built George W. Vanderbilt's "Biltmore". It had forty master bedrooms and a library of 250,000 volumes. A domain of more than feudal size, 203 square miles, surrounded this château, and the first professional American forester, Gifford Pinchot, managed the forest with a staff and a budget larger than those of the United States Department of Agriculture, which he afterwards joined. J. Pierpont Morgan spent relatively few millions on architecture, but he bought rare books, manuscripts, and paintings with the respect for expert advice and avidity for quantity that his customers were supposed to feel for gilt-edged securities. Gutting European castles of entire paneled rooms for installation in new American mansions became commonplace. Some determined millionaires bought entire buildings and had them re-erected stone by stone in the United States.

A serious effort to provide entertainments suited to the grandeur of these premises was climaxed by the titanic struggle between the Astor and Vanderbilt women-folk for social supremacy in New York's "Four Hundred"—a figure arrived at not by gathering provincial nobles into a royal court but by estimating the capacity of Mrs. Astor's ballroom. When the parties became too intolerably stuffy, Mrs. Stuyvesant Fish entered the competition with more relaxed amusements. One party was featured by horses instead of chairs for the diners at table. The possibilities of nights designated as Venetian, Chinese, or Louis Quatorze, all faithfully rendered in guests' costumes, special interior décor, entertainment, and favors, were presently more or less exhausted. Social secretaries were careful to provide the newspapers not only with lists of guests but also with itemized budgets of the host's expenditures.

These goings-on were chiefly promoted by women. Besides paying the bills with whatever satisfaction they could obtain from their size, the husbands, left alone after dinner, discussed money. Henry C. Frick built a magnificent gallery as part of his palace on Fifth Avenue and filled it with paintings that did it justice, but he himself spent his evenings seated on a Renaissance throne reading the *Saturday Evening Post*. Andrew Carnegie in the gardens of his palace a few blocks north sometimes wistfully went to the great iron fence and tried to converse through it with passersby. He was one who found absorbing interest in living up to his own "gospel of wealth" by spending his money on public libraries and other benefactions around the world.

The federal Income Tax Amendment of 1913 was probably the chief destroyer of this experiment in American aristocracy. But in its excessive form it was bound to die anyway because its practitioners, led by Mamie Fish, ceased to believe in it. Herbert Croly saw that the architecture of magnificence, which had suited feudalism because it housed companies of retainers and served as the political headquarters of a region, made no sense for American millionaires. The women clung to their dream long enough to organize a series of matches between their daughters and European nobles. English dukes commanded the highest premiums in this market, and the marriage of Consuelo Vanderbilt to the Duke of Marlborough, with $2.5 million of American railroad shares involved in the arrangements, climaxed the series of international marriages. Presently divorce proceedings of the Duchess indicated that her mother had overpersuaded her. English butlers continued to be regarded as essential for the dignity of American millionaires' establishments.

Even before the First World War began, the hope was failing that acquisition of those aspects of high European civilization which were for sale would create the substance of aristocracy in America. The formidable Mrs. Oliver Hazard Perry Belmont led millionaires' wives and daughters to join other women in the fight for suffrage as a more exciting cause than social exclusiveness. Suspicion that the attention which the popular press paid to the doings of Society indicated more ridicule than respect and more anger than envy seeped into the consciousness of the rich. Competitive art-collecting resulted in inflation of values just as if paintings were stocks in a bull market, and the game was good for no more titillation. The seasonal round from New York to Newport to Europe and back again, the pageantry of servants in livery and dowagers in diamonds, the suffocating pomposity of it all could not long survive the revival of the democratic spirit which occurred with the triumph of Progressivism. Success defined as exploits of money-making prowess remained a dominant ideal for the majority of Americans, but translation of such success into Old World symbols of prestige gave way to ideals more useful to American society as a whole.

The Philanthropic Use of Great Wealth

A new statesmanship in philanthropy was inaugurated by John D. Rockefeller when he organized and endowed the General Education Board in 1902 and the Rockefeller Foundation in 1913. He turned over to self-perpetuating groups of professional experts the task of using his vast wealth for publicly useful purposes. It was a kind of confession that, contrary to Carnegie's hope, a rich man is not capable of spending his money wisely, and Carnegie, too, endowed several great foundations. The foundation became the standard institution for the disposal of private fortunes in the United States. It was not an original institution in the history of private wealth, but in America the foundation reached its apogee. The activities of foundations in supporting educational, medical, scientific, and artistic endeavors have been of incalculable value to Americans and other peoples. That they have been administered privately while governed by the terms of state charters makes them an important addition to the pluralist American system. The aims of the foundations in general conformed in an unexpected way to the aims of Progressivism: the improvement of the material and cultural welfare of the people as a whole.

Rockefeller's announcement of a plan to establish a foundation came at a moment when his business methods were being exposed by a New York legislative investigating committee, and it aroused suspicion that his motive was sinister. But this very suspicion made the New York state legislature define the terms of the foundation's charter very carefully to guarantee its proper conduct and freedom from political interest. The growth of foundations was symptomatic of the failure of unmitigated plutocracy in the United States, along with its abortive ideal of creating in the United States a replica of European aristocracy. Then the game of aping European aristocrats in their style of life was taken up by movie stars. They turned it into farce, which the public enjoyed even more than it did the rituals of the Vanderbilts and the Astors.

Declining Prestige of the Very Rich

The essential failure of the plutocracy which had seemed so firmly entrenched when Bryan was defeated in 1896 was its failure to hold public respect. Ten years later hardly a popular magazine in the country failed to attack the rich for Roman luxury, corruption, and enmity to liberty. Besides the documentation of the muckrakers, cartoonists pictured the type of millionaire American as gross and vicious. It required a long campaign of public well-doing for Rockefeller to win the respect of the public. Millionaires as a class never succeeded in re-establishing themselves as a plutocracy. In the 1912 elections even Taft, the candidate of the conservative Republicans, was a Progressive compared to McKinley. Henceforth no important political group or leader would openly represent wealth. In fact, any evidence that it did so was politically disastrous.

By 1919, the magnates of the trusts and Wall Street were well on their way to join every other group that attempted to establish itself as a privileged class in America. The Puritan oligarchs had a religious ideal to justify their supremacy, the Tidewater planters an ideal of public service, and the cotton planters a dream of chivalry to justify slavery and secession. The new industrial and financial titans allowed their wives to pursue the ideal of an aristocratic social life which turned out to be absurd and the shortest-lived of all. Actually business leaders could point to the great rise in productivity of the American economy as their best justification.

CHAPTER 16

The Triumphs of Pragmatism

AFTER THE CIVIL WAR, THE LEADING THINKERS AND artists of the nation identified themselves with the wealthy. In the 1890's a profound change began. The excesses of the plutocracy, the absurdity of the châteaux and social ambitions of the Four Hundred, and the aridity of the genteel tradition in the arts alienated all but the most craven intellectual servants of the rich. The great majority of talented men and women began to identify themselves with the mass of the people and with renovating movements in politics, ranging from mild Progressivism to extreme varieties of socialism.

A few sought refuge in aestheticism from the vulgarity of the wealthy, the inhumanity of industrialism, and the inadequacies of the mass of people. This aestheticism was sometimes linked with ideals of handicrafts as opposed to machine production, with gothic medievalism as opposed to modernism in architecture and philosophy, and with other romantic dreams. Even escapist movements were protests against the status quo. But most creative leaders, like the Progressives of 1912, accepted industrialism and wished only to make it serve human ends.

They found new sources of vitality and inspiration in emotional identification with the people as a whole and with rebellious laborers and farmers in particular. They sought a more satisfying standard of success than money, a richer culture than one determined by material welfare. Henry George, Lester Ward, Stephen Crane, Louis Sullivan, and others had laid the foundations for revolt against cultural conservatism late in the nineteenth century. Now their descendants matched the victories of the Progressives and won effective leadership in all areas of thought and the arts. The result was a burst of achievement that equaled the accomplishments of the era of Jackson and Emerson. In both these greatest periods of American cultural creativity the effort was to build a civilization worthy of humanity under the rule of liberty.

PHILOSOPHY, EDUCATION, ECONOMICS, AND LAW

The Instrumentalism of John Dewey

John Dewey is perhaps the most important philosopher the United States has produced. Although his thought owed much to the pragmatism of William James, he developed a system he called instrumentalism which differs from it in significant respects. These differences express personal contrasts between the two men and also the breakaway of the twentieth century from old moorings. Dewey was the son of a grocer in Burlington, Vermont, where he attended the state university and absorbed the intense respect for the free individual who is a responsible citizen that is taken for granted in the Green Mountains. He also studied in the new graduate school of the Johns Hopkins University, and he taught philosophy in Middle Western universities when that region was torn by the Farmers' Revolt. In 1904, he joined the faculty of Columbia University. There he became the leading American thinker despite extreme shyness and a quite graceless prose style.

James had spoken from the stronghold of New England idealism for the preservation of religion as a most valuable result of his pragmatic test of truth. Dewey with his broad background in rural and Middle Western America cared nothing for religion. He spoke from the nation's metropolis for the application of the method of experimental science to the task of improving society. Ideas could be proved true insofar as they were successful instruments in remolding society. He accepted the industrial age as implying that the individual could now achieve fulfillment only by group action. He was in the great tradition of American liberals who trust human beings to know what is good and to act for it; he completed the secularization of this tradition, based it on scientific method, and added a new social dimension to it.

Dewey was criticized by traditional philosophers. Morris Cohen argued that a great need of mankind is neglected by a philosophy which ignores the desire for understanding of the nature of being (metaphysics) and the universe (cosmology), reduces philosophy to the single branch of the method of knowledge (epistemology), bases ethics on the shaky foundation of that which men regard as good in any particular time and place, and limits the definition of truth to what men consider useful and desirable. But such criticism reasserted the hopes, so far unfulfilled, of establishing agreement on a complete philosophic system, while Dewey in a remarkable way expressed the abandonment by most advanced industrial peoples of interest in abstract truth and their turn to attainable goals. The Progressives were reasserting the supremacy of the human being over all systems and absolutisms external to himself, and Dewey worked out the implications of their position. He admonished them to function collectively only as a means to the end of individual fulfillment and he had little to offer individuals who prefer to withdraw from co-operation with their fellows. At the same time he avoided the error of Marxists who subjected the individual to a collectivism which in practice turns out to be a tyrant's instrument. His philosophy tends to become experimental social science. His conscious followers are found more often among social scientists and reformers than among men of contemplation. His unconscious supporters include that vast majority of Americans who are more interested in useful ideas—from gadgets to political policies, and including all applied sciences and effective economic activity—than they are in meditation.

Dewey practiced what he preached by devoting a major portion of his long life (1859-1952) to the reform of education. He believed that it could be the best means of improving society by giving maximum scope to the freely developing talents and contributions of the oncoming generations. The school, he taught, was not a preparation for life but life itself; conversely, all life is a school. The traditional school should give way to a deliberate reproduction of a free society with discipline reduced to the same minimum required for the maintenance of order by government. This free society should provide opportunity for the creative activity of the child as a member of the group, which would permit him to grow through experience. In books such as *Democracy and Education* (1916), in lectures, and by conducting experimental schools, Dewey led the progressive education movement. It had obvious roots in the work of earlier innovators, but Dewey brought the movement to maturity. The influence of his progressive education can be traced in practices of those who theoretically oppose him. Simple signs of this are the virtual abandonment of corporal punishment of children and of learning by rote, and the substitution of positive motivations, for which "learn by doing" is the slogan. Continuing conflict over the degree to which progressive educational theory and practice are desirable and successful does not alter the fact that minimum reforms were universally adopted. Indeed it may be that the conflict is itself a necessary accompaniment of educators' and parents' adoption of Dewey's proposals for experimentation.

The experimental attitude, with its implication that no truth is final, spread from inductive scientific method into philosophy and education under Dewey's influence, and into politics, the social sciences, the arts, and everyday life. "Experimental" as a value word lost its suggestion of weakness and gained enormous prestige as a sign that dogma and the closed mind were rejected. To overthrow fixed systems of thought and codified ways of doing things and try something new became characteristic of American life in the new century.

The Institutional Economics of Thorstein Veblen

A decisive break with tradition in economic theory was made by Thorstein Veblen. Born in 1857 of Norwegian parents in Wisconsin, he studied philosophy and economics at Carleton College, Minnesota, the Johns Hopkins, Yale, and Cornell. He developed more skepticism than conventional Americanism. He would not conform to the habits, academic or matrimonial, expected of teachers and drifted or was expelled from several universities. In a series of books he rejected all "models" of the economy, whose construction had preoccupied theorists since Adam Smith, on the ground that they were dogmatic abstractions, and proposed instead that economists study the actual facts of economic institutions. His own studies led him to believe that a vital difference had grown up between technology or industry, which was constructive, and business or capitalism, which produced nothing but was purely predatory, reaping profits and wielding power over industry by financial manipulation. In his opinion, technology makes for progress, while finance is reactionary. To set free productive forces, including not only workers but also managers, engineers, technicians, and owners like Henry Ford whose policy was progressive rather than manipulative, should be the purpose of enlightened action.

Veblen's most influential book was his first, *The Theory of the Leisure Class* (1899). It was in effect an answer to those who asked the American plutocracy to take on the graces and responsibilities associated with the English aristocracy. With an Olympian objectivity that concealed deeply satirical anger, Veblen described the businessman as the anthropologist's analogue of a barbaric chieftain and argued that vulgar ostentation was a necessary consequence of the false pecuniary standard of business success. Puritan, Jeffersonian, and Populist antagonism to Wall Street, Fifth Avenue, and Newport is apparent in this most biting of all American indictments of capitalists.

Students and heirs of Veblen made intensive studies of the facts of economic behavior in specific sectors. Robert Franklin Hoxie's *Trade Unionism in the United States* (1917) explored "business unionism" which, under Gompers and the AFL, violated preconceived theories of trade unionism and established an American policy devoted to practical and immediate objectives of better wages, hours, and working conditions. Wesley C. Mitchell, following the injunctions of his teachers Dewey and Veblen, faced the business cycle free of the dogmas both of the classical economists, according to whom depressions were merely a peculiar exception, and of the Marxists, according to whom depressions would inevitably intensify until capitalism destroyed itself. Mitchell simply studied the facts and looked for repetitive relationships among the elements of economic change. He made Columbia University the headquarters of fruitful studies in this field. In *Business Cycles* (1913) and later books he developed the use of statistics and index numbers as the chief weapons for the analysis of past movements in the business cycle and the chief hope of predicting future movements, or at least of detecting early warning signs of impending inflationary and deflationary dangers. Mitchell's work, which is carried on today by a whole corps of researchers, in and out of government, represents the most important development of the institutional school of economics which Veblen founded. It exemplifies the influence of Dewey's injunction to apply the method of experimental science to all fields of knowledge. In its suspicion of theory, its devotion to measurable facts, and its accomplishments in increasing understanding of the economic system with concomitant opportunity to regulate it, this school represents an original American contribution to the world history of economic study.

The Legal Realism of Holmes and Brandeis

The philosophy of Dewey was also illustrated by the new school of judicial interpretation called legal realism. The common law and the Constitution, the two chief formulations of American law, were crystallized in the nineteenth century as absolutes expressing natural law. The immutability of natural law was supported by Greek, Roman, and Christian philosophy, by Newtonian science, by English and American political science, and seemingly by reason itself. According to this doctrine, the duty of the courts, and pre-eminently of the United States Supreme Court, was simply to place any challenged act of a citizen or government alongside the appropriate clause of the written law, compare them, and decide whether the act was legal or illegal. This respect for American written law as crystallized natural law resulted in a reverence for the Constitution and the Supreme Court and for its lesser forms and servants that amounted to fetishism. Such reverence was valuable in helping the difficult operations of the federal system, and it often served the ideal of human liberty which was written into American law so unmistakably; but it also made property rights as important as human rights, so that first slavery and later business corporations found in the courts powerful champions. It required a war to change the courts' views on slavery, and a revolution in the philosophy of law was necessary to re-establish the supremacy of human rights and the people's government over business corporations.

This revolution was unwittingly prepared for by jurists like Joseph Story (1779-1845), who emphasized that law is a product of historical process. In the hands of conservatives this merely strengthened the tendency of the legal profession to make the law a cult involving knowledge of precedents, rituals, and terms from which laymen should be excluded and whose service only lawyers and judges are entitled to supply as priests. By the end of the nineteenth century this kind of historical jurisprudence had been combined with the doctrine of natural law to support extreme conservatism. State and federal laws which experimented in new forms of social welfare were regularly found unconstitutional. Ironically, it was mechanical interpretation of a human right—the right to make a contract—and of the due process clause of the Fourteenth Amendment, which had been intended to protect the freedom of Negroes, that the courts most often invoked to protect corporations and to invalidate laws passed to protect laborers. Such laws were said to deprive corporations of their property without due process of law and to destroy the freedom of laborers to make contracts unfavorable to themselves.

But historical jurisprudence contained a deeper meaning. If law is "discovered" in past custom, obviously it evolved in some relation to the past needs of man and society. Why should the present generation be denied a creative role in establishing customs? This question could destroy the absolutism of natural law and the ritualism of judicial decision by precedent. Oliver Wendell Holmes, Jr., was the first great jurist to draw a full conclusion from the historical-evolutionary view of law. Son and namesake of the famous Boston wit and physician, he combined remarkable intellectual power and literary talent with the moral independence of the greatest New Englanders. As early as 1880 he disclosed a relativist view of law:

> The life of the law has not been logic; it has been experience. The felt necessities of the time, the prevalent moral and political theories, intuitions of public policy, avowed or unconscious, even prejudices which judges share with their fellow-men, have had a good deal more to do than the syllogism in determining the rules by which men should be governed.

This duplicated the pragmatist-instrumentalist rejection of logical deduction from metaphysical principles as the road to truth in philosophy, and substituted inductive experiment. Law itself became a hypothesis in constant process of readjustment to experience. It ceased to be an ultimate restriction on life and became an instrumentality of social evolution. Still the translation of the new philosophy into judicial decisions required more than a half century. Holmes himself, after twenty years of service on the Massachusetts bench, was appointed to the Supreme Court by President Theodore Roosevelt in 1902. Serving there for thirty years until he was ninety, he retired on the eve of the triumph of his heresies during the administration of the second Roosevelt. For all those years he was in the minority on most important issues that came to the Supreme Court; but his dissents were more noteworthy than most pronouncements of the majority. In Holmes modern America produced a jurist whom some authorities considered greater even than John Marshall.

He was not a progressive in social philosophy—indeed there was much of the conservative in his temperament—but he believed that to doubt one's first principles is the mark of a civilized man and that judges are not censors of life. The federal Constitution itself he called "an experiment, as all life is an experiment," and he believed in the right of the people to experiment with new kinds of legislation and of individuals to express new ideas, even if they make fools of themselves—which he denied that anything in the Constitution forbids—and even if the laws or opinions were loathesome to himself. He particularly welcomed experimentation in new legislation by the states, regarding this country as the fortunate possessor of forty-eight laboratories where policies can be tested for general adoption or rejection. It was typical of Holmes that he refused to join the majority of the Court even in the Northern Securities Case (1904), when it decided against the great railroad holding company. In his dissent he argued for the "rule of reason" which Theodore Roosevelt and the Court later made their own.

Equally pragmatic in his view of the law but far more definitely progressive in social philosophy was Louis D. Brandeis. Called the "people's attorney" because he argued so many public causes, he filled with socioeconomic facts the gap in legal argumentation left by Holmes's devaluation of precedents. His brief in arguing before the Supreme Court for the validity of a state law limiting the hours of women's labor (Muller vs. Oregon, 1908) contained a very few references to cases alongside a mountain of evidence that heavy labor by women is injurious to them, to their children, and to society. The "Brandeis brief" spelled out the doctrine that law is the product of experience. Its acceptance by the Supreme Court, and the Senate's reluctant approval of President Wilson's appointment of Brandeis to the Court in 1916, marked victories for sociological jurisprudence as an outgrowth of legal realism.

The Old Guard on the Court usually mustered a majority until 1937. Meanwhile, legal realism and sociological jurisprudence were erected into a learned discipline by Roscoe Pound of the Harvard Law School, while the Yale Law School worked to make law into a true science and called in sociologists, psychologists, and economists to help train its students. Law is the most vital meeting ground of the individual and society, of philosophy and action, and therefore it was appropriate that the development of pragmatism-instrumentalism in philosophy, which makes action the test of truth, and individual and social well-being the aim of action, should be exemplified by a renovation of the American view of law.

History, Anthropology, and Psychology

The implications of the new philosophy and jurisprudence for the ideas of the Constitution were so important that the problem was attacked directly by historians. To most Americans the document was ultimate truth. That the members of the Convention of 1787 were motivated by pure patriotism, guided by pure reason, and inspired by sheer genius when they framed the federal Constitution was a sacred doctrine. The muckrakers of the early twentieth century exposed the way in which modern political history was activated by economic interest. A few writers dared to suggest that the same interest had controlled earlier political events, including the drafting of the Constitution; but it was left for Charles A. Beard to dazzle the Progressives in their climactic year 1913 and shock conservatives by devoting an entire book, *An Economic Interpretation of the Constitution,* to the private finances of the framers of the Constitution and a mechanical explanation of how their fortunes could be affected by the instrument.

Beard disclaimed responsibility for his obvious implication of guilt in the Framers. He ignored the noneconomic consequences of their work in a misleading concentration on one category of causes. His book was severely attacked and in his reply (*The Economic Basis of Politics,* 1922) he cited all the respectable authorities for the economic interpretation of history while neglecting to mention Karl Marx, the most influential one. Beard afterwards denied the possibility of a science of history, declaring that any selection and arrangement of facts, is "controlled inexorably by the frame of reference in the mind of the selecter and arranger." This was a salutary reminder, but it does not relieve the historian of the obligation to be as objective as possible and to use the methods best calculated to secure objectivity.

Other historians avoided the muckraking attitude and engaged in valuable explorations of the economic aspect of historical development. This kind of work dominated American historical studies for a generation. To the frontier interpretation of Turner was added an understanding of the part that the interests of other classes—especially planters, merchants, industrialists, financiers, and skilled and unskilled labor—played in the drama of politics. James Harvey Robinson of Columbia University and Carl Becker of Cornell approached in their work their professed ideal of the "New History" which should comprehend the whole life of man, balancing traditional emphasis on politics not only with new emphasis on economics but also on thought, social life, arts, and religion. Few could embrace so wide an image, none contributed importantly to the philosophy of history, and synthesis was postponed while most historians were content to cultivate highly specialized gardens with a professional expertness which spoke of the domination of graduate school training for the doctorate. History was not a science but it now became a vastly proliferated study in which Americans matched other national schools in learning although not in philosophic profundity. They were, in short, pragmatists —enamored of facts, suspicious of theory. A few, notably Beard and

Becker, restored literary quality to a high position in American historiography.

The Anthropology of Franz Boas

The most important advance in the other social sciences occurred in anthropology. The contribution of America's greatest anthropologist, Franz Boas, was to discredit the scientific pretensions of racism. This doctrine lent support to three policies: segregation and exploitation of the Negro and the Indian in the United States, contempt and exploitation of the New Immigrants from southern and eastern Europe, and imperialism in relations with "lesser breeds without the law." American popular thought was shot through with the assumptions of the immutable superiority of the "race" variously called Anglo-Saxon, Teutonic, Nordic, Aryan, or Northwest European. Progressives were probably more militantly racist than conservatives were. Populist hatred of Wall Street was meshed with anti-Semitism, and hostility to the city became hostility to the latest immigrant nationalities. Theodore Roosevelt and Senator Albert J. Beveridge preached aggressiveness to cautious businessmen as the duty of the superior race to prove its superiority. At the turn of the century the anthropometrists who conducted extremely elaborate studies of the ratio between width and length of head in various human groups had great influence. From their studies it appeared that the heads of most of the currently dominant races were dolichocephalic while the currently weaker peoples were mostly brachycephalic. Franz Boas pointed out the superficiality of racial differences compared to the importance of the factors common to the human species.

He had been born and educated in Germany and joined the faculty of Columbia University in 1896. He was the most influential of a new generation of anthropologists who rejected preconceptions and undertook sympathetic surveys of whole cultures in order to understand their inner coherence. From this point of view, races were not primitive or advanced, superior or inferior, they simply represented different adaptations to environment and different expressions of the human potential for biological and cultural variation. Boas's studies of the Kwakiutl Indians were models of objectivity and penetration. His most influential general book was *The Mind of Primitive Man* (1911). Boas on occasion moved out of the academic world, for example in 1912 when he published a report to the Immigration Commission of the United States Senate proving that the American environment altered immigrant types in ways which racists considered impossible. Once Boas and his followers developed a sound approach to anthropology, an enlightened person had difficulty in justifying feelings of racial superiority. In the second and third decade of the century, Progressives adopted antiracism with immense consequences for the position of the Negro, the Indian, and recent immigrants, and for foreign policy. Ethnocentrism, which was at least as old as the Greeks, who had called all foreigners barbarians, was beginning to be expelled from the American mind.

Sociology profited from this new objectivity. Students of American society went beyond the germinal ideas of William Graham Sumner and Lester Ward to make exact studies of the actualities of group life. The family, the gang, the club, the church, the school, and all other forms of occupational and associational groups came under examination as the mediators between the individual and society. Interviews, questionnaires, and statistics became the material of sociology in America to a degree unknown elsewhere, and few were willing to risk sweeping generalizations. The insights gained by these objective methods generally supported Progressivism in politics. Those trained in sociology who did not themselves become scholars grew into an army of trained "social workers" staffing settlement houses in slums, welfare agencies of government, and, increasingly, private charitable institutions which were formerly operated by intuition. A most striking product of the new sociology was the social map of a city demonstrating block by block the coincidence of statistics of crowding and poverty with disease and crime. Old-fashioned moral exhortations seemed futile in the face of such evidence, and the drive for environmental improvement, by government action if necessary, gained strength. Some argued, from evidence of the persistence of mental and moral qualities through many generations of single families, that heredity rather than environment controlled behavior, but this minority report among the sociologists also supported movements for reform. Mrs. Margaret Sanger, a social worker and district nurse in the New York slums, led the movement to legalize the dissemination of information on methods of birth control. Her magazine, *The Woman Rebel,* founded in 1914, was banned by the Post Office Department. Mrs. Sanger went to jail on this and other occasions, but she steadily gained support. Less successful was the movement which demanded the enforcement by law of the principles of eugenics.

The Psychology of Watson and Freud

During the first years of the twentieth century, psychology, which had so recently won scientific standing as a result of the laboratory methods of William James, fell into a bewildering variety of schools. Just as Dewey built on James in philosophy, so he did in psychology. In an article "The Reflex Arc Concept" (1896) he elaborated James's concept that mind serves the organism functionally by interactions of stimuli and responses towards adaptive ends. Functionalism became the focus of work in most academic centers of research. Only measurable facts satisfied the most rigorous researchers, and, with the aid of a vast proliferation of laboratory apparatus and testing procedures, they piled up mountains of data. Psychologists gained the ability to predict fairly accurately in what kind of job a person could succeed. Functionalism retained the concept of mind while turning towards practical goals, and introspection remained its chief method even while new experimental laboratory techniques were developed.

The new school of behaviorism was much more extreme. Its chief promoter was John B. Watson. In *Behavior: An Introduction to Comparative Psychology* (1914), following the work of the Russian Ivan Pavlov on conditioned reflexes, he applied to human beings the interpretations which he held in common with animal psychologists. Introspection was ruled out, mind and consciousness were irrelevant. The human psyche was treated as a machine to be understood in materialistic terms. The most subtle reaches of psychic activity were believed to vary from simple muscular and motor reflexes only in degree of complexity. According to behaviorism, thought is "nothing but" incipient action of the vocal organs; the emotions are "nothing but" glandular reactions. Watson impressed the public by exaggerated promises that the psychologist could now mold human character at will. Behaviorism appealed to those who could believe in simple formulas and it had a tremendous success among psychologists as well as laymen. Insofar as it encouraged research it was useful, but an element of faddism clung to it and the next generation outgrew it.

A second importation in psychological theory, Freudianism, has had increasing importance in the United States. Beginning as a physician and neurologist in Vienna, Dr. Sigmund Freud devised the psychoanalytic technique of therapy for neurosis and developed a theory of psychology that stressed sexual impulses as the source of much human suffering when suppressed and much human grandeur when sublimated. His image of the structure of the human psyche included the unconscious level of instinctual drives, the superego as the introjected voice of parents and social taboos, and the ego struggling between these two in order to act. This theory could not be proved by ordinary laboratory experiment, but it turned out to be extraordinarily successful as a basis for therapy. The psychoanalyst was able to interpret dreams and inconsequential acts as well as major behavior patterns and show patients their hidden motivations, as a means to help them overthrow obsessions, manias, and abnormal nervous symptoms. The emphasis on the influence of sex on behavior made Freud's struggle for recognition very difficult. But even before he received much recognition abroad, he was invited in 1909 to lecture in the United States as part of the anniversary observance of Clark University by its president, G. Stanley Hall, himself a leading psychologist. There William James told Freud that he expected the new theory to overthrow all others in psychology. Dr. A. A. Brill became the chief American promoter of psychoanalysis and it gradually gained a stronger position in American medical practice than in any other country.

In popularized and often vulgarized form, Freud's theories were taken up avidly by many who viewed all repressions as harmful, all impulsive conduct as beneficial. The younger literary generation particularly welcomed Freudianism. Greenwich Village in New York City became a bohemia of experimentation with unsuppressed desires. The new movements in poetry, playwriting, and the novel were heavily indebted to Freudian psychology for their analysis of character. Despite absurdities and excesses, the Freudian invasion had much to do with the revolution in manners, morals, and literature which, at its best, displaced traditional Puritan hypocrisy and Victorian gentility with a new honesty and realism. Freudian doctrine was pessimistic insofar as it pictured man as the slave of his unconscious impulses; but it also proposed that man by gaining knowledge of these obscure drives could gain new control over himself, and it probably was this hopeful implication of Freudianism that made psychoanalytic therapy so popular in the United States. It held out new means to that happiness which Americans regard as their right and which Europeans scarcely anticipate. After Freudianism had been thoroughly naturalized in this country, a movement developed to purge it entirely of its pessimistic aspect.

Medicine and Science

While psychoanalytic therapy progressed experimentally and won great victories over the most mysterious sectors of mental disease, advances were also made in its treatment by material means. Dr. Adolf Meyer discovered that injection of malarial organisms into the blood could cure certain psychoses. He was a leader in the mental hygiene movement which undertook to educate the public and governments in the prevention and cure of mental disorder. In general medicine perhaps the greatest accomplishment was the reform of medical schools. The great 1910 Report to the Carnegie Foundation by Dr. Abraham Flexner revealed abuses and outlined reforms. As a result, many inferior or fraudulent medical schools closed and the instruction in the remaining institutions vastly improved. A serious consequence, however, was the reduction in the number of doctors graduated each year. While the quality of medical service improved, its declining availability, especially in rural regions, and its growing cost created new problems. Basic medical research progressed with the discoveries of hormones and vitamins, the use of radium and X-ray therapy, and systematized attacks on many diseases by many individuals and agencies, notably the Rockefeller Institute of Medical Research (founded 1901). An outstanding achievement was the discovery in 1915 by Joseph Goldberger of the United States Public Health Service that pellagra, a scourge in the South, is caused by vitamin deficiency in diet.

In pure biological research, Thomas Hunt Morgan made a discovery that balanced the Darwinian emphasis on environment with a new understanding of heredity. As a professor at Columbia University he made the humble fruit fly, *Drosophila,* yield fundamental knowledge of genes as components of chromosomes, and of their linkages and mutations. He founded in 1909 the new science of genetics on a genuinely experimental basis. Its importance to social thought was demonstrated later when one set of totalitarians, the German Nazis, exaggerated the determining power of genes to support racism, while another set, the Russian Communists, denied their significance entirely, and punished geneticists. On another level, the American-born science of genetics permitted the development of hybrid seed for corn and other crops to the great advantage of farmers.

In physics, the great advances of the relativity and quantum theories occurred during this period in Europe, with Robert A. Millikan's measurement of the charge of an electron (1910) as the chief American contribution. The United States acquired the best tool in the world for astronomical study when George Ellery Hale, inventor of the spectroheliograph, opened the Mt. Wilson Observatory (1906) in California, and thus fulfilled the hope of John Quincy Adams that the American experiment in freedom would be justified by "scanning the heavens" and winning eminence in science. During these years American science made the transition from emphasis on inventions to emphasis on pure research— which turned out to be even more fruitful for utilitarian purposes than the "tinkering" tradition of the great inventors.

FERMENT IN RELIGION

The Social Gospel

The prestige of science over all other modes of knowledge grew to such pre-eminence that the proponents of religious faith either advanced from the post-Darwinian reconciliation to make positive use of the methods and findings of science, or blindly rejected them altogether. The former tendency was apparent in the Social Gospel movement. Its first leader was a Congregational minister, George Washington Gladden, whose book, *Being a Christian* (1876), welcomed the findings of science in all fields and joined science to the Gospel of Christ to criticize the evils of society. William Dwight Porter Bliss went farther. He had been born in Constantinople of American missionary parents, and decided during his education in the United States that this country stood in need of Christianization of its economic and social systems. He found inspiration in the socialism of Edward Bellamy and the English Fabians, in the Populism of the Middle West and the Single Tax of Henry George. An Episcopalian minister, he organized the Church Association for the Advancement of the Interests of Labor (1887), the Brotherhood of the Carpenter in Boston, the Society of Christian Socialists, and the American Fabian Society (1895). None of these organizations satisfied him, although the first of them did much to make American clergymen aware of the need for church action in favor of labor. Bliss became editor of the *Encyclopaedia of Social Reform,* first published in 1897, and this monumental work served for the new century some of the purposes of the great French Encyclopaedia in the eighteenth. Its authors included many of the most advanced social scientists. Its program included the whole range of Progressive reforms and a mild variety of evolutionary socialism besides, all in the name of the Founder of Christianity. The new social science thus gained force from the Sermon on the Mount.

A Congregational minister, George D. Herron of Iowa, took up the work of preaching the Social Gospel with great effect until in 1901 a divorce scandal forced him to escape abroad. But he used his second wife's money to found the Rand School of Social Science in New York, and this institution carried on the work of providing scientific bases for reform. Another Congregational minister, Charles M. Sheldon of Topeka, Kansas, wrote a novel, *In His Steps* (1898) which applied Christian love, literally, to the problems of living in modern America to such startling effect that more than 15 million copies were sold and readers imbibed as Christianity what others learned from economists and sociologists.

The greatest preacher of the Social Gospel was Walter Rauschenbusch. After spending most of his life obscurely teaching church history at Rochester Theological Seminary, he suddenly emerged in 1907 with the publication of *Christianity and the Social Crisis* as a prophet with worldwide influence. He analyzed existing ills, chiefly the grinding poverty of the many, as the product of evil institutions rather than evil men. He boldly declared that economic competition, the most prized concept of the defenders of the existing order, was the enemy of Christian brotherhood. It resulted in monopoly and the final stand of autocracy. Profit under monopoly he attacked as a tribute exacted by the powerful from the weak. In 1917, Rauschenbusch stated that "God is against capitalism, its methods, spirit and results." He declared that socialization of natural resources was essential for the creation of a Christian Commonwealth. He blamed the churches for tolerating and even supporting existing institutions that violated the fundamental teachings of Christ. The Social Gospel with Rauschenbusch achieved great influence in transforming the social philosophy of American clergymen and laymen.

Its chief influence was among the best-educated denominations. It was linked with liberalism in theology, the scholarship of the "higher criticism" of the Bible, acceptance of Darwinism, and respect for the methods and findings of science in all fields. It seemed to some leaders of religion to lose sight of man's inherent sinfulness in favor of a secular philosophy, and to betray Christianity itself when it questioned the literal words of the Bible.

Fundamentalism

While the leaders of the Social Gospel pointed to the suffering of the poor in the cities, the poorest—and least-educated—rural religious groups organized a counterattack. Fundamentalism became an organized movement in 1909 when some clergymen, most of them connected with evangelical churches, encouraged by two California oil millionaires, launched a widespread propaganda effort which the latter financed in behalf of their somewhat simplified idea of "the old-time religion." For about a decade they wielded great influence in colleges, theological seminaries, the religious press, the Chautauqua circuit, and revivalist camp meetings. The blatant preaching style of Billy Sunday, who liked to play baseball against the Devil and turned the vocabulary of theology into the latest slang, was the admiration of masses and the model of his colleagues.

William Jennings Bryan demonstrated the intimate link between religious fundamentalism and agrarian discontent. The angers which had been channeled into the politics of Populism and Free Silver were much the same as those which burst out in the Fundamentalist movement. Their central target was the city itself. It was displacing the homestead as the most important site of American life and to farmers it seemed corrupt from the top, where thieving millionaires lived in Babylonian opulence, to the bottom, where the dregs of the worst European nations bred slums, disease, vice, and machine politics. The learning and culture of the cities seemed infected by infidelity. Bryan's failure in politics was the failure of the farmers in their counterattack against the city. He turned to spend most of his energy on the Fundamentalist campaign to save religion from the educated unfaithful. For years between political campaigns he was the star lecturer of the Chautauqua circuit, and after he resigned as President Wilson's Secretary of State in 1915, he led the Fundamentalist campaign against the teaching of evolution in the public schools.

But this could hardly extirpate Darwinism from American thought. The Fundamentalists typically attacked symptoms and often very superficial ones. In the cities the old Puritan Sabbath was no more. The Fundamentalists urged state and local laws against baseball and movies on Sundays. In the cities the traditional American pipe and chewing tobacco were giving way to cigarettes. The Fundamentalists demanded laws against "coffin nails." In some Southern and Western states "blue laws" regulated private conduct as if in caricature of the Puritan oligarchy of Massachusetts-Bay. The greatest success of this kind was the prohibition of alcoholic liquor by national law.

Medievalism

Unlike the Puritanism of the seventeenth century, Fundamentalism was anti-intellectual. At the other extreme of religious life there was an attempt to restore medievalism. This was a concern especially of certain highly cultivated Episcopalians. It had roots in the Romantic Movement in literature and philosophy and a direct antecedent in the Oxford Movement of "High Church" Anglicans which restored some of the rituals and beliefs of the pre-Reformation Church and carried a few back to Roman Catholicism. In the United States some Episcopalians took up a refined medievalism in ritual and architecture. The most earnest admirers of the medieval synthesis developed a social philosophy which, if it did not accept socialism as the modern equivalent of Christ's law of love, revived the ideal of charitable responsibility of the favored for the welfare of the poor.

Strangely enough, it required something like a revival for the Roman Catholic Church in the United States to activate medieval ideals. Late in the nineteenth century the desire of Roman Catholics to accommodate their religious faith to the prevailing concepts of Americanism had given rise to what some Catholics subsequently called the "American heresy." While most Roman Catholics found no conflict between their loyalties to their Church and to the United States, more rigorously intellectual Catholics, who admired the thirteenth century more than the twentieth, cast about for means to restore medievalism to the Church and to society itself. Lacking strength to organize an independent political party and respecting American dislike of religion in politics, Catholic medievalists generally confined themselves to philosophic and aesthetic self-cultivation. Perhaps their greatest influence came from their criticism of modern society.

The hundreds of thousands of immigrants of Roman Catholic faith who arrived each year had little interest in the restoration of medieval institutions and values. Parishes were often organized for immigrants on a language or nationality basis, and parochial schools were built for their children, but religion was presented as in no way contradictory of the fundamental concepts of Americanism. Urban political machines appeared to be largely Catholic. While holding itself aloof from Protestant Fundamentalism, the Roman Catholic Church consolidated its own kind of literalism by disciplining its members in strict obedience. The effects in public life were discernible in Catholic opposition to certain movements, notably Prohibition and birth control. At the same time some clerical leaders, among whom Father John A. Ryan was outstanding, and numerous Catholic politicians were active on many fronts in behalf of labor and welfare legislation. The most influential Catholic cleric was the second American Cardinal, James Gibbons of Baltimore. He advocated the elimination of ethnic boundaries among immigrants, supported organized labor, and upheld the separation of Church and State.

Despite the generally rapid Americanization of Catholic immigrants, their number and their strange nationalities gave rise to a new outburst of nativism. The number of Roman Catholics rose from about 12 million in 1900 to 16 million in 1910. In the Fundamentalist districts of the Middle West an anti-Catholic organization called the American Protective Association gained strength. Founded in 1887 by H. F. Bowers of Iowa, it was never influential as pre-Civil War nativism had been among educated groups.

Judaism

To a considerable extent Jewish immigrants now displaced Catholics as a chief target of prejudice. Judaism at the same time underwent important developments in America which indicated the influence of the new environment. The small Jewish groups in America during the nineteenth century were dominated by immigrants from Germany. Led by Isaac Mayer Wise of Cincinnati, they had evolved by the end of the century a program of Reform Judaism. This was comparable to Protestant liberalism. The Talmud and Messianic doctrine were reduced in importance, many rituals and the segregation of women in the synagogue were abandoned, Sunday instead of Saturday was observed as the Sabbath, and English replaced German and other European languages.

A few leaders opposed this "Americanization," and worked for a return to historical or Conservative Judaism. The influx, among the New Immigrants from Eastern Europe, of Jews who were inferior in education to German Jews and who formed "ghettos" especially in New York and the largest cities, which insulated them against the American environment, stopped the growth of Reform Judaism. Solomon Schechter in the new century became the leader of Conservative Judaism. He reorganized the Jewish Theological Seminary in New York in 1902 and in 1913 achieved a federation of Conservative congregations called the United Synagogue. But Conservative Judaism made many concessions to reform. Even American Orthodoxy, a small faction of ultratraditionalists, did not maintain the full array of orthodox Jewish tenets, rituals, and customs. With the emergence of the second and third generation, Reform Judaism again gained strength. A minority of eastern European Jews were antireligious radicals of one sort or another. But the extremes of religious orthodoxy and political radicalism both steadily gave way before the influences of the new society.

CHAPTER 17

The Birth of Modernism
in the Arts

THE ASCENDANCY OF PROGRESSIVISM IN POLITICS AND pragmatism in thought was paralleled by the triumph of naturalism in literature. Apparent in all three was the preference for facing the "facts of life," particularly the unpleasant ones, over all the pleasant ways of ignoring them or explaining them away. Even the novels of Henry James during his last years, aesthetically perhaps the greatest fiction ever produced by an American, contained a profound condemnation of the shoddy moral codes of materialists. James's most talented follower in portraying upper-class Americans, Edith Wharton, who was born into the old Knickerbocker circle, pictured New York society in *The House of Mirth* (1905) as an aristocracy purely of money. Most of her works carried this moral, but in *Ethan Frome* (1911) she showed her awareness of the other side of the dilemma. This very simple and very great tale of the New England hills ends in tragedy arising out of poverty.

THE NOVEL OF NATURALISM

The great naturalists were closer to social science and propaganda than to art. In *McTeague* (1899), Frank Norris, a Californian of some wealth who studied at Harvard and tried painting in Paris, used a crude distortion of Darwinism, that the brute in man is always ready to overcome his civilization, to demonstrate his essential thesis that poverty degrades. Just thirty years old in 1900 and with only two years of life left, Norris conceived a trilogy of wheat, but he wrote only *The Octopus* (1901) and *The Pit* (1903). In the former the protagonists are the wheat farmers, representing the creative forces of life, and the Southern Pacific Railroad representing the death-dealing power of the machine. In the second vol-

301

ume a Chicago grain speculator's campaign to corner wheat is defeated by the fecundity of nature and the labor of farmers who flood the market. Norris planned the third volume, *The Wolf*, as a study of the movement of the wheat to the hungry masses of Europe and Asia. Here was an attempt to comprehend in literature the new and mighty social and economic tides of modern America.

Jack London, also a Californian, the illegitimate child of an astrologer and a spiritualist, emerged from the poverty of an oyster pirate, seaman, and hobo, to fame and wealth as a popular writer. He added romantic socialism to crude Darwinism to make up an incongruous philosophy of individual adventurism, biological atavism, and social revolution. *The Call of the Wild* (1903), the story of a dog in the far North who reverts to the life of a wolf, can be read as allegory. In *The Sea Wolf* (1904), the story of a ruthless schooner captain, London pits moral decency against primitivism. His great financial success, his conversion to socialism, a second marriage to his "mate-woman," and a project of building a fabulous ranch, "The Valley of the Moon," did not help him in his fight against alcoholism and despair. His adherence lent glamor and prestige to the Socialist Party, but he was unable to incorporate Socialist doctrine in his fiction except indirectly in a novel of the future. *The Iron Heel* (1908), is a picture of socialism three centuries after its victory over "The System," which was a frightening preview of fascism. In his forty-nine published volumes London showed mastery of narrative but fundamental weaknesses in thought.

The greatest of the naturalists was Theodore Dreiser. He was born in Indiana of a poor family fathered by an ineffectual but fanatical German Catholic immigrant. His relationship with his mother gave him some security but the family moved constantly from place to place and suffered social ostracism. To Theodore economic and social success had the value of a spiritual ideal. He earned his living by newspaper work and magazine editing while developing his groping talent as a novelist. *Sister Carrie* was published in 1900 but withdrawn when it was threatened with censorship because of its frank exposition of the way a girl gained social position by exploiting her sexual attraction. A similar study of feminine defiance of strict morality, *Jennie Gerhardt*, was published in 1911, and the next year *Sister Carrie* was reissued. These two books marked an important point in the revolution of American attitudes towards sexual experience and towards the freedom of the artist. A deep honesty in searching for a tenable philosophy redeemed Dreiser's acceptance of biological determinism. The characters in his books, like the author himself, tried to learn more about themselves and society by facing ugly facts; they suffered chiefly from bewilderment at the disparity between the promise and the reality of American life.

In a trilogy based on the life of the street-railway magnate, Charles

T. Yerkes, of which *The Financier* appeared in 1912, *The Titan* in 1914, and *The Stoic* in 1947, Dreiser related social and economic phenomena to the imperious impulses or "chemisms" which drove Frank Cowperwood to power over wealth, women, and fine paintings. In *The Genius* (1915) an artist, lacking Cowperwood's strength, suffers in trying to reconcile his ambition to create beauty in the environment of insensitive America. With *An American Tragedy* (1925) Dreiser achieved recognition as a great novelist, although his fumbling prose style and mental crudity were rather repellent. It was a triumph of force over finesse. His work was crucial in liberating the American novel from the taboos of the nineteenth century. He embraced socialism late in life as a sort of dream which might free mankind from the limitations that he himself exaggerated, but his criticism of American society was more influential than the cure he offered.

The same was doubly true of Upton Sinclair. He was an early convert to socialism. His racy narratives and sociological pictures of contemporary evils brought him a tremendous audience, but American readers paid little attention to his Socialist moral. The son of Southerners fallen on hard times, he hated the poverty of his youth and the liquor that conquered his father. He used the novel frankly as a propaganda vehicle. *The Jungle* (1906), a study of the Chicago stockyards, to his disappointment caused more clamor over bad meat than the plight of the workers. In *Love's Pilgrimage* (1911) he explored the corruption that he observed flowing from capitalism into the church, the school, the press, and the arts. A philosophy which identified evil with the institution of private property provided Sinclair with themes for a long series of novels dealing methodically with one aspect of society after another. To literary critics who complained of his crude propaganda, Sinclair answered with figures which proved that he reached a mass of readers around the world outnumbering the audience of any other American writer. He made the novel of naturalism important as a muckraking instrument with slight consequence for socialism but considerable effect on Progressivism. In the same vein were Ernest Poole's impressive novel, *The Harbor* (1915), and David Graham Phillips' *The Great God Success* (1901), and *Susan Lenox: Her Fall and Rise* (1917).

While the naturalists succeeded in forcing people to look at the seamy side of life, they failed in that important function of art which is to give pleasure. Ordinary readers preferred sugary romance. The American novelist Winston Churchill in *Richard Carvell* (1899) and *The Crisis* (1910), Paul Leicester Ford in *Janice Meredith* (1899), Mary Johnston in *To Have and To Hold* (1900), and Booth Tarkington in *Monsieur Beaucaire* (1900) made the historical romance lighter and brighter than ever. Their success encouraged a corps of writers who fluffed up casual mixtures of love and pseudo-history into giddy and enormously popular soufflés of which George Barr McCutcheon's *Beverley of Graustark* (1905) was the archetype. In these novels the jewels were visibly made of paste, the swords were admittedly toys. Whether laid in the mythical Balkan kingdom of Graustark, or in the Renaissance Italy of F. Marion Crawford's innumerable romances, or in a more prosaic American setting, romantic novels and magazine stories, innocent and escapist, were the preferred fare of the mass of American readers.

THE REBELS—CHIEFLY POETS

A few highly sensitive spirits were repelled by the whole gamut of genteel, naturalistic, and neoromantic literature. They felt alienated from modern civilization. William James had spoken for them when he denounced "the bitch-goddess Success," but his hospitality towards the common experience of modern man left them cold.

James Gibbons Huneker, primarily a music critic but more broadly a purveyor of attitudes toward life, preached taste as the greatest good, art as the worthiest religion, and epicurean sophistication as America's crying need. The best of his many books was *Chopin: The Man and His Music* (1900).

The most talented of his disciples was Henry L. Mencken of Baltimore. With Mencken the rejection of democracy became outright. He adopted the ideas of Friedrich Nietzsche and propagated them among the intelligentsia in this country. In a brilliant prose style of plain, hard texture, Mencken described average Americans—particularly politicians, professors, and preachers—as baboons, and proclaimed the right of the superior man to superior privileges. These privileges turned out to be little more than good food, good music, good literature—usually German, French, Russian, or Scandinavian—and good beer. Mencken remained amused and amusing through a long career and became an important student of the American language. With the Socialist Robert Rives La Monte, he published a correspondence, *Man Versus Men* (1910), which declared witty contempt of the common man and all his prophets, especially Socialists. With the young drama critic George Jean Nathan, he made *Smart Set* a fashionable magazine of the young pre-war intellectuals.

Ambrose Bierce stirred similar attitudes into a bitter brew. A veteran of the Civil War, he became a popular writer for the Hearst newspapers while embellishing the bohemian life of San Francisco. He was obsessed with violence and death. His prose style was brilliant and mordant. *The Devil's Dictionary* (1906) revealed cynicism surpassing misanthropy and approaching horror at life itself, a more devastating rejection of values than any American had dared to pronounce. His short stories were in the Poesque tradition of premature burials and assorted shudders. He disappeared in 1914 without a trace in Mexico—an ending worthy of one of his stories.

Bohemianism and expatriation were more meaningful for this new generation of intellectuals than for any earlier generation of artists and writers. To go to Greenwich Village in New York or to similar quarters of other cities, to sail away to London or Paris, was a necessary gesture. It signified personal defiance of business-minded and Puritan-minded America and a declaration of personal freedom to live according to sexual, aesthetic, and philosophic precepts unacceptable in the rebel's family and home town.

Floyd Dell led a typical migration from Davenport, Iowa, to a district in Chicago where the makers of the "Chicago Renaissance" foregathered in cheap lodgings and congenial restaurants, thence to New York's Greenwich Village before the war, and forward to Paris when the Village was taken over by sightseers and the United States by Prohibitionists. The antics of the Villagers, their experiments in free love, radicalism, and strange styles of behavior, were the externals of a profound revolution in art. American like British poetry had sunk to the status of space-filler for editors seeking to elevate the tone of magazines with effusions on a standard repertory of subjects—nature, love and virtue—in a standardized "poetic" language—e'er, thou, lorn, mourn, ye and eftsoon. The aesthetes now standardized to death the lush emotions and language of Swinburne.

The New Poetry

A small and determined woman who emerged from the cultural uplift in Chicago became the organizer of a rebirth of genuine poetry. In October 1912, Harriet Monroe published the first number of *Poetry: A Magazine of Verse,* the most important such periodical in the English language. It quickly became the vehicle of the two main tendencies of the new American poetry. The one was led by Vachel Lindsay, Edgar Lee Masters, and Carl Sandburg, all of Illinois, in whose plainest life they found great poetry—whether the fulfilled tragedy of Abraham Lincoln in Lindsay's verse and Sandburg's prose, the tragedy of small-town frustration in Masters' *Spoon River Anthology* (1915), or fierce vitality in Sandburg's *Chicago Poems* (1916). All were cast in the language of American common speech heightened to the intensity of art, as in Sandburg's title poem:

> Hog Butcher for the World,
> Tool Maker, Stacker of Wheat,
> Player with Railroads and the Nation's Freight Handler:
> Stormy, husky, brawling,
> City of the Big Shoulders.

This was shocking to genteel taste, but it was not far removed from the Elizabethan pith of Shakespeare. Most popular of the Illinois poets was

Lindsay. Readers were instructed to sing his "General William Booth Enters into Heaven" (1913) to a Salvation Army hymn tune accompanied by drum, banjo, and tambourine, but actually its compelling rhythm needed no accessories. Lindsay toured the country as a vagabond of art, singing, or reciting, or lecturing to anyone who would listen. Lindsay, Masters, Sandburg, and many lesser poets were nativists who sang the glories of America and complained only against betrayals of her best dreams. They sought strength for their art in the common lives of the people, and identified themselves with Progressive movements in politics.

Similar only in its discarding of the worn-out shell of Victorian poetry was the other main tendency in the poetic revolution. Its leaders moved to London, where they initiated a renovation of English as well as American poetry. Later in Paris or Italy they participated in international vanguard movements. T. S. Eliot of St. Louis was the greatest and one of the first of these migrants. Descended from New England Unitarians, he absorbed the most conservative ideas available at Harvard and worked as a bank clerk in London to gain freedom to write. Ezra Pound, a romance-language teacher from Idaho who was expelled from Wabash College, Indiana, in 1908 for unconventionality, joined Eliot in London, virtually took over the editorial leadership of *Poetry* magazine by mail, and became chief disciplinarian of the new movement as well as a poet on his own account. He promoted Imagism, which rejected all poetic values except those of the single, objective image, until it was appropriated and widely publicized by Amy Lowell of Boston. It was Pound who insisted that Harriet Monroe publish Eliot's *The Love Song of J. Alfred Prufrock* in 1915, which begins:

> Let us go then, you and I,
> When the evening is spread out against the sky,
> Like a patient etherised upon a table;

Drily intellectual and to Victorian taste antipoetic, this new voice seemed more disturbingly revolutionary than that of the Chicago poets. Eliot was deeply learned. He used the common language intensified as Dante and Donne had used theirs, and exploited his scholarship in symbols and allusions. His forms were free but controlled by an ear for compulsive rhythms and concealed rhymes. The newness of his poetry and his satires of contemporary life gave him for some time the aura of a radical; but he was in fact a conservative who later formulated for himself a thoroughly medieval philosophy. Ezra Pound, a less original poet, became a more reactionary thinker and moved from hatred of philistine America to support of Mussolini's fascism after the First World War. In Paris, Gertrude Stein of San Francisco performed for American prose similar revolutionary work, but she remained through her long expatriation devoted to the idea of America.

It was no small event in world history when Americans went to London and Paris and took leading parts in creating the new literature of the twentieth century. This literature reached a climax of achievement after the war, but it is significant that neither in form nor idea was it simply a product of that cataclysm. Rather it grew out of the self-critical, profoundly reformist spirit of the Progressive Era. The emergence of Dreiser, Mencken, Masters, and Eliot marked the beginning of a creative era in American literature less dependent on European leadership than were the writers of the Jackson period.

AN AMERICAN ARCHITECTURE

In one other art besides poetry an American emerged early in the twentieth century as a modern master of world stature. Frank Lloyd Wright won his first renown in Europe when a volume of his designs for houses was published in Germany in 1910. Born at Richland Center, Wisconsin, in 1869, he remained a Middle Westerner. His home in Wisconsin, "Taliesin," was an unfolding in stone of his long and astonishing career. He absorbed elements of Japanese and other exotic architectural and decorative disciplines without subordinating himself to any precedent. He carried to fulfillment the revolt of his teacher, Louis Sullivan, against the genteel, the eclectic, and particularly the classical models of the Chicago World's Fair.

Wright's creativity was such that he rarely imitated himself, but decade after decade invented fabulous new solutions for houses, factories, churches, and office buildings. To the functional or "international" style of European modernists, which subordinates human emotion to rational efficiency, Wright opposed "organic" architecture. This called for a fusion of natural site and human imagination, industrial methods and natural materials, and, above all, human emotional needs with functional requirements. He had a sense of the richness of the American potential as profound as Whitman's and a similar aspiration that democracy should fulfill itself not merely by overthrowing aristocratic cultural forms, but by surpassing them. In the central tradition of American democracy, he was a supreme individualist. His career was a war made up of battles against defenders of the traditional, the mediocre, and the false. He won most of these battles, and in the end gained general recognition as the greatest master of modern architecture, a man on the scale of the cultural heroes of history.

His first innovation was the "prairie" house, examples of which, notably the Robie house of 1909, he built in and around Chicago. "Democracy needed something basically better than the box," he said later, "so I started out to destroy the box as building." Inside he broke down the walls that cut houses into small boxes, and made space flow outward from a strong center, usually a great fireplace, to wide eaves like hovering petals, and to walls running out into gardens like roots. In 1904, he built the Larkin Building in Buffalo on the revolutionary principles that a business structure could be beautiful and the employee's physical environment esthetically satisfying. In Oak Park, a suburb of Chicago, Wright built the Unity Church without repeating a single motif of former church architecture, and in 1914 he created the fantastic Midway Gardens on the South Side of Chicago. Two years later he designed the Imperial Hotel in Tokyo on revolutionary engineering principles which were vindicated when it was virtually the only structure left standing by the earthquake of 1923.

Such achievements would have made the name of an ordinary artist, but they were only the first stages of a career that continued past the middle of the century. The ultimate acceptance of his work by the American people as well as by others argues its appropriateness to its time and place, but Americans were very slow to abandon Greek pillars and Gothic arches in favor of something of their own. They clung to "colonial" designs for their homes, as if reluctant to face the new life their own machinery and power had created. For public buildings the classical revival initiated by the Chicago Fair reached a peak of excellence in the designs of the New York firm of McKim, Mead and White. Their Columbia University Library (1893), J. P. Morgan Library in New York (1906), and many other edifices were superb realizations of classical standards. Luxury of materials, soundness of construction, and originality within the frame of Roman and Renaissance precedent as taught by the Paris *Ecole des Beaux-Arts* have never surpassed the work of these men.

The Gothic Revival also approached its final stage. Churches, colleges, and even pinnacles of skyscrapers were adorned with ever more accurate imitations of fourteenth-century monuments. Scholarly fidelity to medieval precedents was reached in the architecture of Ralph Adams Cram. The cadets at West Point were reminded of the glories of chivalry in Cram's Chapel (1904). The detail of St. Thomas's Episcopal Church (1911-1913) in midtown New York suited the surrounding châteaux of millionaires. A site worthy of medieval idealism was offered to Cram on Morningside Heights, New York, overlooking the great metropolis, when the trustees of the new Episcopal Cathedral of Saint John the Divine suddenly discharged Christopher LaFarge in 1907 and gave the half-built Romanesque structure to Cram to finish in Gothic. The latter had become more fashionable. "Style" as something which Americans could shop for among architects and the centuries was perfectly defined by this episode. Cram proceeded to remake the huge structure according to the exact norms of one and another French cathedral, and to "Americanize" the result by picturing Daniel Webster in the medium of fourteenth-century stained glass. The careful reproduction of medieval methods of handwork, so much admired by Cram's generation, could be managed for a time with immigrant labor, but it has become impossibly expensive in our own day, and the great unfinished work stands a monument to American cultural confusion.

The skyscraper itself, whose emergence in the work of Louis Sullivan promised a genuine expression of the realities of American life and of the individuality of the artist, was captured from the Chicago School and brought under the control of genteel Beaux-Arts designers. The tallest and most numerous examples were built in New York. Sullivan himself built there in 1898 a beautifully decorated tower emphasizing the verticality of its steel skeleton (the Bayard or Condict Building on Bleecker Street), but he found no more great opportunities. Some small commissions in the Middle West, particularly banks and business blocks in country towns, displayed his originality, but he died in obscurity in 1924. Daniel H. Burnham in his "Flatiron" Building (1902) set the mode for the new era of temples of business clothed in eclectic historical ornament. The Metropolitan Life Insurance Tower (1906) by N. LeBrun and Sons, and Cass Gilbert's colossal Gothic Woolworth Building (1913), set successive new records for height and with clusters of other mammoth towers in lower and midtown Manhattan made the New York skyline one of the great spectacles of the world. The skyscraper was called America's only contribution to the history of architecture until the work of Wright won recognition.

REVOLUTION IN PAINTING

The greatest American painter of this period was unable to make his living by his work. John Sloan did not sell a single picture until 1913, many years after he had been hailed by critics as the leader of an important new school of American painters. Variously called Realists, "The Eight," and the "Ash-Can School," Sloan, Robert Henri, Maurice Prendergast, George Luks, William Glackens, George Bellows, and others aimed at a lyrical rendering of everyday life, especially in great cities, which the academic-genteel painters regarded as too vulgar for art. French Impressionism had produced American echoes, beginning in 1898 with an exhibition by Childe Hassam, John H. Twachtman, and others making up "The Ten." American Impressionists won considerable public and financial success.

The Realists, on the other hand, worked in the tradition of Winslow Homer, Thomas Eakins, William S. Mount, and the painters of genre subjects. Their work was more honest to the unpleasant sides of ordinary existence, and close in spirit to the naturalism of Theodore Dreiser. Their most important exhibit was held in 1908 at the Macbeth Gallery in New York and aroused wide interest. Academic painters called them "apostles of ugliness." Actually they realized an eloquent new beauty in the faces, actions, and backgrounds of the poorest classes. They differed from former painters of poverty because they did not patronize it as quaint, or prettify it to soothe patrons' sensibilities. Thus they were the counterpart of political Progressives who insisted on the worthiness of hitherto despised groups. Sloan and other Realists identified themselves with reform or socialism. Their work gave importance to the *Masses*, a radical monthly founded in 1910, which Sloan as art editor two years later helped to make an exceptionally vigorous organ of dissent until it was suppressed by the federal authorities for opposing war measures in 1917.

The Realists scarcely had time to win the position their vision and talent merited before American painting was invaded by European Post-Impressionism, a comprehensive term for a bewildering variety of anti-realist movements—the *pointillisme* of Seurat, the cubism of Cézanne, the futurism of Marinetti, the expressionism of Van Gogh, and all the periods and methods of such fecund masters as Matisse, Duchamp, and Picasso. The School of Paris was moving towards abstractionism, the elimination from the canvas of every reference except the purest painterly values of form, color, and composition. The first signs that this violent revolt would find a home in the United States occurred under the encouragement of Alfred Stieglitz, a very great photographer. One of the few points of doctrine all Post-Impressionists held in common was that the camera had made it unnecessary for painters to continue representing what the eye sees.

In 1908, Stieglitz showed at his Little Galleries of the Photo-Secession, at 291 Fifth Avenue, paintings of Henri Matisse. This was the introduction of modern art to America, and critics and public alike were offended. Some other Post-Impressionists were imported by Stieglitz and he also showed the first works of Americans trying to break free of convention—Arthur G. Dove, Marsden Hartley, John Marin, Alfred Maurer, Max Weber, and Georgia O'Keefe. Even to advanced critics like James Huneker the result seemed a scandal. Only the journalist Hutchins Hapgood glimpsed what was afoot. He pleaded in 1912 after seeing canvases of Picasso at "291" for "a larger hospitality—for greater freedom to experiment esthetically and mentally." He said: "We have a background of support now in politics and sociology for the insurgent and the unconventional. It is time that we should have some respectable and official recognition of the art that is unacademic, untraditional, personal."

The answer to his plea burst on America in the most dramatic episode in the history of American taste, the Armory Show of 1913, officially the International Exhibition of Modern Art by the American Painters' and Sculptors' Association. This famous event was initiated by some American Post-Impressionists who wished to demonstrate to the public that their work was paralleled by painters abroad. Organized by Arthur B. Davies,

Walt Kuhn, and others, they leased a regimental armory in New York City and filled its cavernous spaces with paintings and sculptures of the European modernists as well as with their own work. The result was a kind of circus. The public and critics mostly condemned what they saw. Still they were impressed, and American art could never be the same again. *Nude Descending a Staircase* by Marcel Duchamp amused, baffled, and angered, but above all interested, beholders. Droves streamed past the strange productions in New York and in other cities when the show went on the road. Theodore Roosevelt visited the Armory Show on the day Woodrow Wilson was inaugurated President of the United States, and wrote in *The Outlook* more appreciatively about the rebel artists than about his successful rival. The impact of the Armory Show was immediately apparent in furniture design, advertising, interior decoration and the minor arts. In American painting and sculpture a long search for "significant form" produced much that was freakish, but individual expression and free experiment destroyed superimposed "taste" in American art and put it on the road to genuine achievement.

THE NEW THEATER

The New Theater was an application of developments in both literature and visual arts. A new generation of scene designers, beginning with Robert Edmond Jones, made the New Theater an exciting experience of form and color, sometimes more effective than the play that unfolded in front of the sets. The "little theater" movement, similar in its defiance of commercial standards to "little magazines" like *Poetry*, got under way in 1900 with the founding of the Hull House Players in Chicago. In 1912, play production became academically respectable with the founding of the "47 Workshop" at Harvard under Professor George Pierce Baker for the training of playwrights, directors, and designers. Winthrop Ames invaded Broadway with the methods of the New Theater in the same year.

The greatest moment in the emergence of the New Theater was the founding of the Provincetown Players in 1915. In a ramshackle fishhouse on a wharf at the tip of Cape Cod, a dozen talented young people wrote, produced, and acted short plays. Beginning in 1916, they produced ten of Eugene O'Neill's plays, thus opening the door for America's greatest dramatist. Civic and college theaters suddenly blossomed with repertories of important dramas made up chiefly of the works of vital new Europeans, especially George Bernard Shaw and Henrik Ibsen, as well as the classical Sheridan, Shakespeare, and the Greeks. The New Theater was a movement of the vanguard. But now for the first time Americans were creating dramatic art of their own marked by the honesty, intensity, and talent that appeared in great epochs of European history.

The dance, too, was revolutionized. The postures of the Victorians suddenly looked ludicrous when Isadora Duncan, of California and Athens, in classical robes and bare feet, set the art-loving world afire with her passionate freedom of bodily expression. Isadora tried to carry her message of expressive freedom beyond the footlights and into the schools and the whole life of the people. But the officials of New York City were frightened by the idea of advanced souls teaching the joy of uninhibited dance in the public schools. The New Arts did not gain a following among most Americans, who cared more for the movies and the Model T Ford. Nevertheless, in time the work of the "Little Renaissance" of the years around 1912 made its way through devious channels into the consciousness of the nation. As Gertrude Stein said, the Americans were the first to enter the twentieth century, and the advanced arts, progressive politics, and the Model T were all emblems of the new time.

THE MASS MEDIA

Newspapers

The press remained the fundamental vehicle of American communication. The printed word in newspapers and magazines, not yet rivaled by radio or television, reached the apogee of its importance in reflecting and influencing the thinking of the millions. Vitality was the only compliment that could be paid the New Journalism, or Yellow Press, so-called from an early comic feature of the New York *World*, "The Yellow Kid." Economically the New Journalism showed tendencies common to business enterprise by sacrificing quality for the sake of a mass market, using ruthless competitive methods and superior capital resources to put rival newspapers out of business, and combining individual newspapers into great chains. At the same time, syndicated material and press associations tended to standardize the contents of otherwise independent newspapers. Formerly the leaders of journalism had been writers who gained readers by their talent; now leadership was won by businessmen and corporations. The time had arrived when the press was absorbed into the business system as a source of profits. Following its lead, the movies, radio, and television developed successively as mass media which were primarily industries. That cultural activity should come under business control was proof that the United States was developing a new kind of business civilization.

The pioneers of the New Journalism were Joseph Pulitzer and William Randolph Hearst. The former, an immigrant from Hungary, after serving in the Union Army developed the *St. Louis Post-Dispatch* into a powerful organ. Following a local political feud, the tall and red-bearded Pulitzer, intensely energetic and cultivated, invaded New York City, bought the decrepit *World* in 1883, and soon made its circulation skyrocket by alert reporting and sensational stunts and pictures. Even when the cause was a sound reform, Pulitzer injected a brass-band note into his crusades. Editors all over the country studied his technique, and his most ardent imitator, William Randolph Hearst, went far beyond his relative restraint and decency.

The heir of a western mining fortune, Hearst was expelled from Harvard because of the vulgarity of a practical joke he played on the faculty. His father gave him the *San Francisco Examiner,* and, after he came into his father's millions, he bought the *New York Journal* in 1895 and tried to outdo the inventor of the new sensationalism. One of his devices was to buy away from Pulitzer and other competitors their best writers and artists. In the race for supremacy he would even hire such authors as Stephen Crane and Mark Twain.

Hearst exploited various reforms not merely in ordinary news and features and cartoons, but by making news. The newspaper itself, for example, obtained a court injunction to prevent a gas-franchise deal. Similarly, Hearst organized his reporters as a crew of detectives to pursue murderers and make crime news more exciting. He hired thugs to frighten vendors into favoring the *Journal,* and preachers to provide religious material for the editorial page.

Hearst challenged Pulitzer to a circulation duel over the events leading up to the Spanish-American War, which he treated as his private party. He is said to have persuaded the artist Frederic Remington, who cabled from Cuba in 1897 that everything was quiet and that he wished to return: "Please remain. You furnish the pictures and I'll furnish the war." No other newspaperman could keep up with Hearst's impudent stunts, but almost all newspapers were cowed by his claim of a monopoly of patriotism into dosing their pages with the same jingoism.

The whole affair troubled thoughtful citizens by suggesting that demagogues of wealth could create and control public opinion on such a grave issue as war. After the debauch of 1898, Pulitzer withdrew from competition in degradation of the press and made the *World* a responsible journal of liberal politics and high standards. Hearst developed ambitions for political office which were frustrated mostly because his journalistic smears made politicians afraid of him. Then he created a chain of newspapers in the chief cities and modeled them on the *Journal,* presently adding to his holdings a large number of magazines. He became the archetype of the dangerous lord of the press. His personal unpopularity through his long life among leaders in all fields was very great.

Pulitzer sought to raise the standards of the profession by endowing the School of Journalism at Columbia University in 1912 and establishing annual prizes for writing in many fields. Adolph S. Ochs, during the same years that witnessed Hearst's abuses of freedom of the press,

developed the *New York Times* into one of the most distinguished newspapers ever published, so notable for the accuracy and thoroughness of
its material that it was and still is generally accepted as a newspaper
of historical record. Nor was it unprofitable. Edward W. Scripps and
Frank A. Munsey organized great chains of newspapers in rivalry with
Hearst, although their standards were higher.

While no owner or corporation came close to monopoly control of
the American press, the decline in the number of newspapers, and their
growing dependence on a few syndicates and press associations for most
of their material, defined chief characteristics of the modern era. The
syndicates provided a substitute for the personal appeal of the old
editors by selling the output of columnists who were allowed to display
temperament and to sign their names. Outstanding reporters also were
given "by-lines." Editors and owners were now generally unknown to
their own readers. Like any other corporation heads, they controlled their
staffs by their power to hire and fire. All journalists, in short, had become
employees. The most obvious consequence was that American newspapers increasingly supported conservatism in politics.

They also provided increasing quantities of sheer entertainment—
any and all kinds of text and pictures that required no thought but gave
diversion to the workman returning home on the trolley car and to the
entire family on Sunday. In 1896, Hearst's Sunday *Journal* issued an eight-
page comic supplement in colors. He hired away from Pulitzer the artist
Richard F. Outcault with his "Yellow Kid" drawings of the antics of
Hogan's Alley children. The next year the *Journal* began publication
of the first true comic strip, the "Katzenjammer Kids," by Rudolph Dirks.
Each sequence narrated a trick played by Hans and Fritz upon the
Captain and the Inspector. The popularity of this feature encouraged
the creation of "Foxy Grandpa," "Buster Brown," "Bringing up Father,"
"Krazy Kat," 'Mutt and Jeff," "Happy Hooligan," and dozens of other
"funnies." Editors discovered that these were the most popular offerings
in their papers. Many observers deplored the comics, but they were
a new kind of urban folk art deeply expressive of the emerging commercial mass culture. Whatever most Americans may have thought of
paintings, they loved the comic strips at first sight.

Magazines

Magazines followed the lead of the newspapers and tried to gain
popularity. Respectable old monthlies like the *Century, Harper's* and
Scribner's lost circulation while the new and lower-priced *McClure's,
Cosmopolitan, Munsey's, Collier's, Saturday Evening Post,* and *Leslie's
Weekly* won hundreds of thousands of readers and rich advertising
harvests by catering to the taste for pictures and lively reading matter.
For a few years after the turn of the century, muckraking helped build

the circulations of the mass magazines; but by 1910 they had largely turned to straight entertainment for their appeal. Fiction was their chief material, and here a wide gulf opened between "serious" writing, whether genteel or advance-guard, and the slick, machine-made commodity for mass consumption requiring only elementary feeling and no thought. Americans especially delighted in the trick ending which O. Henry brought to a perfection resembling the operation of some clever mechanical gadget. In the new magazines, as in most best-selling novels, fiction ceased to be an illumination of life and turned into a distraction from it. Pictures were lavishly used to illustrate fiction. *Puck, Judge* and the old *Life* offered photographs, political cartoons, and humorous drawings with a minimum of reading matter. At their best they achieved satire of manners, and in the drawings of Charles Dana Gibson and lesser artists they created types of feminine beauty which the nation's young girls tried hard to match.

The coverage of the weekly *Literary Digest* and the monthly *Review of Reviews* ranged from trivia to significant intellectual, artistic, and political events. "Home" magazines flourished anew with the success of the *Ladies Home Journal* under Edward W. Bok, *The Delineator*, which was edited from 1907 to 1910 by Theodore Dreiser, and the *Woman's Home Companion*. For children there was the *Youth's Companion* or *St. Nicholas*, for farmers the *Farm Journal*, for the literary *The Dial*, for the religious *The Christian Century* and countless denominational publications. Every imaginable special-interest group or organization had a magazine or newspaper. Machines to bale discarded reading matter had to be provided. The printed word had become prodigiously available, whatever questions might be asked about its quality.

Movies

The demand for mass entertainment was met by a totally new industry when the moving picture was used first in 1903 by Edwin S. Porter as producer to film a story, *The Great Train Robbery*. Here was the comic strip actually in motion, popular fiction that was easier to enjoy than by reading, drama cheap enough for the millions to afford. The thirst for movies was so great that almost 10,000 "nickelodeons" were showing films within five years. From these simple halls exhibitors soon moved into quarters that outshone legitimate theatres in gaudiness, while holding admissions down to a level that threatened to put the "live" theatre out of business. The business of production moved from New York City to Hollywood, California, for the sake of more sunshine, and there a colony of stars provided an extra dividend of entertainment by their highly-publicized private lives.

The silent films encouraged vivid pantomime and concentrated on "slapstick" comedy. Mack Sennett was the greatest producer of these comedies, and Charlie Chaplin developed his art as actor in them to the superlative power which made him one of the best of mimes and a profound satirist. The popular melodrama of the stage was translated into films, at first in serials like Pearl White's *Perils of Pauline,* and the star system was developed by the new industry to the point where Mary Pickford ("America's Sweetheart"), Douglas Fairbanks, Norma Talmadge, Lillian and Dorothy Gish, and their successors did not need to portray any character except their well-advertised Hollywood personalities. Millions loved these stars as the people of former societies loved saints, knights, or princes.

To produce films, companies were organized that resembled manufacturing corporations more than theater troupes, and they went through evolutions characteristic of American business. The Edison, Biograph, and Vitagraph Companies formed a trust in 1909. A lawsuit brought by William Fox ended this monopoly. "Block-booking," which started in 1912, made exhibitors the pawns of producers so that the worst of the film output was shown indiscriminately with the best. This system could not be squared with the argument that public taste was to blame for low-quality pictures, and it was belatedly attacked in 1948 by the federal government as a violation of the antitrust laws. By that time most film companies were dependent on Wall Street banks for capital, and bankers were found in the strange position of arbiters of art, not as a Medician adornment, but to "protect their investment." The people flocked to the movies without much regard for the artistic or social qualms of critical observers. For them the stars became the arbiters of manners and morals. In the "Western," starring such folk heroes as William S. Hart and Tom Mix, and in sex dramas, starring a succession of "great lovers," the industry discovered new formulas for financial success. The impact of the movies on political thought was demonstrated by *The Birth of a Nation,* produced by D. W. Griffith in 1915 and artistically superior, but troubling to many because it glorified the terroristic role of the Ku Klux Klan during Reconstruction days.

The movies precipitated the question of social control over the new mass media in acute form. Outraged parents demanded and in some states obtained censorship by public authority, but this was perhaps more dangerous than useful. Nor was organized pressure by private groups satisfactory to those who subscribed to dissimilar aesthetic and moral standards. Probably there was no solution except the endless effort to improve universal education.

Jazz

In music, too, there began a great departure from traditional standards. The music called "classical," had never been popular and the popular music of nineteenth-century song, operetta, and dance became "semiclassical" when jazz was born. This has been called the only truly original contribution of the United States to the history of art. Scholars dispute the question of its origin, but African tribal, Latin-American folk, military band, and Protestant hymn music all played a part. The post-Civil War Negro was the organizer of the new musical idiom. It is said that Negroes obtained discarded Confederate Army band instruments and, lacking formal instruction, improvised their way to a clowning version of ordinary music. Syncopation, rhythm, and "blues" harmony were emphasized as a new way of "ragging" any melody. The style made its way into the musical underworld of cities, and there a few composers and musicians were producing ragtime by the turn of the century. The mood of ragtime was irreverent and orgiastic. Irving Berlin mastered it along with many other styles in a long career as the most successful song writer of all time. His *Alexander's Ragtime Band* (1911) was the most popular, although not the best of the ragtime tunes. Ragtime as composed music had its headquarters in New York. It initiated a dance craze that began with a group of new steps, the Bunny Hug, the Turkey Trot, the Grizzly Bear and the Fox Trot, competition among which was handily won by the last.

Another strain in the formation of jazz originated in New Orleans among Negro bands that devised a style to cheer up the mourners after funerals, and then found employment as "tail-gate" bands which were hauled about the city on wagons to advertise low resorts. When the United States Navy in 1917 closed "Storyville," the vice district of New Orleans, some of the musicians, including the historic Original Dixieland Jazz Band, moved to Chicago where they became popular entertainers, particularly for gangsters of the new era. Their first imitators were delinquent high school students; and presently jazz bands appeared everywhere. A third strain originated in the compositions of William C. Handy of Memphis, the Negro "Father of the Blues." This was the melancholy complement of bouncy ordinary jazz, and had roots in the work songs and spirituals of slavery times. Handy's *The Memphis Blues* (1913), *St. Louis Blues* (1914), and *Beale Street Blues* (1917) are masterpieces combining the honesty of folk music with considerable musical sophistication.

Jazz was a creation of the least-educated classes and it had ties with vice, but its power was not less for these origins. It conquered first the American public and then a large part of the world as the authentic musical expression of today's mass civilization. It defied "good" taste, and Americans themselves mostly disregarded its importance until French critics hailed it as a great new art form. Along with the New Journalism, comic strips, and the movies, jazz defined the actual as opposed to the received culture of most twentieth-century Americans. The most traditional critic could not deny the amazing vitality of these forms.

CHAPTER 18

Woodrow Wilson and the New Freedom, 1913-1917

WOODROW WILSON TURNED OUT TO BE THE SPOKESMAN of Progressivism in its years of greatest achievement. As President he is most remembered in connection with the First World War and its aftermath. The failure of his peace plans makes his achievement in international affairs problematical. On the other hand, the passage of time has underlined the importance of the legislative achievements of his first years in the White House. They constitute a substantial part of the permanent adaptation of American government to the realities of modern society.

The New Freedom was the climax of the Progressive Era. The legislative enactments which made up the New Freedom satisfied only a part of the demands of Progressives, and they failed to impress radicals. Conservatives, on the other hand, were appalled by what they regarded as drastic and dangerous departures from sound principles of governmental respect for Big Business. Wilson's program can best be understood as one of moderate reform in the great Anglo-American tradition of a middle way between extremes of radicalism and conservatism.

In the conditions of the twentieth century, this meant a middle way between the rule of finance capitalism and a revolt against capitalism in favor of some sort of socialism. Wilson at first hoped that he could restore the supremacy of small competitive business and the farmer. This hope was more nostalgic than practical. The New Freedom turned out to be virtually indistinguishable from Theodore Roosevelt's New Nationalism. The federal government could not destroy Big Business and restore simple competition, nor could it ignore labor in favor of the farmer. What it could do was strengthen the authority of the federal government to prevent abuses by the most powerful private groups, and to counterbalance the weakness of other groups.

This eminently pragmatic procedure was unsatisfying to doctrinaires of all persuasions. It sought to retain all the positive values of private ownership while establishing benefits for the people as a whole which Socialists claimed could only be achieved through governmental ownership of the means of production. It was a distinctive American development—even Great Britain followed a more anticapitalist path towards social welfare. Theodore Roosevelt as President had made the first important contributions to this new American system, and Franklin D. Roosevelt made the largest additions to it. Standing between these men in time, Woodrow Wilson also stands between them in achievement. The peculiar nature of the creative American administrations of the twentieth century is that they have tinkered their way to a reconciliation between a government based on eighteenth-century conditions and ideas and a mass industrial society the most advanced in the world. To this extraordinary and distinctive process Woodrow Wilson, despite some defects of personality, brought rare qualities of inspiration and guidance during the halcyon years before the First World War.

WILSON THE LEADER

Woodrow Wilson was the first professional scholar to become President of the United States. Born of Scottish stock, in Staunton in the Valley of Virginia four years before Lincoln's first election, he was the son and grandson of Presbyterian divines. Spending his early years in Georgia at Augusta, in South Carolina at Columbia, and in North Carolina at Wilmington, he absorbed traditional Southern political ideas along with his father's strict Calvinism. He graduated from Princeton and studied law at the University of Virginia. Failing to make a quick success in law practice in Atlanta, he turned to the study of history and political science at The Johns Hopkins University. His doctoral thesis, *Congressional Government* (1885), was brilliant, and his fame as a teacher rapidly grew after he joined the Princeton faculty. His study led him to the significant criticism of the American form of government that its division of powers among the three branches leaves it without responsible leadership unless the President exerts initiative. This view was Jacksonian in its emphasis on the Executive, while not incompatible with a Jeffersonian emphasis on state-rights.

Wilson was elected president of Princeton in 1902 and for a few years enjoyed great success. He introduced the preceptorial system of instruction and strengthened the faculty, but failed in his attempt to establish a residential system which would have done away with the exclusive student eating clubs. His purpose was not so much to democratize as to intellectualize the life of the college and reduce social and athletic activities to subordinate positions—a novel idea at the time, which most of the Princeton alumni resented. Many people throughout his life disliked Wilson because he seemed to identify his own opinions with God's. But he also possessed great magnetic power which he best exerted in public speaking. He presented his forward-looking educational ideas with notable effectiveness. He could never accommodate himself to opposition, however, and this led to numerous quarrels. The most decisive of these occurred when he tried to establish his own policy for a new graduate school at Princeton. Dean Andrew F. West, after procuring a handsome gift for the school, bested Wilson on this issue and in 1910 he resigned to accept the Democratic nomination for the governorship of New Jersey.

To the larger public Wilson appeared to have been defeated at Princeton by vested alumni interests and financial power, but the Democratic bosses who nominated him for governor because of his eminent respectability had reason to assume that he was a political conservative. He had attacked the initiative, referendum, and recall; he had termed himself a "fierce partisan of the open shop;" he had wished to "knock Mr. Bryan once for all into a cocked hat." But when he assumed the actual responsibilities of political leadership he awoke to the moral superiority and growing popularity of Progressivism. Soon after he took office, he broke with the machine bosses, gained control over the Democratic Party of New Jersey by direct appeals to the people, and put through the legislature a sweeping reform program. New Jersey, hitherto regarded as the "mother of trusts," was now described as another Wisconsin. In less than two years Wilson became a conspicuous contender for the presidency. He gathered about himself astute advisers led by Colonel Edward M. House of Texas and George Harvey, editor of *Harper's Weekly*. In the national party he had to contend with Speaker Champ Clark of Missouri, an influential Congressional politician who had inherited most of Bryan's following, as well as with city bosses like Charles F. Murphy of Tammany Hall. Bryan himself went over to Wilson during the Democratic National Convention of 1912 at Baltimore, and Wilson's managers won over the city leaders. He gained the nomination against the will of Bryan's fanatical agrarian followers, but he formulated a national reform program that brought Populism and Bryanism up to date.

As he defined it in his campaign oratory, Wilson's New Freedom differed from the New Nationalism of Roosevelt, which by 1912 reflected the neo-Hamiltonianism of Herbert Croly. Louis D. Brandeis was the chief theorist of a neo-Jeffersonianism that Wilson made his own. Roosevelt called Wilson a "rural Tory" devoted to the outgrown doctrine of laissez faire. Wilson retorted: "As to the monopolies, which Mr. Roosevelt proposes to legalize and to welcome, I know that they are so many cars of juggernaut, and I do not look forward with pleasure to the time when the juggernauts are licensed and driven by commissioners of the United States."

As the campaign progressed, Roosevelt made more extreme promises of social justice for workmen and farmers. Wilson pronounced dire prophecies of slavery under Big Business and Big Government if Roosevelt were elected, urging the necessity to save free enterprise as the key to all freedom. At the same time Wilson, too, spoke out for measures of social justice.

That Wilson did speak for an agrarian and Jeffersonian ideal is indicated by the fact that with his inauguration a group of Southerners came to national power. Besides House, who was the President's intimate adviser and confidential diplomatic agent, these included: William G. McAdoo, originally of Georgia, whom Wilson appointed Secretary of the Treasury; William F. McCombs of Arkansas, an early political manager for Wilson; Walter Hines Page of North Carolina, editor of *World's Work*, whom the new President sent to the Court of St. James's; and Josephus Daniels, editor of the Raleigh, North Carolina, *News and Observer*, who became Secretary of the Navy. Albert S. Burleson of Texas, the new Postmaster General, used the patronage ruthlessly to coerce Congressmen into voting for Wilson's program. He influenced the administration not to remove conservatives from the Democratic state and local party machines. The Secretary of Agriculture was David F. Houston, originally of North Carolina, an economist who clung to laissez-faire principles. Most of these men fell short of the Progressivism for which the country had voted, but they helped make Wilson leader of the Democratic Party in the Southern wing which controlled the most influential positions in Congress by virtue of seniority. Representative Carter Glass of Virginia, the chief legislative architect of the Federal Reserve System, was fairly conservative.

Wilson's other Cabinet appointees were disappointing to Progressives, although they included able men: Secretary of War Lindley M. Garrison, a judge from New Jersey; Secretary of the Interior Franklin K. Lane, a brilliant Californian; and Secretary of Labor William B. Wilson, who, beginning as a miner at the age of nine, had risen to leadership in the United Mine Workers with incidental imprisonment for defying an injunction. Secretary of State Bryan had no special competence in diplomacy; like Seward he was given the chief post in the Cabinet because he had been displaced as leader of the party by the new President, but unlike Seward he failed to grow in office to meets its exacting demands. The real test of Wilson's allegiance to the Northern urban Progressive element was his attitude towards Louis D. Brandeis. The stature of the "people's attorney" as the champion of human rights against property interests, and Wilson's personal debt to him for the philosophy of the New Freedom, led the President-elect at first to plan his appointment as Attorney General. House dissuaded him. Then Wilson thought he would make Brandeis Secretary of Commerce. Not only House but party politicians and Big Business objected strenuously. Wilson gave in and appointed William C. Redfield, a conventional politician from Brooklyn. But in 1916 he appointed Brandeis to the Supreme Court.

Wilson's relations with the Cabinet and Congress suggested that he preferred the subordination of others to their objective advice, and that he relied too much on respect for his own righteousness as a basis for loyalty. His moralizing was resented by many politicians, while his idealism seemed inconsistent to others. He could be very uncompromising in the pursuit of some goals and at the same time abandon entirely other goals which seemed equally important to Progressives of longer standing. Yet Woodrow Wilson was a great leader, a great executive, and a great reformer. At his best during the prewar years, he knew how to express and effectuate the desires and needs of the people as a whole. His rapid conversion to Progressivism was one example of the millions of such conversions which the same few years produced. His insistence on personal domination of Cabinet, Congress, and Party did not differ in degree from that of most of the greatest Presidents of the United States. His self-righteousness is not separable from the general source of the American character in Puritanism, with all its moral elevation and its vindictiveness against wrongdoers. A major secret of his public appeal was his confident assumption of high-minded leadership.

During the weeks before his inauguration, rumors circulated that he was planning a sweeping batch of reform laws and that Wall Street would stage an economic crisis to discipline him. He answered publicly that in such case he promised businessmen "a gibbet as high as Haman's." It was not conventional for a President-elect to threaten his countrymen with Old Testament thunder. In his Inaugural Address he spoke more humbly:

> This is not a day of triumph; it is a day of dedication. Here muster, not the forces of party, but the forces of humanity. Men's hearts wait upon us; men's lives hang in the balance; men's hopes call upon us to say what we will do. Who shall live up to the great trust? Who dares fail to try? I summon all honest men, all patriotic, all forward-looking men, to my side. God helping me, I will not fail them, if they will but counsel and sustain me.

On that same day, March 4, 1913, Wilson called Congress into special session to give him the laws which would reassert the supremacy of human rights over property interests in the policy of the United States government.

From Competition to Regulation

President Wilson immediately dramatized his commitment to the principle of executive leadership by restoring the practice, which Jefferson had stopped, of delivering Presidential messages to Congress in person. He believed that the British Cabinet system of direct leadership in Parliament was superior to the American separation of powers. He did not attempt a constitutional amendment because he concluded that the American President has sufficient power if he will use it. This is true only so long as Congress is *willing* to accept a President's leadership. That was the case when Wilson was inaugurated. The Democrats had fair majorities in both houses, many of the members were young and ardent Progressives, and the older party leaders were generally convinced that it was time for action. Furthermore, a number of the Republicans were Progressives. Wilson might have tried for a nonpartisan coalition, but, as in his Cabinet appointments, he decided to work with his party as it stood. He decided to use the patronage unsparingly to whip recalcitrant Democrats into line. Appointments were postponed while the administration watched the votes of Representatives and Senators on key measures.

The Underwood Tariff

He delivered his program to Congress like a school teacher's assignments to pupils. On April 8, in his first address to Congress, he asked for tariff reform. The next day, to the consternation of old-line legislators, he appeared in the corridors of the capitol to confer with party leaders, and he developed a disconcerting way of showing up unexpectedly at committee meetings. Step by step Wilson supervised the progress of a tariff bill bearing the name of Chairman Oscar W. Underwood of the House Ways and Means Committee. It put wool and sugar on the free list, along with manufactures controlled by trusts—most importantly, iron and steel,—gave little or no protection to consumers' goods such as food, clothes, and farm machinery, and made American products which faced no competition from abroad free or virtually so. Those American industries which faced genuine competition by foreign products in the American market were given enough protection to equalize competition. All duties were made *ad valorem* so that no tricks could be played with "small" rates which would be actually high by percentage. The average reduction in rates brought them down to 30 per-cent from the 40 per-cent level in the Payne-Aldrich Tariff Act of 1909, but this does not reflect the immense significance of placing key products on the free list.

So drastic was the reduction that a loss of $100 million in revenue was anticipated, and to make up for this Representative Cordell Hull of Tennessee, an indefatigable exponent of low tariffs, added to the Underwood Bill provision for an income tax. The Sixteenth Amendment, authorizing such a tax, had just been ratified on February 25. This first income tax law laid only 1 per cent on individual and corporate incomes over $4000. The surtaxes were not severe: 1 per cent on incomes above $20,000, 2 per cent above $50,000, 3 per cent above $75,000, 4 per cent above

$100,000, 5 per cent above $250,000 and 6 per cent above $500,000. But these surtaxes did express the principle of taxation in proportion to wealth. They were not as steep as La Follette, Norris, and some Progressive Democrats had demanded. Yet later analysts, particularly opponents of the income tax, have declared that it is the keystone in the construction of the modern welfare state.

The House passed the Underwood Bill on May 8. The test lay in the Senate where the Republican Old Guard could muster support among Democrats from sugar and wool states. Wilson went to work on these Democrats with the greatest vigor and effect, so that some, like Thomas J. Walsh of Montana, publicly reversed their positions. Lobbyists were being sent to Washington in platoons. Wilson told the country that the people had no lobby, while artificial opinion was being created by groups interested only in profits. Some Senators thought to embarrass the President by proposing an investigation of these charges, but the Progressives agreed to one. The country was shocked by the spectacle of Senators admitting to a committee, not only that lobbyists tried to influence their votes, but also that they themselves owned sugar and sheep lands, coal and steel stocks. In the light of this publicity a vote against the Underwood Bill was now a very difficult action for certain Senators. Republicans sought to delay matters by lengthy discussion of the rates one by one. But the President won over all the Democrats except the two from Louisiana. The bill passed, and Wilson signed it on October 2, 1913.

The Underwood Tariff was the first important reduction of rates and the first genuine blow against the protective principle since 1857. The outbreak of world war in the ensuing summer created an abnormal situation in which this policy was denied a fair test, but the passage of the Act was a startling achievement. People who remembered the defeats of Cleveland and all the dreary tariff fights, decade after decade, could hardly believe that the "Scholar in the White House" had outmaneuvered all the lobbyists, all the protected interests, all the log-rollers and fixers who had their own way for so long, and laid an income tax on wealth besides.

The Federal Reserve System

Already Wilson had Congress deeply immersed in the struggle for banking and currency reform. On June 23, 1913, his second message defined the terms of a bill he would accept. Bankers themselves, after the Panic of 1907 had dramatized the inflexibility of the country's banking and money system, had taken the lead in moving for centralized control which had been lacking ever since Jackson destroyed the Second Bank of the United States. Congress had responded by creating in 1908 the National Monetary Commission, made up of Senators and Representatives headed by Senator Aldrich. For four years the Commission studied the banking systems of the world and in 1912 made a report in forty volumes. This pointed out the inability of American banks to make use of their reserves in time of crisis, their inability to borrow against the repayment of sound loans made to businessmen and farmers, the lack of credit facilities in the South and West, and the illogic of the existing method of expanding and contracting credit and currency, not according to the needs of the economy, but according to the quantity of government bonds held by national banks, under the system designed to help the federal government during the Civil War.

The report recommended a National Reserve Association with fifteen branches all to be controlled by private bankers. This would be a bankers' bank, holding some of the reserve funds of member banks, and discounting loans in order to make cash available to them when they needed it. For the latter purpose it would issue paper money. It would hold the deposits of the federal government, although the government's share in the control of the system would be subordinate to that of private bankers. This plan was drawn up by Paul M. Warburg of Kuhn, Loeb and Company, a leading Wall Street firm, and the American Bankers' Association approved it. Called the Aldrich Plan, it amounted to a resurrection of the old Bank of the United States, as Progressives were quick to point out, and a handing over to private bankers of the government's funds and money powers.

What this would mean in the conditions of the twentieth century had been forcibly exposed in the same year of 1912 by the Pujo Investigation by the House of Representatives into the "Money Trust." The Pujo Committee inquired into the most disturbing charges of muckrakers and reformers: namely, that a private monopoly over the financial life of the nation was pyramided on the manufacturing trusts. The Committee found that a tiny group of Wall Street bankers wielded control over a vast congeries of banking, insurance, and manufacturing enterprises. Three banks, J. P Morgan and Company, the Rockefeller-controlled National City Bank, and George F. Baker's First National Bank, owning combined resources of $632 million, were affiliated with lesser banks and insurance companies which raised the total to more than $2 billion. The partners of the three banks held 341 directorships in 112 corporations with capitalization of $22 billion. A fourth group joined Kuhn, Loeb and Company to the vast Harriman interests. The men who stood at the pinnacle of the national financial pyramid were primarily investment bankers who marketed securities to the public. Because they wanted these securities to be sound, their use of their power was sober and, within the limits of investors' interests, generally responsible. What was appalling was not anything morally scandalous in the conduct of these financiers, but the sheer power they wielded.

Before Wilson was inaugurated, Chairman Carter Glass and the Democratic members of the House Banking and Currency Committee proposed a system no less privately-controlled, but decentralized so that, as Glass hoped, no one bank could ever dominate it. This proposal expressed the Jeffersonian-Wilsonian oppostion to Big Business and Big Government alike. Whether it would have done anything to decentralize the actual power of Wall Street as revealed by the Pujo Investigation is doubtful. Opposition to the Glass scheme developed when Bryan called for government control over the system along with government retention of the power to issue currency. President-elect Wilson suggested to Glass that a general supervisory board be placed as a "capstone" of the system, leaving it privately-controlled. Glass agreed, although this made the system hardly distinguishable from the Warburg-Aldrich plan. In fact, Warburg and other bankers now endorsed the Glass proposal. News of it leaked out and caused a furor among Progressives.

By June 1913 Wilson found to his surprise that Bryan and Secretary of the Treasury McAdoo were at the head of a revolt of Progressives. Brandeis explained to him why, in view of the Democratic Party's historic policy and numerous recent commitments, the rebels must be heeded. Wilson, quick to learn, thereupon obtained concessions from Glass and pronounced to Congress on June 23: "The control of the system of banking and of [currency] issue which our new laws are to set up must be public, not private, must be vested in the Government itself, so that the banks may be the instruments, not the masters, of business and of individual enterprise and initiative."

This was not enough for Progressives. They also opposed private control of the branch reserve banks, and the issuance of currency solely on the basis of commercial loans. They wanted guarantees against the interlocking directorates which the Pujo Committee had revealed, and they wanted short-term farm loans to be discounted as well as commercial loans, and currency to be issued on farm paper equally with commercial paper. Wilson personally entered the battle. He promised the rebels that a prohibition of interlocking directorates would be included in a new antitrust law. He then accepted provisions to make short-term farm loans eligible for discount. Though this left the branch banks under private control, it satisfied Bryan and enough of the rebels to win a strong majority in the House on September 18.

Promptly the American Bankers' Association began a bitter campaign against the bill. The bankers objected to government control of the central Reserve Board and spoke scornfully of "corn-tassel currency." Wilson and the Progressives stood by the crucial provisions until on December 19, 1913, the Senate voted in their favor, 54 to 34. The Federal Reserve Act was a great victory for Progressives. The law established a minimum of governmental control over the nation's banking system. The

Federal Reserve Board functions as an independent agency whose seven (later eight) governors are appointed by the President with the consent of the Senate and serve terms of 14 years so that they are relatively free of political pressure. The new system provided the flexibility and centralization which bankers had wanted but turned over these great powers to officials charged with the public interest. It was not a "government bank" such as most other nations have at the apex of their economies. But the advantages of membership in one of the 12 regional Federal Reserve Banks led most American banks to join the System, and the government as a result gained *indirect* authority over most banking operations in the United States.

Furthermore, the power of the Board to alter reserve requirements and rediscount rates turned out to have influence on the economy as a whole. Reduction of reserve requirements and the rediscount rate tends to make credit cheaper and thereby stimulates economic activity. Conversely, raising the reserve requirements and the rediscount rate discourages economic activity. It is doubtful that the authors of the Act understood that the indirect controls over banking could influence the business cycle itself. The Board failed to use its controls in this sense until after a decade of experience.

The Federal Reserve System has its greatest meaning as an original experiment in the relations between private business enterprise and government. Avoiding both the extremes of laissez faire advocated by bankers and of government ownership which Socialists advocated, or even of total *direct* control, which radical Progressives like LaFollette wanted, the System is a successful American invention, mingling minimum governmental authority in the public interest with private ownership of banks in a way that may be illogical but, with experience, has won the support of bankers as well as the people at large. It was a crucial step in establishing governmental regulation of American business enterprise.

Farm Loan Banks

One large banking problem which the Federal Reserve Act left unsolved was that of long-term farm credit. Bankers charged exorbitant interest for the one- to five-year mortgages which were the most important form of farm borrowing. Lack of liquidity makes such loans dangerous for ordinary banks, which must consider such factors as possible demands by depositors, unforeseeable climatic events, and turns in the economic cycle. Only the federal government possesses resources of credit equal to the risks of long-term farm loans, and all three parties in 1912 promised some sort of action. Wilson at first supported a plan which would set up a new system of land banks operating under federal charters but subject to private control. The Progressives in the House and Senate saw this as a betrayal which would force the farmer to pay exorbitant interest for the profit of bankers. Again they rebelled and drew up a bill to make the federal government owner of the banks, furnishing their capital, and operating the system. This time Wilson and conservative Democrats led by Glass temporarily defeated the Progressives on the ground that the extension of government credit to a favored class was unjustifiable. But in January 1916, Wilson changed his mind; he fought for the Progressives' bill through the spring, and signed it on July 17. The result was a system of twelve regional Federal Farm Loan Banks operating under federal control and using governmental credit to make long-term, low-interest mortgage loans to farmers. This competition with conventional banks had a remarkable effect in lowering their interest rates. The essential meaning was *indirect* control over credit, supplementing the Federal Reserve System. It was a historic measure of aid to farmers in their ancient struggle as debtors against exploitation by private creditors.

The Clayton Anti-Trust Act

Late in 1913 when the Underwood Tariff and Federal Reserve Acts were out of the way, the President turned to the third of the great items of his program, the enactment of a strong federal law against business monopolies. In a preliminary skirmish in June he had straddled the special issue of the application of antitrust laws to labor unions. Extreme Progressives insisted that unions must be exempted from the application of the Sherman Anti-trust Act and, in particular, that injunctions and contempt proceedings against strikes and against secondary boycotts should be forbidden to the courts insofar as they were based on the Sherman Act. The courts would remain free to issue injunctions in case of evidence that violence impended, whether from a strike situation or any other source. Democrats had embarrassed President Taft by attaching to an appropriation bill early in 1913 a rider forbidding the Department of Justice to use any of the funds to obtain antiunion injunctions, but Taft had vetoed the whole in order to scotch what he called "class legislation of the most vicious sort." The bill was re-enacted after Wilson was inaugurated, and he signed it, announcing at the same time that he would use general funds to prosecute any violation of the antitrust laws.

In December, Wilson took up the main issue. He found that Progressive opinion in Congress was divided. Some favored his own early view that the terms of the Sherman Anti-trust Act should be defined specifically to prevent the courts from reducing to a shadow the prohibition of conspiracies in restraint of trade. In particular they wanted interlocking directorates to be prohibited, and the "rule of reason," which the Supreme Court had announced in 1911, to be defined in such a way that the courts could not use it to make a distinction in favor of "reasonable" restraint of trade. Progressives of the Roosevelt persuasion, however, believed that legislative definition in such a complicated area was hopeless. They wanted a powerful federal trade commission to regulate business and stop monopolistic practices. In January 1914 came a dramatic announcement by J. P. Morgan and Company that the partners were resigning from thirty directorships. This was a conciliatory gesture to Wilson, but he went to Congress with a precise recommendation of his own brand of antitrust legislation. Chairman Henry D. Clayton of the House Judiciary Committee drew up a bill in Wilson's terms. The committee offered another one to create a federal trade commission, not as a powerful independent agency such as the Roosevelt Progressives wanted, but as an adjunct of the Department of Justice.

Labor leaders were opposed to the main Clayton Act because it contained no exemption of unions. Wilson agreed to an amendment limiting the issuance of injunctions in labor disputes, providing for jury trials in cases of criminal contempt, and declaring that neither labor unions nor farmers' organizations were illegal combinations in restraint of trade when they used legal methods to achieve legal goals. The ground on which this exemption was justified was that labor, contrary to the Marxian doctrine which businessmen's practice tended to support, is not a commodity, but human life. Therefore, it should not be subjected to the regulations appropriate for property, but be granted special privilege as a human right. As doctrine, this was worthy of Gompers' praise of the Clayton Act as "Labor's Magna Carta," though its specific terms against injunctions were not strong enough to suit union leaders and extreme Progressives.

The Clayton Act as finally passed and signed in October 1914 contained, besides the labor and farm exemptions, prohibition of interlocking directorates in corporations worth $1 million or more and of the purchase of stock by one corporation in a competing corporation. It forbade price differentials—high prices where no competition existed and low prices elsewhere—and it outlawed exclusive distributors' contracts preventing them from handling competitors' products. Officials of corporations were made personally responsible for violations of the law, and injured parties were offered a wide array of methods of obtaining legal redress, including three-fold damages for price discriminations or exclusive contracts. To obviate the hardship of seeking court action, the Federal Trade Commission was authorized to issue cease-and-desist orders against violators of the law.

The Federal Trade Commission

This body was the result of a startling shift of course by Wilson. It was apparently Louis D. Brandeis who now convinced him that he should adopt the essence of the New Nationalism. A powerful trade commission authorized to regulate all business activities was embodied in a new bill. Wilson, in June 1914, made this his chief proposal while allowing the antitrust provisions of the Clayton Bill to be weakened by provisos, such as that offenses must "substantially lessen competition," which were invitations for emasculating interpretations. Wilson staged a major fight in favor of the Brandeis-inspired Trade Commission. On September 10 he signed the law. It provided for a commission of five members with authority to require business reports by corporations, to investigate their operations, and to issue cease-and-desist orders against unfair business practices. These orders were subject to judicial review and it was hoped that they would not have to be used. Rather the sponsors wished the FTC to obtain co-operative compliance with fair trade principles.

The creation of the Federal Trade Commission illustrated most plainly the drift of the Wilson administration towards adoption of the contention of Croly and Roosevelt that consolidation of American business had proceeded so far, and was so valuable to the country's productive capacity, that action designed to restore competition among small units in the main sectors of industry was positively dangerous, however appealing it might be as a promise to revive an earlier age of history. In its final form the Federal Reserve Act also implied the abandonment of the hope to restore competition among smaller units of the banking structure and a facing up to the problems of making Big Government capable of regulating Big Finance. Wilson made this shift "unconsciously," in the sense that he had not planned it and did not offer philosophic reasons for it. For practical reasons he came to view the development of Big Government as the only possible progressive way of dealing with the problems created by Big Business.

Towards Social Justice

While the Clayton Act and the Federal Trade Commission Act increased government authority to end business abuses, the former lacked decisive strength, and the FTC was staffed by President Wilson with officials who were inefficient or unwilling to use their power. At the same time, deeper forces were at work to moderate the reformist pace of the administration and allow a breathing spell for conservatives. An economic recession began late in 1913 which businessmen blamed on the administration's tariff and antitrust policies, although it was actually worldwide. Wilson became conciliatory towards businessmen and went out of his way to reiterate assurances that the administration was friendly to their interests. Prosecutions of trusts were moderated by an offer of advice by the Deparment of Justice on ways to avoid difficulty. This marked a shift towards indirect regulation and away from the use of the antitrust laws to break up big businesses into small ones.

Wilson appointed businessmen, including Paul M. Warburg, who had opposed the Progressive features of the Federal Reserve System, as members of the Federal Reserve Board. Then, in August 1914, the outbreak of the World War distracted attention from domestic problems and placed a premium on national unity. Wilson interpreted this situation as requiring a reduction of the antagonisms which Progressivism aroused among conservatives. In the fall, the administration faced its first election test and conciliation seemed in order.

Thus it was that the initial phase of the New Freedom ended late in 1914. But Wilson had already begun to move towards new goals of social justice on which the various kinds of Progressives had been agreed in 1912. Labor was raised in 1913 from the status of a bureau in the Department of Commerce and Labor to a separate Department with a Secretary in the Cabinet. The Newlands Act of July 1913 created a four-member Board of Mediation and Conciliation to settle disputes between railroad managers and their employees. This signified that the federal government regarded its responsibility in strike situations as extending beyond the maintenance of law and order. The federal government now began to exercise influence to obtain fair negotiations in labor disputes, although it still refrained from the use of power to require collective bargaining.

The elections of 1914 were favorable to the administration. The next year it began to go further in developing measures for social justice. Sailors on merchant ships were among the most severely exploited workers under the United States flag, and the federal government's unquestioned authority over foreign commerce encouraged Progressives to demand reform. President Taft had pocket-vetoed a seaman's bill, but President Wilson in March 1915 signed Senator La Follette's Seaman's Act. This provided for improved living and safety conditions, protection against despotic captains, a nine-hour day in port, and freedom from the near-slavery devices common in sailors' labor contracts.

As the 1916 presidential campaign got under way, the railroad brotherhoods prepared to call a general strike for the eight-hour day and other demands. Failing to convince the railroad managers that they should make concessions, Wilson rushed the Adamson Act through Congress and signed it on September 3. This imposed the eight-hour day for all railroad workers with time-and-a-half pay for overtime work. The operators refused to obey the law, calling it unconstitutional, and a strike threatened in March 1917, when the nation faced war with Germany. On March 19, the Supreme Court (Wilson vs. New) ruled by a vote of five to four that the law was valid on the ground that the authority of Congress over interstate transportation facilities is absolute. The struggle

of labor for the eight-hour day, which had begun in the turbulent days
of the Haymarket Riot, turned an important corner towards success.

On September 1, 1916, Wilson signed the Keating-Owen Child Labor
Act which prohibited the shipment in interstate commerce of products
manufactured by child labor. The National Child Labor Committee was
one of the most effective reform organizations of the period. With word
and photograph it brought home to the consciences of voters and lawmakers the appalling spectacles of small children tending vast ranges
of textile machinery, and young boys working long hours in coal mines.
By the time that Wilson was inaugurated, most of the states had some
sort of law to reduce the evil, but enforcement was in many cases feeble
and employers could shop among the states and move plants to places
where they could hire children. A federal law could not reach purely local
situations and had to be related to interstate commerce. When a child-
labor bill was introduced in Congress in January 1914, Wilson did not
support it because he thought it unconstitutional. But, in July 1916, he
was warned that Progressives regarded such a law as a test of the administration which might determine the outcome of the elections in the
fall. The President suddenly overcame his scruples, went to the capitol,
and secured the conversion of enough Southern Senators, who were
fully aware of the desire of their states to draw textile mills away from
New England on the promise of cheap labor, to pass the bill.

But the Supreme Court was not convinced. The law went well beyond
the Adamson Act to regulate the conditions of manufacture within a state
prior to the entry of products into interstate commerce, and the Court
declared it unconstitutional in June 1918 (Hammer vs. Dagenhart) by
a five to four vote with Holmes and Brandeis dissenting. In 1919, a second
Child Labor Act was designed to satisfy the Court by using the taxing
power of the federal government to lay prohibitive levies on the products
of child labor in interstate commerce. But in 1922 the Court, now led by
ex-President Taft as Chief Justice, struck down this law (Bailey vs.
Drexel Furniture) on the ground that its purpose did not differ from the
original one. Not until the administration of Franklin D. Roosevelt was
there effective federal legislation against child labor which met judicial
approval.

Woman suffrage emerged during the Wilson administration as a burning issue. It commanded the support not only of strong women's organizations but of an increasing number of men who identified this cause
with Progressivism as an expansion of human rights, and a just recognition
of the new generations of women who were proving their competence in
business, higher education, and the professions. The upsurge of Progressivism brought woman suffrage in eleven states by 1914. By this time
the women's organizations, led by Carrie Chapman Catt, were concen-
trating on an amendment to the federal Constitution. The violent methods

of the British suffragettes were not much imitated in this country, although some women were jailed. Rather, the British example lent social prestige to the movement. Women of education and position found it galling to see hod-carriers vote while they were turned away from the polls. The radical young Max Eastman organized men in favor of women's votes and in 1912 marched with them in the face of jeers in a great suffrage parade in New York City.

The suffragists besieged President Wilson. Occasionally he explained that he would not support an amendment because it had not been promised in the Democratic platform. This question embarrassed the Democratic Party because its Southern wing bitterly opposed woman suffrage. When the United States entered the World War, suffragists picketed the White House in favor of their own democratic war aim. Some were jailed, but as women rapidly took the place of men in munitions and other factories, and staffed dozens of special organizations to help win the war, including a brigade of "yeomanettes" in the Navy, the suffrage movement, which had suffered more from ridicule than any serious masculine argument, acquired patriotic dignity.

Wilson in 1917 came out in favor of the suffrage amendment, and it passed Congress in June 1919. The Nineteenth Amendment forbade the states to deny or abridge the right of citizens to vote "on account of sex." In August 1920, three-fourths of the states having ratified it, the Amendment was proclaimed in force. The advocates of woman suffrage had prophesied that women would use the vote to clean out corruption and machine bosses, to further humanitarian legislation, and to ensure world peace. The first President elected with the help of women's votes on a national scale was Warren G. Harding. Students had difficulty in discovering during the following decades any particular effect of women's votes besides an increase in the size of the electorate. But no one suggested that women were *more* to blame than men for the failures of American politics, and no one advocated repeal of the Amendment. In the activities of the League of Women Voters and other groups, some of the hopes of the suffragists were fulfilled.

THE LIMITS OF WILSONIAN REFORM

The Color Line

Wilson's indifference to reforms in favor of Negroes reflected the predominant sentiment of his time, which was shared at first by most Progressives. Ray Stannard Baker, afterwards the authorized biographer of Wilson, called attention to the situation of the Negroes in a series of articles in *McClure's* and the *American Magazine* which were published in a book entitled *Following the Color Line* (1908). But Progressives generally accepted the color line during the first decade of the century, and it is a striking fact that, during the Progressive Era, the status of Negroes fell to the lowest point since the days of slavery. External signs of this were the culmination of the movement in the South to disfranchise Negroes by state law, the passing of Jim Crow laws there, and various forms of discrimination in other parts of the country.

Contrary to a common impression, these Southern laws did not immediately follow Reconstruction. The disfranchisement movement had its formal beginning in Mississippi in 1890, but it did not gain great impetus until after the Populist revolt, when the one-party system was temporarily threatened and Negro votes were sought by both Populists and conservatives. Corruption and coercion were conspicuous accompaniments of these efforts. The elimination of these votes, which might constitute the balance of power, was afterwards urged in the name of white solidarity by leaders who were far more hostile to Negroes than either the Redeemers or the Populists had been. The former in varying degree carried on the old paternalistic tradition, which assumed white dominance but frowned on personal unfriendliness, while the latter made a genuine if abortive attempt to promote interracial co-operation among farmers. The new crop of leaders included demagogues who owed their political success almost wholly to the exploitation of racial antagonism. Among the advocates of disfranchisement in this period, however, were men like Hoke Smith of Georgia and Charles B. Aycock and Josephus Daniels of North Carolina, who were Progressive on most of the issues of the time.

Disfranchisement did not become section-wide until the imperialist era, when the philosophy of white and "Aryan" superiority came into full flower in the country as a whole. By 1910, eight southern states had disfranchised Negroes in new constitutions or constitutional amendments. Such devices as the poll tax and the white Democratic primary were used in these and other states to accomplish the same purpose. Many of these laws were ingenious. Avoiding direct reference to race and color, they imposed requirements for voters which Negroes would have difficulty in meeting and which put them virtually at the mercy of local election officials. At the same time, loopholes were left through which unqualified white men could pass. One of these was the "Grandfather Clause"—by means of which a man might gain the suffrage because of his grandfather's status as a voter or Confederate soldier. A clause of this sort in the Oklahoma constitution was declared unconstitutional by the United States Supreme Court in 1915, but otherwise the courts upheld the disfranchisement policy. So did predominant white opinion in the North as well as the South.

In the 1890's, various Gulf states passed laws requiring the separation of white and colored pasengers on the railroad trains. In the older states many regarded this as quite unnecessary. South Carolina, North Carolina, and Virginia did not yield to the movement until the end of the century (1898-1900). Segregation was next extended to waiting rooms, street cars, and residential districts, the trend being to make it universal. In 1917, the Supreme Court ruled against residential restrictions, but these were effectively reimposed by private covenants. In the South these codes were more rigidly enforced than the black codes of slavery times had been, and they applied to all persons with a trace of Negro ancestry.

From the end of Reconstruction to the First World War the most important figure in American Negro history was Booker T. Washington, born a slave in Virginia the same year that Woodrow Wilson was born in a Presbyterian manse in that state. He established Tuskegee Institute in Alabama in 1881 and made it a noted center of vocational training, at a time when there was growing emphasis on practical education in schools for whites. His advice to his own people was: "Cast down your bucket where you are." His first and major aim was to make them good workmen, and he instilled in thousands of them the spirit of craftsmanship. He sought to prepare them for citizenship but did not directly seek it for them. His approach was economic and he was an exponent of gradualism. In all his relations with the whites he was prudent and conciliatory, with the result that among them he became the recognized leader of his race. An eloquent speaker as well as a high-minded man, he was exceedingly successful in his appeals to Northern philanthropy. Considering his times, he followed the most promising line of policy, and he was a genuinely constructive figure, but before the end of his life (1915) he was severely criticized by other leaders of his race for pursuing too limited a course and not being bold enough.

Chief of his critics was William E. B. DuBois, born in Massachusetts and educated at Fisk University in Tennessee and at Harvard, where he took a Ph.D. degree in history. The title of Booker Washington's best-known book, *Up from Slavery* (1901), suggested his experience and philosophy, but those of DuBois were different. As a student at Fisk he found himself in a segregated society such as he had not been accustomed to in the Berkshires of New England, and he had a similar experience when, after leaving Harvard and studying abroad, he became a professor of history and economics at Atlanta University. There he shocked the cautious Negro leaders over whom Booker T. Washington was a benevolent dictator by severely criticizing the latter's emphasis on vocational as compared with "liberal" education, his gradualism, and his seeming acceptance of inferior status for the Negro. In 1903, DuBois published *The Souls of Black Folk*, a book which inspired new confidence among the younger generation of educated Negroes and some progressive whites. This led to a meeting at Niagara Falls, under the leadership of DuBois, and what was called the Niagara Movement. In 1906, a manifesto was issued at Harper's Ferry, where John Brown had begun his rebellion. This demanded immediate suffrage for the Negro, the abolition of the Jim

Crow system, and the enforcement of laws against rich as well as poor, against white as well as black.

The young militants made little headway until an event in Springfield, Illinois, in 1909, the centenary of Lincoln's birth, demonstrated that the problem of the Negro was not confined to the South any more than it was being solved by the gradualist policy. The prejudice of Northerners, when Negroes migrated to their vicinities to find jobs in industry, convinced the militants of the futility of Washington's hope to gain white sympathy by limiting Negro ambition to economic betterment. For two days in Springfield race riots, lynchings, and burnings drove Negroes in terror from their homes. Out of the revulsion came a famous "Call" signed by white Progressives and Negro militants for a conference to initiate reformist action on a new basis. The conference led to the organization of the National Association for the Advancement of the Colored People in 1910. Its first group of officers included only one Negro, DuBois. Oswald Garrison Villard, heir of a railroad fortune and publisher of the *New York Evening Post* and *The Nation,* was a prominent member. This organization slowly displaced the Washington leadership and doctrine and eventually became one of the most successful reformist pressure groups in American history.

The first effort of the vigorous young movement to make national gains came in the campaign of 1912. With the migration of Negroes into northern industrial centers, their votes began to make them interesting to politicians of both parties. Roosevelt when President had aroused a storm of protest by inviting Booker T. Washington to dine in the White House. The Republican Party enjoyed the traditional loyalty of Negroes. But Wilson, without touching the Southern system of disfranchisement, tried to win Negro votes in the North by promising sympathy for the NAACP program so that Villard, DuBois, and other leaders worked for his election. After the inauguration, Villard proposed to the President that he appoint a National Race Commission to study the entire problem. Wilson refused, admitting that he feared to antagonize Southern Democrats in Congress whose support he needed on other issues.

Far from doing anything to advance the Negro, Wilson allowed Southern Cabinet members, led by Postmaster General Burleson, to federalize the Jim Crow system by instituting segregation of Negro employees in governmental offices, rest rooms, and restaurants. In the South, Negro employees of the federal government were discharged or reduced to menial jobs. Wilson frankly expressed approval of the federal segregation policy and declared that he instituted it in the Negro's own interest. But many of his supporters were antagonized by his policy and the NAACP led a vigorous protest. Wilson was surprised, and after 1913 the spread of segregation in federal offices was stopped. The events of 1913 marked the high point of white supremacy in post-Civil War history.

The part of the Negro in the First World War did not win him any benefits: the armed forces remained strictly segregated and Negroes were used mostly for labor battalions in the Army, and exclusively as mess boys in the Navy. This situation was a strange outcome of Wilson's promise that the New Freedom included benefits for all disadvantaged groups. It marked the narrowest limitation of his liberalism. The Wilson administration did nothing to discourage a new outbreak of race riots in the North, lynchings in the South, and a revival of the Ku Klux Klan.

Immigration Policies

Racism was directed against the New Immigrants only less virulently than against the Negroes. But in this area, which interested his Southern supporters less than the Negro question, President Wilson was more responsive to reformist thought. The American Federation of Labor, on the other hand, took the lead in demanding an end to immigration, or at least restrictions of it, because the great crowds surging into the labor market lowered wage scales, made employers indifferent to working conditions, and strengthened the unorganized section of the labor force. At the same time, the AFL showed little interest in unionizing immigrant labor and most unions positively barred Negroes from membership. In the heavy industries where immigrants concentrated, the AFL chose only the most skilled trades for its organizational efforts. Its immigration policy reflected the tendency of the AFL to separate itself from the majority of the working class and to create favored conditions for the "aristocracy of labor." Insofar as this policy was directed against southern and eastern Europeans, it appealed to anti-Catholic and anti-Jewish sentiments of older American groups, and they strengthened the demand for a change in governmental immigration policy.

A literacy test was included in the Burnett Immigration Bill that passed Congress in January 1915. But President Wilson had promised foreign-language groups during the campaign of 1912 that he would oppose such a restriction, and he vetoed the bill. He said of it: "Those who come seeking opportunity are not to be admitted unless they have already had one of the chief of the opportunities they seek, the opportunity of education. The object of such provisions is restriction, not selection." Two years later Congress again passed the bill, and Wilson vetoed it again, but this time Congress overrode the veto. This was only the beginning of immigration restrictions to stem the tide after the War.

Wilson Opposes Prohibition

Prohibition turned out to be the last reform issue Wilson had to deal with. The movement to outlaw "Demon Rum" had by 1900 produced statewide results in Maine, Vermont, New Hampshire, North Dakota, and Kansas. This cause was neglected or positively opposed by most of the leaders of the Progressive Movement, as they placed the blame for economic and social ills on the abuses of businessmen and the corruption of politicians. But evangelical and rural religious groups continued to place their main faith in regeneration of mankind by policing personal habits. Despairing of voluntary temperance or abstinence, they agitated militantly for Prohibition by law. Such groups had been important in Populism and they remained a force to be reckoned with in both parties. Politicians, particularly in the Southern and the Plains states and the hill country of New England, became prohibitionists for political purposes without regard to their personal habits. The Anti-Saloon League was connected with evangelical sects, the Methodist Episcopal Church maintained a Temperance Society which was actually a prohibitionist organization, and women were powerfully combined in the Women's Christian Temperance Union. These and lesser organizations made an amendment of the federal Constitution their chief objective after the Supreme Court decided in 1898 (Rhodes *vs.* Iowa) that dry state governments could not prevent the shipment in interstate commerce of liquor to their inhabitants for personal use.

The Webb-Kenyon Interstate Liquor Act was passed over President Taft's veto on March 1, 1913, to forbid such shipments. By this time the Prohibition movement had gained momentum equal to or surpassing any other reform. Fund drives, innumerable meetings with religious revivalist overtones, powerful lobbies in state capitals and in Washington, and propaganda that covered the country like a blanket, with new emphasis on "scientific" arguments against the evils of alcohol added to the old moral and social arguments, all gained strength with the rise of Progressivism. It was a reform much easier for plain people to understand than the difficult problems of economic and political reform. It was openly directed against the city as the headquarters of vice, and covertly at immigrant groups, especially Catholics. The addiction of many country people to "white mule" and other home-made potations, either to avoid the expense of good liquor or to circumvent prohibition laws, was less offensive than the city saloon, a genuine social sore and focus of political corruption.

Wayne B. Wheeler became the outstanding leader of the new generation of prohibitionists, and many preachers were enlisted in the crusade. The dry forces came to be feared by politicians everywhere except in the largest cities. There the political machines of both parties stayed unabashedly wet. The prohibitionists were most successful in forcing politicians to take a stand. Special appeals were made to the fear that liquor contributed to racial conflict in the South and to industrialists' problem of inefficient work on Mondays, when employees were recovering from pay-day sprees. The rising agitation led to Prohibition laws in seven southern states by 1915, and the total of dry states numbered twenty-six when the United States entered the War.

As in the case of woman suffrage, war conditions produced clinching arguments for a constitutional amendment. The shortage of grain made its diversion to brewers and distillers inhumane as well as unpatriotic. The Lever Food and Fuel Control Act of August 10, 1917, forbade the use of foodstuffs for distilled liquors and also the importation of the latter. The brewing of beer was largely in the hands of Americans of German origin, and this was played upon to discredit the beverage. The need for increased industrial production made Prohibition seem justified as a means of eliminating drunkenness. In these circumstances Congress, on December 18, 1917, approved the Eighteenth Amendment. This prohibited the "manufacture, sale, or transportation of intoxicating liquors within, the importation thereof into, or the exportation thereof from the United States . . . for beverage purposes."

President Wilson did not approve the Prohibition Amendment, although it was supported by some members of the administration, particularly Josephus Daniels, who had abolished the officers' wine mess on warships shortly after he took office. But presidential agreement is not necessary for an amendment to the Constitution. By January 1919, it had been approved by three-quarters of the states and was ratified. Then Congress after prolonged debate passed the implementing Volstead Bill. This provided a strict definition of "intoxicating" as any beverage containing more than one-half of 1 per cent of alcohol, and created the office of Commissioner of Prohibition in the Bureau of Internal Revenue to enforce the law. President Wilson vetoed the bill but it was passed over his veto on October 28, 1919.

This was the most extreme attempt in history by the federal government to control personal behavior. It was at least partially responsible for one of the worst eras of lawlessness in American history. It was a sorry finale to the reform legislation of the Wilson administration. The President's refusal to support Prohibition was courageous and far-sighted. But his championship of personal freedom in this case was more than offset by the grave abuses of personal and civil liberties of which his administration was guilty during and after the War. The ardor for reform which had produced the Underwood Tariff, the Federal Reserve System, the Federal Farm Loan Act, the Clayton Anti-trust Act, the Federal Trade Commission, the Income Tax Act, the Adamson Act, and the Woman Suffrage Amendment seemed to be transformed during the War into a frenzy of intolerance among both officials and the people.

CHAPTER 19

First Experiments in Foreign Policy

WHEN HE WAS INAUGURATED, PRESIDENT WILSON intended to eliminate the evils of American imperialism, to secure the reign of world peace by a new system of conciliation, and to extend the blessings of democracy wherever possible in the world. The initial foreign policies of his administration were overshadowed by the unforeseen advent of the World War, and to Latin-American patriots they seemed little different from imperialism, but they were a significant experiment in new ways to use the growing power of the United States.

To Wilson and Secretary of State Bryan anti-imperialism seemed the natural counterpart abroad of the New Freedom at home. They thought it high time to launch upon a new, moral course of conduct in foreign as well as domestic policy. They saw a dangerous aggrandizement of the national government in Roosevelt's imperialism and New Nationalism alike. Thus the initial Wilsonian program of restoring competition and the reign of Small Business at home was paralleled by plans to liquidate imperialist positions abroad and restore the sovereignty of weak nations.

GROPING FOR A POLICY

Dollar Diplomacy was the latest product of Republican imperialism and Wilson set out quickly to abolish it. One week after his inauguration he announced that governmental support of private interests abroad would cease. One more week and he publicly told the syndicate of Wall Street bankers, who had been encouraged by the Taft administration to participate in a six-power loan to China as a means of increasing United States diplomatic influence, that the terms of the loan injured Chinese sovereignty and might result in intervention by the United States. Therefore, he said, the project would not be supported by the new administration. The bankers withdrew the next day without reluctance.

This sensational repudiation of "immoral" foreign policy impressed the public. But in Central America and the Caribbean islands the new President found his anti-Wall Street moralism in conflict with the strategic interests of the nation. Wilson and Bryan decided they could not liquidate Dollar Diplomacy in Nicaragua without some provision for American control over the canal route. The Taft administration left behind it a treaty project which would give the United States a permanent option on the canal route and leases on strategic naval sites at both ends in return for $3 million. With this the Nicaraguan government could pay back loans from American bankers. Anti-imperialist Democrats in the Senate had defeated the treaty, but the new administration was anxious to prevent other naval powers from gaining control of an Isthmian route.

Bryan proposed to Wilson the allocation of money to Latin-American governments to free them from the influence of private European and American bankers and at the same time strengthen the political influence of the United States. This proposal anticipated the policy of foreign aid that the United States adopted during and after the Second World War. But, as in domestic policy, Wilson at first thought he could reduce the power of private economic interests without increasing the activity of the federal government, and he rejected Bryan's idea. The upshot was surprising: Bryan and Wilson, in June 1913, not only accepted the original terms of the treaty but added a provision giving the United States a quasi-protectorate over Nicaragua. The United States would have the right to intervene to maintain orderly government, to protect property, and to maintain the country's independence. This matched Roosevelt's Platt Amendment in Cuba. Wilson was so confident of the righteousness of his purposes that he abandoned in practice his opposition to policies which he had believed to be evil when Republican administrations pursued them. The turnabout aroused antagonism not only in Latin America but among Democratic Senators. They prevented ratification until the quasi-protectorate feature of the Bryan-Chamorro Treaty was eliminated. Then it was ratified in February 1916.

The practical control by the United States over the Nicaraguan government was not affected by the elimination of the offending clauses from the treaty. United States Marines continued to support American supervision of the Nicaraguan customs and debts service, and they supported any local administration that Washington selected. In elections in 1916, the United States Minister to Nicaragua effectively threatened that, if the candidate of the Liberal Party won, the United States would not recognize his government. The Wilson administration professed approval

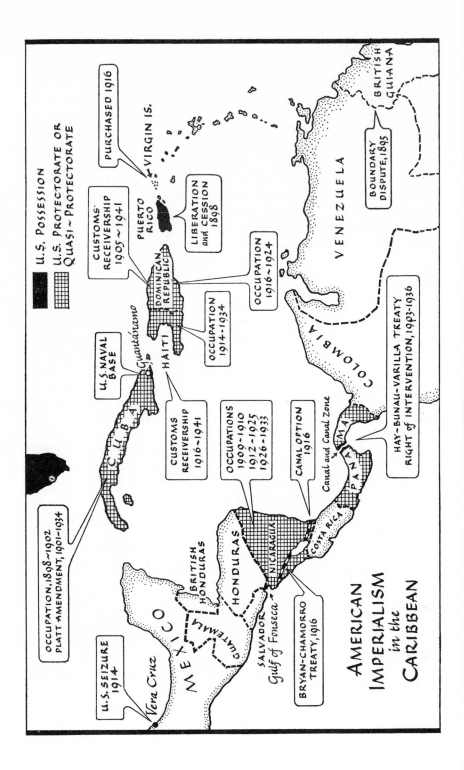

AMERICAN IMPERIALISM in the CARIBBEAN

U.S. POSSESSION

U.S. PROTECTORATE OR QUASI~PROTECTORATE

PURCHASED 1916

VIRGIN IS.

BRITISH GUIANA

BOUNDARY DISPUTE, 1895

VENEZUELA

CUSTOMS RECEIVERSHIP 1905~1941

PUERTO RICO

LIBERATION and CESSION 1898

OCCUPATION 1916~1924

DOMINICAN REPUBLIC

OCCUPATION 1914~1934

HAITI

Guantánamo

U.S. NAVAL BASE

C U B A

CUSTOMS RECEIVERSHIP 1916~1941

OCCUPATIONS 1909~1910 1912~1925 1926~1933

CANAL OPTION 1916

Canal and Canal Zone

P A N A M A

COLOMBIA

HAY~BUNAU~VARILLA TREATY RIGHT of INTERVENTION, 1903-1936

OCCUPATION, 1898~1902 PLATT AMENDMENT, 1901~1934

COSTA RICA

NICARAGUA

HONDURAS

BRITISH HONDURAS

GUATEMALA

SALVADOR

Gulf of Fonseca

BRYAN~CHAMORRO TREATY, 1916

M E X I C O

Vera Cruz

U.S. SEIZURE 1914

of the judicial process to settle international disputes, but it seemed hypocritical when it ignored a decision of the Central American Tribunal of Justice that the leases of naval base sites to the United States in the Bryan-Chamorro Treaty were invalid.

Nicaragua was strategically important because that country offered an alternative to the Panama Canal. Haiti and the Dominican Republic were important because they flanked water routes to the Isthmus. Drastic action in Haiti was encouraged by intrigues of the German government. Here the Wilson administration worked intimately with the National City Bank of New York. A series of ineffective revolutionary governments were urged without success to accept a convention giving the United States a naval base, and control over Haitian customs according to a plan of the New York bankers. Bryan opposed direct intervention, but after he resigned a particularly atrocious series of political murders led President Wilson to order United States Marines to take over in August 1915. A new government favorable to the United States was elected, and it signed a protectorate treaty in September.

In the neighboring Dominican Republic the existing United States customs receivership was manipulated by Bryan's appointee, Minister James M. Sullivan, an ex-prize fighter and a Bryan Democrat of New York City, to suit his own purposes. His brother Tim Sullivan obtained lucrative construction contracts there. This shift from the Wall Street to the Tammany type of control did not include efficient use of political influence by Minister Sullivan. The country fell into civil war. President Wilson dismissed Sullivan in the summer of 1914 and provided American supervision of elections in the fall. But civil war began again in May 1916. Wilson ordered the Marines to land. By the end of the year Captain Harry S. Knapp of the United States Navy commanded a military government in the little republic.

These interventions did not serve the interests of Wall Street. Several times Bryan prevented Latin-American governments from making concessions to American bankers. But the Wilson administration in practice compromised small sovereignties even farther than Wall Street required. Wilson, on October 27, 1913, in a famous speech at Mobile, Alabama, tried to reassure Latin Americans that his policy remained anti-imperialist. He promised that Latin America would be liberated from the stranglehold of foreign capitalists and asserted that the United States did not covet one foot of Latin-American territory. But he also warned that the United States intended to maintain leadership in Latin America. In two dramatic instances Wilson proved that he regarded stable Latin-American governments as the juridical equals of the United States. In 1914, he accepted the offer of Argentina, Brazil, and Chile to mediate in a dispute between the United States and Mexico, and in the same year his government negotiated a treaty with Colombia virtually apologizing for Theodore Roosevelt's aid to the Panama revolt of 1903. The latter display of humility was frustrated by Roosevelt's friends in the Senate until a treaty without apology, but awarding Colombia $25 million, was ratified in 1921. In 1916, furthermore, Wilson attempted to allay Latin-American fears of Yankee imperialism by negotiating a pact among the 21 republics containing mutual guaranties of territorial integrity and political independence under republican forms of government, along with promises to settle all disputes by peaceful means and to refrain from aiding enemies of the signatory governments. Colombia had proposed such a pact, but Taft had refused it. Wilson pursued it strongly until the Chilean government discouraged him because it would interfere with Chilean aims in a boundary dispute with Peru. Then the Latin-American Pact was superseded in Wilson's mind by the plan for similar provisions in a universal League of Nations.

Critics pointed to the undeniable fact that the Wilson administration actually increased the coercive influence of the United States in neighboring republics to the south. But a real change occurred in the purpose for which American power was used. Secretary Bryan typically refused a Haitian offer of exclusive franchises for American investors, declaring that the administration felt obliged to protect Haiti from exploitation by Americans. When the government decided to buy the Virgin Islands from Denmark, the motive was exclusively strategic. In 1867, the United States had failed to conclude an agreement to pay Denmark $7.5 million for them; but after the outbreak of the World War, fear that Germany might get hold of the Islands led the Wilson administration to pay Denmark $25 million. A treaty of annexation was ratified on August 4, 1916. Domination over the inhabitants or exploitation of them was certainly not the purpose of this territorial acquisition. The strengthening of the power position of the United States in Central America and the Caribbean was obvious, however, and it made Latin American nationalists and American anti-imperialists indifferent to the distinctions between the Wilsonian and earlier methods of extending American influence. Still it was power for the sake of security that the Wilson administration groped for during these years, and if security had been obtainable by means of the internationalist technique of the Latin-American Pact, Wilson would presumably have been willing to abandon unilateral methods.

THE MEXICAN TEST

In Mexico the potentialties of Wilson's new foreign policy were most dramatically tested and there its fundamental error was unmistakably revealed. Since relations with Mexico were in crisis when he was inaugurated, the situation was ready-made for an exercise of the new idealism. The dictator Porfirio Díaz during a long tenure as President of Mexico had encouraged foreign promoters, chiefly American, to take ownership, often by shady methods, of large segments of Mexico's economy—especially railroads, mining and oil lands, and great acreages of ranch and farm lands. He was overthrown in 1911 by a liberal movement headed by Francisco I. Madero. The new government seemed to be pursuing Mexican counterparts of American progressive policies. But Madero had only a backward peasantry and a tiny middle class with which to combat the powerful clerical, military, and aristocratic landowning classes, and he faced determined opposition to all reform on the part of foreign owners and business interests.

The question was whether these foreign groups would be able to induce their governments, in the first place the United States, to support them against a Mexican government of reform and national vindication. It was an early example of the revolts of underdeveloped countries against imperialism which have increasingly challenged the great democratic powers during this century, and all of Latin America watched the outcome. President Taft's ambassador, Henry Lane Wilson, opposed Madero and encouraged a counterrevolution under Victoriano Huerta, a general who promised to revive the Díaz policies. Huerta betrayed and murdered President Madero early in February 1913. The American Ambassador frantically urged Taft to recognize his government, but the Department of State wished first to obtain a promise of favorable terms for the settlement of minor questions, and Taft gave over the problem to his successor.

The traditional policy of recognizing any *de facto* government, without inquiring into the justice of its accession or policies, was now reversed by Wilson and Bryan. They ignored the pressure of financial interests led by Speyer and Company, bankers of New York. Wilson said privately that he would not recognize a "government of butchers." He placed his hopes in a new Maderist revolutionary movement that developed under the leadership of Venustiano Carranza. The British and other governments recognized Huerta. Wilson saw this as a result of the need of the British Navy for Mexican oil. His own interest, he said, was in the "submerged eighty-five per cent of the people of that Republic who are now struggling toward liberty." He brought the British into line with his policy possibly as part of an understanding on other matters. In his speech at Mobile in October 1913, he explained: "We dare not turn from the principle that morality and not expediency is the thing that must guide us and that we will never condone iniquity because it is most convenient to do so." In November, he sent a confidential agent to offer Carranza the aid of the American Army and Navy to protect the Constitutionalists, especially against European intervention, while elections were held which by all indications would displace Huerta.

Wilson, in short, offered a virtual guarantee of success to Carranza in return for acceptance of his advice on how to restore constitutional government. Carranza refused. This was the first indication that even the Maderists were nationalists first and democrats second. Carranza wanted nothing from the United States except diplomatic recognition and the right to buy arms.

In February 1914, Wilson gave in to the latter demand and thus abandoned the appearance of nonintervention. Spreading disorder resulted in property losses in Mexico and murders of Americans. New groups rose under the social-revolutionary Zapata in the South and the rambunctious Francisco ("Pancho") Villa in the North. Racial contempt for Mexicans made it difficult for most Americans to share Wilson's faith that good could come out of the revolution. Unforeseen by everyone was the ominous rallying to Huerta's support of many Mexicans whose distrust of him was overcome by their hatred of United States interference in their domestic affairs. Wilson evidently welcomed an opportunity which arose in April 1914 to unite American opinion behind a more forceful policy. Huerta refused to order a 21-gun salute to the American flag, as apology for the arrest of some American sailors by one of his colonels in Tampico, unless an American warship would return the salute gun for gun. Wilson feared this would constitute recognition. Resorting to this old-fashioned punctilio, Wilson asked Congress for authority to punish Huerta with armed force. While that body debated, he learned that a German ship loaded with munitions for the Huerta government was approaching Vera Cruz. Without waiting for Congress, he ordered the Navy to occupy that city. It did so by April 22, killing 126 and wounding 195 Mexicans, while 19 Americans were killed and 71 wounded. Wilson reiterated his hatred of war. The American people were confused, while Europeans ridiculed the President for hypocrisy, and in many Latin-American cities demonstrations against the United States broke out. Most ominously, Carranza sided with Huerta, demanding that Wilson evacuate Vera Cruz immediately. In vain Bryan explained to Carranza that the occupation was directed only against Huerta. Carranza like most Mexicans saw it as a violation of Mexican sovereignty.

Naval occupation of Vera Cruz could accomplish nothing. The President and his advisers were discussing an armed expedition to Mexico City when Argentina, Brazil, and Chile offered their services as mediators. Wilson accepted with relief. He was determined to use the mediation to eliminate Huerta and win the acceptance by Carranza of a thorough-going program of reform founded on land distribution and capped by constitutional rectitude. The ABC mediators organized a meeting of American and Mexican delegates at Niagara Falls late in May 1914. Huerta admitted that he faced military defeat. Carranza was persuaded to send delegates to Niagara, and the effort of Wilson was directed to making him agree to stop the fighting and initiate Wilson's program. In return the President would in effect award Carranza victory in the civil war. Carranza absolutely refused. As a Mexican patriot, he preferred the risk of defeat to a victory compromised by acceptance of the tutelage of the Colossus of the North. Baffled, Wilson could only stand aside while Carranza fought his own way to victory and took Mexico City in August.

The world thought this a victory for Wilson's policy, but behind the scenes the administration was encouraging Pancho Villa, who carefully nourished the belief that he would be more amenable to guidance from Washington. Carranza was weakened within his own government by the adherence of his chief lieutenant, Álvaro Obregón, to Wilson's plan. A coalition of the Villista and Zapatista groups, representing the deeper forces of agrarian revolution, gained control of Mexico City and Carranza retreated to Vera Cruz in the wake of the American naval forces when they evacuated the city in November 1914. The Wilson administration now supported the Villista government with its ready promises of reform. But Carranza early in 1915 adopted reformist agrarian and labor aims and rallied most of the more responsible and effective forces of the revolution to his side, while Villa turned out to be a virtual bandit.

The political life of Mexico was more complicated than Wilson imagined. His new protegé was defeated in central Mexico and retired to the northern province of Chihuahua. Wilson belatedly tried to shift to a policy of neutrality among the contending forces in Mexico. Sentiment in the United States for intervention to establish law and order was whipped up by the newspapers of Hearst, whose vast land holdings in Mexico were threatened by the social revolutionaries; by Theodore Roosevelt who upbraided Wilson for not using the Big Stick in Mexico as he would have done; and by Roman Catholics who were antagonized by the anticlericalism of the Carranzistas. Wilson, in June 1915, told the Mexican leaders they must stop fighting or the United States would force peace on the country. Villa agreed but Carranza refused. At the same time the *Lusitania* crisis with Germany made it essential to solve the Mexican problem, in particular because German intrigues in Mexico were designed to distract the United States by fomenting a war between it and Mexico. The new Secretary of State, Robert Lansing, decided that the Carranza government must be recognized as offering Mexico's best hope of civil peace. Wilson agreed and, as a result, faced the hostility of the Roman Catholic hierarchy and other interventionist groups and a large segment of the press in the election campaign of 1916.

THE PUNITIVE EXPEDITION

Wilson gained no surcease. Villa, feeling betrayed by Washington, turned to deliberate provocations of war. He murdered Americans in

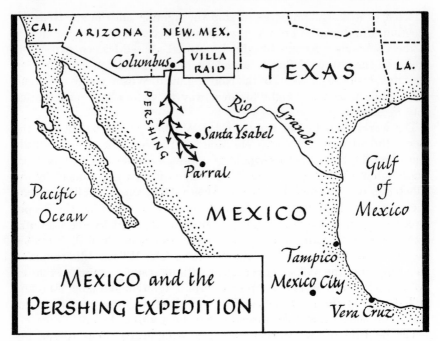

MEXICO and the
PERSHING EXPEDITION

the northern states of Mexico, and when this brought no armed reaction, he crossed the border on March 9, 1916, burned Columbus, New Mexico, and killed 19 Americans. The American election campaign was now beginning, and the demand for intervention spread from Wilson's opponents to many of his supporters. Anxiously he inquired of the Carranza government whether it would approve a punitive military expedition into Mexico to apprehend Villa. In return for a promise of reciprocal rights for Mexico to pursue bandits into the United States, Carranza's subordinates agreed. Brigadier General John J. Pershing was given command of 5000 troops and he entered Mexico on March 15, 1916, with strict orders to avoid conflict with the Carranza authorities.

Carranza in giving consent had thought only in terms of small forces in hot pursuit of bandits. Pershing's force was soon raised to 11,000, it organized what amounted to an occupation of northern Mexico as Villa retreated southward, and Wilson stationed 150,000 National Guardsmen at the border. The Americans thought that Carranza would welcome the opportunity to capture Villa as they pushed him into the Carranzistas' arms, but in this, too, they showed a lack of understanding. The Mexicans, including Carranza, preferred Villa to any foreign invader. The Carranza forces ignored the Villistas. Pershing in desperation moved deeper into Mexico without getting any closer to Villa. On April 12, at Parral, Carranza's troops fired on a small detachment of American soldiers.

The next day Carranza's government demanded the withdrawal of the punitive expedition.

While the Wilson administration maneuvered for a face-saving way out, Villistas increased the pressure of American public opinion for full-scale war by raids across the border into Texas. Wilson sent a new force in pursuit of these raiders, and the War College began to make plans for general war. Carranza gave orders to his forces to resist any further movement of Pershing's troops in any direction except retreat northwards. Wilson called out 100,000 additional National Guardsmen, and ordered warships to both coasts of Mexico. Fighting occurred at Mazatlán and Carrizal. The latter affair was at first understood by Wilson to be the result of aggression by Carranzistas, and he prepared to send a war message to Congress, but a more accurate report soon revealed that the Americans had incited the clash. This report was spread in American newspapers, the issue was taken up by antiwar groups, and Wilson, in a remarkable display of integrity, reversed himself and denied publicly that "the glory of America would be enhanced by a war of conquest in Mexico." He accepted an offer of Carranza on July 4, 1916, to negotiate with a view to ending all the troubles.

Commissioners of both governments met in the United States. The product of months of discussion was rejected by Carranza on December 27 because it attached to the agreement to withdraw American forces from Mexico conditions involving Mexican treatment of American property. Nevertheless, in January 1917, when the entry of the United States into the European War was imminent, Wilson ordered Pershing to come home. On March 13 the United States recognized the Carranza government *de jure*. Without the advice of Wilson, Mexico proceeded to organize a constitutional convention and hold new elections, and to progress on the difficult path of democracy and social reform. Her actions included harsh measures against American economic interests.

Wilson could claim that he had kept European interference away from Mexico during her years of crisis, but he had also increased the distrust of Yankee imperialism on the part of Mexicans and other Latin Americans. That his intention, very unlike that of imperialism by the usual definition, was to guide Mexico towards true independence and democracy, meant nothing to Mexicans. Inherent in Wilson's attitude was the relegation of Mexicans to an inferior status that justified tutelage. Mexicans discounted heavily Wilson's assumption of American moral and political superiority. They remembered with bitterness the loss of half their country to the United States in 1848. Their sense of material and military weakness in the face of their northern neighbor made them more rather than less sensitive to American slights. The failure of Wilson's Mexican policy was a failure of understanding. It typified and climaxed the Latin-American policy of the United States after 1898, which seemed to present a total contrast between America's lofty purposes and her actual abuse of the sovereignty of small nations. More years and further tragedies were required before Americans and their government learned the expediency as well as the justice of genuine respect for Latin-American rights.

In actuality Wilson's lofty purposes were not entirely contradicted. He did accept mediation; he did turn to negotiation when jingos were screaming for war and revenge against him at the polls; he did accept defeat in Mexico when Mexican patriots demonstrated their determination. He accepted defeat, it should be noted, before the German policy of fomenting war between Mexico and the United States was fully revealed on March 1 in the Zimmerman Note, which made the wisdom of his acceptance doubly clear. To Wilson, too, belongs the credit for ending governmental support of private American promoters and property owners who sought to rifle Mexico of her most valuable resources. The new Mexican Constitution of 1917 contained provisions for the economic as well as political redemption of Mexican nationality. The Mexicans owed something to Wilson even though they violently repelled him in the role of schoolmaster. Finally, Wilson intended the Latin-American Pact of 1916 to eliminate for the future troubles like those he had in Mexico. The nobility as well as the mistakes in the Wilsonian conduct of foreign relations were all apparent in the Latin-American crisis, most poignantly in Mexican policy, before the great Calvinist teacher led the nation into a far more difficult venture in international leadership.

First Efforts for World Peace

Wilson's European policy started and ended in efforts to organize world peace. Presidents Roosevelt and Taft had negotiated arbitration treaties with the leading governments of the world, but they both failed because of the jealousy of Senators who feared the undermining of their own authority in foreign relations. Secretary of State Bryan took a new tack which avoided the technical difficulties of arbitration. He proposed to the nations of the world that each enter into a treaty of conciliation with the United States providing that any dispute which did not yield to other pacification must be turned over to a permanent investigatory commission. The parties would agree to refrain from war for a year until the commission should make its recommendation for a peaceful settlement. The theory was that by this time the parties would have cooled off and reasonable counsels would prevail. It implied that war is a product of momentary emotions rather than more enduring causes.

This doubtful proposition led some Americans to lampoon the program as a typical product of a pacifist and prohibitionist—"Grape Juice

Diplomacy." But Bryan during 1913 and 1914 got "cooling-off" treaties with thirty governments, including Great Britain and France. No treaties were made between foreign countries, and Germany refused to make a treaty with the United States. Although Bryan always believed he had made a great contribution to peace, neither the outbreak of war among the European powers in 1914 nor the conflict between the United States and Germany was affected by his treaties.

On a concrete issue of considerable sensitiveness, the Wilson administration showed that it did place reason and honor above emotion and self-interest. Congress, in August 1912, had exempted American-owned ships making coastwise voyages from payment of tolls on the nearly-finished Panama Canal. The British Foreign Office strongly protested this as a violation of the Hay-Pauncefote Treaty of 1901 which guaranteed equal tolls for ships of all nations. Irish-American Democrats led the demand to defy Britain, and the Roosevelt Progressives were not far behind. The Democratic platform of 1912 supported the exemption. Wilson approved it during the campaign. After his inauguration, however, he decided that the British were in the right. He did not make an issue of the question until after Congress had enacted his initial program of domestic reforms. Then on March 5, 1914, he personally delivered to Congress a message requesting repeal of the exemption. He said that the United States was "too big, too powerful, too self-respecting a Nation" to insist on its own interpretation of its promises. This was the authentic note of Wilsonian idealism and it gained the day when the Senate voted to repeal on June 11, 1914. Whether Wilson had obtained from Britain a promise to support his policy in Mexico in return for repeal of the Canal tolls exemption is not entirely clear. But the incident ended the last in a long series of Anglo-American disputes just a few weeks before the beginning of the World War. It won prestige for Wilson in Europe as a moral leader capable of admitting his own and his country's error and rectifying it—in profound contrast to the behavior of the leaders of other nations that fateful summer.

Wilson and Bryan tried also to conciliate the Japanese government but did not succeed quite so well. Japanese pride was offended by a movement in California to prevent Japanese residents from owning land. The movement was supported by both Democratic and Progressive Republican politicians, and Wilson did not oppose it. He only suggested that a restrictive law be phrased so as to offend Japan as little as possible and avoid overt violation of the Japanese-American treaty of Amity and Commerce of 1911. He doubted whether the treaty power of the federal government supersedes state authority over land ownership. He sent Secretary Bryan to plead with the California lawmakers for moderation, but, in May 1913, they defiantly passed a bill denying landownership to persons "ineligible to citizenship"—which could only mean Japanese.

The anger of Japanese nationalists made war seem possible. The United States Joint Board of the Army and the Navy recommended naval dispositions to defend the Philippines, but Wilson forbade any action. The Japanese government proposed a new treaty strengthening the mutual guarantee of landowning rights, and Wilson and Bryan agreed to negotiate such a treaty when political conditions permitted. Repeated postponement by the United States led Japan to withdraw the proposal, in order to avoid humiliation. Anti-Americanism remained strong among the sensitive Japanese—the first nonwhite people to build a modern nation—and it plagued relations between the two countries when they faced the crises of the First World War.

SELECT BIBLIOGRAPHY

General Statement

READING IN MORE DETAILED WORKS CAN ENORMOUSLY ENRICH AND ENLIVEN the story which is inevitably compressed in a book like this; and original sources can provide a vividness of impression that secondary narratives rarely convey. Part of the continuing appeal of historical study arises from the fact that there is always something more which anybody can learn about the past and that the closer one gets to the actual people and events the more vivid and real they become. To some extent every student can become an explorer in his own right, and in the investigation of some appealing topic can taste the joy of discovery.

The purpose of the present bibliography is to acquaint the student and reader with the most useful aids—stress being laid on those that are most accessible—and, without making any pretence of exhaustiveness, to mention selected books which can be read to advantage and sources which can be explored with relative ease. Comments are frequently attached—sometimes as a sort of warning but more often as an invitation to particular items in the historical feast.

First, there is a relatively brief list of works bearing on the whole or most of this volume; then, both general and specific suggestions are given chapter by chapter. These can be richly supplemented from the bibliographical items and suggestions in many of the listed books.*

Basic Reference Works

The most important single bibliographical aid is the *Harvard Guide to American History* (1954) edited by Oscar Handlin. Besides excellent chapters on the materials and tools of American history and convenient lists of books in various categories, it contains suggestions for reading on the various periods and topics which go far beyond any that can be given here.

Every historical shelf should have the *Encyclopedia of American History* (1953), edited by R. B. Morris, a handy volume which is invaluable for facts and dates. The arrangement is both chronological and topical.

Among the larger reference works with which students should familiarize themselves is the *Dictionary of American Biography* (20 vols., 1928-36), edited by Allen Johnson and Dumas Malone; supplementary volumes edited by H. E. Starr (1944), and R. L. Schuyler (1958). This co-operative work provides rich personal materials for the whole of American history. A good way to turn mere names into real persons is to look them up in this collection of articles. Those desiring to read further will find suggestions in the bibliogra-

* The introductory part of this Bibliography repeats, with some omissions and additions, the corresponding section of the Bibliography for Books I-III.

phies. (A selected list of biographies is given in the *Harvard Guide*, pp. 190-206).

The *Dictionary of American History* (5 vols., 1940), edited by J. T. Adams, is abridged in *Concise Dictionary of American History* (1962), edited by Wayne Andrews. The *Encyclopedia of the Social Sciences* (15 vols., 1930-34), edited by E. R. A. Seligman, is a work of much wider scope.

Fascinating statistical materials can be found in the publications of the Bureau of the Census, *A Century of Population Growth . . . 1790-1900* (1909), and *Historical Statistics of the U.S., Colonial Times to 1957: A Statistical Abstract Supplement* (1960). The *Biographical Directory of the American Congress, 1774-1949* (1950), is a big and awkward but useful volume. Besides giving the lists of members of the successive Congresses (and also of executive officers), it contains brief biographical sketches.

Good maps are of the first importance. Two older collections have not yet been excelled for general historical use: W. R. Shepherd, *Historical Atlas* (1911), which deals with Europe as well as America; and *Harper's Atlas of American History* (1920), consisting of maps from the old *American Nation* series. Later school atlases of wide use include: C. E. and E. H. Lord, *Historical Atlas of the United States* (1944); and J. T. Adams, *Atlas of American History* (1943). The fullest and most authoritative work is C. O. Paullin, *Atlas of the Historical Geography of the United States* (1932), edited by J. K. Wright. While too big and cumbersome for frequent use, this is valuable for boundary disputes and other matters of concern to advanced students and specialists.

Much work has been done in making old and recent pictures available. The first extensive modern compilation was *The Pageant of America* (15 vols., 1926-29), edited by R. H. Gabriel. The *Harvard Guide*, pp. 65-66, has a list of later general collections. Some works of special value dealing with particular periods or subjects will be referred to hereafter at appropriate points. Naturally, pictorial records became more accurate as well as more extensive with the development of photography, but the older paintings and prints often convey a delightful sense of their own day.

Convenient Collections of Documents and Readings

The best general collection of documents in convenient form and a strong contender for any historian's bookshelf is *Documents of American History* (7 edn., 1963), edited by H. S. Commager. Besides official documents, this contains party platforms, important speeches, etc. It can be supplemented by L. B. Evans, *Cases on American Constitutional Law*, revised edition by C. G. Fenwick (1948); and by *Cases in Constitutional Law*, by Robert E. and Robert F. Cushman (1958), both of which are fuller in a more limited field. Treaties and diplomatic documents can be best consulted in R. J. Bartlett, ed., *The Record of American Diplomacy* (1950), a book which should stand on the shelf with Commager.

A rich collection of readings bearing especially on social and intellectual matters is *American Issues*, Vol. I, "The Social Record" (rev. edn., 1955), edited by Willard Thorp, Merle Curti, and Carlos Baker. Another good collection, which is more economic and political in emphasis, is *The Shaping of the American Tradition* (1947), edited by L. M. Hacker, whose relatively long introductions are illuminating and provocative. The older and less accessible work, G. S. Callender, ed., *Selections from the Economic History of the United States, 1765-1868* (1909), contains, besides readings, brief but unusually penetrating introductions which comprise a summary of economic history.

The Making of American History (rev. edn., 1954), edited by Donald Sheehan, is an anthology which contains 35 long extracts from historical writers dealing with major topics. Some of these will be specifically referred to hereafter. *Understanding the American Past* (1954), edited by E. N. Saveth, is a similar work.

Problems in American Civilization: Readings Selected by the Department of American Studies, Amherst College (1947- to date) comprise a useful series of paper-bound booklets. Each deals with a particular topic and contains selections from authors with varying views. Somewhat more than a dozen have been issued to date and they offer one of the best methods of studying controversial questions. Individual booklets will be mentioned hereafter.

Larger General Histories

Every student and serious reader should become acquainted with major long histories and series, and should dip into them to some extent. The present list is confined to works or sets covering the whole or most of American history.

The Chronicles of America (50 vols., 1918-21), edited by Allen Johnson, comprise an unusually readable series of small volumes which inevitably vary in quality. Six supplementary volumes (1950-51), edited by Allan Nevins, carry the story to 1945.

A History of American Life (13 vols., 1927-48), edited by A. M. Schlesinger and D. R. Fox, is the standard series for social history. The bibliographies are excellent.

The old series, *The American Nation: A History* (26 vols., 1904-08; additional vol., 1918), edited by A. B. Hart, has a distinguished position in American historiography and certain volumes are still of great value. *The New American Nation Series*, edited by H. S. Commager and R. B. Morris, to comprise about 40 vols., is in process. The volumes are of a handy size and contain full and up-to-date bibliographies.

A History of the South, edited by W. H. Stephenson and E. M. Coulter (1947-   ), projected in 10 vols., of which 3 fall in the period after 1865, is an admirable series, now almost done. The bibliographies are detailed and comprehensive.

Topical Histories

GEOGRAPHY AND ABORIGINES

There is need for a readable work on American historical geography in convenient size. The two following books are useful for reference: J. R. Smith and M. O. Phillips, *North America* (rev. edn., 1940), a lengthy regional treatment of the United States, Canada, and Central America; R. H. Brown, *Historical Geography of the United States* (1948), a sound work, following the order of settlement. Rachel Carson, *The Sea around Us* (1951), is fascinating. An excellent account of the Indians is R. M. Underhill, *Red Man's America* (1953); important documents are in *The Indian and the White Man*, edited by W. E. Washburn (1964).

SETTLEMENT AND IMMIGRATION

Most general works pay attention to the process of settlement. Specialized studies are O. A. Winther, *The Transportation Frontier* (1964) and R. W. Paul, *Mining Frontiers* (1963). A comprehensive book is R. A. Billington, *Westward Expansion: A History of the American Frontier* (1949), dealing with transportation and land policies. *The Frontier in America* (1921), a collection of essays by F. J. Turner, is a classic.

The larger problems of immigration are illuminated by M. L. Hansen, *The Immigrant in American History* (1941), edited by A. M. Schlesinger and J. F. Kennedy, *A Nation of Immigrants* (1959) by a future President. A good general treatment is Carl Wittke, *We Who Built America: The Saga of the Immigrant* (1939).

ECONOMIC AND FINANCIAL HISTORY

Among general economic histories in one volume are H. U. Faulkner, *American Economic History* (8 edn., 1959); E. C. Kirkland, *A History of American Economic Life* (3 edn., 1951); F. A. Shannon, *America's Economic Growth* (rev. edn., 1951), and Robert R. Russel, *A History of the American Economic System* (1964). The older and more restricted works, D. R. Dewey, *Financial History of the United States* (12 edn., 1934), and F. W. Taussig, *Tariff History of the United States* (7 edn., 1923) are still useful handbooks.

INTELLECTUAL HISTORY

Merle Curti, in *The Growth of American Thought* (2 edn., 1951), covers the whole period systematically and has unusually valuable bibliographies for his chapters. V. L. Parrington, *Main Currents in American Thought* (3 vols., 1927-30), is a highly stimulating work and a delight to read, even when one disputes the author's judgment. R. H. Gabriel, *The Course of American Democratic Thought* (2 edn., 1956), deals admirably with the period after 1815.

LITERARY HISTORY

Abundant materials are available in R. E. Spiller and others, *Literary History of the United States* (3 vols., 1948), the third volume of which is an elaborate bibliography; and A. H. Quinn, ed., *The Literature of the American People* (1951).

LABOR

F. R. Dulles, *Labor in America* (1949), is a convenient general treatment. J. R. Commons *et al.*, *History of Labor in the United States* (4 vols., 1918-1935), is rich in materials on the later nineteenth and early twentieth centuries.

CONSTITUTIONAL HISTORY AND PARTIES

For general use the best works on their subject are C. B. Swisher, *American Constitutional Development* (1943); and A. H. Kelly and W. A. Harbison, *The American Constitution: Its Origins and Development* (1948). A. C. Mc-Laughlin, *A Constitutional History of the United States* (1935) becomes less valuable after the early national period. W. E. Binkley, *American Political Parties: Their Natural History* (3 edn., 1958), is a good survey.

DIPLOMACY

General treatments are: J. W. Pratt, *A History of United States Foreign Policy* (1955); S. F. Bemis, *A Diplomatic History of the United States* (rev. edn., 1950); T. A. Bailey, *A Diplomatic History of the American People* (7 edn., 1964); Alexander De Conde, *History of American Foreign Policy* (1963); R. W. Leopold, *Growth of American Foreign Policy* (1962), emphasizing the period since 1889. Anyone wishing to inquire into the activities of some particular man should see S. F. Bemis, ed., *The American Secretaries of State and Their Diplomacy* (10 vols., 1927-29); Vol. XI, edited by R. H. Ferrell (1963), is the first of 6 additional volumes.

RELIGION, SCIENCE, AND EDUCATION

General treatments are disappointing, but the following works are useful: W. W. Sweet, *The Story of Religion in America* (rev. edn., 1939); D. J. Struik, *Yankee Science in the Making* (1948); E. P. Cubberly, *Public Education in the United States* (rev. edn., 1934); E. E. Slosson, *The American Spirit in Education* (1921, *Chronicles of America*). M. E. Curti, *Social Ideas of American Educators* (1935), is excellent. Richard Hofstadter and Wilson Smith, eds., *American Higher Education: A Documentary History* (1961), is basic. J. W. Smith and A. L. Jamison, eds., *Religion in American Life*, Vols. I, II, IV (1961), is a significant contribution.

ARCHITECTURE AND ART

The main lines of development are shown in T. F. Hamlin, *The American Spirit in Architecture* (1926); T. F. Tallmadge, *The Story of Architecture in America* (rev. edn., 1936); W. C. Andrews, *Americans, Ambition and Architecture* (1955); Samuel Isham, *The History of American Painting*, supplemented by Royal Cortissoz (1927); and O. W. Larkin, *Art and Life in America* (1949).

MILITARY AND NAVAL

The fruitfulness of scholarship in this field is best shown in specialized studies. General works do not yet fully reflect it, but the following are useful: W. A. Ganoe, *A History of the United States Army* (1942); O. L. Spaulding, *The United States Army in War and Peace* (1937); D. W. Knox, *A History of the United States Navy* (rev. edn., 1948); H. H. and Margaret Sprout, *The Rise of American Naval Power, 1776-1918* (1939). The old army textbook, M. F. Steele, *American Campaigns* (2 vols., last edn., 1922), is still helpful.

Part I. The Era of Reconstruction, 1865–1877

General

This list for the era as a whole is followed by more specific suggestions for particular chapters.

NARRATIVES, CHIEFLY POLITICAL

W. A. Dunning, *Reconstruction: Political and Economic, 1865-1877* (1907, *American Nation*), requires supplementation in the light of later studies and changed attitudes but is still an excellent account of political events. J. F. Rhodes, *History of the United States*, covers the period in Vols. V-VII. With Dunning, this work set the tone of historical interpretation for a generation. J. G. Randall, in *The Civil War and Reconstruction* (1937), Chs. 30-37, is concise and judicious, but hardly as good as on the Lincoln era. C. G. Bowers, *The Tragic Era* (1929) is readable but reflects the anti-Republican partisanship of its author. R. S. Henry, *The Story of Reconstruction* (1938), is more reliable, though less vivid.

ECONOMIC AND SOCIAL

Allan Nevins, *The Emergence of Modern America, 1865-1878* (1927, *History of American Life*), is an admirable supplement to the political histories and has a full bibliography. T. C. Cochran and William Miller, *The Age of Enterprise: A Social History of Industrial America* (1942), covers a longer period and is therefore much less detailed for this one. V. S. Clark, *The History of Manufactures in the United States* (3 vols., 1929), is a standard work but is largely factual. D. R. Dewey, *Financial History of the United States*, is invaluable for this period and later ones. With respect to Western developments, the same can be said for R. A. Billington, *Westward Expansion*, and F. L. Paxson, *History of the American Frontier* (1924).

1. RECONSTRUCTION OF THE UNION

Special

INTERPRETATIONS OF RECONSTRUCTION

The interpretation associated with the name of Dunning was perpetuated and elaborated by his students at Columbia, who wrote monographs on many individual southern states. The most important of these, along with others, are listed in the bibliography of E. M. Coulter, *The South during Reconstruction, 1865-1877* (1947, Vol. VIII of *A History of the South*), a full-bodied work that is essentially in the Dunning tradition. Adherents of Dunning have laid great emphasis on the political aspects and political motivation of Radical Reconstruction; to them the Congressional policy has appeared as virtually unmitigated folly, resulting in chaos. Revisionist trends are well described in H. K. Beale, "On Rewriting Reconstruction History," *American Historical Review*, XLV (1939-40), 807-827. One major trend, shown notably by C. A. and Mary Beard in *The Rise of American Civilization* (1927, one-volume edition, 1930), Ch. 18, has been towards a greater economic emphasis. The Beards describe the Civil War and Reconstruction as "The Second American Revolution," leading to the complete dominance of the Northern economic system. This concept has been taken over by a number of historians, including Southerners. Another recent tendency, also marked among Southerners, has been to recognize that there were some enduring social gains in the South itself, and to attempt to do fuller justice to the freedmen. The interpretation of events in the terms of class struggle, however, by W. E. B. DuBois, in *Black Reconstruction: An Essay toward a History of the Part which Black Folk Played in the Attempt to Reconstruct Democracy, 1860-1880* (1935), is extreme, and that of F. S. Allen, *Reconstruction: The Battle for Democracy, 1865-1876* (1937), is more so. To Negro historians the Dunning tradition is unacceptable; their position is stated moderately by J. F. Franklin in *Reconstruction After the Civil War* (1961). One of the best-balanced accounts by a Southern historian is that of F. B. Simkins in *History of the South* (1963), chs. 16-19; see also his "New Viewpoints of Southern Reconstruction" in *Jour. of Sou. History*, Feb. 1939.

NATIONAL POLITICS AND POLITICIANS

G. F. Milton, *The Age of Hate: Andrew Johnson and the Radicals* (1930), is one of several books tending to resuscitate Johnson. H. K. Beale, *The Critical Year: A Study of Andrew Johnson and Reconstruction* (1930), emphasizes the part played by economic forces in Johnson's political defeat. See also D. M. DeWitt, *The Impeachment and Trial of Andrew Johnson* (1903). Among helpful biographical works are R. N. Current, *Old Thad Stevens* (1942); W. B. Hesseltine, *Ulysses S. Grant, Politician* (1938); Stewart Mitchell, *Horatio Seymour of New York* (1938). E. L. Pierce, *Memoir and Letters of Charles Sumner* (4 vols., 2 edn., 1894), is extensive but uncritical. The development of Congressional policy and the interplay of Congressional personalities are illuminated by *The Journal of the Joint Committee of Fifteen on Reconstruction* (1914), edited by B. B. Kendrick. See also P. S. Pierce, *The Freedmen's Bureau* (1904). E. L. McKitrick, *Andrew Johnson and Reconstruction* (1960), and La Wanda and J. H. Cox, *Politics, Principle, and Prejudice, 1865-1866* (1963), reflecting a current trend, are critical of Johnson.

CONSTITUTIONAL DEVELOPMENTS

These are of great importance and are dealt with in the general constitutional histories of Swisher, Kelly and Harbison, and McLaughlin, as they are in Charles Warren, *The Supreme Court in United States History*, II, Chs. X, XX, XXXII; and most critically in Louis Boudin, *Government by Judiciary*, II (1932), Ch. XII. More specialized studies include: H. E. Flack, *The Adoption of the Fourteenth Amendment* (1909), with which may be coupled W. A. Dunning, *Essays on the Civil War and Reconstruction* (1904), and J. W. Burgess, *Reconstruction and the Constitution* (1902).

THE SOUTH DURING RECONSTRUCTION

The fullest over-all description is that of Coulter. Among many contemporary accounts, that of A. W. Tourgee, *A Fool's Errand, by One of the Fools* (enlarged edn., 1880), reflects the point of view of a frustrated Radical; while that of J. S. Pike, *The Prostrate State: South Carolina under Negro Government* (reprint, 1935), is probably the best-known picture of the abuses of Radical government. S. D. Smedes, *Memorials of a Southern Planter* (1887) is a classic account. Edmund Wilson, *Patriotic Gore* (1962) is brilliant analysis of leaders and misleaders. The undoing of Reconstruction is described in S. F. Horn, *Invisible Empire: The Story of the Ku Klux Klan, 1866-1871* (1939); and the older work by J. C. Lester and D. L. Wilson, *Ku Klux Klan* (1905), which some prefer. On education see H. L. Swint, *The Northern Teacher in the South, 1862-1870* (1941), and E. W. Knight, *The Influence of Reconstruction on Education in the South* (1913).

COLLECTIONS OF SOURCES

The indispensable sourcebook, full of human interest as well as important documents, is W. L. Fleming, *Documentary History of Reconstruction: Political, Military, Social, Religious, Educational, and Industrial* (2 vols., 1906-07). The older and more limited work of Edward McPherson, *The Political History of the United States of America during the Period of Reconstruction* (1875), is still useful.

2. POSTWAR ECONOMIC EXPANSION

Special

RAILROADS

John Moody, *The Railroad Builders* (1919, *Chronicles of America*) is brief and popular. R. H. Holbrook, *The Story of the American Railroads* (1947), and R. E. Riegel, *The Story of the Western Railroads* (1926), are good general accounts. See also L. R. Hafen, *The Overland Mail, 1849-1869* (1929); and Edward Hungerford, *Wells Fargo* (1947). The biographies of the great railroad builders in their epic age are generally disappointing, and the wise procedure would be to start with the articles in the *Dictionary of American Biography.* C. F. and Henry Adams, *Chapters of Erie* (1871) is a classic exposé.

INDUSTRY

Ida M. Tarbell, *The History of the Standard Oil Company* (2 vols., 1904) reflects the mood of the muckraking era in which the book was written. Allan Nevins, in *John D. Rockefeller: The Heroic Age of American Enterprise* (2 vols., 1940) is more favorable. P. H. Giddens, in *The Birth of the Oil Industry* (1938), covers the early years. A violent contemporary attack on monopolies, especially Standard Oil, is H. D. Lloyd, *Wealth against Commonwealth* (1894). B. J. Hendrick, *The Life of Andrew Carnegie* (2 vols., 1932) is full and well written though rather uncritical. *The Autobiography of Andrew Carnegie* (1920), edited by J. C. Van Dyke, reveals the philosophy of the man. E. C. Kirkland, *Industry Comes of Age . . . 1860-1897* (1961), is a good general account.

Finance and Currency

D. R. Dewey, *Financial History of the United States* can be supplemented by A. D. Noyes, *Forty Years of American Finance* (1909) and more specialized studies. The currency will be covered more fully hereafter. On the Greenbacks, see A. B. Hepburn, *History of the Currency* (1915), Chs. 12, 14. Charles Fairman's admirable study, *Mr. Justice Miller and the Supreme Court* (1939), deals with the legal-tender cases, along with many other questions which the constitutional histories treat in less detail.

Westward Movement

The general accounts in Billington, *Westward Expansion,* and Paxson, *History of the American Frontier,* can be richly supplemented by more detailed studies. One of the most striking of these is W. P. Webb, *The Great Plains* (1931); a selection from this, "The Cattle Kingdom," is reprinted in Sheehan, *The Making of American History,* pp. 443-478. Over against this should be set a work by one of Webb's major critics, F. A. Shannon, *The Farmer's Last Frontier: Agriculture, 1860-1897* (1945). Everett Dick, in *The Sod-House Frontier, 1854-1890* (1937), describes the common life. Its drudgery and its heroism are nowhere better related than in the autobiographical work of Hamlin Garland, *A Son of the Middle Border* (1917). Other useful works are J. C. Malin, *The Grasslands of North America* (1948); Lewis Atherton, *The Cattle Kings* (1961); R. W. Paul, *Mining Frontiers of the Far West, 1848-1880* (1963). For government land policy, see R. M. Robbins, *Our Landed Heritage: The Public Domain, 1776-1936* (1942).

3. FOREIGN AFFAIRS AND NATIONAL POLITICS

Special

Foreign Affairs

Fuller than the accounts in the general diplomatic histories of Bailey, Bemis, and Pratt are the treatments of Seward and Fish in S. F. Bemis, *American Secretaries of State and Their Diplomacy,* Vol. VII. Invaluable for both foreign and domestic matters is Allan Nevins, *Hamilton Fish: The Inner History of the Grant Administration* (1936). Among scholarly treatments of particular questions are: V. J. Farrar, *The Annexation of Russian America to the United States* (1937); Goldwin Smith, *The Treaty of Washington* (1941); William D'Arcy, *The Fenian Movement in the United States, 1858-1886* (1947); L. B. Shippee, *Canadian-American Relations, 1849-1874* (1939); C. C. Tansill, *The United States and Santo Domingo, 1798-1873* (1938).

DOMESTIC POLITICS

Few comments on the public scene are more penetrating, and none are more devastating, than those in *The Education of Henry Adams* (1918); see especially Ch. 17 on President Grant. The biography by the younger C. F. Adams of his father, *Charles Francis Adams* (1900), has value for both foreign and domestic affairs. *The Reminiscences of Carl Schurz* (3 vols., 1907-08) include in Vol. III an account by Frederick Bancroft and W. A. Dunning of the distinguished career of this frustrated public man. J. G. Blaine, *Twenty Years in Congress* (2 vols., 1884-86), is colorful like the man himself, and like him must be viewed critically. The corruption of the era is vividly depicted in the cartoons of Thomas Nast. These can be seen in the files of *Harper's Weekly*, edited by G. W. Curtis, the civil service reformer; see the years 1869-1872 for the crusade against the Tweed Ring. For his entire career, see A. B. Paine, *Thomas Nast: His Period and His Pictures* (1904). Special political studies of value include E. D. Ross, *The Liberal Republican Movement* (1919); and F. E. Haynes, *Third Party Movements* (1916). See also the pertinent chapters in the old but still useful work, C. R. Fish, *The Civil Service and the Patronage* (1904).

4. THE END OF AN ERA

Special

POLITICAL EVENTS, 1876-1877

These receive considerable attention in the general histories, and in biographies such as C. R. Williams, *The Life of Rutherford Birchard Hayes* (2 vols., 1914); and C. C. Flick, *Samuel Jones Tilden* (1939). These books and P. L. Haworth, *The Hayes-Tilden Disputed Election* (1906; rev. edn., 1927), should be supplemented by C. V. Woodward, *Reunion and Reaction: The Compromise of 1877 and the End of Reconstruction* (1951), which throws new light, chiefly economic, on the motives of both parties to the compromise. See also L. B. Richardson, *William E. Chandler, Republican* (1940).

THE REDEEMERS AND SOUTHERN HOME RULE

C. V. Woodward's, *Origins of the New South, 1877-1913* (1951, Vol. IX of *A History of the South*) supersedes all previous accounts. Chs. 1-3 bear directly on these events, and the work can be consulted profitably about all phases of Southern life in the generation after Reconstruction. The sensitive study of reconciliation by P. H. Buck, *The Road to Reunion* (1937), deals with the development of the romantic tradition of the plantation by literary men. See also the pioneer work of F. P. Gaines, *The Southern Plantation: The Development and Accuracy of a Tradition* (1924); R. B. Nixon, *Henry W. Grady: Spokesman of the New South* (1943); and, for the lingering tradition of plantation gentility in the twentieth century, the beautiful book of W. A. Percy, *Lanterns on the Levee: Recollections of a Planter's Son* (1941). A study of unusual interest and poignancy is H. M. Jarrell, *Wade Hampton and the Negro: The Road Not Taken* (1949).

CULTURE

Further suggestions for reading in literature and the arts and in the history of thought are given in connection with Chapter 10, which covers a much richer period. See also the admirable bibliographies for Chs. 19-20 of Curti's *The Growth of American Thought*. Works of particular interest here are Frank Freidel, *Francis Lieber* (1947); Bernard DeVoto, *Mark Twain's America* (1932); Lewis Mumford, *The Brown Decades* (1932); and the early chapters in Parrington, *Main Currents in American Thought*, Vol. III. The postwar period begins with Ch. 11 in F. R. Dulles, *America Learns to Play: A History of Popular Recreation, 1607-1940* (1940). Among many works bearing on the significant developments in higher education the following are specially commended: D. C. Gilman, *Launching a University* (1906); W. A. Neilson, *Charles W. Eliot: The Man and His Beliefs* (1926), which is more illuminating than the formal biography by Henry James, *Charles W. Eliot* (2 vols., 1930); Andrew D. White, *Autobiography* (2 vols., 1915). J. W. Draper, *History of the Conflict between Religion and Science* (1874) is significant as a pioneer work; A. D. White, *A History of the Warfare of Science with Theology* (2 vols., 1906) is fuller. The controversial subject of Christian Science can be approached through the article on Mary Baker Eddy in the *Dictionary of American Biography*; though far from satisfactory to Christian Scientists, it is more restrained than other widely circulated accounts by persons outside the fold, such as E. F. Dakin, *Mrs. Eddy* (rev. edn., 1930). S. C. Cole, *The History of Fundamentalism* (1931) is useful.

Part II. The Triumph of Business, 1877-1900

General

NARRATIVES, CHIEFLY POLITICAL

J. F. Rhodes, *History of the United States from Hayes to McKinley* (1919), is supplementary to his seven volumes on the years from 1850 to 1876. H. J. Ford, *Cleveland Era* (1919), is more superficial than Nevins' biography of the Democratic President. Matthew Josephson, *The Politicos, 1865-1896* (1938), emphasizes the unedifying aspects of the political history.

ECONOMIC AND SOCIAL

A. M. Schlesinger, *The Rise of the City, 1878-1898* (1933, *History of American Life*), is indispensable. See also E. C. Kirkland, *Industry Comes of Age* (1961) and C. N. Glaab, *The American City* (1963). T. C. Cochran and William Miller. *The Age of Enterprise: A Social History of Industrial America* (1942) is brilliant and objective. Samuel Hays, *The Response to Industrialism, 1885-1914* (1957) is a brief and excellent interpretation. Matthew Josephson, *The Robber Barons: The Great American Capitalists, 1861-1901*

(1934), is not objective but it is entertaining. The muckraking study by Gustavus Myers, *History of the Great American Fortunes* (3 vols., 1910), has value but should be balanced against more temperate authorities. The evolution of many historians' views on the rise of Big Business may be traced by comparing two works by L. M. Hacker: *The Triumph of American Capitalism* (1940), and *American Capitalism: Its Promise and Accomplishment* (1957).

5. THE LEADERSHIP OF INDUSTRY

Special

TRUSTS

Early treatments which remain useful are A. S. Dewing, *Corporate Promotions and Reorganizations* (1914); W. Z. Ripley, *Trusts, Pools, and Corporations* (1916); J. W. Jenks and W. E. Clark, *The Trust Problem* (5th edn., 1929); and Eliot Jones, *The Trust Problem in the United States* (1921). Ida Tarbell abandoned the muckraker's stance in *The Nationalizing of Business, 1878-1898* (1936, *History of American Life*), and *The Life of Elbert H. Gary: The Story of Steel* (1925). Allan Nevins revised his biography of Rockefeller in *Study in Power: John D. Rockefeller: Industrialist and Philanthropist* (2 vols., 1953). The details of Standard Oil Company history are in R. W. and M. E. Hidy, *Pioneering in Big Business, 1882-1911: History of the Standard Oil Company (New Jersey)* (1955). Allan Nevins, *Abram S. Hewitt: With Some Account of Peter Cooper* (1935) is an interesting introduction to the steel industry. Later stages of the story of steel are in the candid *Autobiography of Andrew Carnegie;* Tarbell's *Gary;* Abraham Berglund, *The United States Steel Corporation* (1907); Lewis Corey's critical study, *The House of Morgan* (1930); and F. L. Allen's admiring biography, *The Great Pierpont Morgan* (1949).

RAILROADS

The best account of the climactic years of consolidation is E. G. Campbell, *The Reorganization of the American Railroad System, 1893-1900* (1938). Corey's *House of Morgan* illuminates the techniques of financial control. Works by an early expert are W. Z. Ripley, *Railroads: Rates and Regulation* (1915), and *Railroads: Finance and Organization* (1915). The role of railroads in opening up the West is described in R. C. Overton, *Burlington West: A Colonization History of the Burlington Railroad* (1941), and J. G. Pyle, *The Life of James J. Hill* (2 vols., 1917). A subject often neglected is well treated in C. R. Fish, *The Restoration of the Southern Railroads* (1919). J. B. Hedges, *Henry Villard and the Railroads of the Northwest* (1930), is a work of scholarly merit. Further aspects of consolidation are detailed in George Kennan, *E. H. Harriman* (2 vols., 1922).

Electricity

Attractive accounts of the new uses of electric power are in the collection edited by W. B. Kaempffert, *Popular History of American Inventions* (2 vols., 1924); a handy survey is Holland Thompson, *The Age of Invention* (1921, *Chronicles of America*). The articles on Alexander Graham Bell and Theodore N. Vail in the *Dictionary of American Biography* should be consulted. Horace Coon, *American Tel and Tel* (1939), is a good example of the modern vogue for corporation histories.

The Fourteenth Amendment and the Supreme Court

Special studies of the difficult and important question of the origins of the Amendment are: H. J. Graham, "The 'Conspiracy Theory' of the Fourteenth Amendment," *Yale Law Review*, XLVII and XLVIII (1938); L. B. Boudin, "Truth and Fiction About the Fourteenth Amendment," *New York University Law Review* (1938); A. C. McLaughlin, "The Court, the Corporation, and Conkling," *American Historical Review* (1940); and Jacobus tenBroek, *The Antislavery Origins of the Fourteenth Amendment* (1951). For judicial interpretation of the Amendment during this period, see appropriate chapters in the constitutional histories by Swisher, Kelly and Harbison, and McLaughlin. Perhaps the clearest account of individual decisions of the Supreme Court is in Charles Warren, *The Supreme Court in United States History* (Vol. III, 1922). Also useful is H. C. Hockett, *The Constitutional History of the United States* (2 vols., 1939). Individual jurists may be studied in C. B. Swisher, *Stephen J. Field: Craftsman of the Law* (1930), and Charles Fairman, *Mr. Justice Miller and the Supreme Court* (1939).

6. LABOR AND IMMIGRATION

Special

Depression and Violence, 1873-1877

The great strikes of this and later periods are described in Samuel Yellen, *American Labor Struggles* (1936). Norman Ware, *The Labor Movement in the United States, 1860-1895* (1929), deals thoroughly with the organizational efforts of labor. A key figure in this stage of the story is well presented in J. P. Grossman, *William Sylvis* (1945). J. W. Coleman's study, *The Molly Maguire Riots* (1936), reads like a detective story.

Labor Begins to Organize

To supplement accounts of the Knights of Labor in general labor histories, the autobiographies of their leader should be consulted: T. V. Powderly, *Thirty Years of Labor* (1889), and *The Path I Trod* (1940), the latter edited by H. J. Carman and others. A revealing account of the impact of the Haymarket Riot is Everett Carter, "The Haymarket Affair in Literature," *American Quar-*

terly, II (1950), 270. The Governor of Illinois explained his position in J. P. Altgeld, *Reasons for Pardoning* (1893). Samuel Gompers, *Seventy Years of Life and Labor* (2 vols., 1925), is an outstanding document. C. A. Madison, *American Labor Leaders* (1950), offers the radical view of Gompers and others.

TURMOIL OF THE NINETIES

The Homestead Strike and other violent episodes in labor history are dealt with in Louis Adamic, *Dynamite* (1931). George Harvey is sympathetic to his subject in *Henry Clay Frick* (1928). An extraordinarily vivid impression of the anarchists and one of their firebrands may be gained from Emma Goldman, *Living My Life* (2 vols., 1931). Almont Lindsay, *The Pullman Strike* (1942) is a thorough treatment. Ray Ginger, *The Bending Cross: A Biography of Eugene Victor Debs* (1949 is valuable not only on Debs but on unionism and socialism in general. Cleveland defended his action in the Pullman Strike in *The Government in the Chicago Strike of 1894* (1913), while Altgeld is defended in H. Barnard, *Eagle Forgotten: The Life of John Peter Altgeld* (1938). The "armies" of unemployed are described in D. L. McMurry, *Coxey's Army* (1929). The ideas of Edward Bellamy are studied in A. E. Morgan, *The Philosophy of Bellamy* (1945), and equivalent service is performed by G. R. Geiger in *The Philosophy of Henry George* (1931).

THE NEW IMMIGRANTS

The best authority is Oscar Handlin. In *The Uprooted* (1951), he breaks new ground by bringing psychological and sociological insights to bear upon the immigrants themselves. See also the same author's collection of materials, *Immigration as a Factor in American History* (1959). Attitudes of earlier immigrants to the newcomers are thoroughly explored in John Higham, *Strangers in the Land* (1955). R. L. Garis, *Immigration Restriction* (1927), covers the story of legislation. Among the many studies of particular groups the following are specially valuable: Jerome Davis, *The Russian Immigrant* (1922); Thomas Capek, *The Czechs in America* (1920); B. J. Hendrick, *The Jews in America* (1923); R. F. Foerster, *The Italian Emigration of Our Times* (1919); H. P. Fairchild, *Greek Immigration to the United States* (1911); and W. I. Thomas and F. Znaniecki, *The Polish Peasant in Europe and America* (5 vols., 1918-1920). Herman Feldman, *Racial Factors in American Industry* (1931), is revealing on the exploitation of national antagonisms among the immigrants. The American Protective Association can be studied in H. J. Desmond, *The A.P.A. Movement* (1912). Carey McWilliams, in *A Mask for Privilege: Anti-Semitism in the United States* (1948), writes as a member of the generation that was appalled by Hitlerism.

7. THE POLITICS OF BUSINESS, 1877-1890

Special

HAYES ADMINISTRATION

The best biography is H. J. Eckenrode, *Rutherford B. Hayes: Statesman of Reunion* (1930). Herbert Agar, *The Price of Union* (1950), contains penetrating analyses of politics during these and later years. D. B. Chidsey, *The Gentleman from New York: A Life of Roscoe Conkling* (1935), is a fairly objective account of a key figure. An early proponent of silver may be studied in W. V. Byars, *An American Commoner: The Life and Times of Richard Parks Bland* (1900). John Sherman, *Recollections of Forty Years* (2 vols., 1895), is useful.

GARFIELD AND ARTHUR ADMINISTRATIONS

R. G. Caldwell, *James A. Garfield: Party Chieftain* (1931), and G. F. Howe, *Chester A. Arthur* (1934), supplement the articles in the *Dictionary of American Biography*. D. S. Muzzey, *James G. Blaine* (1934), is the best biography of any politician of these years. Civil service reform and mugwumpery are illuminated in C. M. Fuess, *Carl Schurz: Reformer* (1932). See also C. R. Fish, *The Civil Service and the Patronage*. A. F. Tyler, *The Foreign Policy of James G. Blaine* (1927), is comprehensive.

THE FIRST CLEVELAND ADMINISTRATION

Allan Nevins, *Grover Cleveland: A Study in Courage* (1932) is invaluable for understanding of the man and of both his terms as President. Ida M. Tarbell, *The Tariff in Our Times* (1911), is excellent on Cleveland's revival of the issue. H. S. Drinker, *The Interstate Commerce Act* (1909), treats the early years of that law. W. D. Puleston, *Mahan* (1939), is especially good on Mahan's influence on naval policy. Mahan's own writings are cumbersome in style, but the effort to read his seminal book, *The Influence of Sea Power upon History, 1660-1783* (1890), will be rewarded. Bailey, *Diplomatic History*, gives an entertaining account of early relations with Samoa and Hawaii.

THE HARRISON ADMINISTRATION

On pensions, see J. W. Oliver, *History of the Civil War Military Pensions* (1917). N. W. Stephenson, *Nelson W. Aldrich: A Leader in American Politics* (1930), is objective on this powerful Senator. Dewey, *Financial History*, contains the best account of the monetary issue. To Sherman's *Recollections* may be added the biography, T. E. Burton, *John Sherman* (1906). Early years of the Sherman Anti-Trust Act are described in A. H. Walker, *The Sherman Law* (1910). No adequate full-length biography of Harrison has appeared.

8. THE REBELLIOUS FARMERS, 1873-1892

Special

GRIEVANCES OF THE FARMERS

The general economic histories of Faulkner, Kirkland, and Shannon can be profitably consulted on this subject. E. L. Bogart, *Economic History of American Agriculture* (1923), is not entirely out of date. Shannon, *The Farmer's Last Frontier: Agriculture, 1860-1897*, is excellent. Special regions and crops may be studied in M. E. Jarchow, *The Earth Brought Forth* (1949), on Minnesota; E. D. Ross, *Iowa Agriculture* (1951); C. V. Woodward, *Origins of the New South;* J. C. Malin, *Winter Wheat in Kansas* (1944); Dorothy Giles, *Singing Valleys* (1940), on corn; and J. C. Robert, *Story of Tobacco* (1949). Preoccupation with economic matters should not obscure the intensely human dimension of the farm problem. Insight into this can be obtained in no better way than by reading some of the many excellent literary works it inspired. Hamlin Garland, *A Son of the Middle Border*, Willa Cather, *My Ántonia* (1918), and Ole Rolvaag, *Giants in the Earth* (1927), are superb.

THE GRANGES AND THE FARMERS' ALLIANCES

S. J. Buck, *The Granger Movement* (1913), is authoritative, and the same author's *Agrarian Crusade* (1921) carries the story of farmers' organizations into later stages. C. C. Taylor, *Farmers' Movement* (1953), is a recent synthesis.

BEGINNINGS OF POPULISM

J. D. Hicks, *The Populist Revolt* (1955, originally published in 1931), is definitive. Nathan Fine, *Labor and Farmer Parties in the United States, 1828-1928* (1928) is particularly good on the Populists. Iowa serves F. E. Haynes as a laboratory for his study, *Third Party Movements Since the Civil War* (1916). Among numerous biographical works on the Populist leaders the following are specially interesting: F. B. Simkins, *Pitchfork Ben Tillman, South Carolinian* (1944); C. V. Woodward, *Tom Watson: Agrarian Rebel* (1938); F. E. Haynes, *James B. Weaver* (1919); and J. D. Hicks, "The Political Career of Ignatius Donnelly," *Mississippi Valley Historical Review*, VIII, 80.

9. FROM POPULISM TO HIGH REPUBLICANISM

Special

Many of the titles recommended for the two preceding chapters continue to be valuable for this one. Hicks, *The Populist Revolt*, and Nevins, *Grover Cleveland*, are of first importance.

SECOND CLEVELAND ADMINISTRATION

A special study of value is G. H. Knoles, *The Presidential Campaign and Election of 1892* (1942). The best book on the Panic of 1893 is F. B. Weberg, *The Background of the Panic of 1893* (1929). Sidney Ratner, *American Taxation* (1941), is good on the income-tax feature of the Wilson-Gorman Tariff Act and its invalidation by the Supreme Court.

ELECTION OF 1896

W. E. Binkley, *American Political Parties* (1943), contains a brilliant analysis of inner-party factions and sectional alignments in this election campaign. S. L. Jones, *Presidential Election of 1896* (1964) is a fine study. Richard Hofstadter, in *The Age of Reform* (1955), adds a new social-psychological dimension. H. D. Croly, *Marcus Alonzo Hanna* (1912), rescued this business-man-turned-politician from the muckrakers and cartoonists. M. R. Werner, *Bryan* (1929), is popular; Paxton Hibben, *Peerless Leader* (1929), is more analytical. The atmosphere of the Free Silver crusade should be sampled in W. H. Harvey, *Coin's Financial School* (1894).

MCKINLEY AND THE HIGH REPUBLICANS

C. S. Olcott, *Life of William McKinley* (2 vols., 1916) is useful but dull. Interesting portraits of this President are found in W. A. White, *Masks in a Pageant* (1928), by the famous Kansas editor, and in Josephson, *The Politicos*. Croly's *Hanna* is indispensable. The sketches of Mr. Dooley by Finley Peter Dunne, originally published in newspapers and later collected in many volumes, provide incomparable satirical humor on public affairs. For this period, see F. P. Dunne, *Mr. Dooley in Peace and in War* (1899). A fine new biography is Margaret Leech, *In the Days of McKinley* (1959).

10. THE BEGINNINGS OF CRITICAL REALISM

Special

THOUGHT, FROM SOCIAL DARWINISM TO PRAGMATISM

This subject has claimed the attention of some of the most talented American historians. H. S. Commager, *The American Mind* (1950), is designed to complete the vast canvas which V. L. Parrington did not live to finish. The latter's third volume, *The Beginnings of Critical Realism in America, 1860-1920*, under the general title *Main Currents in American Thought* (3 vols. in one, 1930), contains little more than the author's notes. Its weakness is that it confuses standards of criticism, identifying liberal-reformist ideas with literary excellence. Richard Hofstadter, *Social Darwinism in American Thought* (rev. edn., 1955), is a brilliant example of the new emphasis on the history of ideas by the younger generation of historians. M. G. White, *Social Thought in America* (1949), an excellent survey, actually concentrates upon this period. Valuable for its exposition of relationships between ideas and politics is E. F. Goldman, *Rendezvous with Destiny* (1952). Daniel Aaron, *Men of Good Hope* (1951), is a penetrating study of leading personalities. Excerpts from the writings of outstanding thinkers of the period are readily available in *American Thought: Civil War to World War I* (1954), with a notable introduction by the editor, Perry Miller. The course of sociologists' thought is illuminated in Charles Page, *Class and American Sociology: From Ward to Ross* (1940). Outstanding studies of individuals are R. B. Perry, *The Thought and Charater of William James* (2 vols., 1935); Samuel Chugerman, *Lester F. Ward: The American Aristotle* (1939); C. A. Barker, *Henry George* (1955); and W. H. Jordy, *Henry Adams: Scientific Historian* (1952). A collection of writings on the frontier thesis is in *The Turner Thesis Concerning the Role of the Frontier in American History* (1949), edited by G. R. Taylor. But reading about these seminal thinkers should never preclude exploration of their own writings, the most important of which, with dates of original publication, are mentioned in the text.

A QUARTER-CENTURY OF LITERATURE

Alfred Kazin, *On Native Grounds* (1942), is the best history of American literature since 1890. Van Wyck Brooks, *New England: Indian Summer* (1940), and *The Confident Years: 1885-1915* (1952), are warm-hearted evocations of literary life. On Emily Dickinson, G. F. Whicher, *This Was a Poet* (1938), and Genevieve Taggard, *The Life and Mind of Emily Dickinson* (1930), are more rewarding than the "official" biography by M. D. Bianchi, *Life and Letters of Emily Dickinson* (1924). The study by Van Wyck Brooks, *The Ordeal of Mark Twain* (1920), stressing his "frustration," should be compared with Bernard DeVoto, *Mark Twain's America* (1932) and L. J. Budd, *Mark Twain: Social Philosopher* (1963). The most brilliant short criticism of *Huckleberry Finn* is the introduction to an English edition (Cresset Press, London, 1950) by Twain's fellow Missourian, T. S. Eliot. L. J. Edel, *Henry James: The Untried Years: 1843-1870* (1953), is the masterly first volume of a biography-in-progress. Quentin Anderson, *The American Henry James* (1957), explores the influence of his father's ideas on the novelist, and argues that the latter was never expatriated spiritually. Van Wyck Brooks, *The Pilgrimage of Henry James* (1925), is a famous study. F. O. Matthiessen, *Henry James: The Major Phase* (1946), is the best study of James's last novels. D. G. Cooke, *William Dean Howells* (1922), is the standard biography. John Berryman, *Stephen Crane* (1950), is excellent.

THE ARTS TO THE CHICAGO EXPOSITION

John Maass, *The Gingerbread Age* (1957), is amusing. E. R. and J. Pennell, *Life of James McNeill Whistler* (1919), should be supplemented with Whistler's loving exposition of his own temperament in *The Gentle Art of Making Enemies* (1890). Lloyd Goodrich, *Thomas Eakins* (1933), is authoritative on the great painter. Useful biographies are W. H. Downes, *The Life and*

Works of Winslow Homer (1911), and F. F. Sherman, *Albert P. Ryder* (1920). On architecture, prevailing taste may be studied in a book by the leading critic of the period: Montgomery Schuyler, *American Architecture* (1892). Larkin, *Art and Life in America,* is particularly good on the Chicago School and the World's Fair, while Wayne Andrews, *Americans: Ambition and Architecture* (1955), is brilliant on the plutocrats' dream of architectural grandeur. H. R. Hitchcock, *The Architecture of H. H. Richardson and His Times* (1936), is a model study. L. H. Sullivan, *Autobiography of an Idea* (1924), is a prime source on the great Chicago ancestor of modern architects. See also Sullivan, *Kindergarten Chats on Architecture, Education, and Democracy* (1934). J. M. Fitch, *American Building: The Forces That Shaped It* (1948), is an important interpretation.

Part III. Imperialism and Progressivism, 1896-1917

General

The best general survey of the period is in two excellent volumes of *The New American Nation Series*: G. E. Mowry, *The Era of Theodore Roosevelt, 1900-1912* (1958), and A. S. Link, *Woodrow Wilson and the Progressive Era, 1910-1917* (1954). H. U. Faulkner, *The Decline of Laissez Faire, 1897-1917* (1951), deals with economic and social history, and the same author, in *The Quest for Social Justice, 1898-1914* (1931), broke new ground in depicting the Progressive Movement. The fads and fancies of the American people are entertainingly recorded by a journalist, Mark Sullivan, in *Our Times: The United States, 1900-1925* (6 vols., 1926-1935).

11. THE EMERGENCE OF AN IMPERIAL POWER

Special

THE NEW EXPANSIONISM, HAWAII

J. W. Pratt, in *Expansionists of 1898* (1936), gives a masterly account of the ideas that inspired the new expansionism. He disproves the contention that businessmen as a group favored war with Spain. E. R. May, *Imperial Democracy: The Emergence of America as a Great Power* (1961), is specially good on European attitudes. A. K. Weinberg, in *Manifest Destiny* (1935), dissects the ideas embodied in this phrase. Dexter Perkins, in *The Monroe Doctrine, 1867-1907* (1937), traces the imperialists' use and misuse of the Doctrine. S. K. Stevens, *American Expansion in Hawaii, 1842-1898* (1945), and R. S. Kuykendall and A. G. Day, *Hawaii* (1948), provide broad historical backgrounds. On Cleveland's Hawaiian policy, see Nevins, *Grover Cleveland.* S. B. Dole, *Memoirs of the Hawaiian Revolution* (1936), is by the president of the short-lived republic.

Latin America and the Monroe Doctrine

To Muzzey's *Blaine*, and the works of Perkins and Nevins cited above, should be added S. F. Bemis. *The Latin American Policy of the United States* (1943). The Olney Note is expertly interpreted by G. B. Young, in "Intervention under the Monroe Doctrine," *Political Science Quarterly*, LVII (1942).

Cuban Crisis and the Spanish-American War

L. H. Jenks, *Our Cuban Colony* (1928), emphasizes the development of American interests in the island. Pratt, *Expansionists of 1898*, is authoritative on American opinion. J. E. Wisan, *The Cuban Crisis as Reflected in the New York Press* (1934), describes the exploitation of the crisis by newspapers. The role of leading imperialists may be explored in Puleston, *Mahan*, H. F. Pringle, *Theodore Roosevelt* (1931), and C. G. Bowers, *Beveridge and the Progressive Era* (1932). *The Letters of Theodore Roosevelt* (8 vols., 1951-1954), edited by E. E. Morison and J. M. Blum, are invaluable for this and later periods. Important themes are well handled in H. K. Beale, *Theodore Roosevelt and the Rise of America to World Power* (1956), and G. C. O'Hara, *Theodore Roosevelt and the Rise of the Modern Navy* (1943). The Spanish-American War is described, not unjustly, in the spirit of comedy by Walter Millis in *The Martial Spirit* (1931), and with lavish illustrations in Frank Freidel, *The Splendid Little War* (1958). R. S. West, *Admirals of American Empire* (1948), is authoritative on Dewey and other commanders. The Spanish side of the struggle is illuminated in Orestes Ferrara, *The Last Spanish War* (1937).

The Triumph of Imperialism and the Colonial Experiment

The transformation of American opinion in midwar is made clear in Pratt, *Expansionists of 1898*. F. E. Chadwick, *The Relations of the United States and Spain: The Spanish American War* (Vol. II, 1911), details the negotiation of the peace treaty. Agitation against an American empire is described in two articles by F. H. Harrington: "The Anti-Imperialist Movement in the United States, 1898-1900," *Mississippi Valley Historical Review* (1935), and "Literary Aspects of American Anti-Imperialism, 1898-1902," *New England Quarterly* (1937). W. M. Calcott, in *The Caribbean Policy of the United States, 1890-1920* (1942), surveys the Cuban problem in the context of the development of policy towards the Isthmus and the Caribbean area as a whole. J. W. Pratt, *America's Colonial Experiment* (1950), is the best history of the subject.

China and the Open Door

F. R. Dulles, in *America's Rise to World Power, 1898-1954* (1955), studies the general problem of United States efforts to assume the responsibilities of a world power. The ideas that inspired American policy are richly set forth in R. E. Osgood, *Ideals and Self-Interest in America's Foreign Relations: The*

Great Transformation of the Twentieth Century (1953). Osgood argues that such commitments as the Open Door were dangerously unrealistic, and his book is the most valuable historical study by a member of the school of "realist" critics of American foreign policy headed by Hans J. Morgenthau at the University of Chicago. An excellent account of the immediate circumstances of the Open Door Notes is in A. W. Griswold, *The Far Eastern Policy of the United States* (1938). Tyler Dennett, *Americans in Eastern Asia* (1922), tells the fascinating story of contacts with the Orient, and incidentally demonstrates that the Open Door was no sudden revolution in United States policy. The same author's *John Hay: From Poetry to Politics* (1933), is an expert biography of this important Secretary of State.

12. THEODORE ROOSEVELT'S SQUARE DEAL

Special

ROOSEVELT AND THE PRESIDENCY

To H. F. Pringle, *Theodore Roosevelt* (1931), should be added the penetrating interpretation by J. M. Blum, *The Republican Roosevelt* (1954), and the brilliant chapter on Roosevelt in Richard Hofstadter, *The American Political Tradition and the Men Who Made It* (1948), and W. H. Harbaugh, *The Life and Times of Theodore Roosevelt* (1961). Roosevelt's *Autobiography* (1913) is wonderfully expressive of the spirit of the man. Next to Roosevelt himself, probably no one enjoyed his presidency more than newspaper cartoonists. Their work is assembled in a vivid book by Albert Shaw, *A Cartoon History of Roosevelt's Career* (1910). P. C. Jessup, *Elihu Root* (2 vols., 1938), is a learned biography of an important Cabinet member.

GOVERNMENT AND BUSINESS

The best history of the Roosevelt and Taft administrations is Mowry, *The Era of Theodore Roosevelt*. It analyzes carefully the evolution of Roosevelt's views and policies. B. H. Meyer, *A History of the Northern Securities Case* (1906), supplements treatments in general works. H. B. Thorelli, *Federal Antitrust Policy* (1955), is particularly good on the prosecutions by the Roosevelt administration. A. E. Suffern, *Conciliation and Arbitration in the Coal Industry in America* (1915), is useful for Roosevelt's role in settling the anthracite strike. Also helpful is Edward Berman, *Labor Disputes and the President of the United States* (1924).

CONSERVATION

Gifford Pinchot, *Breaking New Ground* (1947), tells the striking story of the most conspicuous conservationist. B. H. Hibbard, *A History of Public Land Policies,* is best on reclamation. Broader in scope are H. W. Fairbanks, *Conservation Reader* (1920), and C. R. Van Hise and Loomis Havemeyer, *Conservation of Natural Resources in the United States* (1930).

The Muckrakers

C. C. Regier, *The Era of the Muckrakers* (1932) is the standard work, but the student should not overlook the books by the muckrakers themselves which are mentioned in the text. An exceptionally fine work is Lincoln Steffens, *Autobiography* (1931), valuable for the accounts of the muckraking movement and of the author's disillusionment with reform. William Allen White, *Autobiography* (1946), is an important document by one who did not lose his faith in democracy. Novels by Brand Whitlock, *The Thirteenth District* (1902); Theodore Dreiser, *The Financier* (1912), and *The Titan* (1914); Winston Churchill (not to be confused with the eminent British statesman, Sir Winston S. Churchill), *Coniston* (1906); Booth Tarkington, *The Turmoil* (1915); and W. A. White, *A Certain Rich Man* (1909) reflect the muckraking spirit. Louis Filler, *Crusaders for American Liberalism* (1939), contains a good account of the movement.

Roosevelt's Second Term

To the works already mentioned by and about Roosevelt should be added two which are especially good on later stages of his career: G. E. Mowry, *Theodore Roosevelt and the Progressive Movement* (1947), and Lewis Einstein, *Roosevelt: His Mind in Action* (1930). R. M. La Follette, *Autobiography* (1913), contains a sharp analysis of Roosevelt's tendency to compromise as well as a valuable account of the prewar career of his eminent rival for leadership of the Progressive forces. F. L. Allen, *The Lords of Creation* (1935), is very readable on business leaders. The same author's *Morgan,* and Lewis Corey, *House of Morgan* (1934), contain important accounts of the financier's role in the Panic of 1907.

13. IMPERIALISM AND DOLLAR DIPLOMACY, 1901-1913

Special

The Panama Canal

Gerstle Mack, *The Land Divided* (1944), and D. C. Miner, *The Fight for the Panama Route* (1940), are authoritative. L. M. Gelber, *The Rise of Anglo-American Friendship* (1938), deals well with a much misunderstood topic. Philippe Bunau-Varilla, *Panama: The Creation, Destruction, and Resurrection* (1914), less than candid, is nevertheless an important source.

The Roosevelt Corollary

Dexter Perkins, *The Monroe Doctrine, 1867-1907,* is supplemented by the same author's fine study of general policy, *The United States and the Caribbean* (1947). A muckraking account of American business interests in the Caribbean area and elsewhere, which fails to show that these interests played a significant role in the formulation of United States policy, is Scott Nearing and Joseph Freeman, *Dollar Diplomacy* (1925).

The Far East

A. W. Griswold, *The Far Eastern Policy of the United States* (1938), is the best general account. Tyler Dennett, *Roosevelt and the Russo-Japanese War* (1925), tells the official story of the Portsmouth Conference, while Eleanor Tupper and G. E. McReynolds, in *Japan in American Public Opinion* (1937), reveal the transformation wrought by Japanese victories. T. A. Bailey, *Theodore Roosevelt and the Japanese-American Crisis* (1934), is first-rate on the immigration and segregation episodes as well as the cruise of the Great White Fleet. Much insight into Far Eastern affairs as they concerned the United States during these years is found in Herbert Croly, *Willard Straight* (1924).

Europe

J. B. Brebner, *The North Atlantic Triangle* (1945), is masterly on this as on other periods of Anglo-Canadian-American relations; he places the story in the setting of the German threat. Allan Nevins, in *Henry White* (1930), describes the Algeciras Conference from the viewpoint of the senior American delegate. European views are revealed in E. N. Anderson, *The First Moroccan Crisis, 1904-1906* (1930). J. B. Scott, *The Hague Peace Conferences of 1899 and 1907* (1909), was written without benefit of essential sources. More recent studies which emphasize American hopes are Merze Tate, *The Disarmament Illusion* (1942), and M. E. Curti, *Peace or War: The American Struggle, 1636-1936* (1936).

Dollar Diplomacy

The best general account of diplomacy during the Taft administration is the essay by H. F. Wright, "Philander Chase Knox," in *American Secretaries of State and Their Diplomacy*, IX (1929), edited by S. F. Bemis. Croly, *Willard Straight,* is indispensable on Dollar Diplomacy. B. H. Williams, *Economic Foreign Policy of the United States* (1929), is more trustworthy than Nearing and Freeman, *Dollar Diplomacy*. Griswold, *Far Eastern Policy* and Bemis, *Latin American Policy,* are the best surveys.

The Mexican Revolution

J. F. Rippy, *The United States and Mexico* (1931), contains lurid details of events in Mexico and the activities of Ambassador H. L. Wilson. *The United States and Mexico* (1953), by H. F. Cline, is excellent.

Canadian Reciprocity

The story of the failure of the Taft administration in this episode is found in L. E. Ellis, *Reciprocity, 1911* (1939).

Arbitration Treaties

W. S. Holt, *Treaties Defeated by the Senate* (1933), illustrates the Senate's use of its power over foreign relations on this and other occasions.

14. THE PROGRESSIVES AND PRESIDENT TAFT

Special

THE PROGRESSIVE MOVEMENT

This subject receives the major attention of Richard Hofstadter, in *The Age of Reform* (1955), and no other book analyzes the Progressive Movement so profoundly. E. F. Goldman, *Rendezvous with Destiny* (1952), is a rich collection of details on Progressivism. John Chamberlain, *Farewell to Reform* (1932), stresses the limitations of the movement as viewed during the Great Depression. Key statements of Progressive doctrine by contemporaries are Herbert Croly, *The Promise of American Life* (1909), Walter Lippmann, *Preface to Politics* (1913) and *Drift and Mastery* (1914), W. E. Weyl, *The New Democracy* (1912), and Woodrow Wilson, *The New Freedom* (1913). On special topics see R. C. Brooks, *Corruption in American Politics* (1910); J. D. Barnett, *Operation of the Initiative, Referendum, and Recall in Oregon* (1915); Tao-Shuen Chang, *History and Analysis of Commission and City Manager Plans* (1918); C. W. Patton, *The Battle for Municipal Reform* (1940); Jacob Riis, *How the Other Half Lives* (1890) and *The Battle with the Slums* (1902); John Spargo, *The Bitter Cry of the Children* (1906); E. C. Stanton, *History of Woman Suffrage* (6 vols., 1881-1922); Eleanor Flexner, *Century of Struggle* (1959), the best short history of the woman's rights movement; and P. H. Douglas, *Real Wages in the United States: 1890-1926* (1930). Good studies of Progressivism on the state level are: G. E. Mowry, *The California Progressives* (1951); R. E. Noble, *New Jersey Progressivism before Wilson* (1946); E. N. Doan, *The La Follettes and the Wisconsin Idea* (1947); R. S. Maxwell, *La Follette and the Rise of the Progressives in Wisconsin* (1956); and W. A. Flint, *The Progressive Movement in Vermont* (1941). R. B. Nye, *Midwestern Progressive Politics* (1951), emphasizes municipal reform. A convenient collection is *The Progressive Movement*, edited by R. Hofstadter (1963). The following are valuable: M. J. Pusey, *Charles Evans Hughes* (2 vols., 1951); E. A. Fitzpatrick, *McCarthy of Wisconsin* (1944); Tom Johnson, *My Story* (1911); F. C. Howe, *Confessions of a Reformer* (1925); Morris Hillquit, *Loose Leaves from a Busy Life* (1934); and Brand Whitlock, *Forty Years of It* (1913). The reformer as a type is pictured in Arthur Mann, *Yankee Reformers in the Urban Age* (1954), Louis Filler, *Crusaders for American Liberalism* (1950), and A. M. Schlesinger, *The American as Reformer* (1950).

THE TAFT ADMINISTRATION AND DOMESTIC AFFAIRS

The authoritative biography is H. F. Pringle, *The Life and Times of William Howard Taft* (2 vols., 1939). In his book, *The Presidency* (1916), Taft gives his own views. See also R. W. Leopold, *Elihu Root and the Conservative Tradition* (1954). K. W. Hechler, *Insurgency: Personalities and Politics of the Taft Era* (1940), is particularly good on the rebellion of the Progressives. On the Payne-Aldrich Tariff, see Taussig, *Tariff History*, and Stephenson,

Nelson W. Aldrich. On Cannonism, see Chang-Wei Chiu, *The Speaker of the House of Representatives Since 1898* (1928), and on Cannon himself, Blair Bolles, *Tyrant From Illinois* (1951). A special study of great value is A. T. Mason, *Bureaucracy Convicts Itself: The Ballinger-Pinchot Controversy of 1910* (1941). Pinchot defended himself in *The Fight for Conservation* (1910).

ELECTION OF 1912

General works on the period and biographies and autobiographies of leaders already cited illuminate many sides of the struggle of 1912. To them should now be added the first volume of the brilliant biography of Woodrow Wilson by A. S. Link, *The Road to the White House* (1947), which carries the subject to his election. Wilson's *The New Freedom* conveys the quality of his mind and rhetoric. A. T. Mason, *Brandeis* (1946), reveals an important source of Wilson's ideas. Champ Clark, *My Quarter Century of American Politics* (2 vols., 1920), and W. J. Bryan, *A Tale of Two Conventions* (1912), are important sources on Democratic Party politics.

15. ECONOMIC AND SOCIAL LIFE IN THE NEW CENTURY

Special

MASS PRODUCTION FOR THE MASS MARKET

Siegfried Giedion, in *Mechanization Takes Command* (1948), analyzes decisive steps in the technology of mass production. A. F. Burns, in *Production Trends since 1870* (1934), discusses components of prosperity during this period. Arundel Cotter, *Authentic History of the United States Steel Corporation* (1916), and J. W. Hammond, *Men and Volts: The Story of General Electric* (1941), deal with two key corporations. D. L. Cohn, *Combustion on Wheels* (1944), is an entertaining account of the automobile; E. D. Kennedy, *The Automobile Industry* (1941), is perhaps the best study of its manufacture. Among the many biographies of Henry Ford, several of varying views may be selected: W. C. Richards, *The Last Billionaire* (1948), W. A. Simonds, *Henry Ford* (1943), and K. T. Sward, *The Legend of Henry Ford* (1948). The most scholarly work, based on Ford's papers, is Allan Nevins and F. E. Hill, *Ford* (2 vols., 1954). An expert treatment of the building and financing of automobile roads is F. L. Paxson, "The Highway Movement," *American Historical Review*, LI (1946). For aviation, the Wright brothers tell their own story in engrossing fashion in *Miracle at Kitty Hawk: The Letters of Wilbur and Orville Wright*, edited by F. C. Kelly (1951); this supplements Kelly's *The Wright Brothers* (1943). See also Jeremiah Milbank, Jr., *The First Century of Flight in America: An Introductory Survey* (1943). Paul Schubert, in *The Electric World: The Rise of Radio* (1928), describes the beginnings of wireless transmission.

LABOR RADICALISM

Contemporary expositions of labor problems are found in Robert Hunter, *Poverty* (1904), John Ryan, *A Living Wage* (1906), L. B. More, *Wage Earners' Budgets* (1907), F. H. Streightoff, *The Standard of Living among Industrial People* (1911), T. C. McMahon, *Women and Economic Revolution* (1912), and W. J. Lauck and Edgar Sydenstricker, *Conditions of Labor in American Industries* (1917). D. H. Grover, *Debaters and Dynamiters* (1964) is the story of the sensational Haywood trial. The connection between labor exploitation and the turn to socialism is illustrated in two books by John Spargo: *The Bitter Cry of the Children* (1906), and *Socialism* (1910). D. J. Saposs, *Left Wing Unionism* (1926), details the efforts to tie American trade unionism to radicalism in politics. P. F. Brissenden, *I.W.W.* (1919), was written at the moment of the Wobblies' defeat. Morris Hillquit, *History of Socialism in the United States* (1910), is a text by a leader of the Socialist Party. Essays in *Socialism and American Life* (2 vols., 1952), edited by D. D. Egbert and Stow Persons, deal with every variety of socialism, and the bibliography in the second volume is exhaustive. Theodore Draper's description of the "Old Left" in *The Roots of American Communism* (1957), is brilliant on radicalism at the end of this period and the effects on it of the Russian Bolshevik Revolution. Ray Ginger, *The Bending Cross: Debs* (1949), is the best biography of the most important American Socialist. Ira Kipnis, *The American Socialist Movement* (1952), D. A. Shannon, *The Socialist Party of America: A History* (1955), R. E. Riegel, *American Feminists* (1963), are useful.

THE PLUTOCRACY

Dixon Wecter, *The Saga of American Society* (1937), is the only attempt to survey the history of the social élite. The files of *Town and Country* magazine provide vivid images of the efforts of the plutocrats to become aristocrats; the centenary history of this organ of Society is Basil Rauch, "The First Hundred Years," *Town and Country* (December 1946). The continuing self-sufficiency of the Boston Brahmins is amusingly portrayed by Cleveland Amory, *The Proper Bostonians* (1947), and with irony in the novel by J. P. Marquand, *The Late George Apley* (1937). Amory also describes the decline of the plutocrats and their playgrounds in *The Last Resorts* (1948). The effort of millionaires to amass collections of Old Masters and other art objects is entertainingly told in A. L. Saarinen, *The Proud Possessors* (1959). Nevins, *Rockefeller*, contains the best account of the oil magnate's philanthropies, particularly the establishment of the foundations. Very interesting new gound is broken by Merle Curti, *American Philanthropy Abroad* (1963). In a class by himself, as a critical intelligence significant of his time but never "typical" of it, is the descendant of Presidents, Henry Adams. Ernest Samuels is writing a splendid multivolume biography of which *The Young Henry Adams* (1948), and *Henry Adams: The Middle Years* (1958), have appeared. An attractive short biography is Elizabeth Stevenson, *Henry Adams* (1956). H. D. Cater's collection of letters, *Henry Adams and His Friends* (1947), places one in a brilliant circle. But none of these books should be allowed to supersede Adams' own masterpiece, *The Education of Henry Adams*.

16. THE TRIUMPHS OF PRAGMATISM

Special

PHILOSOPHY

No better introduction to the life and work of John Dewey can be suggested than the collection of essays, *The Philosophy of John Dewey* (1951), edited by P. A. Schilpp, containing favorable as well as adverse criticisms of Dewey's thought by a number of distinguished philosophers; it begins with a biographical sketch by his daughter Jane M. Dewey, and ends with an important reply to his critics by Dewey himself. The bibliography of Dewey's writings found in this volume will lead the student into further readings.

EDUCATION

M. E. Curti, *The Social Ideas of American Educators* (1935), reveals the centrality of Dewey's ideas in the ferment of modern thought on education.

ECONOMICS

Joseph Dorfman, *Thorstein Veblen and His America* (1934), is a magisterial biography of this original thinker. David Riesman, *Thorstein Veblen* (1953), is an interesting brief interpretation. Even the student without special training in economics will gain much by reading Veblen's own writings. A good selection and introduction are found in *What Veblen Taught* (1936), edited by W. C. Mitchell. A. F. Burns, *Wesley Clair Mitchell* (1952), is a biography of Veblen's chief follower by a student of Mitchell who became economic adviser to President Eisenhower.

LAW

The beautiful prose of Justice Holmes makes the reading of his opinions a pleasure. They are conveniently collected in *Dissenting Opinions of Mr. Justice Holmes* (1929), edited by Alfred Lief (1929). His mind and spirit can be apprehended in his correspondence with a distinguished British jurist, *The Holmes-Pollock Letters*, edited by M. D. Howe (2 vols., 1941). Max Lerner has edited a collection of writings, *The Mind and Faith of Justice Holmes* (1943). An attractive novelized biography is C. D. Bowen, *Yankee From Olympus* (1944). A. T. Mason, *Brandeis: A Free Man's Life* (1946), supersedes in most respects Alfred Lief, *Brandeis: The Personal History of an American Ideal* (1936). The thought of Brandeis can best be studied in *The Social and Economic Views of Mr. Justice Brandeis* (1930), edited by Lief. Excellent recent studies of legal realism and sociological jurisprudence are

K. S. Carlston, *Law and Structures of Social Action* (1946), and A. D. Smith, *The Right to Life* (1955).

HISTORY

C. A. Beard's *Economic Interpretation of the Constitution* has recently been subjected to searching criticism even with respect to its factual data by R. E. Brown, *Charles Beard and the Constitution* (1956). See also *Charles A. Beard: An Appraisal* (1954), edited by H. K. Beale. Beard's rejection of the ideal of objectivity was set forth by him in "That Noble Dream," *American Historical Review*, XLI (1935). J. H. Robinson, *The New History* (1912), is the manifesto of the movement bearing that name, and M. G. White, *Social Thought in America*, contains a fine account of it. H. H. Bellot, *American History and American Historians* (1952), a general survey, is particularly valuable for this period. A good special study of Beard and Carl Becker is Cushing Strout, *The Pragmatic Revolt in American History* (1958).

ANTHROPOLOGY

A splendid brief introduction to the life and work of the great anthropologist is M. J. Herskovits, *Franz Boas: The Science of Man in the Making* (1953). Boas's epochal study for the Senate Commission on Immigration, *Changes in Bodily Form of Descendants of Immigrants* (Senate Document 208, 61st Congress, 2nd Session, 1911), was reprinted in 1912. His findings on race were summarized by him in the article "Race," *Encyclopedia of the Social Sciences*. A good survey of the history of sociological thought during these years is Page, *Class and American Sociology: From Ward to Ross*. R. U. Dugdale's famous study of delinquency in one family, *The Jukes* (1895), encouraged believers in heredity, although Dugdale himself did not neglect the influence of environment. Margaret Sanger, *An Autobiography* (1938), is an important document of the movement for birth control.

PSYCHOLOGY

A. A. Roback, *History of American Psychology* (1952), is specially good on behaviorism. C. P. Oberndorf, *A History of Psychoanalysis in America* (1953), is an interesting study in the migration of ideas. Oscar Cargill, *Intellectual America: Ideas on the March* (1941), contains an excellent account of the early influence of Freud's ideas in America. F. J. Hoffman, *Freudianism and the Literary Mind* (1945), is concerned chiefly with the spread of Freudianism among American writers.

MEDICINE AND SCIENCE

Abraham Flexner, *I Remember* (1940), tells the story of reform of medical education. Two useful works are Albert Deutsch, *The Mentally Ill in America: A History of Their Care and Treatment from Colonial Times* (1937), and H. E. Sigerist, *American Medicine* (1934). Benjamin Harrow, *Vitamins* (1921), describes this important American discovery. Paul De Kruif, *Microbe*

Hunters (1926), is a melodramatic account of scientists' discoveries. Bernard Jaffe, *Men of Science in America* (1944), and D. J. Struik, *Yankee Science in the Making* (1948), are interesting.

FERMENT IN RELIGION

W. W. Sweet, *The Story of Religion in America* (1939) should be supplemented by the chapters on the Social Gospel in R. H. Gabriel, *The-Course of American Democratic Thought* (rev. edn., 1956), and E. F. Goldman, *Rendezvous with Destiny* (·1952). C. H. Hopkins, *The Rise of the Social Gospel in American Protestantism, 1865-1915* (1940), is the standard work. J. A. Ryan, *Social Doctrine in Action* (1941), is the autobiography of the Catholic priest who led the fight to apply in America the "Social Gospel" doctrines of the Encyclical *De Rerum Novarum* by Pope Leo XIII. Essays in *Reform Judaism* (1949), edited by B. J. Bamberger, indicate the relation between this movement and the Social Gospel. S. G. Cole, *History of Fundamentalism* (1931), is authoritative. William Elliott, *Life of Father Hecker* (1891), treats the founder of the Paulist Fathers in Chicago, whose eagerness to accommodate Catholicism to Americanism caused a controversy which was settled by an Apostolic letter from Pope Leo XIII to Cardinal Gibbons. A fountainhead of medievalism among American Roman Catholics is J. J. Walsh, *The Thirteenth, Greatest of Centuries* (1920). Theodore Maynard, *American Catholicism* (1941), is the standard survey. The chief agency of anti-Catholicism is studied in H. J. Desmond, *The A.P.A. Movement* (1912). David Philipson, *The Reform Movement in Judaism* (1931), is still useful. Good new studies are W. S. Hudson, *American Protestantism* (1960), N. Glazer, *American Judaism* (1962), and J. T. Ellis, *American Catholicism* (1963).

17. THE BIRTH OF MODERNISM IN THE ARTS

General

The best survey of prose literature during the period is Kazin, *On Native Grounds*. G. C. Knight, *The Strenuous Age in American Literature* (1954), explores the first decade of the century. The third volume of Spiller *et al.*, *Literary History of the United States*, contains extensive bibliographical material on leading authors of poetry and prose. J. D. Hart, *The Oxford Companion to American Literature* (1956), is remarkably complete, containing factual data on minor as well as major writers, schools, movements, magazines, and related topics. A new survey of the culture of the period is Henry May, *The End of American Innocence* (1959). Louis Filler, *Randolph Bourne* (1943), is a provocative study of a leader of thought.

Special

THE NOVEL OF NATURALISM

Matthew Josephson, *Zola and His Time* (1928), discusses the influence of European writers on the American Naturalists. Kazin, *On Native Grounds,* brilliantly contrasts Edith Wharton and Theodore Dreiser. Ernest Marchand, *Frank Norris: A Study* (1942), is the most recent biography. Irving Stone, *Sailor on Horseback: The Biography of Jack London* (1938), is colorful and objective. The slow growth of Theodore Dreiser's reputation is a fascinating study which may be traced in essays on him listed in Spiller, *Literary History*, Vol. III. Upton Sinclair's autobiography, *American Outpost: A Book of Reminiscences* (1932), is revealing. Best-selling novels of this and other periods are entertainingly discussed in F. L. Mott, *Golden Multitudes* (1947).

THE REBELS OF POETRY

Stirrings of new tendencies in literature may be apprehended in the autobiographies of J. G. Huneker, *Old Fogy* (1913), and *Steeplejack* (1920); H. L. Mencken, *Newspaper Days* (1941), and *Heathen Days* (1943); Floyd Dell, *Homecoming* (1933); and Harriet Monroe, *A Poet's Life* (1937). Horace Gregory and Marya Zaturenska, *History of American Poetry* (1946), is excellent on the beginnings of the modern movement. Developments in Chicago are elaborately set forth in B. I. Duffey, *The Chicago Renaissance* (1954). One of the Chicago poets wrote discriminatingly on another in E. L. Masters, *Vachel Lindsay: A Poet in America* (1935). Carl Sandburg's memoir, *Always the Young Strangers* (1953), is a wonderful account of his youth in a Swedish working-class family. A major gap in the history of modern American literature is the absence of biographical material on T. S. Eliot. Writings on his poetry and criticism are already enormous. The best of these is perhaps F. O. Matthiessen, *The Achievement of T. S. Eliot* (2 edn., 1947). A distinguished group of critics contributed essays to *T. S. Eliot: A Selected Critique* (1948), edited by Leonard Unger. R. H. Robbins, *The T. S. Eliot Myth* (1951), is an attack, sometimes niggling, occasionally effective particularly when the target is Eliot's ventures into social and political thought. American contributions to the new poetry, including those by Amy Lowell and Ezra Pound, are discussed in Glenn Hughes, *Imagism and the Imagists* (1931). An excellent introduction is *Modern Poetry: American and British* (1951), edited by Kimon Friar and J. M. Brinnin.

ARCHITECTURE

Frank Lloyd Wright, *An Autobiography* (1943), is a great document which no student of modern American culture should neglect. The best study of his work is H. R. Hitchcock, *In the Nature of Materials, 1887-1941: The Buildings of Frank Lloyd Wright* (1942). The final glories of the traditional school of design are made clear in *A Monograph of the Work of McKim, Mead and White, 1879-1915* (1914-1915). Biographical accounts are Charles Moore, *The Life and Times of C. F. McKim* (1929), and C. C. Baldwin, *Stanford White* (1931). R. A. Cram, *The Gothic Quest* (1907) and *My Life in Architecture* (1936), are important statements of faith. Henry Adams, *Mont-Saint-Michel and Chartres* (1904), is one of the most eloquent celebrations of medievalism ever written. T. F. Hamlin, *The American Spirit in Architecture* (1926), is excellent on this period. W. A. Starrett, *Skyscrapers* (1928), is useful.

REVOLUTION IN PAINTING

Jerome Mellquist, *The Emergence of an American Art* (1942), traces the stages
in the evolution of modernism from Whistler and the Realists to the Armory
Show and American Post-Impressionism. Rudi Blesh, *Modern Art USA: Men,
Rebellion, Conquest, 1900-1956* (1956), begins with "291" and proceeds
mostly by means of anecdotes to the newest schools of Abstract Expressionism.
The story of the Armory Show is told by Walt Kuhn, one of its painter-
organizers, in a pamphlet, *Twenty-Five Years After: The Story of the Armory
Show* (1938). Rudolph Rosenthal and H. L. Ratzka, *The Story of Modern
Applied Art* (1948), contains a skimpy chapter on modern design in the
United States, but is rich in suggestions of its trans-Atlantic sources.

THE NEW THEATER

Susan Glaspell, *The Road to the Temple* (1926), an idealized biography of
the author's husband, George Cram Cook, is a valuable source on the Provincetown Players, for which she wrote plays. A. S. Downer, *Fifty Years of American
Drama, 1900-1950* (1951), is a brief and effective history. Contemporary surveys are Sheldon Cheney, *The New Movement in the Theatre* (1914) and
T. H. Dickinson, *The Insurgent Theater* (1914), while the story of the most
famous group is told in Helen Deutsch and Stella Hanau, *The Provincetown:
A Story of a Theatre* (1931). E. A. Engel, *Haunted Heroes of Eugene O'Neill*
(1953), and D. V. Falk, *Eugene O'Neill and the Tragic Tension* (1958), are
valuable studies. Isadora Duncan, *My Life* (1927), reveals the turbulent career
of the great dancer and her passion for art. Gertrude Stein's function as a catalyst
of modernism in writing and painting is somewhat exaggerated in her fascinating
autobiography, written as though by her companion, *The Autobiography of
Alice B. Toklas* (1933); her life and work are brilliantly assessed by J. M.
Brinnin, *The Third Rose: Gertrude Stein and Her World* (1959). Mabel
Dodge Luhan, who had a special talent for attracting to her salon at 23 Fifth
Avenue the leaders of the vanguard in art and ideas, in the third volume of her
Intimate Memories, entitled *Movers and Shakers* (1936), conveys the ferment
of the years just before the First World War.

THE MASS MEDIA

Three books by Gilbert Seldes record his efforts to achieve an attitude towards
the new media at once critical and hopeful: *The Seven Lively Arts* (1924),
which opened people's eyes to the possibilities of the movies, the comic strips,
jazz, and other forms; *The Great Audience* (1950), which blames not the
public but the businessmen at the top for the low quality of most movie,
radio, and television fare; and *The Public Arts* (1956), in which he once more
states reasons for hope. F. L. Mott is the standard historian of American newspapers and magazines; see his *American Journalism* (1950), a survey, and
A History of American Magazines, 1885-1905 (Vol. IV, 1957), a mine of information on the new magazines and editorial policies of these years; another
volume is to come. D. C. Seitz, *Joseph Pulitzer: His Life and Letters* (1924),
and Oliver Carlson and E. S. Bates, *Hearst: Lord of San Simeon* (1936),

bracket the beginnings of Yellow journalism. Allan Nevins, *The Evening Post: A Century of Journalism* (1922), and Meyer Berger, *The Story of the New York Times* (1951), are excellent accounts of quality newspapers. An exceptionally readable and important personal document by the editor of the *Ladies' Home Journal* is Edward Bok, *The Americanization of Edward Bok* (1920). The great period of the comic strips is celebrated by E. E. Cummings in his introduction to a volume of reproductions of perhaps the best of all funnies, George Herriman, *Krazy Kat* (1946). American movies have been scrutinized by many historians; a start can be made by reading Lewis Jacobs, *The Rise of the American Film* (1939), a serious study; L. C. Rosten, *Hollywood: The Movie Colony, The Movie Makers* (1941), on the lighter side; and M. D. Haettig, *Economic Control of the Motion Picture Industry* (1944), on the business side. A revealing introduction to the history of jazz is found in the collection of essays, *Jazzmen* (1939), edited by Frederic Ramsey and C. E. Smith. Winthrop Sargeant, *Jazz: Hot and Hybrid* (1939), is an academic analysis of the sources of jazz. Rudi Blesh and Harriet Janis, *They All Played Ragtime* (1950), and Barry Ulanov, *A History of Jazz* (1957), are important recent histories.

18. WOODROW WILSON AND THE NEW FREEDOM, 1913-1917

Special

Wilson the Leader: The authorized biography is R. S. Baker, *Woodrow Wilson: Life and Letters* (8 vols., 1927-1939). Far more penetrating is the work of A. S. Link, whose *The Road to the White House* (1947), and *Wilson: The New Freedom* (1956), are the first two volumes of a biography-in-process which is already a major contribution to historical literature. Link has also written a volume for the New American Nation Series entitled *Woodrow Wilson and the Progressive Era: 1910-1917* (1954), the best general study of the Wilsonian climax of Progressivism. A good short biography is H. C. F. Bell, *Woodrow Wilson and the People* (1945). On Wilson's associates the following are especially useful: For Bryan, Paxton Hibben and C. H. Grattan, *The Peerless Leader* (1929); Mason, *Brandeis;* J. M. Blum, *Joe Tumulty and the Wilson Era* (1951); Josephus Daniels, *The Wilson Era* (2 vols., 1944-1946); and *The Intimate Papers of Colonel House* (4 vols., 1926-1928), edited by Charles Seymour. The varieties of Progressivism should be studied in Croly, *The Promise of American Life* (1909), which reflected and influenced the ideas of Theodore Roosevelt; L. D. Brandeis, *Business—A Profession* (1914); Theodore Roosevelt, *The New Nationalism* (1910); and Wilson, *The New Freedom* (1913). See also William Diamond, *Economic Thought of Woodrow Wilson* (1943). Special interest attaches to Herbert Hoover, *The Ordeal of Woodrow Wilson* (1958). A keen recent analysis is J. M. Blum, *Woodrow Wilson and the Politics of Morality* (1956).

From Competition to Regulation

On the Underwood Tariff, see F. W. Taussig, *Some Aspects of the Tariff Question* (1915). The early history of income taxes is told by the distinguished economist, E. R. A. Seligman, *The Income Tax* (1914). Senator Carter Glass told the story of the passage of the Federal Reserve Act in *An Adventure in Constructive Finance* (1927). L. D. Brandeis, *Other People's Money* (1913), is based on the findings of the Pujo Committee. The operation of the Federal Reserve System may be studied in H. P. Willis, *The Federal Reserve System* (1923), and S. E. Harris, *Twenty Years of Federal Reserve Policy* (2 vols., 1933). E. S. Sparks, *History and Theory of Agricultural Credit* (1932), places in context the story of the Farm Loan Bank Act of 1916; Clara Eliot, *The Farmer's Campaign for Credit* (1927), is also valuable. The Clayton Antitrust Act is dealt with in J. D. Clark, *The Federal Trust Policy*; contemporary opinions are set forth in a volume published by the American Academy of Political and Social Science, *Industrial Competition and Combination* (1912). T. C. Blaisdell, *The Federal Trade Commission* (1932), and N. B. Gaskill, *Regulation of Competition* (1936), are useful on the FTC.

Towards Social Justice

La Follette's Weekly is a rich source on Progressivism at large. The fight for the Seamen's Act can be followed in it, as can all the causes La Follette championed. The story of the Adamson Act and its relation to the election campaign is best told by Link, in *Wilson and the Progressive Era*. R. G. Fuller, *Child Labor and the Constitution* (1923), deals with the two laws against child labor signed by Wilson. After women won the vote, the suffragist leader Carrie Chapman Catt collaborated with N. R. Shuler in writing *Woman Suffrage and Politics* (1926). A popular account of the movement is I. H. Irwin, *Angels and Amazons* (1933). An exhaustive collection of materials is *History of Woman Suffrage* (6 vols., 1881-1922), edited by leaders of the movement, E. C. Stanton, S. B. Anthony, and M. J. Gage.

The Limits of Wilsonian Reform

C. Vann Woodward, *The Strange Career of Jim Crow* (1955), corrects popular errors about the origins and timing of segregation laws in the South. J. H. Franklin, *From Slavery to Freedom: A History of American Negroes* (1947), is the best survey. On ideologies and their conflict see August Meier, *Negro Thought in America, 1880-1915* (1963), and the autobiography of W. E. B. DuBois, *Dusk of Dawn* (1940). Disfranchisement is well treated in Paul Lewinson, *Race, Class, and Party* (1932), and brilliantly related to Southern politics in V. O. Key, *Southern Politics* (1949). O. G. Villard drew attention to the extension of segregation in the federal government in "The President and the Segregation at Washington," *North American Review* (December 1913). W. S. Bernard, *American Immigration Policy* (1950), details the important struggles over restriction during the Wilson era. J. A. Krout, *The Origins of Prohibition*

(1925), is the best study. Justin Steuart, *Wayne Wheeler, Dry Boss* (1928), reveals the ideas and methods of a militant Prohibitionist.

19. FIRST EXPERIMENTS IN FOREIGN POLICY

Special

GROPING FOR A POLICY

Harley Notter, *The Origins of the Foreign Policy of Woodrow Wilson* (1937), and W. H. Callcott, *The Caribbean Policy of the United States, 1890-1929* (1942), are valuable. The Bryan-Chamorro Treaty may be studied in I. J. Cox, *Nicaragua and the United States, 1909-1927* (1927). Particular interest attaches to Sumner Welles, *Naboth's Vineyard: The Dominican Republic, 1844-1924* (1928), because its author, as President F. D. Roosevelt's Under Secretary of State, helped to build the Good Neighbor Policy; his book is a scholarly criticism of all varieties of interventionism. R. L. Buell, *The American Occupation of Haiti* (1929), is the standard study. C. C. Tansill, *The Purchase of the Danish West Indies* (1932), is authoritative.

WILSON'S MEXICAN POLICY

John Reed, *Insurgent Mexico* (1914), is one of the few contemporary efforts to understand the Mexican Revolution. Frank Tannenbaum, *The Mexican Agrarian Revolution* (1929), is a sensitive study of the deeper aspirations of the Mexican people. H. B. Parkes, *A History of Mexico* (1938), is the best survey. These books prepare the student to understand Wilson's Mexican policy, which is set forth in ample detail in Rippy, *The United States and Mexico*, and Cline, *The United States and Mexico*.

FIRST EFFORTS FOR WORLD PEACE

The best analysis of Bryan's "cooling-off" treaties is M. E. Curti, "Bryan and World Peace," *Smith College Studies in History* (1931). Gerstle Mack, *The Land Divided* (1944), gives an account of the Panama Canal tolls controversy with Great Britain. E. O. Reischauer, *The United States and Japan* (1950), places the California land controversy in perspective. Insight into the local situation is found in a contemporary study for the Federal Council of the Churches: H. A. Millis, *The Japanese Problem in the United States* (1915).

APPENDICES

DECLARATION OF INDEPENDENCE

In Congress, July 4, 1776

A DECLARATION BY THE REPRESENTATIVES OF THE UNITED STATES OF AMERICA, IN CONGRESS ASSEMBLED

WHEN, IN THE COURSE OF HUMAN EVENTS, IT BECOMES NECESSARY FOR ONE people to dissolve the political bands which have connected them with another, and to assume, among the powers of the earth, the separate and equal station to which the laws of nature and of nature's God entitle them, a decent respect to the opinions of mankind requires that they should declare the causes which impel them to the separation.

We hold these truths to be self-evident:—That all men are created equal; that they are endowed by their Creator with certain unalienable rights; that among these are life, liberty, and the pursuit of happiness. That, to secure these rights, governments are instituted among men, deriving their just powers from the consent of the governed; that, whenever any form of government becomes destructive of these ends, it is the right of the people to alter or to abolish it, and to institute a new government, laying its foundation on such principles, and organizing its powers in such form, as to them shall seem most likely to effect their safety and happiness. Prudence, indeed, will dictate, that governments long established should not be changed for light and transient causes; and accordingly all experience hath shown that mankind are more disposed to suffer while evils are sufferable, than to right themselves by abolishing the forms to which they are accustomed. But when a long train of abuses and usurpations, pursuing invariably the same object, evinces a design to reduce them under absolute despotism, it is their right, it is their duty, to throw off such government, and to provide new guards for their future security. Such has been the patient sufferance of these colonies; and such is now the necessity which constrains them to alter their former systems of government. The history of the present King of Great Britain is a history of repeated injuries and usurpations, all having in direct object the establishment of an absolute tyranny over these states. To prove this, let facts be submitted to a candid world.

He has refused his assent to laws the most wholesome and necessary for the public good.

He has forbidden his governors to pass laws of immediate and pressing importance, unless suspended in their operation till his assent should be obtained; and when so suspended, he has utterly neglected to attend to them.

He has refused to pass other laws for the accommodation of large districts of people, unless those people would relinquish the right of representation in the legislature—a right inestimable to them, and formidable to tyrants only.

He has called together legislative bodies at places unusual, uncomfortable, and distant from the depository of their public records, for the sole purpose of fatiguing them into compliance with his measure.

He has dissolved representative houses repeatedly, for opposing, with manly firmness, his invasions on the rights of the people.

He has refused, for a long time after such dissolutions, to cause others to be elected, whereby the legislative powers, incapable of annihilation, have returned to the people at large for their exercise; the State remaining, in the mean time, exposed to all the dangers of invasions from without, and convulsions within.

He has endeavored to prevent the population of these States; for that purpose obstructing the laws for the naturalization of foreigners; refusing to pass others to encourage their migration hither, and raising the conditions of new appropriations of lands.

He has obstructed the administration of justice, by refusing his assent to laws for establishing judiciary powers.

He has made judges dependent on his will alone for the tenure of their offices, and the amount and payment of their salaries.

He has erected a multitude of new offices, and sent hither swarms of officers to harass our people and eat out their substance.

He has kept among us in times of peace, standing armies, without the consent of our legislatures.

He has affected to render the military independent of, and superior to, the civil power.

He has combined with others to subject us to a jurisdiction foreign to our constitutions, and unacknowledged by our laws; giving his assent to their acts of pretended legislation:

For quartering large bodies of armed troops among us;

For protecting them, by a mock trial, from punishment for any murders which they should commit on the inhabitants of these States;

For cutting off our trade with all parts of the world;

For imposing taxes on us without our consent;

For depriving us, in many cases, of the benefits of trial by jury;

For transporting us beyond seas, to be tried for pretended offences;

For abolishing the free system of English laws in a neighboring province, establishing therein an arbitrary government, and enlarging its boundaries, so as to render it at once an example and fit instrument for introducing the same absolute rule into these colonies;

For taking away our charters, abolishing our most valuable laws, and altering, fundamentally, the forms of our governments;

For suspending our own legislatures, and declaring themselves invested with power to legislate for us in all cases whatsoever.

He has abdicated government here, by declaring us out of his protection, and waging war against us.

He has plundered our seas, ravaged our coasts, burned our towns, and destroyed the lives of our people.

He is at this time transporting large armies of foreign mercenaries to complete the works of death, desolation and tyranny, already begun with circumstances of cruelty and perfidy scarcely paralleled in the most barbarous ages, and totally unworthy the head of a civilized nation.

He has constrained our fellow-citizens, taken captive on the high seas, to bear arms against their country, to become the executioners of their friends and brethren, or to fall themselves by their hands.

He has excited domestic insurrection among us, and has endeavored to bring on the inhabitants of our frontiers the merciless Indian savages, whose known rule of warfare is an undistinguished destruction of all ages, sexes, and conditions.

In every stage of these oppressions we have petitioned for redress in the most humble terms; our repeated petitions have been answered only by repeated injury. A prince whose character is thus marked by every act which may define a tyrant, is unfit to be the ruler of a free people.

Nor have we been wanting in our attentions to our British brethren. We have warned them, from time to time, of attempts by their legislature to extend an unwarrantable jurisdiction over us. We have reminded them of the circumstances of our emigration and settlement here. We have appealed to their native justice and magnanimity; and we have conjured them, by the ties of our common kindred, to disavow these usurpations, which would inevitably interrupt our connections and correspondence. They, too, have been deaf to the voice of justice and consanguinity. We must, therefore, acquiesce in the necessity which denounces our separation, and hold them, as we hold the rest of mankind, enemies in war, in peace friends.

We, therefore, the Representatives of the United States of America, in General Congress assembled, appealing to the Supreme Judge of the world for the rectitude of our intentions, do, in the name and by the authority of the good people of these colonies, solemnly publish and declare, That these united Colonies are, and of right ought to be, free and independent states; that they are absolved from all allegiance to the British crown, and that all political connection between them and the state of Great Britain is, and ought to be, totally dissolved; and that, as free and independent states, they have full power to levy war, conclude peace, contract alliances, establish commerce, and do all other acts and things which independent states may of right do. And, for the support of this declaration, with a firm reliance on the protection of Divine Providence, we mutually pledge to each other our lives, our fortunes, and our sacred honor.

The foregoing Declaration was, by order of Congress, engrossed, and signed by the following members:

JOHN HANCOCK

NEW HAMPSHIRE
JOSIAH BARTLETT
WILLIAM WHIPPLE
MATTHEW THORNTON

MASSACHUSETTS BAY
SAMUEL ADAMS
JOHN ADAMS
ROBERT TREAT PAINE
ELBRIDGE GERRY

RHODE ISLAND
STEPHEN HOPKINS
WILLIAM ELLERY

CONNECTICUT
ROGER SHERMAN
SAMUEL HUNTINGTON
WILLIAM WILLIAMS
OLIVER WOLCOTT

NEW YORK
WILLIAM FLOYD
PHILIP LIVINGSTON
FRANCIS LEWIS
LEWIS MORRIS

NEW JERSEY
RICHARD STOCKTON
JOHN WITHERSPOON
FRANCIS HOPKINSON
JOHN HART
ABRAHAM CLARK

PENNSYLVANIA
ROBERT MORRIS
BENJAMIN RUSH
BENJAMIN FRANKLIN
JOHN MORTON
GEORGE CLYMER
JAMES SMITH
GEORGE TAYLOR
JAMES WILSON
GEORGE ROSS

DELAWARE
CAESAR RODNEY
GEORGE READ
THOMAS M'KEAN

MARYLAND
SAMUEL CHASE
WILLIAM PACA
THOMAS STONE

CHARLES CARROLL, of
  Carrollton

VIRGINIA
GEORGE WYTHE
RICHARD HENRY LEE
THOMAS JEFFERSON
BENJAMIN HARRISON
THOMAS NELSON, JR.
FRANCIS LIGHTFOOT LEE
CARTER BRAXTON

NORTH CAROLINA
WILLIAM HOOPER
JOSEPH HEWES
JOHN PENN

SOUTH CAROLINA
EDWARD RUTLEDGE
THOMAS HEYWARD, JR.
THOMAS LYNCH, JR.
ARTHUR MIDDLETON

GEORGIA
BUTTON GWINNETT
LYMAN HALL
GEORGE WALTON

THE
CONSTITUTION
OF THE
UNITED STATES OF AMERICA

WE, THE PEOPLE OF THE UNITED STATES, IN ORDER TO FORM A MORE PERFECT union, establish justice, insure domestic tranquillity, provide for the common defence, promote the general welfare, and secure the blessings of liberty to ourselves and our posterity, do ordain and establish this constitution for the United States of America.

ARTICLE I
SECTION 1

ALL LEGISLATIVE POWERS HEREIN GRANTED SHALL BE VESTED IN A CONGRESS OF the United States, which shall consist of a Senate and a House of Representatives.

SECTION 2

The House of Representatives shall be composed of Members chosen every second Year by the People of the several States, and the Electors in each State shall have the Qualifications requisite for Electors of the most numerous Branch of the State Legislature.

No Person shall be a Representative who shall not have attained to the Age of twenty-five Years, and been seven Years a Citizen of the United States, and who shall not, when elected, be an Inhabitant of that State in which he shall be chosen.

[Representatives and direct Taxes shall be apportioned among the several States which may be included within this Union, according to their respective Numbers, which shall be determined by adding to the whole Number of free Persons, including those bound to Service for a Term of Years, and excluding Indians not taxed, three fifths of all other Persons.]* The actual Enumeration shall be made within three Years after the first Meeting of the Congress of the United States, and within every subsequent Term of ten Years, in such Manner as they shall by Law direct. The Number of Representatives shall not exceed one for every thirty Thousand, but each State shall have at Least one

* Repealed by Section 2 of Amendment XIV.

Representative; and until such enumeration shall be made, the State of New Hampshire shall be entitled to chuse three, Massachusetts eight, Rhode-Island and Providence Plantations one, Connecticut five, New-York six, New Jersey four, Pennsylvania eight, Delaware one, Maryland six, Virginia ten, North Carolina five, South Carolina five, and Georgia three.

When vacancies happen in the Representation from any State, the Executive Authority thereof shall issue Writs of Election to fill such Vacancies.

The House of Representatives shall chuse their Speaker and other Officers; and shall have the sole Power of Impeachment.

SECTION 3

The Senate of the United States shall be composed of two Senators from each State, [chosen by the Legislature thereof,]* for six Years; and each Senator shall have one Vote.

Immediately after they shall be assembled in Consequence of the first Election, they shall be divided as equally as may be into three Classes. The Seats of the Senators of the first Class shall be vacated at the Expiration of the second Year, of the second Class at the Expiration of the fourth Year, and of the third Class at the Expiration of the sixth Year, so that one-third may be chosen every second Year; [and if Vacancies happen by Resignation, or otherwise, during the Recess of the Legislature of any State, the Executive thereof may make temporary Appointments until the next Meeting of the Legislature, which shall then fill such Vacancies.]†

No person shall be a Senator who shall not have attained to the Age of thirty Years, and been nine Years a Citizen of the United States, and who shall not, when elected, be an Inhabitant of that State for which he shall be chosen.

The Vice President of the United States shall be President of the Senate, but shall have no Vote, unless they be equally divided.

The Senate shall chuse their other Officers, and also a President pro tempore, in the Absence of the Vice President, or when he shall exercise the Office of President of the United States.

The Senate shall have the sole Power to try all Impeachments. When sitting for that Purpose, they shall be an Oath or Affirmation. When the President of the United States is tried, the Chief Justice shall preside: And no Person shall be convicted without the Concurrence of two thirds of the Members present.

Judgment in Cases of Impeachment shall not extend further than to removal from Office, and disqualification to hold and enjoy any Office of honor, Trust or Profit under the United States: but the Party convicted shall nevertheless be liable and subject to Indictment, Trial, Judgment and Punishment, according to Law.

SECTION 4

The Times, Places and Manner of holding Elections for Senators and Representatives, shall be prescribed in each State by the Legislature thereof; but the Congress may at any time by Law make or alter such Regulations, except as to the Places of chusing Senators.

* Replaced by Section 1 of Amendment XVII.
† Changed by Clause 2 of Amendment XVII.

The Congress shall assemble at least once in every Year, and such Meeting*
shall [be on the first Monday in December] unless they shall by Law appoint a
different Day.

SECTION 5

Each House shall be the Judge of the Elections, Returns and Qualifications
of its own Members, and a Majority of each shall constitute a Quorum to do
Business; but a smaller Number may adjourn from day to day, and may be
authorized to compel the Attendance of absent Members, in such Manner, and
under such Penalties as each House may provide.

Each House may determine the Rules of its Proceedings, punish its Members
for disorderly Behavior, and, with the Concurrence of two thirds, expel a
Member.

Each House shall keep a Journal of its Proceedings, and from time to time
publish the same, excepting such Parts as may in their Judgment require
Secrecy; and the Yeas and Nays of the Members of either House on any question shall, at the Desire of one fifth of those present, be entered on the
Journal.

Neither House, during the Session of Congress, shall, without the Consent
of the other, adjourn for more than three days, nor to any other Place than
that in which the two Houses shall be sitting.

SECTION 6

The Senators and Representatives shall receive a Compensation for their
Services, to be ascertained by Law, and paid out of the Treasury of the United
States. They shall in all Cases, except Treason, Felony and Breach of the
Peace, be privileged from Arrest during their Attendance at the Session of
their respective Houses, and in going to and returning from the same; and for
any Speech or Debate in either House, they shall not be questioned in any
other Place.

No Senator or Representative shall, during the Time for which he was
elected, be appointed to any civil Office under the Authority of the United
States, which shall have been created, or the Emoluments whereof shall have
been encreased during such time; and no Person holding any Office under the
United States, shall be a Member of either House during his Continuance in
Office.

SECTION 7

All Bills for raising Revenue shall originate in the House of Representatives;
but the Senate may propose or concur with Amendments as on other Bills.

Every Bill which shall have passed the House of Representatives and the
Senate, shall, before it become a Law, be presented to the President of the
United States; If he approve he shall sign it, but if not he shall return it,
with his Objections to that House in which it shall have originated, who shall
enter the Objections at large on their Journal, and proceed to reconsider it. If
after such Reconsideration two thirds of that House shall agree to pass the Bill,
it shall be sent, together with the Objections, to the other House, by which it
shall likewise be reconsidered, and if approved by two thirds of that House, it

* Changed by Section 2 of Amendment XX.

shall become a Law. But in all such Cases the Votes of both Houses shall be determined by Yeas and Nays, and the Names of the Persons voting for and against the Bill shall be entered on the Journal of each House respectively. If any Bill shall not be returned by the President within ten Days (Sundays excepted) after it shall have been presented to him, the Same shall be a Law, in like Manner as if he had signed it, unless the Congress by their Adjournment prevent its Return, in which Case it shall not be a Law.

Every Order, Resolution, or Vote to which the Concurrence of the Senate and House of Representatives may be necessary (except on a question of Adjournment) shall be presented to the President of the United States; and before the Same shall take Effect, shall be approved by him, or being disapproved by him, shall be repassed by two thirds of the Senate and House of Representatives, according to the Rules and Limitations prescribed in the Case of a Bill.

Section 8*

The Congress shall have Power To lay and collect Taxes, Duties, Imposts and Excises, to pay the Debts and provide for the common Defence and general Welfare of the United States; but all Duties, Imposts and Excises shall be uniform throughout the United States;

To borrow Money on the credit of the United States;

To regulate Commerce with foreign Nations, and among the several States, and with the Indian Tribes;

To establish an uniform Rule of Naturalization, and uniform Laws on the subject of Bankruptcies throughout the United States;

To coin Money, regulate the Value thereof, and of foreign Coin, and fix the Standard of Weights and Measures;

To provide for the Punishment of counterfeiting the Securities and current Coin of the United States;

To establish Post Offices and post Roads;

To promote the Progress of Science and useful Arts, by securing for limited Times to Authors and Inventors the exclusive Right to their respective Writings and Discoveries;

To constitute Tribunals inferior to the supreme Court;

To define and punish Piracies and Felonies committed on the high Seas, and Offences against the Law of Nations;

To declare War, grant Letters of Marque and Reprisal, and make Rules concerning Captures on Land and Water;

To raise and support Armies, but no Appropriation of Money to that Use shall be for a longer Term than two Years;

To provide and maintain a Navy;

To make Rules for the Government and Regulation of the land and naval Forces;

To provide for calling forth the Militia to execute the Laws of the Union, suppress Insurrections and repel Invasions;

To provide for organizing, arming, and disciplining the Militia, and for governing such Part of them as may be employed in the Service of the United States, reserving to the States respectively, the Appointment of the Officers,

* Paragraphs 1-17 of Section 8 contain the "enumerated powers" of Congress.

and the Authority of training the Militia according to the discipline prescribed by Congress;

To exercise exclusive Legislation in all Cases whatsoever, over such District (not exceeding ten Miles square) as may, by Cession of particular States, and the Acceptance of Congress, become the Seat of the Government of the United States, and to exercise like Authority over all Places purchased by the Consent of the Legislature of the State in which the Same shall be, for the Erection of Forts, Magazines, Arsenals, dock-Yards, and other needful Buildings;—And

To make all Laws which shall be necessary and proper* for carrying into Execution the foregoing Powers, and all other Powers vested by this Constitution in the Government of the United States, or in any Department or Officer thereof.

SECTION 9†

The Migration or Importation of such Persons as any of the States now existing shall think proper to admit, shall not be prohibited by the Congress prior to the Year one thousand eight hundred and eight, but a Tax or duty may be imposed on such Importation, not exceeding ten dollars for each Person.

The Privilege of the Writ of Habeas Corpus shall not be suspended, unless when in Cases of Rebellion or Invasion the public Safety may require it.

No Bill of Attainder or ex post facto Law shall be passed.

No Capitation, or other direct, tax shall be laid, unless in Proportion to the Census or Enumeration herein before directed to be taken.

No Tax or Duty shall be laid on Articles exported from any State.

No Preference shall be given by any Regulation of Commerce or Revenue to the Ports of one State over those of another: nor shall Vessels bound to, or from, one State, be obliged to enter, clear, or pay Duties in another.

No Money shall be drawn from the Treasury, but in Consequence of Appropriations made by Law; and a regular Statement and Account of the Receipts and Expenditures of all public Money shall be published from time to time.

No Title of Nobility shall be granted by the United States: And no Person holding any Office of Profit or Trust under them, shall, without the Consent of the Congress, accept of any present, Emolument, Office, or Title, of any kind whatever, from any King, Prince, or foreign State.

SECTION 10‡

No State shall enter into any Treaty, Alliance, or Confederation; grant Letters of Marque and Reprisal; coin Money; emit Bills of Credit; make any Thing but gold and silver Coin a Tender in Payment of Debts; pass any Bill of Attainder, ex post facto Law, or Law impairing the Obligation of Contracts,§ or grant any Title of Nobility.

No State shall, without the Consent of the Congress, lay any Imposts or Duties on Imports or Exports, except what may be absolutely necessary for

* The "coefficient clause" (or "Elastic Clause" or "Necessary and Proper" clause) of the Constitution.
† This section imposes certain limitations on the powers of Congress.
‡ This section imposes certain limitations on the States.
§ The "Obligation of Contract" clause.

executing it's inspection Laws: and the net Produce of all Duties and Imposts, laid by any State on Imports or Exports, shall be for the Use of the Treasury of the United States; and all such Laws shall be subject to the Revision and Control of the Congress.

No State shall, without the Consent of Congress, lay any Duty of Tonnage, keep Troops, or Ships of War in time of Peace, enter into any Agreement or Compact with another State, or with a foreign Power, or engage in War, unless actually invaded, or in such imminent Danger as will not admit of delay.

ARTICLE II

Section 1

The executive Power shall be vested in a President of the United States of America. He shall hold his Office during the Term of four Years, and, together with the Vice President, chosen for the same Term, be elected, as follows:

Each State shall appoint, in such Manner as the Legislature thereof may direct, a Number of Electors, equal to the whole Number of Senators and Representatives to which the State may be entitled in the Congress: but no Senator or Representative, or Person holding an Office of Trust or Profit under the United States, shall be appointed an Elector.

[The electors shall meet in their respective States, and vote by ballot for two Persons, of whom one at least shall not be an Inhabitant of the same State with themselves. And they shall make a List of all the Persons voted for, and of the Number of Votes for each; which List they shall sign and certify, and transmit sealed to the Seat of the Government of the United States, directed to the President of the Senate. The President of the Senate shall, in the Presence of the Senate and House of Representatives, open all the Certificates, and the Votes shall then be counted. The Person having the greatest Number of Votes shall be the President, if such Number be a Majority of the whole Number of Electors appointed; and if there be more than one who have such Majority, and have an equal Number of Votes, then the House of Representatives shall immediately chuse by Ballot one of them for President; and if no Person have a Majority, then from the five highest on the List the said House shall in like Manner chuse the President. But in chusing the President, the Votes shall be taken by States, the Representation from each State having one Vote; A quorum for this Purpose shall consist of a Member or Members from two thirds of the States, and a Majority of all the States shall be necessary to a Choice. In every Case, after the Choice of the President, the Person having the greatest Number of Votes of the Electors shall be the Vice President. But if there should remain two or more who have equal Votes, the Senate shall chuse from them by Ballot the Vice President.]*

The Congress may determine the Time of chusing the Electors, and the Day on which they shall give their Votes; which Day shall be the same throughout the United States.

No Person except a natural born Citizen, or a Citizen of the United States, at the time of the Adoption of this Constitution, shall be eligible to the Office of

---

* Superseded by Amendment XII.

President; neither shall any Person be eligible to that Office who shall not have attained to the Age of thirty five Years, and been fourteen Years a Resident within the United States.

In Case of the Removal of the President from Office, or of his Death, Resignation or Inability to discharge the Powers and Duties of the said Office, the same shall devolve on the Vice President, and the Congress may by Law provide for the Case of Removal, Death, Resignation or Inability, both of the President and Vice President, declaring what Officer shall then act as President, and such Officer shall act accordingly, until the Disability be removed, or a President shall be elected.

The President shall, at stated Times, receive for his Services, a Compensation, which shall neither be encreased nor diminished during the Period for which he shall have been elected, and he shall not receive within that Period any other Emolument from the United States, or any of them.

Before he enter on the Execution of his Office, he shall take the following Oath or Affirmation:—"I do solemnly swear (or affirm) that I will faithfully execute the Office of President of the United States, and will to the best of my Ability, preserve, protect and defend the Constitution of the United States."

SECTION 2

The President shall be Commander in Chief of the Army and Navy of the United States, and of the Militia of the several States, when called into the actual Service of the United States; he may require the Opinion, in writing, of the principal Officer in each of the executive Departments, upon any Subject relating to the Duties of their respective Offices, and he shall have Power to grant Reprieves and Pardons for Offences against the United States, except in Cases of Impeachment.

He shall have Power,* by and with the Advice and Consent of the Senate, to make Treaties, provided two thirds of the Senators present concur; and he shall nominate, and by and with the Advice and Consent of the Senate, shall appoint Ambassadors, other public Ministers and Consuls, Judges of the supreme Court, and all other Officers of the United States, whose Appointments are not herein otherwise provided for, and which shall be established by Law: but the Congress may by Law vest the Appointment of such inferior Officers, as they think proper, in the President alone, in the Courts of Law, or in the Heads of Departments.

The President shall have Power to fill up all Vacancies that may happen during the Recess of the Senate, by granting Commissions which shall expire at the End of their next Session.

SECTION 3

He shall from time to time give to the Congress Information of the State of the Union, and recommend to their Consideration such Measures as he shall judge necessary and expedient; he may, on extraordinary Occasions, convene both Houses, or either of them, and, in Case of Disagreement between them, with Respect to the Time of Adjournment, he may adjourn them to such Time as he shall think proper; he shall receive Ambassadors and other public Min-

---

* The "Treaty Making Power" is contained in this sentence.

isters; he shall take Care that the Laws be faithfully executed, and shall Commission all the Officers of the United States.

SECTION 4

The President, Vice President and all civil Officers of the United States, shall be removed from Office on Impeachment for, and Conviction of, Treason, Bribery, or other high Crimes and Misdemeanors.

ARTICLE III

SECTION 1

The judicial Power of the United States, shall be vested in one supreme Court, and in such inferior Courts as the Congress may from time to time ordain and establish. The Judges, both of the supreme and inferior Courts, shall hold their Offices during good Behaviour, and shall, at stated Times, receive for their Services, a Compensation, which shall not be diminished during their Continuance in Office.

SECTION 2

The judicial Power shall extend to all Cases, in Law and Equity, arising under this Constitution, the Laws of the United States, and Treaties made, or which shall be made, under their Authority;—to all Cases affecting Ambassadors, other public Ministers and Consuls;—to all Cases of admiralty and maritime Jurisdiction;—to Controversies to which the United States shall be a Party;—to Controversies between two or more States;—between a State and Citizens of another State;—between Citizens of different States,—between Citizens of the same State claiming Lands under Grants of different States, and between a State, or the Citizens thereof, and foreign States, Citizens or Subjects.

In all Cases affecting Ambassadors, other public Ministers and Consuls, and those in which a State shall be Party, the supreme Court shall have original Jurisdiction. In all the other Cases before mentioned, the supreme Court shall have appellate Jurisdiction, both as to Law and Fact, with such Exceptions, and under such Regulations as the Congress shall make.

The Trial of all Crimes, except in Cases of Impeachment, shall be by Jury; and such Trial shall be held in the State where the said Crimes shall have been committed; but when not committed within any State, the Trial shall be at such Place or Places as the Congress may by Law have directed.

SECTION 3

Treason against the United States, shall consist only in levying War against them, or in adhering to their Enemies, giving them Aid and Comfort. No Person shall be convicted of Treason unless on the Testimony of two Witnesses to the same overt Act, or on Confession in open Court.

The Congress shall have Power to declare the Punishment of Treason, but no Attainder of Treason shall work Corruption of Blood, or Forfeiture except during the Life of the Person attainted.

ARTICLE IV

SECTION 1

Full Faith and Credit shall be given in each State to the public Acts, Records, and judicial Proceedings of every other State. And the Congress may by general Laws prescribe the Manner in which such Acts, Records and Proceedings shall be proved, and the Effect thereof.

SECTION 2

The Citizens of each State shall be entitled to all Privileges and Immunities of Citizens in the several States.

A person charged in any State with Treason, Felony, or other Crime, who shall flee from Justice, and be found in another State, shall on Demand of the executive Authority of the State from which he fled, be delivered up, to be removed to the State having Jurisdiction of the Crime.

No Person held to Service or Labour in one State, under the Laws thereof, escaping into another, shall, in Consequence of any Law or Regulation therein, be discharged from such Service or Labour, but shall be delivered up on Claim of the Party to whom such Service or Labour may be due.

SECTION 3

New States may be admitted by the Congress into this Union; but no new State shall be formed or erected within the Jurisdiction of any other State; nor any State be formed by the Junction of two or more States, or Parts of States, without the Consent of the Legislatures of the States concerned as well as of the Congress.

The Congress shall have Power to dispose of and make all needful Rules and Regulations respecting the Territory or other Property belonging to the United States; and nothing in this Constitution shall be so construed as to Prejudice any Claims of the United States, or of any particular State.

SECTION 4

The United States shall guarantee to every State in this Union a Republican Form of Government, and shall protect each of them against Invasion; and on Application of the Legislature, or of the Executive (when the Legislature cannot be convened) against domestic Violence.

ARTICLE V

The Congress, whenever two thirds of both Houses shall deem it necessary, shall propose Amendments to this Constitution,* or, on the Application of the Legislatures of two thirds of the several States, shall call a Convention for proposing Amendments, which, in either Case, shall be valid to all Intents and Purposes, as Part of this Constitution, when ratified by the Legislatures of three fourths of the several States, or by Conventions in three fourths thereof, as the one or the other Mode of Ratification may be proposed by the Congress; Provided that no Amendment which may be made prior to the Year One thousand eight hundred and eight shall in any Manner affect the first and fourth

* The Amending power.

Clauses in the Ninth Section of the first Article; and that no State, without its Consent, shall be deprived of its equal Suffrage in the Senate.

ARTICLE VI

All Debts contracted and Engagements entered into, before the Adoption of this Constitution, shall be as valid against the United States under this Constitution, as under the Confederation.

This Constitution, and the Laws of the United States which shall be made in Pursuance thereof; and all Treaties made, or which shall be made, under the Authority of the United States, shall be the supreme Law of the Land; and the Judges in every State shall be bound thereby, any Thing in the Constitution or Laws of any State to the Contrary notwithstanding.

The Senators and Representatives before mentioned, and the Members of the several State Legislatures, and all executive and judicial Officers, both of the United States and of the several States, shall be bound by Oath or Affirmation, to support this Constitution; but no religious Test shall ever be required as a Qualification to any Office or public Trust under the United States.

ARTICLE VII

The Ratification of the Conventions of nine States, shall be sufficient for the Establishment of this Constitution between the States so ratifying the Same.

DONE in Convention by the Unanimous Consent of the States present the Seventeenth Day of September in the Year of our Lord one thousand seven hundred and Eighty seven and of the Independence of the United States of America the Twelfth. IN WITNESS whereof We have hereunto subscribed our Names.

G° WASHINGTON
Presid^t and deputy from Virginia

NEW HAMPSHIRE	JOHN LANGDON
	NICHOLAS GILMAN
MASSACHUSETTS	NATHANIEL GORHAM
	RUFUS KING
CONNECTICUT	WM. SAML. JOHNSON
	ROGER SHERMAN
NEW YORK	ALEXANDER HAMILTON
NEW JERSEY	WIL: LIVINGSTON
	DAVID BREARLEY
	WM. PATERSON
	JONA: DAYTON
PENNSYLVANIA	B FRANKLIN
	THOMAS MIFFLIN
	ROBT. MORRIS
	GEO. CLYMER
	THOS. FITZSIMONS
	JARED INGERSOLL
	JAMES WILSON
	GOUV MORRIS

DELAWARE	GEO: READ GUNNING BEDFORD jun JOHN DICKINSON RICHARD BASSETT JACO: BROOM
MARYLAND	JAMES McHENRY DAN OF ST. THOS. JENIFER DANL. CARROLL
VIRGINIA	JOHN BLAIR — JAMES MADISON JR.
NORTH CAROLINA	WM. BLOUNT RICHD. DOBBS SPAIGHT HU WILLIAMSON
SOUTH CAROLINA	J. RUTLEDGE CHARLES COTESWORTH PINCKNEY CHARLES PINCKNEY PIERCE BUTLER
GEORGIA	WILLIAM FEW ABR BALDWIN

Attest WILLIAM JACKSON *Secretary*

AMENDMENTS
ARTICLE I

Congress shall make no law respecting an establishment of religion, or prohibiting the free exercise thereof; or abridging the freedom of speech, or of the press; or the right of the people peaceably to assemble, and to petition the Government for a redress of grievances.

ARTICLE II

A well regulated Militia, being necessary to the security of a free State, the right of the people to keep and bear Arms, shall not be infringed.

ARTICLE III

No Soldier shall, in time of peace, be quartered in any house, without the consent of the Owner, nor in time of war, but in a manner to be prescribed by law.

ARTICLE IV

The right of the people to be secure in their persons, houses, papers, and effects, against unreasonable searches and seizures, shall not be violated, and no Warrants shall issue, but upon probable cause, supported by Oath or affirmation, and particularly describing the place to be searched, and the persons or things to be seized.

ARTICLE V

No person shall be held to answer for a capital, or otherwise infamous crime, unless on a presentment or indictment of a Grand Jury, except in cases arising in the land or naval forces, or in the Militia, when in actual service in time of War or public danger; nor shall any person be subject for the same offence to be twice put in jeopardy of life or limb; nor shall be compelled in any Criminal Case to be a witness against himself, nor be deprived of life, liberty, or property, without due process of law; nor shall private property be taken for public use, without just compensation.

ARTICLE VI

In all criminal prosecutions, the accused shall enjoy the right to a speedy and public trial, by an impartial jury of the State and district wherein the crime shall have been committed, which district shall have been previously ascertained by law, and to be informed of the nature and cause of the accusation; to be confronted with the witnesses against him; to have compulsory process for obtaining Witnesses in his favor, and to have the Assistance of Counsel for his defence.

ARTICLE VII

In suits at common law, where the value in controversy shall exceed twenty dollars, the right of trial by jury shall be preserved, and no fact tried by a jury shall be otherwise re-examined in any Court of the United States, than according to the rules of the common law.

ARTICLE VIII

Excessive bail shall not be required, nor excessive fines imposed, nor cruel and unusual punishments inflicted.

ARTICLE IX

The enumeration in the Constitution, of certain rights, shall not be construed to deny or disparage others retained by the people.

ARTICLE X

The powers not delegated to the United States by the Constitution, nor prohibited by it to the States, are reserved to the States respectively, or to the people.

[THE FIRST TEN ARTICLES PROPOSED 25 SEPTEMBER 1789; DECLARED IN FORCE 15 DECEMBER 1791]*

ARTICLE XI
[DECLARED RATIFIED 8 JANUARY 1798]

The Judicial power of the United States shall not be contrued to extend to any suit in law or equity, commenced or prosecuted against one of the United States by Citizens of another State, or by Citizens or Subjects of any Foreign State.

ARTICLE XII
[DECLARED RATIFIED 25 SEPTEMBER 1804]

The Electors shall meet in their respective states, and vote by ballot for President and Vice-President, one of whom, at least, shall not be an inhabitant of the same state with themselves; they shall name in their ballots the person voted for as President, and in distinct ballots the person voted for as Vice-President, and they shall make distinct lists of all persons voted for as President, and of all persons voted for as Vice-President, and of the number of votes for each, which lists they shall sign and certify, and transmit sealed to the seat of the Government of the United States, directed to the President of the Senate;— The President of the Senate shall, in the presence of the Senate and House of Representatives, open all the certificates and the votes shall then be counted;— The person having the greatest number of votes for President, shall be the President, if such number be a majority of the whole number of Electors appointed; and if no person have such majority, then from the persons having the highest numbers not exceeding three on the list of those voted for as President, the House of Representatives shall choose immediately, by ballot, the President. But in choosing the President, the votes shall be taken by states, the representation from each state having one vote; a quorum for this purpose shall consist of

* These amendments bind only the National Government, but these rights are not infrequently binding against State authority because of the Court's interpretation of the "due process clause" of Amendment XIV.

a member or members from two-thirds of the states, and a majority of all the states shall be necessary to a choice. And if the House of Representatives shall not choose a President whenever the right of choice shall devolve upon them, before the fourth day of March next following, then the Vice-President shall act as President, as in the case of the death or other constitutional disability of the President. The person having the greatest number of votes as Vice-President, shall be the Vice-President, if such number be a majority of the whole number of Electors appointed, and if no person have a majority, then from the two highest numbers on the list, the Senate shall choose the Vice-President; a quorum for the purpose shall consist of two-thirds of the whole number of Senators, and a majority of the whole number shall be necessary to a choice. But no person constitutionally ineligible to the office of President shall be eligible to that of Vice-President of the United States.

ARTICLE XIII
[DECLARED RATIFIED 18 DECEMBER 1865]
SECTION 1

Neither slavery nor involuntary servitude, except as a punishment for crime whereof the party shall have been duly convicted, shall exist within the United States, or any place subject to their jurisdiction.

SECTION 2

Congress shall have power to enforce this article by appropriate legislation.

ARTICLE XIV
[DECLARED RATIFIED 28 JULY 1868]*
SECTION 1

All persons born or naturalized in the United States, and subject to the jurisdiction thereof, are citizens of the United States and of the State wherein they reside. No State shall make or enforce any law which shall abridge the privileges or immunities of citizens of the United States; nor shall any State deprive any person of life, liberty, or property, without due process of law; nor deny to any person within its jurisdiction the equal protection of the law.

SECTION 2

Representatives shall be apportioned among the several States according to their respective numbers, counting the whole number of persons in each State, excluding Indians not taxed. But when the right to vote at any election for the choice of electors for President and Vice-President of the United States, Representatives in Congress, the Executive and Judicial officers of a State, or the members of the Legislature thereof, is denied to any of the male inhabitants of such State, being twenty-one years of age, and citizens of the United States, or in any way abridged, except for participation in rebellion, or other crime, the basis of representation therein shall be reduced in the proportion which the

---

* Prior to date of ratification of the twenty-eighth state, Ohio and New Jersey "withdrew" their earlier assents to the amendment. Congress passed a joint resolution on July 21, 1868 declaring the amendment a part of the Constitution and directing the Secretary of State to promulgate it as such. On July 13th South Carolina ratified and on July 21 Georgia added its ratification.

number of such male citizens shall bear to the whole number of male citizens twenty-one years of age in such State.

Section 3

No person shall be a Senator or Representative in Congress, or elector of President and Vice-President, or hold any office, civil, or military, under the United States, or under any State, who, having previously taken an oath, as a member of Congress, or as an officer of the United States, or as a member of any State legislature, or as an executive or judicial officer of any State, to support the Constitution of the United States, shall have engaged in insurrection or rebellion against the same, or given aid or comfort to the enemies thereof. But Congress may by a vote of two-thirds of each House, remove such disability.

Section 4

The validity of the public debt of the United States, authorized by law, including debts incurred for payment of pensions and bounties for services in suppressing insurrection or rebellion, shall not be questioned. But neither the United States nor any State shall assume or pay any debt or obligation incurred in aid of insurrection or rebellion against the United States, or any claim for the loss or emancipation of any slave; but all such debts, obligations and claims shall be held illegal and void.

Section 5

The Congress shall have power to enforce, by appropriate legislation, the provisions of this article.

ARTICLE XV

[DECLARED RATIFIED 30 MARCH 1870]

Section 1

The right of citizens of the United States to vote shall not be denied or abridged by the United States or by any State on account of race, color, or previous condition of servitude.

Section 2

The Congress shall have power to enforce this article by appropriate legislation.

ARTICLE XVI

[PROPOSED 12 JULY 1909; DECLARED RATIFIED 25 FEBRUARY 1913]

The Congress shall have power to lay and collect taxes on incomes, from whatever source derived, without apportionment among the several States, and without regard to any census or enumeration.

ARTICLE XVII

[DECLARED RATIFIED 31 MAY 1913]

The Senate of the United States shall be composed of two senators from each State, elected by the people thereof, for six years; and each Senator shall have one vote. The electors in each State shall have the qualifications requisite for electors of the most numerous branch of the State legislature.

When vacancies happen in the representation of any State in the Senate, the executive authority of such State shall issue writs of election to fill such vacancies: PROVIDED, That the legislature of any State may empower the executive thereof to make temporary appointments until the people fill the vacancies by election as the legislature may direct.

This amendment shall not be so construed as to affect the election or term of any senator chosen before it becomes valid as part of the Constitution.

ARTICLE XVIII*
[DECLARED RATIFIED 29 JANUARY 1919]

After one year from the ratification of this article, the manufacture, sale, or transportation of intoxicating liquors within, the importation thereof into, or the exportation thereof from the United States and all territory subject to the jurisdiction thereof for beverage purposes is hereby prohibited.

The Congress and the several States shall have concurrent power to enforce this article by appropriate legislation.

This article shall be inoperative unless it shall have been ratified as an amendment to the Constitution by the legislatures of the several States, as provided in the Constitution, within seven years from the date of the submission hereof to the States by the Congress.

ARTICLE XIX
[PROPOSED 4 JUNE 1919; DECLARED RATIFIED 26 AUGUST 1920]

The right of citizens of the United States to vote shall not be denied or abridged by the United States or by any States on account of sex.

The Congress shall have power, by appropriate legislation, to enforce the provisions of this article.

ARTICLE XX
[DECLARED RATIFIED 6 FEBRUARY 1933]

SECTION 1

The terms of the President and Vice-President shall end at noon on the twentieth day of January, and the terms of Senators and Representatives at noon on the third day of January, of the years in which such terms would have ended if this article had not been ratified; and the terms of their successors shall then begin.

SECTION 2

The Congress shall assemble at least once in every year, and such meeting shall begin at noon on the third day of January, unless they shall by law appoint a different day.

SECTION 3

If, at the time fixed for the beginning of the term of the President, the President-elect shall have died, the Vice-President-elect shall become President. If a President shall not have been choosen before the time fixed for the beginning of his term, or if the President-elect shall have failed to qualify, then the Vice-President-elect shall act as President until a President shall have qualified;

* Repealed by section 1 of Amendment XXI.

and the Congress may by law provide for the case wherein neither a President-elect nor a Vice-President-elect shall have qualified, declaring who shall then act as President, or the manner in which one who is to act shall be selected, and such person shall act accordingly until a President or Vice-President shall have qualified.

Section 4

The Congress may by law provide for the case of the death of any of the persons from whom the House of Representatives may choose a President whenever the right of choice shall have devolved upon them, and for the case of the death of any of the persons from whom the Senate may choose a Vice-President whenever the right of choice shall have devolved upon them.

Section 5

Sections 1 and 2 shall take effect on the 15th day of October following the ratification of this article.

Section 6

This article shall be inoperative unless it shall have been ratified as an amendment to the Constitution by the legislatures of three-fourths of the several States within seven years from the date of its submission.

ARTICLE XXI

[DECLARED RATIFIED 5 DECEMBER 1933]

Section 1

The eighteenth article of amendment to the Constitution of the United States is hereby repealed.

Section 2

The transportation or importation into any State, Territory or possession of the United States for delivery or use therein of intoxicating liquors, in violation of the laws thereof, is hereby prohibited.

Section 3

This article shall be inoperative unless it shall have been ratified as an amendment to the Constitution by convention in the several States, as provided in the Constitution, within seven years from the date of the submission hereof to the States by the Congress.

ARTICLE XXII

[DECLARED RATIFIED 1 MARCH 1951]

Section 1

No person shall be elected to the office of President more than twice, and no person who has held the office of President, or acted as President, for more than two years of a term to which some other person was elected President shall be elected to the office of the President more than once. But this article shall not apply to any person holding the office of President when this article was proposed by the Congress, and shall not prevent any person who may be holding the office of President, or acting as President, during the term within which this Article becomes operative from holding the office of President or acting as President during the remainder of such term.

SECTION 2

This Article shall be inoperative unless it shall have been ratified as an amendment to the Constitution by the legislatures of three-fourths of the several States within seven years from the date of its submission to the States by the Congress.

ARTICLE XXIII

[DECLARED RATIFIED 3 APRIL 1961]

SECTION 1

The District constituting the seat of Government of the United States shall appoint in such manner as the Congress may direct:

A number of electors of President and Vice President equal to the whole number of Senators and Representatives in Congress to which the District would be entitled if it were a State, but in no event more than the least populous State; they shall be in addition to those appointed by the States, but they shall be considered, for the purposes of the election of President and Vice President, to be electors appointed by a State; and they shall meet in the District and perform such duties as provided by the twelfth article of amendment.

SECTION 2

The Congress shall have power to enforce this article by appropriate legislation.

ARTICLE XXIV

[DECLARED RATIFIED 5 FEBRUARY 1964]

SECTION 1

The right of citizens of the United States to vote in any primary or other election for President or Vice President, for electors for President or Vice President, or for Senator or Representative in Congress, shall not be denied or abridged by the United States or any State by reason of failure to pay any poll tax or other tax.

SECTION 2

The Congress shall have power to enforce this article by appropriate legislation.

UNRATIFIED AMENDMENTS

Twenty-two Amendments have been ratified by the required three-fourths of the states, 5 others have been submitted to the States but have not been ratified.

In *Coleman vs Miller*, 307 U.S. 433, (1939) the U.S. Supreme Court ruled that the reasonableness of time for ratification was a political question to be determined by Congress.

THE TWO UNRATIFIED AMENDMENTS OF THE PROPOSED BILL OF RIGHTS (1789)

ARTICLE I

After the first enumeration required by the first article of the Constitution, there shall be one Representative for every thirty thousand, until the number shall amount to one hundred, after which the proportion shall be so regulated by Congress, that there shall be no less than one hundred Representatives, nor less than one Representative for every forty thousand persons, until the number of Representatives shall amount to two hundred; after which the proportion shall be so regulated by Congress, that there shall not be less than two hundred Representatives for every fifty thousand persons.

ARTICLE II

No law varying the compensation for the services of the Senators and Representatives shall take effect, until an election of Representatives shall have intervened.

THE UNRATIFIED AMENDMENT RELATING TO TITLES OF NOBILITY OF FOREIGN GOVERNMENTS
(proposed by 2nd Session of the 11th Congress)

Resolved by the Senate and House of Representatives of the United States of America in Congress assembled (two-thirds of both Houses concurring), That the following section be submitted to the legislatures of the several states, which, when ratified by the legislatures of three-fourths of the states, shall be valid and binding, as a part of the constitution of the United States.

If any citizen of the United States shall accept, claim, receive or retain any title of nobility or honour, or shall, without the consent of Congress, accept and retain any present, pension, office of emolument of any kind whatever, from any emperor, king, prince or foreign power, such person shall cease to be a citizen of the United States, and shall be incapable of holding any office of trust or profit under them, or either of them.

The Unratified 13th Amendment (proposed by the 36th Congress, March 2, 1861)

This was signed by President Lincoln the day after the seizure of Fort Sumter. This is the only proposed amendment ever signed by the President. The President's signature is not considered necessary because of the constitutional provision that two-thirds of both Houses of Congress must concur before the amendment can be submitted to the States for ratification.

Resolved by the Senate and House of Representatives of the United States of America in Congress assembled, That the following article be proposed to the Legislatures of the several States as an amendment to the Constitution of the United States, which, when ratified by three-fourths of said Legislatures, shall be valid, to all intents and purposes, as part of the said Constitution, viz:

ARTICLE XIII

No amendment shall be made to the Constitution which will authorize or give to Congress the power to abolish or interfere, within any State, with the domestic institutions thereof, including that of persons held to labor or service by the laws of said State.

The Unratified Child-labor Amendment (proposed by the 1st Session of the 68th Congress in June 1924)

Resolved by the Senate and House of Representatives of the United States of America in Congress assembled (two-thirds of each House concurring therein), That the following article is proposed as an amendment to the Constitution of the United States, which, when ratified by the legislatures of three-fourths of the several States, shall be valid to all intents and purposes as a part of the Constitution:

ARTICLE ———

Section 1. The Congress shall have power to limit, regulate, and prohibit the labor of persons under 18 years of age.

Section 2. The power of the several States is unimpaired by this article except that the operation of State laws shall be suspended to the extent necessary to give effect to legislation enacted by the Congress.

STATES OF THE UNION, 1787-1917

State	Date Admitted	Rank in Population 1900	Rank in Population 1950
THE ORIGINAL THIRTEEN*			
Delaware	1787	44	46
Pennsylvania	1787	2	3
New Jersey	1787	16	8
Georgia	1788	11	13
Connecticut	1788	29	28
Massachusetts	1788	7	9
Maryland	1788	26	24
South Carolina	1788	24	27
New Hampshire	1788	37	44
Virginia	1788	17	15
New York	1788	1	1
North Carolina	1789	15	10
Rhode Island	1790	35	36
Vermont	1791	39	45
Kentucky	1792	12	19
Tennessee	1796	14	16
Ohio	1803	4	5
Louisiana	1812	23	21
Indiana	1816	8	12
Mississippi	1817	20	26
Illinois	1818	3	4
Alabama	1819	18	17
Maine	1820	31	35
Missouri	1821	5	11
Arkansas	1836	25	30
Michigan	1837	9	7
Florida	1845	33	20
Texas	1845	6	6
Iowa	1846	10	22
Wisconsin	1848	13	14
California	1850	21	2
Minnesota	1858	19	18
Oregon	1859	36	32
Kansas	1861	22	31
West Virginia	1863	28	29

* Arranged in the order of their ratification of the Constitution.

| State | Date Admitted | Rank in Population | |
		1900	1950
Nevada	1864	48	48
Nebraska	1867	27	33
Colorado	1876	32	34
North Dakota	1889	40	41
South Dakota	1889	38	40
Montana	1889	42	42
Washington	1889	34	23
Idaho	1890	45	43
Wyoming	1890	47	47
Utah	1896	41	38
Oklahoma	1907	30	25
New Mexico	1912	43	39
Arizona	1912	46	37

MAJOR EXECUTIVE OFFICERS
OF THE
UNITED STATES, 1865-1921

President		*Term*
ANDREW JOHNSON* of Tennessee		1865-69
Secretary of State	William H. Seward of N.Y.	1865-69
Secretary of the Treasury	Hugh McCulloch of Ind.	1865-69
Secretary of War	Edwin M. Stanton† of Pa.	1865-68
	John M. Schofield of Ill.	1868-69
Attorney General	James Speed of Ky.	1865-66
	Henry Stanbery of Ohio	1866-68
	William M. Evarts of N.Y.	1868-69
Postmaster General	William Dennison of Ohio	1865-66
	Alexander W. Randall of Wis.	1866-69
Secretary of the Navy	Gideon Welles of Conn.	1865-69
Secretary of the Interior	James Harlan of Iowa	1865-66
	Orville H. Browning of Ill.	1866-69

ULYSSES S. GRANT OF ILLINOIS		1869-77
Vice-President	Schuyler Colfax of Ind.	1869-73
	Henry Wilson†† of Mass.	1873-75

* Acceded April 15, 1865
† Suspended August 12, 1867-January 13, 1868, Ulysses S. Grant serving *ad interim.*
†† Died Nov. 22, 1875.

| *Secretary of State* | Hamilton Fish of N.Y. | 1869-77 |

Secretary of the Treasury	George S. Boutwell of Mass.	1869-73
	William A. Richardson of Mass.	1873-74
	Benjamin H. Bristow of Ky.	1874-76
	Lot M. Morrill of Me.	1876-77

Secretary of War	John A. Rawlins of Ill.	1869
	William T. Sherman of Ohio	1869
	William W. Belknap of Iowa	1869-76
	Alphonso Taft of Ohio	1876
	James D. Cameron of Pa.	1876-77

Attorney General	Ebenezer R. Hoar of Mass.	1869-70
	Amos T. Akerman of Ga.	1870-71
	George H. Williams of Ore.	1872-75
	Edwards Pierrepont of N.Y.	1875-76
	Alphonso Taft of Ohio	1876-77

Postmaster General	John A. J. Creswell of Md.	1869-74
	James W. Marshall of Va.	1874
	Marshall Jewell of Conn.	1874-76
	James N. Tyner of Ind.	1876-77

| *Secretary of the Navy* | Adolph E. Borie of Pa. | 1869 |
| | George M. Robeson of N.J. | 1869-77 |

Secretary of the Interior	Jacob D. Cox of Ohio	1869-70
	Columbus Delano of Ohio	1870-75
	Zachariah Chandler of Mich.	1875-77

| RUTHERFORD B. HAYES of Ohio | | 1877-81 |

| *Vice-President* | William A. Wheeler of N.Y. | 1877-81 |

| *Secretary of State* | William M. Evarts of N.Y. | 1877-81 |

| *Secretary of the Treasury* | John Sherman of Ohio | 1877-81 |

| *Secretary of War* | George W. McCrary of Iowa | 1877-79 |
| | Alexander Ramsey of Minn. | 1879-81 |

Attorney General	Charles Devens of Mass.	1877-81
Postmaster General	David M. Key of Tenn.	1877-80
	Horace Maynard of Tenn.	1880-81
Secretary of the Navy	Richard W. Thompson of Ind.	1877-80
	Nathan Goff, Jr. of W. Va.	1881
Secretary of the Interior	Carl Schurz of Mo.	1877-81

JAMES A. GARFIELD° of Ohio   1881

Vice-President	Chester A. Arthur of N.Y.	1881
Secretary of State	James G. Blaine of Me.	1881
Secretary of the Treasury	William Windom of Minn.	1881
Secretary of War	Robert T. Lincoln of Ill.	1881
Attorney General	Wayne MacVeagh of Pa.	1881
Postmaster General	Thomas L. James of N.Y.	1881
Secretary of the Navy	William H. Hunt of La.	1881
Secretary of the Interior	Samuel J. Kirkwood of Iowa	1881

CHESTER A. ARTHUR† of New York

Secretary of State	Frederick T. Frelinghuysen of N.J.	1881-85
Secretary of the Treasury	Charles J. Folger†† of N.Y.	1881-84
	Hugh McCulloch of Ind.	1884-85
Secretary of War	Robert T. Lincoln of Ill.	1881-85
Attorney General	Benjamin H. Brewster of Pa.	1882-85

° Died September 19, 1881 from an assassin's bullet.
† Acceded Sept. 20, 1881
†† Died 1884

Postmaster General	Thomas L. James of N.Y.	1881
	Timothy O. Howe of Wis.	1882-83
	Walter Q. Gresham of Ind.	1883-84
	Frank Hatton of Iowa	1884-85
Secretary of the Navy	William E. Chandler of N.H.	1882-85
Secretary of the Interior	Samuel J. Kirkwood of Iowa	1881
	Henry M. Teller of Colo.	1882-85

GROVER CLEVELAND of New York		1885-89
Vice-President	Thomas J. Hendricks* of Ind.	1885
Secretary of State	Thomas F. Bayard of Del.	1885-89
Secretary of the Treasury	Daniel Manning of N.Y.	1885-87
	Charles S. Fairchild of N.Y.	1887-89
Secretary of War	William C. Endicott of Mass.	1885-89
Attorney General	Augustus H. Garland of Ark.	1885-89
Postmaster General	William F. Vilas of Wis.	1885-88
	Don M. Dickinson of Mich.	1888-89
Secretary of the Navy	William C. Whitney of N.Y.	1885-89
Secretary of the Interior	Lucius Q.C. Lamar of Miss.	1885-88
	William F. Vilas of Wis.	1888-89
Secretary of Agriculture	Norman J. Colman of Mo.	1889

BENJAMIN HARRISON of Indiana		1889-93
Vice-President	Levi P. Morton of N.Y.	1889-93
Secretary of State	James G. Blaine of Me.	1889-92
	John W. Foster of Ind.	1892-93

* Died Nov. 25, 1885

Secretary of the Treasury	William Windom of Minn.	1889-91
	Charles Foster of Ohio	1891-93
Secretary of War	Redfield Proctor of Vt.	1889-91
	Stephen B. Elkins of W.Va.	1891-93
Attorney General	William H. H. Miller of Ind.	1889-91
Postmaster General	John Wanamaker of Pa.	1889-93
Secretary of the Navy	Benjamin F. Tracy of N.Y.	1889-93
Secretary of the Interior	John W. Noble of Mo.	1889-93
Secretary of Agriculture	Jeremiah M. Rusk of Wis.	1889-93

GROVER CLEVELAND of New York   1893-97

Vice-President	Adlai E. Stevenson of Ill.	1893-97
Secretary of State	Walter Q. Gresham of Ill.	1893-95
	Richard Olney of Mass.	1895-97
Secretary of the Treasury	John G. Carlisle of Ky.	1893-97
Secretary of War	Daniel S. Lamont of N.Y.	1893-97
Attorney General	Richard Olney of Mass.	1893-95
	Judson Harmon of Ohio	1895-97
Postmaster General	Wilson S. Bissell of N.Y.	1893-95
	William A. Wilson of W.Va.	1895-97
Secretary of the Navy	Hilary A. Herbert of Ala.	1893-97
Secretary of the Interior	Hoke Smith of Ga.	1893-96
	David R. Francis of Mo.	1896-97
Secretary of Agriculture	Julius Sterling Morton of Neb.	1893-97

WILLIAM McKINLEY° of Ohio   1897-1901

Vice-President	Garrett A. Hobart† of N.J.	1897-99
	Theodore Roosevelt of N.Y.	1901
Secretary of State	John Sherman of Ohio	1897-98
	William R. Day of Ohio	1898
	John Hay of D.C.	1898-1901
Secretary of the Treasury	Lyman J. Gage of Ill.	1897-1901
Secretary of War	Russell A. Alger of Mich.	1897-99
	Elihu Root of N.Y.	1899-1901
Attorney General	Joseph McKenna of Cal.	1897-98
	John W. Griggs of N.J.	1898-1901
	Philander C. Knox of Pa.	1901
Postmaster General	James A. Gary of Md.	1897-98
	Charles Emory Smith of Pa.	1898-1901
Secretary of the Navy	John D. Long of Mass.	1897-1901
Secretary of the Interior	Cornelius N. Bliss of N.Y.	1897-98
	Ethan A. Hitchcock of Mo.	1898-1901
Secretary of Agriculture	James Wilson of Iowa	1897-1901

THEODORE ROOSEVELT of New York   1901-09

Vice-President	Charles Warren Fairbanks of Ind.	1905-09
Secretary of State	John Hay of D.C.	1901-05
	Elihu Root of N.Y.	1905-09
	Robert Bacon of N.Y.	1909
Secretary of the Treasury	Lyman J. Gage of Ill.	1901-02
	Leslie M. Shaw of Iowa	1902-07
	George B. Cortelyou of N.Y.	1907-09

° Died September 14, 1901 from an assassin's bullet.
† Died Nov. 21, 1899

Secretary of War	Elihu Root of N.Y.	1901-04
	William H. Taft of Ohio	1904-08
	Luke E. Wright of Tenn.	1908-09
Attorney General	Philander C. Knox of Pa.	1901-04
	William H. Moody of Mass.	1904-06
	Charles J. Bonaparte of Md.	1906-09
Postmaster General	Charles Emory Smith of Pa.	1901-02
	Henry C. Payne of Wis.	1902-04
	Robert J. Wynne of Pa.	1904-05
	George B. Cortelyou of N.Y.	1905-07
	George von L. Meyer of Mass.	1907-09
Secretary of the Navy	John D. Long of Mass.	1901-02
	William H. Moody of Mass.	1902-04
	Paul Morton of Ill.	1904-05
	Charles Bonaparte of Md.	1905-06
	Victor H. Metcalf of Cal.	1906-08
	Truman H. Newberry of Mich.	1908-09
Secretary of the Interior	Ethan A. Hitchcock of Mo.	1901-07
	James R. Garfield of Ohio	1907-09
Secretary of Agriculture	James Wilson of Iowa	1901-09
Secretary of Commerce and Labor	George B. Cortelyou of N.Y.	1903-04
	Victor H. Metcalf of Cal.	1904-06
	Oscar S. Straus of N.Y.	1906-09

WILLIAM H. TAFT of Ohio		1909-13
Vice-President	James S. Sherman* of N.Y.	1909-12
Secretary of State	Philander C. Knox of Pa.	1909-13
Secretary of the Treasury	Franklin MacVeagh of Ill.	1909-13
Secretary of War	Jacob M. Dickinson of Tenn.	1909-11
	Henry L. Stimson of N.Y.	1911-13
Attorney General	George W. Wickersham of N.Y.	1909-13

* Died Oct. 30, 1912

Postmaster General	Frank H. Hitchcock of Mass.	1909-13
Secretary of the Navy	George von L. Meyer of Mass.	1909-13
Secretary of the Interior	Richard A. Ballinger of Wash.	1909-11
	Walter L. Fisher of Ill.	1911-13
Secretary of Agriculture	James Wilson of Iowa	1909-13
Secretary of Commerce and Labor	Charles Nagel of Mo.	1909-13

WOODROW WILSON of New Jersey   1913-21

Vice-President	Thomas R. Marshall of Ind.	1913-21
Secretary of State	William Jennings Bryan of Neb.	1913-15
	Robert Lansing of N.Y.	1915-20
	Bainbridge Colby of N.Y.	1920-21
Secretary of the Treasury	William Gibbs McAdoo of N.Y.	1913-18
	Carter Glass of Va.	1918-20
	David F. Houston of Mo.	1920-21
Secretary of War	Lindley M. Garrison of N.J.	1913-16
	Newton D. Baker of Ohio	1916-21
Attorney General	James C. McReynolds of Tenn.	1913-14
	Thomas W. Gregory of Texas	1914-19
	A. Mitchell Palmer of Pa.	1919-21
Postmaster General	Albert Sidney Burleson of Texas	1913-21
Secretary of the Navy	Josephus Daniels of N.C.	1913-21
Secretary of the Interior	Franklin K. Lane of Cal.	1913-20
	John Barton Payne of Ill.	1920-21
Secretary of Agriculture	David F. Houston of Mo.	1913-20
	Edwin T. Meredith of Iowa	1920-21
Secretary of Commerce	William C. Redfield of N.Y.	1913-19
	Joshua W. Alexander of Mo.	1919-21
Secretary of Labor	William B. Wilson of Pa.	1913-21

JUSTICES OF THE UNITED STATES SUPREME COURT, 1865-1917

Name

Salmon P. Chase (CHIEF JUSTICE) of Ohio	1864-73
James M. Wayne of Ga.	1835-67
Samuel Nelson of N.Y.	1845-72
Robert C. Grier of Pa.	1846-70
Nathan Clifford of Me.	1858-81
Noah H. Swayne of Ohio	1862-81
Samuel F. Miller of Iowa	1862-90
David Davis of Ill.	1862-77
Stephen J. Field of Cal.	1863-97
William Strong of Pa.	1870-80
Joseph P. Bradley of N.J.	1870-92
Ward Hunt of N.Y.	1873-82
Morrison R. Waite of Ohio (CHIEF JUSTICE)	1874-88
John M. Harlan of Ky.	1877-1911
William B. Woods of Ga.	1881-87
Stanley Matthews of Ohio	1881-89
Horace Gray of Mass.	1882-1902
Samuel Blatchford of N.Y.	1882-93
Lucius Q. C. Lamar of Miss.	1888-93
Melville W. Fuller of Ill. (CHIEF JUSTICE)	1888-1910
David J. Brewer of Kan.	1890-1910
Henry B. Brown of Mich.	1891-1906
George Shiras, Jr. of Pa.	1892-1903
Howell E. Jackson of Tenn.	1893-95
Edward D. White of La.	1894-1910
Rufus W. Peckham of N.Y.	1896-1909
Joseph McKenna of Cal.	1898-1925
Oliver W. Holmes of Mass.	1902-32
William R. Day of Ohio	1903-22
William H. Moody of Mass.	1906-10
Horace H. Lurton of Tenn.	1910-14
Charles E. Hughes of N.Y.	1910-16
Willis Van Devanter of Wy.	1911-37
Joseph R. Lamar of Ga.	1911-16
Edward D. White of La. (CHIEF JUSTICE)	1910-21
Mahlon Pitney of N.J.	1912-22
Jas. C. McReynolds of Tenn.	1914-41

Louis D. Brandeis of Mass.   1916-39
John H. Clarke of Ohio   1916-22

INDEX